An Introduction to the Maronite Faith

Joseph Azize (Fr Yuhanna Azize)

Connor Court Publishing

Published in 2017 by Connor Court Publishing
Second Edition 2018 by Connor Court Publishing

Connor Court Publishing Pty Ltd
PO Box 7257
Redland Bay QLD 4165
sales@connorcourt.com
www.connorcourtpublishing.com.au

Phone 0497 900 685

ISBN: 978-1-925501-56-8

Cover design, Maria Giordano. Photo: The altar of the church of St Mama, Ehden in Lebanon, is illuminated by a sunburst entering the three windows above it – a natural symbol of the Holy Trinity (see p.281)

Printed in Australia

Practically all Bible quotations are from the Douay-Dhiems as modified by the author in accordance with the original sources and modern English style.

Nihil Obstat:	+ Bishop Antoine-Charbel Tarabay Maronite Bishop of Australia, Eparchy of St Maroun
Imprimatur:	+ Bishop Antoine-Charbel Tarabay Maronite Bishop of Australia, Eparchy of St Maroun 30 March 2017

The *Nihil obstat* and the *Imprimatur* together comprise a declaration that a book or pamphlet is considered to be free from doctrinal and moral error. It is not implied that those who have granted the *Nihil obstat* and the *Imprimatur* agree with the contents, opinions or statements expressed.

Dedicated to His Excellency Bishop Antoine-Charbel Tarabay

With Filial Gratitude and Priestly Reverence

Table of Contents

Foreword

This wonderful introduction to the Maronite tradition of the Christian faith comes at a very opportune time. Hitherto an introductory yet systematic introduction to the beliefs and practices the Maronites has been lacking in English or rather inaccessible to English-speakers. Abbot Paul Naaman has explored Maronite origins as an outcrop of the great Antiochene and Syriac-based branch of the early church, and discussed the historical evidence for St Maroun and his monastic movement (fourth-to-fifth centuries), and the fabled migration to the Mounts Lebanon. Butros Dau and Matti Moosa are two familiar names who have attempted to trace the course of the Maronites through history, also in English. Many other historical researches are in French, however, and the mass of liturgical materials and patriarchal, eparchial and diocesan instructions, much in Arabic and not just Syriac, have barely received English (as a against French) translations. Being an eager custodian for the well-endowed Selby Old Foundation for the purchase of books on Eastern Christianity, for Fisher Library at the University of Sydney, I am myself only too well aware of student needs for a better understanding of the problems and complexities of the Near and Middle East. Fr Dr Azize's context in the Australian diaspora of this vital part of the Lebanese community has helped prompt a work that can not only be of incalculable value to all Maronites far and away from their homeland but also to all those who have yearned for a better knowledge of this ecclesiastical lineage, at the very least for its social role in its Lebanese context.

Many, of course, considering the immense crowd welcoming Pope John Paul II to Beirut in 1997, will want to know from this book what the actual relationship between the Roman and Maronite communities are, and what is an 'Eastern Catholic' or for that matter 'uniate church.'

On this matter Fr Dr Azize ploughs a special course: his purpose is to introduce what is *distinctive* about Maronite theology, spirituality, liturgy, approach to the saints, and ethics. His is a work of clarification about the integrity of the this venerable Levantine faith, which can stand proud, even in its relative smallness, independently of pressure from the largest single organization of earth (yes, the Western or Latin Catholic Church). This shows that our author has performed an act of respect and love toward the special treasures and diversity of the (orthodox) Christian faith, and gives us an awareness of sensitivities and nuances we need to know in today's multicultural societies.

Surely the most intriguing emphasis in Fr Dr Azize's introductory coverage concerns typological interpretation as central to Maronite faith. I have often wondered how, on the way to Emmaus, the resurrected Jesus could have possibly had enough time to explain to his two companions "all the passages referring to himself in every part of the scriptures" (Luke 24: 27). In any case, not a little of the Old Testament books look to be quite irrelevant to Him. Unlocking the key to the myriad of typological connections, however, is the obvious answer, and pre-figural reflections of the Christ to come, even oppositional impetuses that we can see through in the light of Christ, and thus both ante-type and antitype (if we may put it this way), fill the whole *praeparatio evangelii*. An attentive missiologist can even say that such preparation may be found in any religion, philosophy or ideology before and after the Incarnation, for the clear implication of the Gospel message that the typos of perfection in Christ allows for discernment between all that offers truth, justice, peace, and love and what does not. And how crucial this is for our time.

I commend this much needed study very highly indeed.

Garry Trompf
Emeritus Professor in the History of Ideas
University of Sydney

Introduction

What is the Maronite Catholic faith? It is a Church which professes the same creed as the Universal Catholic Church. It is an expression of the revelation and sacramental dispensation of Our Lord Jesus Christ, addressed to a people who shared the Aramaic language and culture of the Semitic world into which He Himself was born. If we think of it as a tree, then its seed was planted by the teaching of Our Lord Jesus Christ, as passed on through His apostles. In the person of St Maroun of Syria, that seed put down roots. Then, through his disciples, who journeyed to Lebanon, a sapling shot up from the soil of Lebanon. Finally, a full-grown cedar appeared, tended by St Yuhanna Maroun (a monk from a Syrian monastery named after St Maroun), who was elected Patriarch of Antioch to preserve the Christian faith.

No "Maronite Church" was ever founded on a given day of a certain year. Rather, an important portion of the Christian Church of Syria removed to the mountains of Lebanon. Then, in communion with the Christian Church there (which owed its origins to the disciples of St Maroun), they continued to live as the Church they had been in Syria. They handed on not only the faith but also the forms and ecclesiastical hierarchy that they knew. They always considered themselves to be in unity with Rome and through Rome with the Universal Church. They retained their Aramaic tongue, and used Syriac (which is a dialect of Aramaic written in a script fashioned in Edessa). Isolated from the world outside by geography and their religious opponents, they preserved their faith in all its ancient monastic purity.

The Maronite Church therefore forms a religious and spiritual bridge spanning the epoch of Our Lord with the ages which have followed it.

This is manifested most clearly in the Syriac tradition of the Maronite Church, as I shall attempt to demonstrate in this book. We shall see direct continuity between our modern faith and that expressed in the New Testament and in early church documents such as the letters of St Ignatius of Antioch (died by 117) and the *Odes of Solomon*, which probably hail from the same time as St Ignatius.

Not only does the Maronite Church claim unity with the Universal Catholic Church, but that claim is recognised by the Apostolic See of Rome, which in turns calls the Maronite Church one of its family. This mutual recognition was given a glorious symbolic solidity when in 2011, a statue of St Maroun was placed in the last remaining empty niche in the outer wall of St Peter's Basilica, Rome.

Why then, this book? As a Maronite priest, working especially with English-speaking Australians, it was found necessary to provide for them a resource which sets out the basic outlines of the Maronite faith, answering questions such as the following: what is distinctive about the Maronite faith, its liturgy, and its theology? Which of the many features characteristic of the Maronite Church are essential to it, and which are not? Can our teachings be explained to the contemporary, English-speaking world in a way which is not only true to the traditions of the Church, but also practical?

To some extent, therefore, this book is felt to be the answer to a personal challenge. So it is not a catechism (a book which systematically sets out the faith), but rather an individual approach and interpretation. Two further matters need to be noted about that last point.

First, a catechism could never convey what I wanted to communicate, namely, that the Maronite faith is a way of life first and foremost, rather than a philosophy or a system of doctrines which when once accepted direct one's behaviour. It is not that we lack a philosophy, or doctrines, or that the faith does not guide our behaviour. It possesses a deep philosophy (which we call *typology*, and to which I aim to introduce the reader), it has many doctrines (too many to exhaustively cover in this book), and it should, if it means anything to us, profoundly affect our behaviour. Neither do I mean to imply that other forms of Christianity are not ways of life. But there is a distinctiveness about the intensity of the Maronite way of life which I attempt to set out in lesson 23, such that its spirituality is a complete way of life for the faithful. It is therefore found in their homes and kitchens, and enters into all their social dealings. The Maronite faith, properly understood, is lived, and reorients the whole of our lives towards God. It will take time for the ideas presented here to seep into the reader's heart and produce lasting change, but it is well worthwhile commencing that great work now. At this very instant.

Secondly, because, about three hundred years ago, the Maronite Church was subject to a wave of reform at the behest of the Latin Church, altering our ideas of liturgy, spirituality and theology, it will take time to recover and produce something authentically and distinctively Maronite. Many workers must put their hands to the wheel, and produce their own interpretations. If this volume inspires or provokes others with deeper knowledge than myself to write and so to supersede this book completely, I will be the first to thank them. I offer this as a further reason for penning an individual approach to the orthodox faith, rather than attempting an impersonal catechism.

The impulse for this book was a series of courses for a certificate of Maronite Studies which I planned, and in which I was ably assisted by my friend Peter El Khouri, who has written the companion volume to this book. Both our books are based on the notes we produced for those courses. At the same time, I was tasked with looking after instruction for Adult Baptism, the teaching of the faith to adults in preparation for their reception into the church. We at the Adult Baptism team found that we needed resources which could be used to prepare lessons to teach these adults the basics of the Christian faith from a Maronite Catholic perspective. It also appeared that some adults who had been baptised as Catholics were in need of further instruction, having been given insufficient Catholic instruction in their school years. Few will ever be able to acquire an all-round knowledge of the faith, beyond the most superficial, if they did not receive a good Catholic education at school.

There are some excellent introductions to the Catholic faith, but, so far as I am aware, only one was written for a specifically Maronite audience, and this is unavailable in Australia. Besides, it seemed good to write a book based on the Syriac way of thinking, explaining typology in more detail, and eschewing reliance on Western writings.

There is always the vexed question of judgment: what should be included and what excluded? Even once a topic has been selected for treatment, what should be said about it and what omitted? No two minds will come to the same conclusion at every stage, for very long. Some topics are absolutely basic, such as God and the Trinity, the Sacraments and the Bible. Others have often been omitted, such as the environment, and others have not, so far as I am aware, been given even the rather pithy treatment they have been given here.

Then there is the question of controversy. A work such as this one defeats its purpose if it is combatively controversial. However, a book which is too safe risks losing its integrity if it avoids issues which could be considered controversial. I do not aim to enter controversy or to avoid it. I merely seek to pass on the faith, accurately, faithfully, and in contemporary terms addressing contemporary issues.

The author is a Catholic priest who considers himself a servant of the Word of God, of the sacraments and the sacramental, rather than traditionally-minded, although more often than not he will take a traditional stand. But what is primary is the sacramentality of the faith. The author believes in the sacramental dispositions made by Our Lord Jesus Christ and that the essences of these sacraments cannot be changed by us, if we are to remain faithful to the faith – and we must.

The sacramental economy is part of revelation, because it was revealed to us by the Lord Himself. Even if the form of the sacraments has been humanly developed, for some more than for others, yet we cannot fashion new sacraments or change or dispense with those existing.

It is *precisely* because the doctrinal and sacramental base of the Church is immutable that we can develop the superstructure with confidence, sometimes even into scarcely envisaged areas, such as the social teaching of the Church on labour and capital. Then some topics, such as pornography, which are dealt with here, have always been condemned by the Church, but not having been nearly so prevalent as they are now, less needed to be said about them in the past. So we should not be afraid to countenance fresh horizons and new applications of that inestimable gift which is the faith in all its many dimensions. In all this, we are not adding anything to the fundamental principles of the faith, or changing its doctrines.

Prejudices go in all directions: we should never complacently imagine that we alone are objective. Too often, in rejecting one error, or correcting one imbalance, we fall into another. But the Lord calls us with the voice of truth. Jesus Christ incarnated and guarantees the truth. The revealed faith is the ultimate criterion for the judgments which we make today, even if we must apply the principles of the faith (which can never contradict those of reason) to novel situations. Since the faith is also inculturated (that is, finds expression in and through human cultures), it also needs a certain adaptation. Cultural influences, especially ideological, philosophical and political currents, can cause trends and movements to arise in the Church, affecting even the refined study of theology. Some modern trends are, in my opinion, simply wrong and even possibly dangerous. The superficiality of so much modern talk, even influential talk, is saddening. Suffice it to say, I have endeavoured to look for the deep realities and the principles, and to relate together the spirituality, language, liturgy and theology of the Church. The writer does not believe that anything he has suggested here is inconsistent with, let alone contrary to, the teachings of the Church, and submits himself to its judgment.

Now, for one explanatory matter: footnotes. I have used footnotes for four reasons: first, to give references beyond mere biblical citations, second, to provide definitions, third to offer short explanations of unusual terms and phrases, and fourth, to include material which, while relevant, and of some interest, is not so important that it had to go into the text. I have been more inclined to use footnotes if the facts I speak of are the sorts of things which I think people might appreciate a reference for, e.g. they are either little known, or controversial.

This book is respectfully dedicated to His Excellency Bishop Antoine-Charbel Tarabay, Eparch of Australia, who consented to my writing the book, and has always placed a high priority upon the faith and formation in the faith. His Excellency's forbearance with my many faults is humbly appreciated. May I hope that He in whose name this endeavour was undertaken, may be abundantly merciful to His poor and wretched servant. He who sees all and searches all hearts knows that something, at least, in the writer is truly as sincere as it is possible for him to be.

Lesson 1

God, the Individual, and the Church

from **Jacob of Sarug's *Homilies on Praise at Table***

> O discerning ones, come and be refreshed spiritually
> at the banquet prepared for us physically!
> Body and soul both seek life from God:
> the body (seeks) food, and the soul (seeks) the Word by which it
> may live.
> We should not be concerned only with building up the body,
> but with the soul, for it is more precious than earthly things.
> It is not by bread and water alone that we have life,
> but by the Word of the Lord, for it is an immense treasure.
> After all, very many foods are very enjoyable,
> yet after a day they mean nothing to those who have eaten them.
> … In the dining room bread lies heavy on them who eat it,
> but from instruction the soul acquires wings to fly![1]

Jacob of Sarug (pronounced Sa-rooj) is one of the most important writers in the Syriac tradition. He was born in about 451 and died in

---

[1]   Jacob of Sarug's *Homilies on Praise at the Table*, ed. and trans. Jeff W. Childers, Gorgias, Piscataway, 2016: "Homily 141: On Praise at the Table 3 – The Word of Life and Moderation," 1-10 and 17-18. I have added the two words "seeks" within brackets in line 4. "Sarug" is also often spelled "Serugh".

about 521, being made a bishop only about two years before his death. His feast is 29 November in the Syriac Orthodox Church. Although he was not a Maronite, the Baptism Liturgy he wrote is the basis of the Maronite one, and it is believed that much of our Divine Sacrifice of the Mass was at least strongly influenced by his distinctive spirit and style.[2]

Here, when Jacob refers to the banquet prepared for us *physically* which can refresh us *spiritually*, he means the Eucharist. The "Eucharist" or "the Thanksgiving" is another name for the sacrament in which we receive Christ Himself in the form of bread. It is also another name for the celebration of the Divine Sacrifice of the Mass in which the bread and wine are consecrated as the Body, Blood, Soul and Divinity of Our Lord. The "Word of Life" of which he speaks is *both* the Eucharist and the teaching of the Lord found in its purest form in the Gospels of the New Testament. As we shall soon learn, Jesus Christ Himself is referred to as the "Word of God."

We shall come very soon to the Gospels and the New Testament, but for now the important point is that by hearing the Word of God, and learning what He wants us to understand so that we can come to know him, we can find a comprehension of the world and of God's plan for it and for us, and so an internal peace. We can learn to walk the safe path which leads us to heaven. And the gate through which we enter to take our first steps on the path is *baptism*, which is why this course of lessons was first designed for those who seek baptism, and for those who have been baptised, and wish to know more about their Maronite Catholic faith.

---

[2] When we attempt to return to and rediscover our Syriac roots, the main Syriac authors we use are Aphrahat, St Ephrem and Jacob of Sarug. A fourth Christian thinker, Narsai, is also important, especially for the liturgy.

1.1 Introduction

All Maronites are Catholic but not all Catholics are Maronite. All Catholics, taken together, form the Universal Catholic Church, of which the Pope (who is the Bishop of Rome) is the head. Around 90% of all Catholics are Latin Catholics, even though their Church today hardly ever uses the Latin language in its liturgies. The rest of the Catholics are Maronite, Melkite, Ukrainian, Coptic Catholic, Armenian Catholic and so on. Each of these forms a Church, and each Church has its own:

1. Liturgy.
2. Discipline.
3. Spirituality.
4. Theology.

The unique Maronite Liturgy is celebrated each day in its Churches, and can be found in its Missals or "Mass Books." The present day English version is called *The Book of Offering*. Worship is so important to us, because the worship of God is the highest activity a human being is capable of. We shall have much to say about this, particularly in lesson 17 on the Eucharist.

In terms of discipline, the Maronite Church is Eastern, which means that, among other things, it allows married men to be ordained to the diaconate and then to the priesthood. All Eastern Catholic Churches have this same discipline, while the Latin allows the married men to be ordained only in extraordinary circumstances, and on a case by case basis.[3]

Our Maronite spirituality is possibly the most *monastic* spirituality in all the Catholic Church because all our priests were originally monks. As a result of this, we are influenced by the special *intensity* of

---

[3] The best known contemporary example is when many Anglicans joined the Catholic Church's Ordinariates, specially established for them. Since many of them were already married, the Pope allowed them to continue both as priests and as married men

the monastic way of life, which leads us to balance the active life with the contemplative life. In recent years, the emphasis, not only in the Church but throughout the world has shifted towards the active. It may well be that we now need to draw fresh nourishment from our roots, for just that monastic-inspired tradition is historically suited to us and our religious culture. But this may also be what the contemporary world needs. The world needs to stand back from the dizzying circuit of life, and ask *why* it is that we live; that is, what purpose are our busy lives meant to serve?

This book is a work of *theology*, the study of God and the study of the world in so far as it is related to God. Theology tells us who God is, who we are from His perspective, and what we should do to be able to enjoy life with God.

Theology is a culturally conditioned study, just as music is. Different cultures use different scales of music, different instruments and have very different ways of performing music (for example, some cultures have a five note scale, others an eight note scale, and so on). Yet, there is also considerable overlap. The same is true in theology. I think it is fair to say that there is a great deal uniting all Catholic theology, whether Latin (Western), or Greek or Syriac (the two main Eastern styles). Whereas the Latin style is, to a good extent, based on a *legal* approach, with definitions and tight logic, the Greek approach is based on *philosophy* and the exploration of concepts through the philosophy of the Fathers. But the Latins also have philosophy, and the Greeks also have law. It is a question of emphasis.

Maronite theology, being a Syriac theology, should be a science and an art in which *typology* takes equal place with *law* and *philosophy*. It has not yet done so, but we can move towards this. I shall explain typology later on, but briefly, it draws the meaning from the life of Christ and the sacraments He instituted, and applies that meaning to all of existence.

It is true that many see our theology as exactly the same as the Latin, and to a significant extent, they are correct. Certainly, *there can be no contradictions between our Churches on theology.* But we can regain our distinctive theological inheritance. One point must be clearly made: the Maronite Church is a Chalcedonian Church, just as Catholic Churches are all Chalcedonian Churches. What this means is that it accepts the teachings of the great ancient councils of the Christian Church. Of these, by far the most important were the first three: the Councils of Nicaea (325), Ephesus (431) and Chalcedon (451). If one attempted to reduce the complex issues and conclusions of these Councils to the single most significant phrase, it might be this: *they held that Our Lord Jesus Christ is both truly divine and truly human.*[4]

A short word has to be said about the Monothelite controversy. The Council of Chalcedon had achieved some clarity about the two natures of Christ, but it did not achieve unity for all Christianity. To bring all Christians together, whatever their views on the natures of the Lord, a new doctrine was invented, today called "Monotheletism", that is, that Our Lord had only one will. The Monothelite idea is often called a "heresy", but in fact it was closer to a doctrinal error. It was and remains so difficult to grasp that if one were to ask contemporary educated Catholics whether the Lord had one will or two, many say that He would have had but one will. In the ancient world, there was no chance that the average person could understand the arguments for and against. They may, however, have been devoted to their liturgy, and that may sometimes have been changed to reflect Monothelite ideas. In that case, their attachment was not to a doctrine they could not understand, but to a prayer in which only a well-trained theologian could spot the error.

---

[4]   Karl-Heinz Uthemann, "History of Christology to the seventh century", in *The Cambridge History of Christianity: Constantine to c.600,* edited Augustine Casiday and Frederick W. Norris, Cambridge University Press, Cambridge, 2007, 460-500, 490. The position of the Maronites touching the "Monothelite" controversy is dealt with by Peter El Khouri in his book, which is a companion volume to this one.

Now, however, I wish to take you to the heart of what it means to be a Christian by telling one of the parables or coded teaching stories of Our Lord. This will tell us, in one very memorable tale, a great deal about our relationship with God.

First of all, note that the parable comes from "Luke 15." This means chapter 15 of the Gospel of St Luke, which is in the New Testament. The Old and New Testaments form the two parts of the *Bible*. We shall return to this later, but it is enough to know that the Bible is the sacred book of the Catholic Church. Secondly, note that before each verse there is a number in superscript. This tells you which verse of the chapter we are reading. By using the fourfold division into two Testaments, the many books in each Testament, and then the chapters and verses of each book, you can easily navigate your way around the Bible.

1.2 The Parable of the Prodigal Son (Luke 15)

[11] And he (Jesus) said: "There was a man who had two sons; [12] and the younger of them said to his father: "Father, give me the share of property that falls to me." And he divided his living between them. [13] Not many days later, the younger son gathered all he had and took his journey into a far country, and there he squandered his property in loose living.

[14] And when he had spent everything, a great famine arose in that country, and he began to be in want. [15] So he went and joined himself to one of the citizens of that country, who sent him into his fields to feed swine. [16] And he would gladly have fed on the pods that the swine ate; and no one gave him anything.

[17] But when he came to himself he said: "How many of my father's hired servants have bread enough and to spare, but I perish here with hunger! [18] I will arise and go to my father, and I will say to him: "Father, I have sinned against heaven and before you; [19] I am no longer worthy to be called your son; treat me as one of your hired servants.""

[20] And he arose and came to his father. But while he was yet

at a distance, his father saw him and had compassion, and ran and embraced him and kissed him. [21] And the son said to him: "Father, I have sinned against heaven and before you; I am no longer worthy to be called your son."

[22] But the father said to his servants: "Bring quickly the best robe, and put it on him; and put a ring on his hand, and shoes on his feet; [23] and bring the fatted calf and kill it, and let us eat and make merry; [24] for this my son was dead, and is alive again; he was lost, and is found." And they began to make merry.

Questions for Contemplation

1. What, if anything, does this parable mean to me?
2. In particular, does the figure of the father mean something to me?
3. Can I identify, in any way, with the prodigal son?

1.3 Every thing and every one comes from God, and returns to God.

The desire to love God is innate in each of us: it comes from God Himself. God has created us not only with these fleshly bodies which will one day decay and pass into dust, but also with immortal souls, and these will live in eternity. In the Syriac tradition, the Holy Spirit, which is one of the three persons of God, is said to be *"the soul of the soul."* That is, God lives inside us, in a manner which we can love, respect and revere, but not understand.

Further, God has planted in each of us an organ which speaks with His own voice: that organ is conscience. Conscience tells us what to do in any situation. These ideas can be expanded, and must be expanded to become practical. First, the desire to love God has to be given a form and a method in our lives: God calls us to love and worship Him in accordance with the way which He himself has shown us. Christianity is the way which God established to show us how to love and worship

Him: as Jesus (who is God) stated: "You are Peter, and upon this rock I build my Church" (Matthew 16:18).[5] In other words, Jesus deliberately founded a Church.[6]

You will shortly learn more about the mystery of the Trinity (that is, how God can be three persons in one divinity: Father, Son and Holy Spirit), and especially who Jesus is and what He did and taught when He was on earth. You will also find out about the Church which He founded to carry on the work of sanctifying, teaching and governing the people of God. The Church compiled the Bible, and adjudicated on the question of which books should and should not be included within it. So, too, it is the Church which safeguards and interprets the Bible, the greatest single source book for the holy life.

The other important aspect which we have mentioned, that of conscience, will also be dealt with. But we will teach you what it is to have a formed well-formed conscience, and to use it correctly. Everyone has a conscience, but that does not mean that they can necessarily use it correctly, any more than people can think logically with the brains they were born with. Just as you can learn the art of thinking rationally, so too, you can learn how to form and then hear the voice of your conscience, and to free it from the confusing lies and mistakes which often "cloud," as we say, the mirror of conscience.

Now we come to the most important aspect of all: everything we have been speaking about, loving and serving God, hearkening to our consciences and learning the moral life, are all steps on the way to *holiness*. To love and serve God is to have holiness: no doubt. But we seek to grow in these things. To put it another way: we opened by saying that God has given us the desire to love and worship Him. More specifically, He sent His Son to make it possible for us to join

---

[5] "Matthew" is another book from the New Testament. It is a shorthand way of referring to the "Gospel of St Matthew."

[6] Incidentally, before they were known as "Christians," the followers of Jesus were known as those on "the way" (see Acts 11:26 and Acts 9:2).

Him in heaven, where we may eternally enjoy the "sight" of God in the "beatific vision."

By founding the Church for this purpose, we can even say that God desired that the ordinary way of people coming to Him would be through the Christian faith. So the desire to be Christian is somewhere within everyone's heart. The Catholic Church is the only Church which stands directly in the lineage of Our Lord himself, being the Church He founded on Peter. The bishops who govern the Church today are the successors of the apostles, the twelve chief disciples of the Lord.

Another way of speaking of holiness is to speak of us becoming formed in the image of God. It is taught in the Book of Genesis, the first book in the Old Testament, that: "God created man in His image; in the divine image He created him: male and female He created them" (Genesis 1:27). However, through sin (disobedience to the will of God), that image of God which is in us became distorted. As we say in the prayer before the Institution Narrative (which shall be explained in the future) from the Anaphora of St John:[7]

> For our salvation You sent Your Son into the world; He descended, became flesh, suffered, and was crucified for us *who had distorted His image.* (italics added)

So, we have the image of God as a sort of basic pattern: this enables us to recognise His presence in goodness, truth and beauty. As we shall see, the image of God is a *type*, and we are *antetypes*, meaning that we are formed in that image, but are not identical to it. Our image has been distorted, and our religion shows us how to put it to rights by walking the path of holiness as best we can.

Because that image has been disfigured, so our recognition of the image of God in ourselves and in others is not as fast or accurate as it could be. Through baptism, however, we enter the door upon the

---

[7] The "Anaphora of St John" is one version of the text of the second and most important part of the Divine Sacrifice of the Mass. This shall be further explained in future lessons.

road to life, and the true image of God is restored in us. But it can be lost again, and certainly, we must work to keep the image pure and powerful in us. St Ephrem puts this very well at the end of the first of his *Hymns on the Nativity*:

> ... it is not too difficult for us also to overthrow our evil will.
> Bound is the body by its nature for it cannot grow larger or smaller;
> but powerful is the will for it may grow to all sizes.
> Today the Deity imprinted itself on humanity,
> so that humanity might also be cut into the seal of Deity. (97b-99)[8]

The "will" is stressed because we must exercise our free will in order to walk the path to life, and to follow God's commands. "Will" even strengthens "love," for our emotions can, by themselves, run astray. We need to remind ourselves of the value we place on love, and to use our wills to do those things which make our love stronger, and to avoid those things which weaken it. For example, selfishness and lust will weaken our love. Even if we are married with children, our love for our spouse will be obscured if not effaced by unbridled lust. To keep lust in check needs an unconditional act of the will (e.g. I *will not* watch pornography, I *will not* lust after that woman).

Note, too, how Ephrem says that God has "imprinted" Himself on humanity, the way that a seal would be made by imprinting a design on wax. This is the essential idea behind typology and the typological interpretation of the mysteries of the faith. God is the image, we are the wax, and we and the creation are made in that image. But because God is infinite, we cannot receive all of his image, only part of it. So we are bound to respect each separate creation as representing some unique aspect of God's infinity.

---

[8] *Ephrem the Syrian: Hymns*, ed. and trans. Kathleen E. McVey, Paulist Press, NY, 1989, p. 74.

1.4 The Aim of Human Life

When we speak of the "end of man" we mean nothing other than the purpose for which each person, whether male or female, was created, namely, to know, love and serve God. It is the *end* which gives the purpose and significance of the journey. When we look around the world, we see that everything has a purpose: how often have scientists thought that something had *no* purpose, and then discover that in fact it did have a purpose? Take the example of "junk DNA." It is now known that it *isn't* junk.

The meaning of the world as a whole cannot be found in the world itself. Is the meaning of anything, say, a car, found in itself, or do you need to know who made it and why? Likewise, the meaning of the world must be found outside or beyond the world. There is nothing beyond the universe but God. Again, imagine if you came across a car in the street. Would you think it had just appeared there? Of course not. No more can this world have just appeared here. It was created, by God, the Creator of heaven and earth, and of all things. We know of God by *revelation*, that is, by what God Himself has disclosed to us. The most important revelation of all was the revelation in and through Our Lord, for we can have complete faith in what He taught us.

However, *within* this universe, there is one very special creature: man. Christians believe that, man "is a creature composed of body and soul, and made in the image and likeness of God." We shall come back this later in the course, but for now let us say that the likeness we are speaking of is one of the soul rather than the body. The soul is made in the likeness of God because it is an immortal spirit, with understanding and free will. Aphrahat (c.280-345) teaches, in *Demonstration 17: On Christ, who is the Son of God*:

> He (God) is the father of all creatures on the face of the earth.
> He honours and elevates and glorifies humans more than all of

his creatures ... since he formed them with His holy hands and breathed into them with His Spirit, and His dwelling place was in them from the beginning (6).[9]

Powerful as our reason is, we still cannot learn everything by use of reason alone: we need revelation to teach us things beyond our human power (compare the knowledge of an adult and a baby: it is different not only in degree but in kind). Further, our "free will" is a gift of God, too, enabling us – to the extent that we have not weakened it – to choose one thing instead of another, and to do good or evil.

God should be the centre of each human life, for we teach that God made us to know, love and serve Him in this world, and to enjoy the beatific vision of Him in the next (which is an eternal world). In the previous sentence, we put "knowing" before "loving" because in our experience as adults it is difficult if not impossible to love what one does not know. The more one sees God the more one loves him. This "seeing" is the knowledge of not only the mind but also the soul.

God is infinitely good, true and beautiful. We cannot grasp how good, true and beautiful he is: but we can have greater and greater indications. The more we grow in faith, hope and charity (the three *divine* virtues, because they come from him); the more we sense his goodness, truth and beauty, and the more we come closer to fulfilling the purpose of life.

I would say that all human beings are made to recognise and seek truth, beauty and goodness. And truth, beauty and goodness are found in their perfection only in God. Because God is eternal, He is the only solid basis for any values.

---

[9] *The Demonstrations of Aphrahat, the Persian Sage*, Adam Lehto, Gorgias Press, Piscataway NJ, 2010, pp. 388-389. Aphrahat was one of the first and most important of the Syriac writers. His writings are not as early as the *Odes of Solomon*, but they are earlier than the works of either St Ephrem or Jacob of Sarug.

1.5 The Church

God is absolute. He has no need of us, and yet He has created us, and given us extraordinary privileges. God creates us as individuals: unique creatures who must one day answer to Him for what we have and have not done.[10]

God has designed us as individuals who are made to be in or related to communities, such as our family, our neighbourhood, our village, town or city, our nation and the world. But there is a universal or *catholic* community of which we can be part: the Church. In the Epistles to Timothy (1 Timothy) and Titus (also from the New Testament), St Paul speaks of the need to appoint bishops to structure the Church. Consider these quotes, In both instances, Jesus is speaking:

> Matthew 16 [17]"And Jesus said to him: "Blessed are you, Simon Barjona, because flesh and blood did not reveal this to you, but My Father who is in heaven. [18]I also say to you that you are Peter, and upon this rock I will build My church; and the gates of Hades will not overpower it. [19]I will give you the keys of the kingdom of heaven; and whatever you bind on earth shall have been bound in heaven, and whatever you loose on earth shall have been loosed in heaven."…

> Matthew 18 [15]"If your brother sins, go and show him his fault in private; if he listens to you, you have won your brother. [16] But if he does not listen to you, take one or two more with you, so that by the mouth of two or three witnesses every fact may be confirmed. [17] If he refuses to listen to them, tell it to the church; and if he refuses to listen even to the church, let him be to you as a Gentile and a tax collector. [18] Truly I say to you, whatever you bind on earth shall have been bound in heaven; and whatever you loose on earth shall have been loosed in heaven.

The Church is the mystical body of Christ, which means that it is

---

[10] The judgment of all humanity is found throughout the Bible (especially in the Gospel of John and the Book of Revelation). We shall return to this ethical component later in the course.

Christ in a way which we cannot fully understand, because our senses are limited in what they can know. But we know that this is so because **Our Lord taught the apostles and the apostles taught us.** It was St John, the Beloved Disciple, who more than any other, understood this. Again, it is Our Lord who teaches in the Gospel of St John, chapter 15:

> [1]"I am the true vine, and my Father is the gardener. ... [4]Remain in me, as I also remain in you. No branch can bear fruit by itself; it must remain in the vine. Neither can you bear fruit unless you remain in me. [5]I am the vine; you are the branches. If you remain in me and I in you, you will bear much fruit; apart from me you can do nothing. ... [8]This is to my Father's glory, that you bear much fruit, showing yourselves to be my disciples.

> [9]As the Father has loved me, so have I loved you. Now remain in my love. [10]If you keep my commands, you will remain in my love, just as I have kept my Father's commands and remain in his love. [11]I have told you this so that my joy may be in you and that your joy may be complete. [12]My command is this: Love each other as I have loved you. [13]Greater love has no one than this: to lay down one's life for one's friends.

The Gospel of St John has always been the most important Gospel in the Maronite Church, and here St John brings together the love of God and the love of our fellow men and women. It is necessary to understand that our love for one another cannot be based on anything permanent and unshakeable other than God. He alone does not depend on anything else to verify or validate him. You can always ask "who says so?" or "why should I if I don't want to?" until the answer is that it is God who says so, and that if we wish to be united with Him in heaven, then we have to obey his commandments – and as we shall see, *to obey the commandments of God is to respond to His love as a human being would naturally respond.* There is a lot in this last thought, it raises, for example, the question of what is natural for us.

If a person rejects life with God, and they are entitled to do so (as they have free will), then they cannot be part of the Christian community.

In some instances (such as with Satanists or anyone dedicated to evil), having any close relations with them, except when they express a desire to change their lives, is dangerous.

Everyone who seeks God will find that He has assistance, not least, he will find companions on the way: the Christian Church. Here, the word "Church" includes both the Church on earth, the Church in purgatory, and the Church in heaven: or what is called the "Church Militant," the "Church Suffering" and the "Church Triumphant."

When we consider the Church here on earth, we see a great diversity in human cultures. The Church can work with and through this diversity. This is part of the reason there are 24 different Catholic Churches: each Church can speak to its own people in their own language. Especially with the Eastern Churches, each Church is a part of the people's history, and identity.

We also have help directly from God: our chief helps are the seven sacraments:

Sacraments of Initiation
Baptism
Confirmation
Eucharist

Sacraments of Vocation
Marriage
Holy Orders

Sacraments of Healing
Penance
Anointing of the Sick

The Great Mystery of the Church is the Divine Sacrifice of the Mass. The Eucharist is the high point of the Mass because it is the sacrifice of Our Lord Jesus Christ offered each and every day upon our altars. We shall learn all of this in more detail in future lessons. We are using the word "sacrament" in a very specific way here, but it can also be used in broader ways, too. We need not concern ourselves about those things right now.

1.6 The Divine Path

Many of these ideas come together in the image of the path. Imagine that, like the prodigal son, you have left your father's house, but are now living in a forest. Although you have left him, he send his messenger to you, to point out to you the path home. That path is not always easy, and it is a long one, but it is 100% sure: if you follow it, you know you will find your way out of the forest and back home. If you don't follow it, you can never tell what will happen. You may be able to find your way back to it, or you may not. But the chances are that once you have strayed you will go further and further astray, and end up lost. This is not the *end* you were made for. There are some wonderful verses from number 7 of the *Odes of Solomon* which describe this and more. The book of the *Odes of Solomon* is the earliest surviving Christian hymnal (hymn book). I copy here only some verses from this beautiful piece:

> My joy is the Lord and my course is towards Him, this path of mine is beautiful. (7:2)

> It is a delight and a consolation to the soul to follow the way of the Lord, the road of holiness.

> ... He became like me, that I might receive Him. In form He was considered like me, that I might put Him on. (7:4)

> ... Like my nature He became, that I might understand Him. And like my form, that I might not turn away from Him. (7:6)

This is related to what we saw from the Book of Genesis and the Anaphora of St John, but it adds that because Our Lord took on human form at the time of His incarnation, and so we can be united with Him.

> For He it is who is incorrupt, the perfection of the worlds and their Father. (7:11)

As have seen, our teaching is that God is the perfection of goodness, truth and beauty. Eternal life is life in God (hence the reference to his being "incorrupt").

> He has allowed Him to appear to them that are His own; in order that they may recognize Him that made them, and not suppose that they came of themselves. (7:12)

This is saying, in the poetic words of a long lost period, that the best evidence for the existence of God is historical: that is, we can be sure that God exists because He came down to earth in the person of Our Lord and told us about Himself.

> For towards knowledge He has set His way, He has widened it and lengthened it and brought it to complete perfection.
>
> And has set over it the traces of His light, and it proceeded from the beginning until the end. (7:13-14)

This takes us back to the image of the path, the way to holiness. This magnificent Ode goes on to speak of other wonders, but it is sufficient for us to say gratefully acknowledge that truth of verse 19: "And they shall praise the Lord in His love, because He is near and does see."[11]

---

[11] I am using the translation of James Charlesworth as found at www. theodesproject.com

Lesson 2

Belief and faith

2.1   Creeds

2.2   The Parable of the King Delivering Judgment

2.3   The Nicene Creed

2.4   Faith and Belief

2.1   Creeds

A "creed" is a statement of belief. From the very earliest days of the Church, we find what we call "creedal statements" in Christianity. First, we will take what is by far the most important creedal statement in the Maronite Catholic Church. Indeed, for us, this is *the* Creed. There is no other which can take its place as the foremost declaration of what we believe. It is called "the Nicene Creed."

> We believe in one God, the Father almighty, maker of heaven and earth, of all things visible and invisible.
>
> We believe in one Lord, Jesus Christ, the only-begotten Son of God, born of the Father beyond all ages. God from God, Light from Light, true God from true God, begotten, not made, consubstantial with the Father; through him all things were made. For us men and for our salvation, he came down from heaven; and by the Holy Spirit was incarnate of the Virgin Mary, and became man. For our sake he was crucified under Pontius Pilate, he suffered death and was buried, and rose again on the third day in accordance with the Scriptures. He ascended into heaven and

is seated at the right hand of the Father. He will come again in glory to judge the living and the dead and his kingdom will have no end.

We believe in the Holy Spirit, the Lord, the giver of life, who proceeds from the Father and the Son, who with the Father and the Son is adored and glorified, who has spoken through the Prophets.

We believe in one holy, Catholic, and Apostolic Church. We confess one baptism for the forgiveness of sins and we look forward to the resurrection of the dead and the life of the world to come. Amen.

But there are other creedal statements. For example, in the Gospel of Mark, chapter 12, we read that Our Lord taught:

The first of all the commandments is, Hear, O Israel; The Lord our God is one Lord: And you shall love the Lord your God with all your heart, and with all your soul, and with all your mind, and with all your strength: this is the first commandment.

And the second is like it, namely, you shall love your neighbour as yourself.

There is no other commandment greater than these.

There is a lot more information in this simple creedal statement than one would think at first sight. For example, note how the commandment to love God comes first. Many people might have put it the other way around, but as we shall see over the length of this course, there is a very good reason for how it is written. To be short, the knowledge, love and worship of God is the only the solid foundation for a meaning- and purposeful human life: anything else is liable to change as people change. Interestingly, this commandment is based on a passage from the Old Testament (Deuteronomy 6:4), but Our Lord developed and perfected it. We shall explore the Old Testament a little later, but it is sufficient to say now that laws given to Israel, and recorded in the Old Testament, provide a link between Christianity and its Jewish past.

Another feature of this extract from St Mark's Gospel is that Our Lord introduces the second commandment by saying that it is *like* the first commandment. How, one may ask, is it "like" it? Their *substance* is that they are both commandments to love. They direct the *manner* of this love by enjoining us to do so with all our heart, soul, mind and strength. And they are alike in *aim*, for since we are all made in the image of God (as we shall learn) it follows that by loving our neighbour, we are loving the image of God.

Then: "love" itself is a tremendous mystery and also a challenge. We come to love in lesson in 13, but it is a mystery in that it is part of God, for "God is love" (I John 4:8) and He is the ultimate mystery. Love is also a challenge, one of the greatest and also one of the sweetest, for as St Isaac of Nineveh states: "For someone to say to his brother "Love God" is very easy, but what is necessary is to know how to love Him."[12]

Why does Our Lord refer to Israel in Mark 12? As I see it, there are at least two reasons. First, because what Our Lord says in that first sentence is in fact from the Old Testament, and was part of the revelation to the people of Israel. But secondly, because although Our Lord was founding a new religion, the new Church is to be the new Israel. Just as Israel was the chosen people of God, and *formed a single people,* so too the Church will be the people whom God chooses from all the nations of the world, and they likewise will form a single people.

In the Maronite tradition, the continuity with Israel was taken seriously, partly because we were close to and influenced by the liturgy of Jerusalem (which is why Jerusalem is mentioned in two of our anaphoras – the eucharistic prayers of the Mass – the Anaphoras of St James and St John Maroun). Also, culturally and linguistically we were very close not only to the land of Israel but even to the Jewish people, and they travelled all around the Mediterranean world. It is rather like

---

[12] Sebastian P. Brock, *The Wisdom of Isaac of Nineveh*, Gorgias, Piscataway, 2006, #105, pp. 28-29.

Scottish and English people living in nearby lands, and able to speak to one another in the same language. For this reason, there is a great deal of Old Testament material, and many allusions to the Hebrew patriarchs and prophets in the prayers of the Maronite Mass and the Divine Office (the daily prayers prescribed for the Church, even if they are mostly said by monks and religious).

These creedal statements of what we believe are signposts along the way. We say the Nicene Creed at each and every Mass, but it is still good to stop sometimes and think about what we are saying. Our actions should reflect our beliefs, and the better thought out and understood our beliefs are, the more consistent our actions will be, and the more confidence we will have in life.

In fact, these creeds are liberating, because they free us from confusion and ignorance. To take the example of the way: if someone tells you that you are free to go home, but you do not know in which direction home lies, what use is your freedom? Or if you are free to choose between two different items (let's say vacuum cleaners) but you know nothing about the vacuum cleaners and what they can do, how long they will last, or even their price, what sort of freedom is that?

As these examples show us very clearly, *knowledge* is necessary to freedom, and *ignorance* is its enemy. So too, because God has given us our spiritual freedom, He gives us the knowledge we need. The chief agent for passing this on is His Church, which tells us what has been revealed. With all these teachings, we can be sure of the direction we are to go in if we want to know, love and serve God. This is what the creeds do, which is part of the reason they are so short: the essentials can be communicated in very few words.

Then, to continue our example, what if you were told that you were free to go home, but you were too weak to make a move? Or if your legs were in chains? You need to have the strength and the ability to actually move. So, if freedom requires knowledge to be able to make use of it,

36

it also requires ability, and in this case, the ability is spiritual strength. As we shall see, the Church provides the vehicles of grace which give the soul the possibility of exercising its freedom, and pressing on with hope and confidence, because without these, we may sink all too easily into despair and a feeling of lassitude.

2.2   The Parable of the King Delivering Judgment

What it means to love another for the sake of the image of God in each of us is shown in our parable for this week, from the Gospel of St Matthew, chapter 25. Once more, Jesus speaks, but from here on, to make it a little easier to read, I omit the superscript verse numbers:

> When the Son of Man comes in his glory, and all the angels with him, he will sit on his glorious throne. All the nations will be gathered before him, and he will separate the people one from another as a shepherd separates the sheep from the goats. He will put the sheep on his right and the goats on his left.

> Then the King will say to those on his right: "Come, you who are blessed by my Father; take your inheritance, the kingdom prepared for you since the creation of the world. For I was hungry and you gave me something to eat, I was thirsty and you gave me something to drink, I was a stranger and you invited me in, I needed clothes and you clothed me, I was sick and you looked after me, I was in prison and you came to visit me."

> Then the righteous will answer him: "Lord, when did we see you hungry and feed you, or thirsty and give you something to drink? When did we see you a stranger and invite you in, or needing clothes and clothe you? When did we see you sick or in prison and go to visit you?'

> The King will reply: "Amen I tell you, whatever you did for one of the least of these brothers and sisters of mine, you did for me."

> Then he will say to those on his left: "Depart from me, you who are cursed, into the eternal fire prepared for the devil and his

angels. For I was hungry and you gave me nothing to eat, I was thirsty and you gave me nothing to drink, I was a stranger and you did not invite me in, I needed clothes and you did not clothe me, I was sick and in prison and you did not look after me."

They also will answer: "Lord, when did we see you hungry or thirsty or a stranger or needing clothes or sick or in prison, and did not help you?'

He will reply: "Amen I tell you, whatever you did not do for one of the least of these, you did not do for me."

"Then they will go away to eternal punishment, but the righteous to eternal life." (Matthew 25:31-46)

This should reinforce for us the idea that by loving our neighbour we also love God. It also relates back to the concept of the Church being a people, which we mentioned when we looked at how Our Lord spoke of the people "Israel." We also start to see how what is said in one part of the Gospels will relate forwards or backwards to what is said in other parts. To study the Gospels is to make connections within their pages, and with our lives.

2.3   The Nicene Creed

The Nicene Creed, or, as it is sometimes called, the Niceno-Constantinopolitan Creed, is the most fundamental statement of the faith. The basis of the Creed was laid down in 325, at the Council of Nicaea, when the bishops of the world (such as they then were) came together to define the faith. Then, at the Council of Constantinople in 381, the Creed was adopted in its present form. The main change was that in 381 they added the last paragraph, pertaining to the Church, baptism, resurrection and eternal life.

This Creed is not fundamental to the faith, but also to our Christian unity. A person cannot reject any part of it and yet be considered truly Christian. We affirm the Creed in every single Divine Sacrifice of the Mass and in the baptism liturgy (the Latin church uses it only on Sundays solemn feast days).[13] In order that we may understand it properly when we attend the Divine Sacrifice of the Mass, we will methodically work through it.

Note that the Creed begins by speaking of "God." Because we are human beings, we can never know God in His fullness. Indeed, we do not even know other people in their fullness. But for us to completely understand God would be like expecting a child to completely understand their parents and why they make the decisions and take the actions which they do. God is intrinsically even further above us and our faculties than that example suggests: God is an infinitely perfect spirit.

When we say that He is infinitely perfect, we mean that His perfections are beyond limit (although God in Himself is one, we can distinguish certain qualities in His actions e.g. His goodness, His mercy, His love and so on). Indeed, God in His very essence is beyond our human imaginations. We believe that only God is infinitely perfect: neither angels, nor any saint, not even Our Lady, are infinitely perfect.

Being an infinitely perfect spirit, who depends on no one and nothing else for his existence, God has existed from before all time. In fact, He had no beginning. He always was and always will be. He is everywhere, whole and entire. When we come to speak like this, we are before a mystery: we cannot know how God can exist before time, how He can be without beginning or end, how He can be everywhere, whole and entire. We comprehend the meaning of these words but not how they can be true. We know a little, but not the whole. This is what we mean by a mystery. And the acceptance of mystery is part of the meaning of faith, as we shall see later.

---

[13]   I am not saying one custom is better or worse than another, I am just mentioning the fact as sometimes people become confused or even querulous about the difference between the Mass in the Latin and Maronite Churches. All Catholic Masses are acceptable forms of worship to any Catholic, and attendance at any Catholic Mass satisfies the obligation to hear Sunday Mass.

We need to be clear about this: a mystery is not a black hole in our knowledge. A mystery is a light shining in the darkness which we can see but cannot explain.

Now although God is spirit, and our souls are spirits, there are big differences: God is a "pure spirit" because He has no body. Our souls, however, are not *pure* spirits, because they were created for union with our physical body.

Since God is everywhere, He sees and knows all, even our most private thoughts. We believe that without His constant care for us we could not exist. This is because all existence not only comes from God, but depends upon Him at every moment. God is pure existence. It is not like how we have children, and then the children can survive us. We are always dependent upon God for our very being.

That God created everything, and that He upholds and cares for everything is part of the reason we call Him "Father." But the greatest reason to call Him that is because His own son, Our Lord Jesus Christ, taught us to make so bold as to address Him in that manner. For example, Jesus taught us to pray saying: "Our Father ..."

The other thing which the Creed says about God at the outset is that He is almighty. We can also speak of his being "omnipotent." This means that He can do everything. There is no impossibility with God.

In our Maronite tradition, St Ephrem, in the third of his *Hymns on the Nativity* (the nativity is Christmas, the birth of Our Lord Jesus Christ, celebrated on 25 December), writes:

> Glory to that Hidden One who even to the mind
> is utterly imperceptible to those who investigate Him.
> But by His grace (and) through His humanity
> a nature never before fathomed is (now) perceived ... (stanza 5)[14]

Kathleen McVey, who edited and translated this hymn, states of

---

[14] From Kathleen McVey, *Ephrem the Syrian: Hymns*, Paulist Press, NY, 1989, pp.83-84.

it: "Those who are arrogant enough to investigate God will be utterly incapable of perceiving him. Ephrem's sustained polemic[15] against the "investigators" and the "inquirers" is directed against (those) ... who seek to understand the mysterious essence of God. The proper role of humans is to ponder the symbols God has placed in scripture and nature and the sacraments rather than trying to analyse the nature of God ..."[16]

We shall speak later about this, because it relates to the very distinctive Maronite system called **typology**, which we mentioned in the first lesson. There are symbols, as McVey says, but more important than the symbols are the types which are the pattern of creation, reality and history. The typological approach which is distinctive of the Maronite approach is also authentically true to the New Testament (it is explicitly used by St Peter and St Paul). It is another example of how close we Maronites are to the ancient Judaic tradition.

2.4 Faith and Belief

By faith, we mean completely submitting our intellects, our hearts and our wills to God. This is "the obedience of faith." We obey the teaching of the Church because its truth is guaranteed by God. And God, of course, is Truth itself. In faithful obedience, we can take the Virgin Mary as our role model.

When we have faith, then we have understood something, and on the basis of that understanding, we give God credit for even more. It means that we will commit to the teaching of God, even when it seems hard to understand, or, indeed, mysterious. Sometimes the teaching of the Church will seem wrong: for instance, as it did to those people in cultures where children could be allowed to die (infanticide), or widows might be expected to throw themselves on the funeral fire as their

---

[15] A "polemic" is an argument against another position.
[16] K. McVey, *Ephrem the Syrian: Hymns*, p.84 n.110.

husbands were being cremated (a practice called "sati" or "suttee"). But the teaching of the Church is correct. We follow that teaching because our faith, based on what we have heard and seen so far, tells us that the teaching ultimately comes from God and so cannot be wrong.

Faith is a "free assent," meaning that no one can make an act of faith for us if we have the faculty of reason: only we can do so. Here is a Maronite Act of Faith, meaning that it is something we say with reverent attention, and that its words will help us formulate what we seek:

> Lord, as the sun rises on the earth anew to nourish it with its light,
> so Lord, kindle in me anew the light of faith so that my soul may
> be nourished and the world around me enlightened through me.
> Amen.

Our personal adherence must be to the whole truth which God has revealed. It would be inconsistent and lacking in faith to say that I will accept *this* teaching but not *that* teaching. But even more than a question of doctrines, although these are of great importance, faith is a matter of the heart as well as of the will and the intellect. Sometimes it seems that the least educated and sophisticated people are the strongest in faith, and hence the closest to God.

Sometimes, the terms "faith" and "belief" are used interchangeably. That is a fact of life, and it has to be accepted. Yet, we do not have to follow this. I would prefer to use "belief" for a purely intellectual acceptance, and "faith" for the conviction which fills the whole person, heart and mind together. If I have faith then of course I will believe what I am told by those in whom I have faith. And if I have belief, then I may come to have faith as well as belief. And yet the two are intrinsically different. Faith is belief but it is also more, it is confidence and an emotional commitment to the belief we hold.

For us, faith in God cannot be separated from faith in Our Lord Jesus Christ and in the Holy Spirit. We meet Our Lord Jesus in the Eucharist, and by hearing from the Gospels what He said and did. We are taught by the Holy Spirit in the Scriptures (including the Gospels) more than anywhere else, but also He sometimes acts through individuals, e.g. through St John-Paul II and St Theresa of Calcutta, to give but two recent and well-known examples.

We are encouraged to pray for faith because, although it might seem as if it is a question of our own decision, that is only part of the story. Faith is a supernatural gift from God. It is said that in order to possess the faith, we need the interior help of the Holy Spirit. The faith and the belief of the Church are also essential. It is said that faith precedes, engenders, supports and nourishes our faith. The Church is the mother of all believers. "No one can have God as Father who does not have the Church as Mother" (St. Cyprian).

Finally, faith is necessary for salvation. The Lord himself affirms: "He who believes and is baptized will be saved; but he who does not believe will be condemned" (Mark 16:16). Indeed, in the Maronite tradition, it is said:

> Faith is a basic gift which also seeks a response in faith. (As a gift) it is related to the Trinity and to Christology[17] ... but it is also connected with Scripture, which supplies faith with a point of reference and an objective measure. As a response, in order to act it out and to nourish it, we must proclaim the faith. For this to lead to good results, we must refrain from scrutinizing the faith, but rather approach it with wisdom, and offer it to God. True faith must be proclaimed, lived, and bear fruit. ... The Trinitarian dimension of the faith is that it relates us to the Trinity, the Cross and the Gospel.... Faith may be compared to the way that the sun enables the eye to see, while the eye nonetheless does not look directly at the sun, but rather, all around it. Faith is also like the rock upon which the house is built.[18]

---

[17] We say this because faith comes from God. "Christology" is the study of Christ.
[18] This is a loose translation from pp.476-477 of Fr Tanios Bou Mansour's *La pensée symbolique de Saint Ephrem le Syrien,* Kaslik, 1988. It is a wonderful book, but rather hard to follow. The reference to the house built on the rock is from Matthew 7:24-27.

Questions for Contemplation:

1. Do I understand what faith and belief are?

2. What do I understand, and just as importantly, what do I not understand in the Nicene Creed,?

3. Do I have a desire that God should strengthen my *belief* and my *faith*? This question is the sort of question which should not just be mentally asked and mentally answered. It is good to take it in a quiet moment, and to put it to myself, and to remain present before it.

Lesson 3

One God, the Father Almighty

3.1 Introduction

We open with a reading from the New Testament which tells us something about God and His action in human history through Our Lord Jesus Christ, through Our Lady and the apostles. It describes the situation after the Resurrection, when Our Lord is meeting with the apostles:

> And being gathered together, he (Jesus) commanded them (the apostles), not to depart from Jerusalem, but to await the promise of the Father: "which you have heard from me. For John baptized with water, but you shall be baptized with the Holy Spirit, not many days hence." So, they who were come together, asked him: "Lord, will you then restore the kingdom to Israel?" But he said to them: "It is not for you to know the times or moments, which the Father has set by his own power. But you shall receive the power of the Holy Spirit coming upon you, and you shall be witnesses unto me in Jerusalem, and in all Judea, and Samaria, and even to the uttermost part of the earth."
>
> And when he had said these things, while they looked on, he was

raised up: and a cloud took him up from their eyes. And while they were gazing intently as he was going up to heaven, behold, two men stood by them in white garments. They said: "You men of Galilee, why stand you looking up to heaven? This Jesus who is taken up from you into heaven, shall so come (again), just as you have seen him going into heaven." (Acts 1:4-11)

And when the day of the Pentecost had come, they were all together in one place. Suddenly there came a sound from heaven, as of a mighty wind coming, and it filled the whole house where they were sitting. And there appeared to them parted tongues as of fire, and it sat upon every one of them: And they were all filled with the Holy Spirit, and they began to speak with divers tongues, as the Holy Spirit gave them to speak. (Acts 2:1-4)

In chapter 1 of Acts, we were told that Our Lady and the brethren of the Lord were with them when the Holy Spirit descended. The brethren of the Lord were most likely his half-brothers and sisters (there was no word for half-brother or sibling in Greek, Aramaic or Hebrew).

This story is instructive, because it mentions the Father, the Son and the Holy Spirit, and shows how they work together. The importance of Our Lord's historical mission emerges, as well as his personality, which is very clearly grasped by the apostles. The two harder figures to understand are of course the Father and, most mysterious of all, the Holy Spirit. We can speak of the Father as the Creator, and the Holy Spirit as the Life-Giver, but really, what one person of the Holy Trinity does, all of them do, *for they are One God in three persons.*

3.2 God

The original Nicene Creed says *pisteuomen eis hena theon*, that is: "we believe in One God." That is the Creed which we Maronites say in every Mass. Notice that it is *we* who believe. We are called individually to be Christians, but to be Christian means, among other things. to be a member of God's family. Our Lord came to found a Church which could continue His work, especially by bringing the sacraments to all Christians, and by teaching the Gospel (the Good News) to all the world, whether Christian or not. Thus He said: "You are Peter, and upon this rock I build my Church" (Matthew 16:18).

When we come together, we encourage each other in our faith, and support one another in good and hard times alike. We go to confession (the Sacrament of Reconciliation) individually.[19] But even that sacrament, when one priest hears the confession of one person, exists within a Church context. We are made by nature to live with other people. Even if it is not easy, it is necessary for us as individuals to try to get on with others the way that Christ has commanded us. Even from a natural perspective, we know that living with other people teaches, or rather *can* teach us humility, compromise and cooperation. Selfishness *always* closes us off. To truly be a part of the Church we must struggle with selfishness.

Each Mass, the entire congregation stands up about five minutes before the reading of the Gospel, and three times we chant in Syriac (a form of the language Our Lord spoke) these words: *Qadišat aloho, Qadišat hayeltono, Qadišat lo-moyooto* ("Holy are you, God. Holy are you, Almighty. Holy are you, Immortal").[20] This immediately tells us not three but four (and maybe even more) things of the first importance about God.

1. We adore Him by praising Him for who and what He is.
2. He is holy: holiness is the quality of God's presence.
3. He is Almighty, and we can have confidence in Him.
4. He is Immortal, and He alone can guarantee us eternal life.

---

[19] There is in fact another Rite of Confession (or Reconciliation) which is for celebration in a group. At this stage, it has only been approved for use on the Saturday of Light (the day before Easter Sunday), but it is expected that it shall be soon approved for more frequent use.

[20] When this is chanted, we respond on each of the three occasions: *itraham 3alayn.* This means "have mercy upon us." Only God can forgive our sins and have mercy upon our souls – which is what we mean by this prayer.

A great deal more follows from all of this. For example, because He is so good, then it is the very perfection of all good fortune to be able to see Him in heaven for eternity. Speaking of His incarnation upon the earth, our Entrance Hymn for the feast of the Nativity (Christmas) says:

> O Lord, mighty God, blest are those upon the earth,
> for you granted them to see with their own eyes your eternal majesty!

To be with God in heaven is what we call "the beatific vision." The word "beatific" means "blessed" or "happy." "Happy" is too weak: it is something more like "blissful." Finally, that funny word "holiness" refers to a quality which is probably impossible to define, but which is, as I have said, the quality of God. What is that quality? It includes His goodness, truth and beauty, it brings faith, hope and love, and fills us with patience and reverence. Aphrahat (c.280-345) tells us that Christ "brings near to himself holiness, which is implanted through faith."[21] Holiness brings a deep feeling of peace, and also an understanding that the world has been created by a good God, and that despite all the problems, virtue will triumph.

3.3 Why we Place God First

As we saw in the previous lesson, in the Gospel of St Mark chapter 12, Our Lord taught us:

> The first (of all the commandments) is, Hear, O Israel; The Lord our God is one (Lord): And you shall love the Lord your God with all your heart, and with all your soul, and with all your mind, and with all your strength: this is the first commandment. And the second is you shall love your neighbour as yourself. There is no other commandment greater than these. (Mark 12:39-41)

---

[21] *The Demonstrations of Aphrahat*, Demonstration 1: "On Faith," §4, p. 71.

The beginning of everything is God. As St John says in chapter 1 of his Gospel:

> In the beginning was the Word, and the Word was with God, and the Word was God. He was with God in the beginning. Through Him all things were made; without Him nothing was made that has been made. In Him was life, and that life was the light of all mankind. (John 1:1-4)

This tells us that God is the head and origin of all creation, and that Jesus was with God the Father even in that mystical time. It specifically adds that life is a property of God (remember our Syriac chant about how God is immortal), and that the life of God is our light. "Light" here includes understanding and consciousness. We may be physically blind, but if we have a knowledge of God and His ways, we can still follow the path to heaven more surely than someone with keen vision but no virtue.

It is implicit in St John's Gospel that *life* is more than just the organisation of biological organisms. *Life* is something which commences in God, and our lives are but portions of it. In John 10:10, Jesus states: "I am come that they may have life, and may have it more abundantly." How can we have life more abundantly? Does it mean to be able to jump over fences, and do without sleep at night? This more abundant life is a glimpse of the eternal life which Our Lord promises throughout the Gospel of St John. In John 17:3, Our Lord declares: "Now this is eternal life: That they may know you, the only true God, and Jesus Christ, whom you have sent." In other words, it is not an extension of existence, but an existence transformed by possessing an understanding of God and of Our Lord Jesus Christ.

This is, of course, a part of *holiness*. A person who is holy, or has some holiness, (because no one can say that they are completely holy in this life) understands something about God with a simplicity which goes beyond what any philosopher could tell you. In other words, as we grow as Christians, we grow into a new state of life. It is an interior state - no light appears around your body to make you glow in the dark! But this new life can be seen in its effects: in works of faith, hope, patience and charity.

We place God first because every good thing we can have comes from Him. Only God is permanent. If I look for security, where can I find it? We have a social structure with police, courts, parliaments and laws so that we will be safe in our homes, and our incomes and livelihoods protected. But what if war breaks out? The social structure all crumbles and we have to look for refuge. What about love? My spouse can die; marriages can break down. Children can and perhaps increasingly do refuse to speak with their parents, and vice versa. The reality is *nothing in this world is permanent and therefore we can find no guarantee of security in it.*

It is God and God alone who is unchanging, and who will be there (and be *here*) for us no matter what happens. No matter how difficult the conditions, one can always have the interior life of divine searching. Martyrs about to be executed still have their faith, their hope for eternal life, and their love.

That faith which carried the martyrs triumphantly through their deaths and into heaven, had to be based on something real and solid – and there can be no true foundation for faith other than God himself. Aphrahat describes it this way, using a good practical example from life:

> Faith is composed of many things, and is built up in many ways. For it resembles a building which is constructed through many actions as its edifice rises to the top. … stones are laid as foundations for the building, and then on these stones the whole building rises up until it is finished. … the foundation of all our faith is the true stone, Our Lord Jesus Christ. Faith is placed on the stone, and on faith the whole building rises up until it is completed.[22]

So faith involves an ongoing project, as we learn and as we put our religion into action. But it will always mean constantly returning

---

[22] *The Demonstrations of Aphrahat*, Demonstration 1: "On Faith," §2, p. 68.

to Our Lord Himself. And now we come to one of the most important aspects of faith in the Lord: the fact that He is the Second Person of the Most Holy Trinity.

3.4   The Most Holy Trinity

God is a Trinity. This means that He is Three at the same time that He is One. How can we explain this? We can't. But we have been told enough by Jesus Christ Himself to know that it is true. We also understand enough about ourselves, and about the difference between ourselves and God, to be able to accept that we cannot grasp the Trinity with our minds because our human minds are limited. This is reasonable: we don't all understand why airplanes work, but we know that they usually do, and we trust ourselves to them although we could not possibly follow an explanation by an engineer about how flight is possible. We know that we don't have the education and background to grasp all the details, but that the engineer does. We know this, and so we have trust in him. When it comes to God, this trust is a part of *faith*.

The idea of the Trinity is expressed very well, in several different ways, in the Mass. When the priest prepares the oblations (the offerings of the bread, wine and water) for elevation (raising them before the people) he says:

> In the name of the Father,
> the Living One, for the living;
> and of the only Son,
> the Holy One, begotten of Him,
> and like Him, the Living One, for the living;
> and of the Holy Spirit,
> the beginning, the end, and the perfection
> of all that was and will be in heaven and on earth;
> the one, true, and blessed God without division
> from whom comes life for ever.

We see here once more that God is the source of life; and that He is the beginning and the end, and that although He is three (Father, Son and Holy Spirit), He has no division within Himself. However, as St Ephrem explains it for the Syriac tradition, the three persons of the Most Holy Trinity have the same will but various functions (just as heat and light and different functions of the sun, which is one), and these functions justify the different names.[23]

A question naturally arises, how can we be sure of this doctrine which, at first sight, seems to have little in reason or logic to recommend it? As we have said, we can be sure of it because God tells us so. When did He tell us? First, we observe the Trinity at work in the Holy Scripture, and seeing its operation, we could conclude that God is a trinity. Secondly, Jesus Christ taught us things which explain what we see happening in the New Testament, and these help us to accept the teaching of the Trinity. We see the Trinity at work in the Baptism of the Lord:

> Then Jesus went from Galilee to the Jordan, to John, to be baptized by him. But John forbade Him, saying: "I need to be baptized by you, and you come to me?" Jesus replied to him: "Suffer it to be now, for it becomes us to fulfil all righteousness." Then John permitted him. Having been baptised, Jesus immediately came up out of the water, and behold, the heavens were opened and he saw the Spirit of God descending as a dove and coming to him. And behold, a voice from the heavens said: "This is my Son, the beloved, in whom I am well pleased. (Matthew 3:13-17)

Clearly the voice from heaven referring to "His Son" must be that of the Father. Further, the Spirit is said to be "the Spirit of God," and so it must be divine.

I might add here that the surest way of being persuaded of the existence of God, and of anything about Him (including the doctrine of the Most Holy Trinity), is to look at the life of Jesus Christ.

Returning now to the Holy Spirit, in John 14, not long before his

---

[23] Thomas Kollamparampil, *Salvation in Christ according to Jacob of Serugh,* 398.

Passion and Crucifixion (Our Lord knew that He would be slain by being crucified on a cross), the Lord taught:

> If you love me, keep my commands. And I will ask the Father, and he will give you another advocate to help you and be with you forever - the Spirit of truth whom the world is not able to receive, because it neither sees him nor knows him. But you know him, for he abides with you and he will be within you. I will not leave you as orphans; I am coming to you. In a little, the world will not see me anymore, but you will see me, because I live, you also will live. On that day you will know that I am in my Father, and you are in me, and I am in you. ... The one who loves me will be loved by my Father, and I too will love him and show myself to him. (John 14:15-20 and 21b)

The Church teaches that the Spirit of Truth Our Lord refers to is one and the same as the Holy Spirit who descended on the apostles on the first Pentecost. The apostles were enlightened by the Holy Spirit, and they taught their pupils and so on, all the way down to us.

The Syriac tradition of course lights on the Epiphany at the Baptism of the Lord as the occasion on which the Mystery of the Most Holy Trinity was revealed to humanity through the person of John the Baptist, the first witness to the Trinity. But in addition, Jacob of Sarug, always concerned for the practical reality of the teaching, points out that the Trinity manifested itself in three physical or sensory ways: the Father through His voice; the Son through touch and sensation by being baptised, and the Holy Spirit by becoming visible. So three senses were engaged in this manifestation of the Trinity: sight, touch and hearing.[24] It is a reminder that our senses have been sanctified by the action of the Most Holy Trinity.

We closed the last section by citing Aphrahat on how faith is based on Christ, the foundation stone, upon whom the whole building rises.

---

[24] Quoted by Thomas Kollamparampil, *Salvation in Christ according to Jacob of Serugh,* 168.

Now let us look at St Ignatius of Antioch, who died a martyr's death no later than 117, who used the same image, but in relation to the Most Holy Trinity:

> … you are as stones of the temple of the Father, made ready for the building of God our Father, carried up to the heights by the engine of Jesus Christ, that is the Cross, and using as a rope the Holy Spirit. And your faith is the windlass (winch)[25] and love is the road which leads up to God.[26]

3.5 God Almighty

There are no limits to the power of God. This does not mean that silly questions should be asked, such as: "Can God make a weight which is so heavy that He cannot lift it?" That question is really only a question about our concepts: the idea of a weight so heavy that God cannot lift it is an absurd one. God is not a body, He is spirit, without muscles and bones and so on. How would we know if God had lifted the weight or not? Because the concept of something which an all-powerful being could not do is self-contradictory, we could not recognise it in practice. Many more objections to such an absurd way of thinking could be made. We need to base ourselves on reason, first, and our reason can show us where it can go no further. For example, my reason tells me that I cannot understand nuclear science because I have not studied the relevant subjects. It does tell me that nuclear science is irrational just because if I try to read a treatise by a nuclear scientist, I cannot understand it at all. My reason itself tells me that it (my reason) is limited and why.

So too, my reason tells me that when we speak of "the almighty nature of God" we refer rather to the fact that God, as the perfect spirit

---

[25] A windlass or winch is a device, often a cylinder, used to help to raise heavy items. The rope which holds the heavy item might be passed over the windless to make it easier to move.

[26] Ignatius of Antioch: "Letter to the Ephesians," §9.1, trans. Kirsopp Lake, *The Apostolic Fathers I*, Loeb, Harvard, 1977, 183.

who created the universe, possesses the fullness of power over that creation. He upholds it, He could destroy it. He can alter it, He can touch and affect all matter, all spirit. But my mind also tells me that I, a mere mortal, who has trouble ironing a shirt, or finding just the word I want for this book, cannot expect to fully understand God and how He created the universe. My reason can follow God's revelation. When I ask myself if I believe the testimony of Jesus Christ, the answer is an unambiguous "yes." He is the most extraordinary man who ever lived. How can I not believe Him? But my very reason tells me that how He came to earth and who He really is lies beyond my complete understanding, even more than nuclear physics.

God has willed to allow us free choice, and rarely does he interfere to stop us feeling the effects of our free will. He has created a universe with regularly observable patterns (the laws of science), and with the capacity for *accident*. It is accident and free will which mean that the universe is not a giant clockwork mechanism which no one can alter. But if accident is important, so are the laws which God has placed in the heart of creation, for they allow us to use our minds, to search for the truth, to find as much truth as we can grasp, and to bring order into our lives by trying to align it with truth and reason.

Further, we need to be reminded, and often, that God's plan of salvation will defeat the plans of the devil. The devil was once an angel, perhaps even the brightest of the angels. However, he rebelled against God. Angels, like we human beings, have free will. Not very much is known about when the devil defied God and was thrown from heaven, only what has been revealed to us. But it seems that the devil (also known as "Lucifer" the light bearer, so glorious was he before his rebellion; and "Satan" the opponent, to describe him after his fall) sinned out of *pride*, being unable to imagine that he could be anything other than the greatest. It seems that he even had the audacity to think that he was or might become greater than God Himself. As result, Lucifer was cast into hell.

Our Lord said: "I saw Satan falling from heaven like a flash of lightning" (Luke 10:18). The traditional understanding of this is that Our Lord was describing the plunging of Lucifer into hell. Satan has been defeated, but until the end of this world he has the power to try and seduce us from the truth. However, he cannot harm us unless we place ourselves under his power. If you have any trouble with him, generally a blessing, confession and the Eucharist is all you need to stop his attacks. But if in doubt, speak to a priest. We will deal with the devil and evil more fully in another lesson.

3.6 God the Creator

The fact of creation is astounding. Why is there something instead of nothing? And why is there an enormous sky, a heaving sea, and tremendous mountains instead of dry dust and sterile rocks? You would not accept that a towel just appeared on the floor of your house. You would ask how it got there. If someone answered that things like that just appear from time to time, for no cause and by no agency whatsoever, you would not pay any serious regard to them.

But not only is the creation of the inanimate world astonishing, so is the presence of life. Scientists cannot create life. All that they can do is to alter or move around the existing forms of life. We are taught that the origin of life is in God: he is full of eternal life, and cannot die. This is satisfying: the reason for life cannot be within life, but it must be greater and beyond it.

The third miracle is the existence of divine qualities such as *goodness, love, truth* and *beauty*. From where does goodness come? I could ask the same for love, truth and beauty. I do not accept that these qualities are merely our way of looking at things. When love, truth and beauty are present in a person, they have an effect on other people which is every bit as strong as electricity or some other physical force.

We live in a universe created by God. In this universe we are meant to experience, to be nourished by and to spread, love, truth and beauty – which are all forms of the goodness or holiness of God.

The Catholic faith aims to teach us how to recognise and grow in these qualities, and to spread the good news about them to others. Jacob of Sarug wrote of the wonder of even contemplating the creation, and how that very emotion called him to share it:

> The mind has taken flight into the upper realms, to speak
> about creation and about the beauty of its formation.
> It gazed upon the heavens, the luminaries and their courses,
> how the mind wonders at the marvel of all creation!
> A homily stirred within me that is full of wonder about creation,
> and now it throbs within me to unveil itself to its hearers.[27]

Questions for Contemplation:

Once more, you do not have to come up with an immediate answer in words. To take an example, although you might be able to say that you do believe in God, the question of *how strongly* you believe may be something to remain with.

1. Do I believe in God, and how strongly?
2. Does God being the Creator mean anything to me?
3. What do I make of the Devil? Could I say that I fear him?

---

[27] *Jacob of Sarug's Homilies on the Six Days of Creation: The First Day*, Gorgias, Piscataway, 2009, ll. 49-54.

Lesson 4

Our Lord Jesus Christ

4.1 Introduction

We now speak of the Second Person of the Blessed Trinity: Our Lord Jesus Christ. He was, in a manner which we cannot understand, *both* fully human *and* fully divine. We learn what the Church teaches about Him from the liturgy, commencing with the liturgy for Genealogy Sunday, which is the Sunday immediately before Christmas. In the *Hoosoye*, or incense prayers for forgiveness, we hear:

> Let us glorify the Ancient of Days, born of the Father before all
> ages, who at the appointed time took flesh from the Virgin Mary.
> By His birth He fulfilled the revelation of the Holy Spirit, spoken
> by the prophets.

A tremendous amount of information has been delivered in these two sentences. First of all, note that it is Trinitarian: it says that the Holy Spirit prophesied the birth of Jesus, who was born twice – first, from the Father *before all ages*, and second *in the flesh* from the Virgin

Mary. This points to the critical role of Our Lady in the history of humanity's relationship with God. It also tells us that the Holy Spirit made his prophecies through the prophets, meaning the prophets of the Old Testament. The "Ancient of Days" is referred to in the Book of Daniel, and Daniel was a prophet. In the appendix to this lesson, I explain the Ancient of Days from the Book of Daniel, but first, let us summarise what just one Gospel, the Gospel of St Mark, tells us about Our Lord. This way, we get a good overview of who Our Lord was and what He did, from just one relatively short document, which you can then read for yourself, learning more as you do so.

The Gospel of St Mark commences by declaring that it is the story of the "Gospel of Jesus Christ, the Son of God." So we immediately know that this is no ordinary biography! Although St Mark wrote his Gospel within forty years of the death of Our Lord (i.e. by 70 A.D.), no one really knows how much older it could be, except that it must have been written after St Peter had begun teaching in Rome, not before the year 50.[28]

4.2 The Story of Our Lord, according to St Mark[29]

In the first chapter, the Gospel narrates the story of the Baptism of Our Lord, which we have briefly looked at; and then the Temptation in the desert. The desert in question is near the Jordan River. This river is not like most European streams, one which wanders through pleasant green valleys and verdant hills. It is more like some of the rivers in Australia's outback, running through wild country, often stony, rocky and with little vegetation. So, to leave the Jordan River and arrive at

---

[28] I do not go into the reasons for this dating, but, in this book, the approach taken to dating is invariably that of E. Earle Ellis, *The Making of the New Testament Documents*, Brill Academic Publishers, Inc. Leiden, 1999.

[29] If one reads the Gospels of Ss Matthew, Mark and Luke, they give the impression that Our Lord's ministry on earth took but one year. However, the Gospel of St John, which makes an effort to be precise on this point, shows that His ministry was actually around three years.

the desert need not take very long. There, He was tempted by the devil. Of course, He defeated the devil, and then, St Mark tells us, He began to preach in Galilee. Galilee is a northern area of Israel, which comes right up to the southern border of modern Lebanon. St Mark says that Jesus came teaching this message: "The time is accomplished, and the kingdom of God is at hand: repent, and believe the gospel." So, we see that Our Lord was referring to the fulfilment of some period of time: "the appointed time" of the Maronite liturgy extracted above.

Then Jesus began to call His twelve apostles, commencing with two fishermen: Simon (Peter) and his brother Andrew. Jesus summonsed them, saying: "Come after me, and I will make you fishers of men." He next called James and John the sons of Zebedee, also fishermen. These were the four main apostles. Our Lord then went to the town of Caphernaum, and began to teach in the synagogues (where the Jews met for religious services when not in the Temple of Jerusalem), arousing a good deal of interest. When the demons possessing a man saw Him, they cried out: "What have we to do with you, Jesus of Nazareth? Are you come to destroy us? I know who you are, the Holy One of God" (Mark 1:24). Our Lord expelled the demon, which all caused some astonishment in the synagogue.

We are told that Our Lord continued to go about the countryside, healing and casting out demons. In Mark 2:1-12, there is a story of how a paralysed man who wanted to be cured tried to come to Jesus for healing, but could not approach Him because of the crowds. So the poor man's friends took him up to the roof of the house within which Jesus was, and opening the roof, placed the paralysed man onto a mattress, and then, through the opening, lowered him down before the Lord. Jesus cured him, and also said that his sins were forgiven. This forgiving of sins, or "absolution," upset many of the people there, who objected that no one but God could forgive sins.

These two stories from the beginning of the Gospel of St Mark are reasonably important, because they show that He was God: first from the words of the demons, and secondly from the implication of the Lord's words.

Our Lord then went about Galilee, and completed the selection of the twelve apostles who were to preach the gospel (the good news), and to heal and exorcise (cast out demons) (3:14-15). As He preached, He told His parables, or teaching stories. These are quite distinctive to Our Lord, so we will look at some of them separately.

4.3 The Parables

In lesson 1 we saw the parable of the Prodigal Son. In chapter 4, St Mark relates how Jesus told the Parable of the Sower. This parable is interesting in itself, but, in addition, Our Lord ends by explaining how to understand the parables. The parables include some of the most famous tales in world literature, such as The Prodigal Son, The Good Samaritan and The Ruler's Son. The Parable of the Sower is as follows:

> "Listen to this! Behold, the sower went out to sow; as he was sowing, some seed fell beside the road, and the birds came and ate it up. Other seed fell on the rocky ground where it did not have much soil; and immediately it sprang up because it had no depth of soil. But after the sun had risen, it was scorched; and because it had no root, it withered away. Other seed fell among the thorns, and the thorns came up and choked it, and it yielded no crop. Other seeds fell into the good soil, and as they grew up and increased, they yielded a crop and produced thirty, sixty, and a hundredfold." He said: "He who has ears to hear, let him hear."

> As soon as He was alone, His followers, along with the twelve, began asking Him about the parables. And He said: "To you has been given the mystery of the kingdom of God, but those who are outside get everything in parables…"

> And He said to them: "Do you not understand this parable? How

will you understand all the parables? The sower sows the word. These are the ones who are beside the road where the word is sown; and when they hear, immediately Satan comes and takes away the word which has been sown in them. In a similar way these are the ones on whom seed was sown on the rocky places, who, when they hear the word, immediately receive it with joy; and they have no firm root in themselves, but are only temporary; then, when affliction or persecution arises because of the word, immediately they fall away. And others are the ones on whom seed was sown among the thorns; these are the ones who have heard the word, but the worries of the world, and the deceitfulness of riches, and the desires for other things enter in and choke the word, and it becomes unfruitful. And those are the ones on whom seed was sown on the good soil; and they hear the word and accept it and bear fruit, thirty, sixty, and a hundredfold." (from Mark 4)

Questions for Contemplation:

1. Could I retell this story in my own words?

2. What type or types of seed would I say that I am?

3. What can I do to be like the seed sown on good soil?

4.4 Jesus' Teaching and Actions

There are many other parables in the Gospel of Mark to be explored later. Returning to the historical narrative, of special interest is the recounting of the calming of a storm in chapter 4 of St Mark's Gospel. The apostles were rowing Jesus across the lake (an inland sea), and while He was sleeping, a storm arose. They feared that they were going to sink, and so awoke Him. He ordered the wind and the sea to be still, and they were (4:35-41). Chapter 5 of the Gospel has more healing stories, one of which was an exorcism. In chapter 6, we learn that many people who had known Jesus all His life, even some of His own family, could not accept Him as a great teacher. It is said, with much truth, that "familiarity breeds contempt." After this, Jesus nonetheless sent the twelve apostles out to preach: the time had come for them to turn their hands to spreading the good news. As Jesus became better known, King Herod started to wonder if Jesus were a prophet, and even if He might not be the prophet John the Baptist, whom Herod had had put to death. At this point, St Mark goes back in time to tell us the tragic story of what had happened to John the Baptist. When St Mark returns to the Lord's ministry, the Twelve have returned from their preaching. They saw that Jesus was surrounded by a huge crowd of 5,000 people, which He miraculously fed from five loaves and two fish (Mark 6:34-44). These stories of miraculous feeding were much loved in the early Church, and were often used to decorate the catacombs, the underground cemeteries of the Christians at Rome. After the feeding of the five thousand comes the story of the walking on water, and other memorable incidents. At the beginning of the account, we are told that the Lord had remained on shore while the apostles were on the sea, fishing. A wind came up, which made it hard for them to row, and then:

> … at about the fourth watch of the night, He (Jesus) came to them, walking on the sea; and He intended to pass by them. But when they saw Him walking on the sea, they supposed that it was a ghost, and cried out; for they all saw Him and were terrified. But immediately He spoke with them and said to them: "Take courage; it is I, do not be afraid." Then He got into the boat with them, and the wind stopped; and they were utterly astonished, for they had not gained any insight from the incident of the loaves, but their heart was hardened. (Mark 6:47-52)

It is typical of St Mark to mention that the apostles failed to understand. He, more than any other evangelist, uses the theme of the apostles being out of their depth with the Lord. It is still true today that we do not completely understand our faith. But if we realise this, it may motivate us to strive to understand it better.

When chapter 7 of the Gospel commences, Jesus is in conflict with the Pharisees, who represent part of the religious establishment of Judaism. They complain that Jesus is not keeping all the religious rules. Our Lord replies that they are clinging to exterior things and to human, not divine, traditions. He then makes the famous statement: "Nothing that enters one from outside can defile (i.e. make unclean) that person, but the things that come out from within are what defile." (Mark 7:15). This chapter also shows Our Lord visiting areas outside of Israel, and curing a man in the Decapolis area (modern Jordan), and includes an account of the meeting with Syrophoenician woman (Phoenicia was then part of Syria, so she was probably a Phoenician woman who spoke not the ancient Phoenician language, but rather the Syrian language, known today as Aramaic). The narrative tells us that she was a Gentile. "Gentile" means "non-Jewish." The Gentiles were regarded as "unclean" by the Jews. The Jewish rules of cleanness and purity extended to food, the preparation of food, and many other matters. These rules are a major part of Judaism, as they are of Islam. Now follows the account:

> ... after hearing of Him, a woman whose little daughter had an unclean spirit immediately came and fell at His feet. Now the woman was a Gentile, of the Syrophoenician race. And she kept asking Him to cast the demon out of her daughter. He said to her: "Let the children be satisfied first, for it is not good to take the children's bread and throw it to the dogs." But she answered and said to Him: "Yes, Lord, but even the dogs under the table feed on the children's crumbs." And He said to her: "Because of this answer go; the demon has gone out of your daughter." And going back to her home, she found the child lying on the bed, the demon having left. (Mark 7:25-30)

This is a powerful tale of how, although Jesus came from the Jews, He neither limited His teaching to them nor remained within the parameters of their faith. This disturbed some of the Jews, because they had the idea that they alone had been chosen as the people of God, and were identified with their purity laws, which tended to strengthen their exclusivity. It is common today to say that Jesus was a Jew. This is often used to argue that the Gospels accounts therefore exaggerate what was new in His teaching. It is true that Our Lord was born and raised a Jew, and considered Himself to be of the faith. But it is not the complete and exhaustive truth. He was more than a Jew, and He saw the limitations in Judaism, such as its exclusivity. He brought His new teaching to transcend and perfect Judaism, and to offer the truth to all men.

Then the Gospel of St Mark presents another feeding, this time of four thousand people, with seven loaves and a few fish. It is said that He performed the miracle because He was moved to pity for the crowds (8:1-9). He predicted to them His own coming death and resurrection (8:31-33). A most significant event then occurred, the Transfiguration (Mark 9:2-8), wherein Jesus took Peter, James and John with Him upon a high mountain, and there appeared in His true heavenly form, blinding them with the light. We celebrate this each year on 6 August as a major feast. Our Lord made another prediction of His own death and resurrection, but St Mark tells us that the disciples did not understand, and were afraid to question Him (9:31-32).

There is much more to ponder in the Transfiguration: this is but a brief introduction. But even this introduction can point to a distinctive feature of the Syriac interpretation of the life of the Lord, which is how it always *connects* the episodes of His life together, finding a unity in them. In this instance, Jacob of Sarug gives the inspired opinion that, Our Lord knowing that His disciples would find the Crucifixion hard to understand and accept, wished to show the key apostles (Peter, James and John) who He really was all the time, so that they might believe, especially when He would look least like the Son of God. Jacob wrote:

> When the time of sufferings and of crucifixion came,
> He (Jesus) wanted to show them His great glory on a high mountain.
> In proportion to the magnitude of the insult and disgrace of the Cross,

He magnified the sign of His glory on the mountain and made it manifest to them.

They saw His glory in order that they may not hesitate on account of his humiliation,

so that from His magnificence they might retain love for his feebleness.[30]

This is still true today, for there are moments when we catch a glimpse of the greatness, the holiness, the great supporting power of God. But there are also times when it seems as if it was all a dream. We need to recall and to treasure those moments, so that they remain with us in our time of need. After more teaching and miracles, St Mark tells us of the blessing of the children:

And they brought children to Him so that He might touch them; but the disciples rebuked them. But when Jesus saw this, He was indignant and said to them: "Permit the children to come to Me; do not hinder them; for the kingdom of God belongs to such as these. Amen, I say to you, whoever does not receive the kingdom of God like a child will not enter it at all." And He took them in His arms and began blessing them, laying His hands on them. (Mark 10:13-16)

This is one of the most well-known and best loved passages in all the Gospels, perhaps because in some ways we all see ourselves as children needing the love of God. Another interesting feature is how often Our Lord says "Amen" before declaring anything to His disciples. This was unique to the Lord: no one else ever asserted the truth of what he said by using this Hebrew word, meaning "it is confirmed": "it is true," or – approximately – "may it be." Before Our Lord, it had been used as a response, especially by congregations. It was sort of like saying: "we agree." But it had been a way of confirming what had been said or read by someone else, while Our Lord used it of His own sayings. St Matthew records Our Lord saying "amen" 31 times, St

---

[30] *Jacob of Sarug's Homily on the Transfiguration of Our Lord*, trans. Thomas Kollamparampil, 99-104 (pp.16-18).

Mark has it 13 times, and St Luke on six occasions. But only St John, the evangelist who insists on letting us know that he was there and saw what he describes, depicts Our Lord saying: "amen, amen," on some 25 occasions!

In other words, the use of this word is an actual historic memory of something distinctive about the way Our Lord spoke. No wonder, then, that in the Book of Revelation (the Apocalypse), St John actually records Our Lord speaking in His own name as "the Amen" (Revelation 3:14). It is much to be regretted that zealous modern translators have almost all replaced "amen" with "truly." First of all, the Gospels are written in Greek, but "amen" is not a Greek word. This shows that the evangelists deliberately used a Hebrew word to make it stand out. Second, it was distinctive of the Lord. To keep it is to obliterate the distinctiveness which the evangelists wished to portray, and to lose the memory of His personal manner of speech.[31]

4.6 The Entry to Jerusalem, and the Passion and Death of the Lord

Jesus' most explicit prediction of His death and resurrection comes in Mark 10:32-34, where He prophesied that He would be handed over to the Gentiles (for the Romans were non-Jews or "Gentiles") and they would mock Him, spit upon Him, scourge and then slay Him, but that he would rise after three days. After more healings and teaching, Our Lord entered Jerusalem. This was the chief city of the Jews. Jerusalem was and still is, set upon a mountain. It is still surrounded by walls (at least the Old City is). You could then only enter by a few gates. He entered riding on a young donkey, while people removed their cloaks, cut branches and placed them beneath His feet like a welcome carpet, crying:

Hosanna! Blessed is he who comes in the name of the Lord;

---

[31]   The same

Blessed is the coming kingdom of our father David;
Hosanna in the highest! (Mark 11:9-10)

The next day, He drove the money-changers out from the Temple. When people came to Jerusalem to perform sacrifices, they would have money from different parts of the world. They needed the local currency to purchase the animals to be sacrificed. They obtained this currency from the local money-changers, who had set up their tables in the grounds of the Temple. These courtyards were considered to share in the holiness of the Temple. Our Lord's actions worried the religious authorities, who tried to find a way to shame and to stop Him. In one such case, they tried to trick him:

> Then they sent some of the Pharisees … to Him in order to trap Him in a statement. They came and said to Him: "Teacher, we know that You are truthful and defer to no one; for You are not partial to any, but teach the way of God in truth. Is it lawful to pay a poll-tax to Caesar, or not? Shall we pay or shall we not pay?" But He, knowing their hypocrisy, said to them: "Why are you testing Me? Bring Me a denarius to look at." They brought one. And He said to them: "Whose likeness and inscription is this?" And they said to Him: "Caesar's." And Jesus said to them: "*Render to Caesar the things that are Caesar's, and to God the things that are God's.*" And they were amazed at Him. (Mark 12:13-17)

One feature of this which we should note is that *Our Lord did not have a denarius*. A denarius was a reasonably valuable Roman coin. In St Matthew's Gospel, a denarius is the day's pay for a labourer (Matthew 20:2). In the account of the widow's mite which we shall read below, all that she had to live on was one *quadratus* which was only worth one sixty-fourth of one denarius, which shows how very poor she was. That Our Lord had to ask to be shown such a coin is probably not coincidence: it is more likely to be eloquent proof of His poverty.

Soon after this came the question about the greatest commandment, which we have already looked at. You will recall that Our Lord said that the greatest commandment is to love God and to love your neighbour as yourself (Mark 12:29-31). The scribe who had asked the Lord this question answered rightly, and the Lord replied that he (the scribe) was not far from the Kingdom of God (12:34). This shows that Our Lord was perfectly fair to his opponents, and that not all of them were fools, or evil. Then comes one of my favourite passages, The Widow's Mite:

> And He sat down opposite the treasury, and began observing how the people were putting money into the treasury; and many rich people were putting in large sums. A poor widow came and put in two *lepta* (small bronze coins), which amounted to a *quadratus*. Calling His disciples to Him, He said to them: "Amen, I say to you, this poor widow put in more than all the contributors to the treasury; for they all put in out of their surplus, but she, out of her poverty, put in all she owned, all she had to live on." (Mark 12:41-44)

Chapter 13 of this Gospel is devoted to prophecies concerning the end, the most important of which says that we do not and cannot know when that time will come (Mark 13:34). This passage concludes with a sobering parable:

> It is like a man away on a journey, who upon leaving his house and putting his slaves in charge, assigning to each one his task, also commanded the doorkeeper to stay on the alert. Therefore, be on the alert - for you do not know when the master of the house is coming, whether in the evening, at midnight, or when the rooster crows, or in the morning - in case he should come suddenly and find you asleep. What I say to you I say to all: "Be on the alert!' (Mark 13:34-37)

Then, we are told, one his twelve apostles, Judas Iscariot, made a plot with the priests to betray Jesus to them. On that Thursday night before he died, he had a supper, known as The Last Supper, with His apostles. He predicted His betrayal, and at the meal, this happened:

> While they were eating, He took some bread, and after a blessing He broke it, and gave it to them, and said: "Take it; this is My body." And when He had taken a cup and given thanks, He gave it to them, and they all drank from it. And He said to them: "This

is My blood of the covenant, which is poured out for many. Amen I say to you, I will never again drink of the fruit of the vine until that day when I drink it new in the kingdom of God. (Mark 14:22-25)

This is, of course, the origin of the tradition we use for our Mass.[32] After this, they all went to the Garden of Gethsemane. The most important thing which happened there is that Judas came to Him with soldiers, and He was arrested. Then, He was tried, and as He foretold, He was tortured and then put to death. But on the third day He arose again, and appeared to many. This, then, is a brief general account of what Our Lord did when He was on earth.

Appendix: The Ancient of Days

Chapter 7 of the Book of Daniel, which is in the Old Testament, contains this prophecy of the future: "... Daniel saw a dream ... I kept looking until the thrones (of the kingdoms of the earth) were cast down, and the Ancient of Days was seated. His garments were white like snow, and the hair of his head was like pure wool. His throne was of blazing flames, and his wheels were burning fire. A stream of fire flowed forth and came before him. Thousands ministered to him, and ten thousand stood before him. Judgment was ready, and the books were opened. ... In these visions of the night I then saw, behold! One like the Son of Man came with the clouds, and they brought him to the Ancient of Days. He was given dominion, glory and a kingdom, so that all people, nations and languages should serve him. His dominion is everlasting. It shall not pass away, and his kingdom shall never be destroyed. (Daniel 7:1-2, 9-14)

---

[32] Most modern liturgical scholars do not accept that Our Lord did institute the Eucharist, and deny the historical value of the accounts in the Synoptics and St Paul to that effect. I have attempted an academic answer: Joseph Azize: "The Institution of the Eucharist in the Gospel of John, the *Didache* and Ignatius of Antioch," *Universitas* 2016, 504, 3-35.

The Ancient of Days was sometimes considered to be the Father, and sometimes the Holy Spirit, but as in our Mass, He was usually considered to the Jesus Christ. Note, too that the Ancient of Days is involved in judging. This is most definitely the role of Jesus, as Our Lord said (John 5:21). This is also the basis of the picture of Our Lord which St John gives in the Book of Revelation 1:13-18: "I saw one like a son of man, clothed in a robe reaching to the feet, and girded across His chest with a golden sash. His head and His hair were white like white wool, like snow; and His eyes were like a flame of fire. His feet were like burnished bronze, when it has been made to glow in a furnace, and His voice was like the sound of many waters. In His right hand He held seven stars, and out of His mouth came a sharp two-edged sword; and His face was like the sun shining in its strength. When I saw Him, I fell at His feet like a dead man. And He placed His right hand on me, saying: "Do not be afraid; I am the first and the last, and the living One; and I was dead, and behold, I am alive forevermore, and I have the keys of death and of Hades."

Lesson 5

Our Lord's Life, Death and Purpose

5.1   The Incarnation

Why was Our Lord born into our world? There are several legitimate and complementary ways of looking at this, some of them being more complete than others. But all of them have in common that they discuss the question by reference to *the revelation of God to humanity*, and the desire of God that we should come to know, serve and love Him. That is, in order to unite us to Himself, God sent Our Lord into the world to show to us the way back to our eternal home.

This idea is so tremendous that we become quickly used to it: it is too much to really take in. What we are saying is that Christ willingly came to earth so that we could be united with Him in heaven. This was promised to the prophets of the Old Testament, and was fulfilled on the night when Our Lord was born: Christmas Eve. Let us take just one explanation of His coming or *incarnation* (that is, His becoming human flesh), which we learn from the most uniquely Maronite anaphora of all, the *Šarar*. It says that Our Lord came to establish peace between heaven and earth:[33]

---

[33]   This ancient anaphora is used in Lebanon, but not yet in Australia.

You have generously bestowed on the faithful Church the luminous peace which the highest angels bore to the world with hymns of thanks and worship, and through it her children have acquired enlightened understanding. The peace which was sent by the angel Gabriel to the Virgin Mary, Holy Mother of God, saying to her: "Peace be with you, the Lord is with you, and from you the Saviour of the children of Adam shall appear. The peace which was established between those who dwell on high and those who dwell below, and through which the angels were sent to preach the good news on earth, saying: "Glory to God in the Highest, and on earth peace to men and women of good will."

Why was there any need for Our Lord to establish this peace? The answer is implied in that passage: after the actions of Adam, a Saviour was needed. So what had Adam done? We shall look at this in more detail afterwards, but the simple answer is that Adam and Eve, the first man and woman, sinned. That is, they did something which God had specifically commanded them not to do. As a result, sin entered the world, and humanity, which had been born for immortality, became mortal. We do believe that there were really was an Adam and Eve, and that through their transgression humanity fell from the grace and goodness which it should naturally have possessed. They had lived in a state of bliss or paradise, but after this sin, were expelled from that paradise: "The Garden of Eden." For this reason, their sin is known as "The Fall."[34]

The existence, indeed the dominance of sin among people caused a rupture between humanity and God. The rupture was not complete, there were always men and women who loved and served God. And God did not entirely abandon us. Rather, He chose to send His Son to earth to make peace between humanity and Himself possible. His Son was also to suffer and offer up His own life in atonement for the sin of the world, or more precisely, for those who would, by intention, faith

---

[34] Yet, Our Lord, as recorded in the Gospels, assumes rather than expounds this doctrine. He manifested the truth in Himself. It was for later writers to piece together the analysis.

and good deeds, do His will. So Our Lord:

1. Taught us what to do and what to refrain from doing.
2. Gave us an example of goodness.
3. Suffered and died for us as a sin-offering to God.
4. Rose again from the dead to show that God had accepted the offering.
5. Left behind a visible Church to continue His work.

5.2 The Temptation

We have, by scanning the Gospel of St Mark, obtained an overview of the life of Jesus. We now know that he was incarnated for our sakes. But we must say more about the Lord, for His life and work are central to the faith, and to our destiny – yours and mine. We will begin with the Syriac interpretation of the Temptation of the Lord, an episode which is told in the Gospels of Matthew, Mark and Luke. It was obviously very important, because all three of these evangelists told it. Further, we Maronites have a special day when we recall the Temptation, that day being the last Friday of Lent. The connection with Lent, a time of fasting and mortification,[35] will become apparent when we know what happened at the Temptation. St Matthew states:

> Then Jesus was led up by the Spirit into the wilderness to be tempted by the devil. And after He had fasted forty days and forty nights, He then became hungry. And the tempter came and said to Him: "If You are the Son of God, command that these stones become bread." But He answered and said: "It is written: "Man

---

[35] "Mortification" means bringing the body and its appetites into subjection by denying them something. What we deny them is either something which they can well do without (e.g. lollies), or something which we allow them in sufficient but not copious quantities (e.g. food). Temporarily doing without something (e.g. coffee) will help us remember that we are abstaining, and why, and that we are seeking holiness. It will also develop the will power and may be effective for the forgiveness of sins, should God accept our offering of this penance (which, we believe, He ordinarily would). This is why, in the Mass for the Friday of the Temptation, we sing "Fasting gives light to the mind and brings purity to body and soul. Fasting helps protect our hearts from sinful desires."

shall not live on bread alone, but on every word that proceeds out of the mouth of God."

Then the devil took Him into the holy city and had Him stand on the pinnacle of the temple, and said to Him: "If You are the Son of God, throw Yourself down; for it is written: "He will command his angels concerning you'; and 'On their hands they will bear you up, so that you will not strike your foot against a stone." Jesus said to him: "On the other hand, it is written: "You shall not put the Lord your God to the test.""

Again, the devil took Him to a very high mountain and showed Him all the kingdoms of the world and their glory; and he said to Him: "All these things I will give You, if You fall down and worship me." Then Jesus said to him: "Go, Satan! For it is written: "You shall worship the Lord your God, and serve him only." Then the devil left Him; and behold, angels came and began to minister to Him. (Matthew 4:1-11)

Note that Our Lord was driven into the wilderness by the Spirit, where He would be tempted. This is an example of the co-working of the Persons of the Most Holy Trinity. Note, too, that He rejected the temptation to rule over the world. This episode is important because it sets the tone for the whole of the Gospel account of Our Lord's life. We know from it that:

- He was God, for angels ministered to Him when it was complete (also, each of his three answers to Satan is ambiguous: each can mean that He is God, but does not necessarily have to mean that).
- He had rejected and outsmarted the devil.
- He was beyond any temptation of the body or for power or for wealth and glory.

Jacob of Sarug wrote two homilies on the Temptation. In the first of these he commences with asking the Lord to inspire him (Jacob) so that he may understand by seeing. This is important: as Jacob states, no one can *understand* God and His mysteries, all we can do is ask God to let us see. How does God grant us this sight? *By Himself gazing at us*, so that we are the mirror in which God looks, and so we can tell of the reflection which appears in our souls.[36] This is a beautiful and humble way to pray and to study, remembering that it is God who does the work in us, we simply ask Him and then cooperate. We could all take as our own Jacob's prayer:

> Son of God, look in my soul, and it will be full of your beauties,
> And remain with it, lest it be cut off from your companionship....
> See me, seer of all, fill me with wonder of your power. (lines 23, 24 & 26)

Jacob states that Satan mistakenly thought that he could tempt the Lord and succeed, because he saw that the Lord had a body (ll. 40-74), and that He had been fasting (ll.79-125). When the devil did approach Jesus to tempt Him, he had a chance of success, for Our Lord was genuinely hungry (ll. 193-212). He states that Satan tempted Our Lord three ways: through love of the belly, through love of praise and through love of riches and power, but, in each case, Our Lord showed us how to overcome these temptations (ll. 550-570). This echoes the teaching of St John who warned us against desire of the flesh and of the eyes, and the arrogance of life (1 John 2:16). Significantly for us, Jacob gives this defeating of the devil and showing us how to do so in our turn, as being related to the very reason for Our Lord's incarnation:

> For our sake Our Lord set out into the world,
> And it is more fitting for us than for the angels to praise Him,
> For he was acquiring victory for humanity,
> and for this reason He became man, that he might teach them
> With what weapon they should meet the opponent ... (ll. 550-554)

The second of these homilies has some overlap, and includes a wonderful meditation on the role of the angels at the end of the passage. However, I must include this thought from the first homily, which Jacob delivers almost by the way, as it were:

---

[36] *Jacob of Sarug's Homilies on Jesus' Temptation*, ed. and trans. Adam Carter McCollum, Gorgias Press, Piscataway NJ, 2014, Homily 82, lines 1-10, p. 28.

Truth is more beautiful than any beauty in creation,
And there is no other beauty like it in the world:
The truth of the Creator is his beauty and praise ... (ll. 373-375).

Questions for Contemplation

1. What is meant by temptation?

2. What are the nature of the temptations made to Our Lord?

3. How do I react to temptations in my own life?

5.3 The Plot to Kill the Lord

After the Temptation, Our Lord began teaching and performing miracles, as we have seen in the last lesson. But after a period of up to three years, He went up to Jerusalem knowing that He was to suffer and be put to death. The authorities had made the decision to do so after He had raised His friend Lazarus from the dead. St John, in his Gospel, tells us:

> The chief priests therefore, and the Pharisees, gathered a council, and said: "What can we do, for this man does many miracles? If we let him alone so, all will believe in him; and the Romans will come, and take away our place and nation." But one of them, named Caiaphas, being the high priest that year, said to them: "You know nothing. Neither do you consider that it is expedient[37] for you that one man should die for the people, and that the whole nation perish not." And this he spoke not of himself: but being the high priest of that year, he prophesied that Jesus should die for the nation. And not only for the nation, but to gather together in one the children of God, that were dispersed. From that day therefore they devised to put him to death. (John 11:47-52)

---

[37] Something is "expedient" if it helps us reach an end, e.g. it is expedient to catch a taxi if I have to get somewhere faster than the bus can take me.

There is a great deal to consider in this, but it is ironical[38] that Caiaphas, in recommending that Jesus be put to death, says that it is expedient for one person to die so that the people might live, for this is in fact what happened: Our Lord's self-sacrifice gives us life. But Caiaphas had not meant it like that.

Now those who intended to put the Lord to death were certain religious authorities of the time in Jerusalem, and especially a group named the Pharisees. Oddly, the more the Pharisees have been studied, the more complicated the picture appears. The best source for this group in the time of Our Lord and what they did to Him is actually the New Testament itself. Of the role the Pharisees play in the Gospel of St John, one expert says:

> The Pharisees in John function both as government officials and as the learned doctors of the law who are interested in Jesus' teaching and dispute its truth.... John emphasizes the Pharisees' leadership role in the community. ... they acted as established leaders should; they kept their distance from the newcomer and schemed to blunt his influence and preserve their own. When they took official action it was with the cooperation of the chief priests and other officials. They were not the main political leaders, for the chief priests took over as the main opponents of Jesus in the passion narrative just as in the Synoptic Gospels.[39]

So to maintain their own position, the authorities decided to have Our Lord killed, for He was becoming too well known and highly regarded. In lesson 4, we saw some of the attempts they made to entrap Him. Our Lord of course knew what would happen and He accepted it. For example, in Matthew 16:21 we read: "From that time Jesus began to show His disciples that He must go to Jerusalem and suffer many

---

[38] "Irony" can be saying the opposite of what is meant, e.g. when I make a mistake, I say: "clever!" But it can also be an unintended meaning, which seems to mock what was intended. Here, it was intended to end Jesus and His work, and to save the people through that. But, ironically, the killing of the Lord *fulfilled* His plan of salvation and secured the salvation of the faithful.

[39] Anthony J. Saldarini: "Pharisees" in the *Anchor Bible Dictionary*.

things from the elders and chief priests and scribes, and be killed, and on the third day be raised." This points to the existence of His divine plan. Our Lord consented to this design, which is the central feature of what we call "the divine economy of salvation," the word "economy" initially referring to the overall scheme for management of a house, but here, it is the management and direction of the entire creation.

Jesus did indicate this to His twelve apostles, but they either could not or did not wish to understand. St Luke records:

> Then Jesus took unto him the twelve, and said to them: "Behold, we go up to Jerusalem, and all things shall be accomplished which were written by the prophets concerning the Son of Man. For He shall be delivered to the Gentiles, and shall be mocked, and scourged, and spat upon: and after they have scourged him, they will put Him to death; and the third day He shall rise again." But they understood none of these things, and this word was hid from them, and they did not understand the things that were said. (Luke 11:31-34)

However, Our Lord had His plan, it had to proceed. This is why He decided to have that last meal with the apostles, which we studied in the last lesson, and which is now known as "the Last Supper." After that supper, Our Lord took the apostles to the Garden of Gethsemane, as we saw. There He prayed to the Father: "if you will, remove this chalice from Me. But yet, not My will, but yours be done" (Luke 22:42). By speaking of the "chalice," a ceremonial cup and its contents, Our Lord meant that He would accept what was in store for Him, just as a man might say that he will drink whatever has been poured into a cup for him.

Importantly, it is at the Last Supper that Our Lord instituted the priesthood and the Eucharistic sacrifice. We recall the Last Supper in each and every Mass we say the Institution Narrative, which is the story of how the Eucharist was instituted.

5.4 The Institution Narrative of the Divine Sacrifice of the Mass

The full significance of Our Lord's work is taught in the *Šarar* anaphora,[40] in the most solemn part, which we refer to as the "Institution Narrative." It is one of the unique and distinctive aspects of the *Šarar* that the priest's prayer is addressed directly to the Lord, saying *You* did this on the night of the Last Supper, whereas in the vast majority of anaphoras, it is to the Father, saying of Our Lord that *He* did this and that.[41] The Institution Narrative from the *Šarar* states:

> We make remembrance, Lord, as You taught us: On that night on which You were delivered over to the crucifiers, You took, Lord, bread in Your pure and holy hands. You looked up to heaven, to Your worshipped Father. You blessed +, You sealed +, and You consecrated + it, Lord. You broke it and gave it to Your disciples, the blessed apostles, and You said to them: This bread is My body, which is broken and given for the life of the world. And will be for those who have communion with it, forgiveness of trespasses and the remission of sins. Take and eat of it, and it will be for you unto eternal life.

After the people respond "Amen," the priest continues:

> And likewise with the cup: You thanked +, You praised +, and You said +, Lord: This cup is My blood, the New Covenant, which is shed for many, for the forgiveness of sins. Take and drink from it, all of you. It will be for you for the forgiveness of trespasses and the remission of sins, and unto eternal life.

I think that the most important element here is that Our Lord sacrificed His flesh and His blood to God the Father. *Sacrifice* had been essential to the system set up in Old Testament times, which

---

[40] "Š" is a sign for "sh" as in the English word "English." It is needed because, in Semitic languages, the sounds "s" and "h" may often follow one another, but they should be separately pronounced, for example, the name "ishaq" is not pronounced as if the "sh" was one sound, but as "iss-haq."

[41] The priest addressing the Lord in the second person ("You") making it direct, rather than in the third person ("He"), makes a huge impression on the priest.

was a preparation for the system, or "dispensation"[42] which would be instituted by Our Lord in New Testament times. The sacrifice by Our Lord of His life was the *ultimate* sacrifice to the Father on behalf of sinful mankind. It surpassed the sacrifices of the Old Testament. That ultimate self-offering restored the balance of justice, as it were, and made peace between heaven and earth. Hence St John writes that John the Baptist said of Him: "Behold, the Lamb of God who takes away the sin of the world!" (John 1:29) This is a reference to the sacrifice of the lamb at the time of the first Passover:

> Now the Lord said to Moses and Aaron in the land of Egypt, … "Speak to all the congregation of Israel, saying: "On the tenth of this month they are each one to take a lamb for themselves … You shall keep it until the fourteenth day of the same month, then the whole assembly of the congregation of Israel is to kill it at twilight. Moreover, they shall take some of the blood and put it on the two doorposts and on the lintel of the houses in which they eat it. They shall eat the flesh that same night, roasted with fire, and they shall eat it with unleavened bread and bitter herbs. … and you shall eat it in haste—it is the LORD'S Passover. For I will go through the land of Egypt on that night, and will strike down all the firstborn in the land of Egypt, both man and beast; and against all the gods of Egypt I will execute judgments … The blood shall be a sign for you on the houses where you live; and when I see the blood I will pass over you, and no plague will befall you to destroy you when I strike the land of Egypt. (from Exodus 12:1-13)

The lamb also had a role in the Jewish sacrificial system, and Jesus also identified Himself as the Suffering Servant in Isaiah, but all of this is rather more advanced. It is sufficient to say that Our Lord also accepted that He was offering His life for us: "For the Son of Man did not come to be served, but to serve, and to give His life as a ransom for many" (Mark 10:45). This is what lies behind the terms of the

---

[42] "Dispensation" has a theological meaning of "A religious order or system, conceived as a stage in a progressive revelation, expressly adapted to a particular nation or age." *Shorter Oxford Dictionary*, 1973, p.572.

Institution Narrative in the *Šarar*, which I set out above.

We can also see from the Institution Narrative in the *Šarar* that Our Lord made a *new covenant* with God the Father, which replaced the one Israel had had with God. That covenant was made with Jesus' own blood. This is one aspect of how He made peace between heaven and earth. A covenant is not just a contract, it is a definite agreement in which there is a witness, and the parties bind not only their property (as in a mortgage) or promise to pay money or deliver goods and services, but more importantly, they bind their very *selves*. It is an agreement of *being* before it is an agreement for *doing* something, but of course, if I bind myself I am by that fact indicating what I shall do because what I do manifests or flows from my being. In a covenant, I put *myself* on the line. If I break a contract, I may lose money, or my goods can be sold to recompense the other party for their loss because of my breach. But in a covenant, it is I myself who am lost if I breach it, or redeemed if I keep it.

Under this new covenant: "the Father Himself loves you, because you have loved me and have believed that I came from the Father" (John 16:27). There is a mutuality of person in this covenant of being:

> "But now I come to You; and these things I speak in the world so that they may have My joy made full in themselves. I have given them Your word; and the world has hated them, because they are not of the world, even as I am not of the world. I do not ask You to take them out of the world, but to keep them from the evil one. They are not of the world, even as I am not of the world. Sanctify them in the truth; Your word is truth. As You sent Me into the world, I also have sent them into the world. For their sakes I sanctify Myself, that they themselves also may be sanctified in truth. I do not ask on behalf of these alone, but for those also who believe in Me through their word; that they may all be one; even as You, Father, are in Me and I in You, that they also may be in Us, so that the world may believe that You sent Me. The glory which You have given Me I have given to them, that they may be

one, just as We are one; I in them and You in Me, that they may be perfected in unity, so that the world may know that You sent Me, and loved them, even as You have loved Me. Father, I desire that they also, whom You have given Me, be with Me where I am, so that they may see My glory which You have given Me, for You loved Me before the foundation of the world." (John 17:13-24)

From these words spoken by Jesus, we can see that the reception of the Father is very closely related to the reception of His Word. His "Word" is not the Bible in some simple manner where "written word" *equals* "Word of God," because the Bible had not then been written. The Word of God is rather, Himself, His commandments, and all else which was taught by Our Lord. Together with the Word of God comes *joy*, because one's heart is at peace, knowing that we are doing the right thing. But there is more than this, the Holy Spirit brings joy with Him when He enters us. Joy, like truth, beauty and goodness, is a property of God.

Note that to be part of this covenant with God is to be taken out of the world. We begin to belong to heaven.

5.5 The Resurrection

It is time to return to the Gospel of St Mark, and to focus on the Resurrection of the Lord. However, note that neither St Mark nor any other evangelist ever describes the Resurrection itself. It is referred to, but not from the perspective of any eye-witness. The relevant passage begins in chapter 15, when Pilate, having been informed by a soldier that Jesus has truly died, allows Joseph of Arimathea to take the Lord's body and to place it in a tomb. After that is done, a huge stone was rolled across it. Mark mentions that two of the women saw which tomb Jesus had been laid in. Then comes the account of things to do with the Resurrection:

When the Sabbath was over, Mary Magdalene, and Mary the

mother of James, and Salome, bought spices, so that they might come and anoint Him. Very early on the first day of the week, they came to the tomb when the sun had risen. They were saying to one another: "Who will roll away the stone for us from the entrance of the tomb?" Looking up, they saw that the stone had been rolled away, although it was extremely large. Entering the tomb, they saw a young man sitting at the right, wearing a white robe; and they were amazed. And he said to them: "Do not be amazed; you are looking for Jesus the Nazarene, who has been crucified. He has risen; He is not here; behold, here is the place where they laid Him. But go, tell His disciples and Peter, He is going ahead of you to Galilee. There you will see Him, just as He told you." They went out and fled from the tomb, for trembling and astonishment had gripped them; and they said nothing to anyone, for they were afraid.

Now after He had risen early on the first day of the week, He first appeared to Mary Magdalene, from whom He had cast out seven demons. She went and reported to those who had been with Him, while they were mourning and weeping. When they heard that He was alive and had been seen by her, they refused to believe it. After that, He appeared in a different form to two of them while they were walking along on their way to the country. They went away and reported it to the others, but they did not believe them either. (Mark 16:1-13)

The question whether Jesus rose from the dead is a purely historical one. We have the evidence of the evangelists that He did, and also the fact that the apostles went to the death in the certainty that He had done so. This must be insisted upon: many people have gone to death for their beliefs, and not all of these professed faith in Christ. That is not the point. Whatever those other people believed at the times of their deaths, the point is that the men who did know Our Lord accepted martyrdom because of their belief that He had been raised from the dead and was true God. St Paul stated:

Now if Christ is preached, that He has been raised from the dead, how do some among you say that there is no resurrection of the dead? But if there is no resurrection of the dead, not even Christ has been raised; and if Christ has not been raised, then our preaching is vain, your faith also is vain. Moreover we are even found to be false witnesses of God, because we testified against God that He raised Christ, whom He did not raise, if in fact the dead are not raised. For if the dead are not raised, not even Christ has been raised; and if Christ has not been raised, your faith is worthless; you are still in your sins. Then those also who have fallen asleep in Christ have perished. If we have hoped in Christ in this life only, we are of all men most to be pitied. (1 Corinthians 15:12-19)

So it is that Jesus suffered, died and rose from the dead for us. We all know that He was condemned to suffer and be put to death as a criminal, but the reason that Our Lord allowed this to be done to Him was to reconcile us to the Father. He was the lamb who was sacrificed to save the people.

Lesson 6
The Ascension, Pentecost and the Holy Spirit

6.1   The Lord and the Holy Spirit

6.2   The Ascension

6.3   Pentecost

6.4   The Holy Spirit

6.5   The Parable of the Talents

6.1 The Lord and the Holy Spirit

The Gospel of St John is in many ways the clearest of the Gospels on the relation between Our Lord and the Holy Spirit, so let us methodically follow it. The Gospel of St John begins with a magnificent description of who the Lord is, not as only an earthly man, but in his eternity:

> In the beginning was the Word, and the Word was with God, and the Word was God. He was with God in the beginning. Through him all things were made; without him nothing was made that has been made. In him was life, and that life was the light of all mankind. The light shines in the darkness, and the darkness has not overcome it. (John 1:1-5)

Then, as part of this same passage, we are told about St John the Baptist, and of his own testimony not only to the Lord but also to the Spirit:

> "I saw the Spirit come down from heaven as a dove and remain on Him. And I myself did not know Him, but the one who sent me to baptize with water told me: "The man on whom you see the

Spirit come down and remain is the one who will baptize with the Holy Spirit." I have seen and I testify that this is God's Chosen One." (John 1:32b-35)

Note the element of mutuality: the Spirit came down *from heaven* (showing that He is divine) and rested upon the Lord, and He (the Lord) *will baptise with the Spirit.* They are two different persons, but their work is united. Later on, in a conversation with a man named Nicodemus, Our Lord states:

> ... No one can enter the kingdom of God unless they are born of water and the Spirit. Flesh gives birth to flesh, but the Spirit gives birth to spirit. You should not be surprised at my saying: "You must be born again." The wind blows wherever it pleases. You hear its sound, but you cannot tell where it comes from or where it is going. So it is with everyone born of the Spirit." (John 3:5b-8)

This is further confirmation that the Holy Spirit will be associated with baptism and the regeneration which baptism brings. Our Lord commanded that baptism be observed as the first of the sacraments, the gateway to all the others, but it is the Holy Spirit who operates in the sacrament.

Note, too, that Our Lord speaks of the Spirit as moving in a way beyond our comprehension, working our spiritual rebirth. In other words, to accept the reality of the Spirit, we must open to the reality of the *mystery*. We need to accept that we are in the presence of something which can be logically and rationally spoken of, but which retains an element which transcends (or goes beyond) our reasons.

Then, in a significant section, Our Lord proclaims: "Let anyone who is thirsty come to Me and drink. Whoever believes in Me, as Scripture has said, rivers of living water will flow from within them." By this He meant the Spirit, whom those who believed in Him were later to receive. Up to that time the Spirit had not been given, since Jesus had not yet been glorified. (John 7 37b-39)

This reference to Jesus not having yet been "glorified" is to His not yet having been put to death and risen from the dead. What St John is explaining that even at this point in His earthly ministry, Our Lord had not yet sent or given the Spirit to the faithful, because that would not happen while He (Jesus) was on earth with us. It was only when, towards the end of His earthly life, Our Lord was preparing the disciples for what was to come, that He promised them:

> "If you love me, keep my commands. And I will ask the Father, and He will give you another advocate to help you and be with you forever – the Spirit of truth. The world cannot accept Him, because it neither sees Him nor knows Him. But you know Him, for He lives with you and will be in you." (John 14:15-17)

This fits in with what was said above: the Holy Spirit is not sent while the Lord is on earth ("he lives with you" is a *vivid future*, as if for example someone says "Do that and I go.") Further, the Holy Spirit is not available to everyone: His entering into us is a special gift. Later in the same address, Our Lord says: "But the Advocate (literally, *the Paraclete*), the Holy Spirit, whom the Father will send in my name, will teach you all things and will remind you of everything I have said to you" (John 14:26). Again, the work of the Son and the Spirit is mutual. Then, a little later Our Lord states: "When the Advocate (*Paraclete*) comes, whom I will send to you from the Father, the Spirit of truth who goes out from the Father, He will testify about me" (John 15:26).[43]

I will pause to note that the word *Paraclete* comes from a Greek root meaning "to call to one's side." The Paraclete is the one whom you call to your side, meaning in a general way that he assists you, but then it specifically came to mean the one who consoles you, and the one who is your advocate, your defender. Finally, and most importantly, after He had suffered, died and risen from the dead, Our Lord appeared to the apostles and, among other things:

---

[43] John 16:12-15 continues and completes this teaching.

Again Jesus said: "Peace be with you! As the Father has sent me, I am sending you." And with that He breathed on them and said: "Receive the Holy Spirit. If you forgive anyone's sins, their sins are forgiven; if you do not forgive them, they are not forgiven." (John 20:21-23)

Our Lord *bestowed* the Holy Spirit upon the apostles by blowing upon them: that is, although He did not need to, He chose to use a formal act, *a liturgy*, as a means of showing what He was doing. And with this, came the power to forgive sins, the power which priests use when they hear confessions and grant absolution. It is clear from this overview that the Holy Spirit worked with Our Lord from the beginning of His ministry, but did not directly work with the apostles and the faithful until after the Resurrection of the Lord, when Jesus bestowed the Holy Spirit upon the apostles. But another even greater outpouring of the Spirit was to come at Pentecost.

6.2 The Ascension

The story of the Ascension is told by St Luke. It commences with the Gospel, in which he states that after His death, Our Lord appeared to His apostles, and:

> Then He opened their minds so they could understand the Scriptures. He told them: "This is what is written: The Messiah will suffer and rise from the dead on the third day, and repentance for the forgiveness of sins will be preached in His name to all nations, beginning at Jerusalem. You are witnesses of these things. I am going to send you what my Father has promised; but stay in the city until you have been clothed with power from on high." When He had led them out to the vicinity of Bethany, He lifted up His hands and blessed them. While He was blessing them, He left them and was taken up into heaven. Then they worshiped Him and returned to Jerusalem with great joy. And they stayed continually at the temple, praising God. (Luke 24:45-53)

When Jesus said that He would send to them, He was referring to the Holy Spirit. Then, in the Book of Acts, which St Luke wrote to follow the story of the Gospel by telling of the growth of the Church, he wrote:

> In my former book, Theophilus, I wrote about all that Jesus began to do and to teach until the day He was taken up to heaven, after giving instructions through the Holy Spirit to the apostles He had chosen. After His suffering, He presented himself to them and gave many convincing proofs that He was alive. He appeared to them over a period of forty days and spoke about the kingdom of God. On one occasion, while He was eating with them, He gave them this command: "Do not leave Jerusalem, but wait for the gift My Father promised, which you have heard Me speak about. For John baptized with water, but in a few days you will be baptized with the Holy Spirit."
>
> Then they gathered around Him and asked Him: "Lord, are You at this time going to restore the kingdom to Israel?" He said to them: "It is not for you to know the times or dates the Father has set by His own authority. But you will receive power when the Holy Spirit comes on you; and you will be My witnesses in Jerusalem, and in all Judea and Samaria, and to the ends of the earth."
>
> After He said this, He was taken up before their very eyes, and a cloud hid Him from their sight. They were looking intently up into the sky as He was going, when suddenly two men dressed in white stood beside them. "Men of Galilee," they said: "why do you stand here looking into the sky? This same Jesus, who has been taken from you into heaven, will come back in the same way you have seen Him go into heaven. Then the apostles returned to Jerusalem from the hill called the Mount of Olives, a Sabbath day's walk from the city." (Acts 1:1-12)

This was the last of Jesus' appearances on earth. As St Luke makes very clear, He returned to His Father in heaven. But when He went, He again promised that He would send the Holy Spirit. The Syriac tradition sees in the fact that Jesus ascended from the Mount of Olives, a link between the anointing which is the first stage of baptism and the Ascension, thus Jacob of Sarug states:

> The treasure of oil is on the Mount of Olives for anointing;
> Because Christ too ascended from it towards His Father.
> And ... towards that mountain itself He gathered them
> to supply them with the oil for the signing of the whole earth.[44]

Jacob ends by inviting us to contemplate the *mystery* of the Ascension:

> Rest yourself, O intellect, because the one who ventures advancing and leaping will fall,
> ... The High Priest has entered into the Holy of Holies,[45]
> with His own blood He will reconcile His Father with humanity.
> He is the offering, the High Priest and the libation[46] too,
> ... He descended, visited us, and ascended redeeming us,
> to Him be glory.[47]

In the Maronite liturgy for the Ascension, the emphasis is placed on the Ascension as being when Our Lord fulfilled His promise to go and prepare a place for us:

> My Father's house has many rooms; if that were not so, would I have told you that I am going there to prepare a place for you? And if I go and prepare a place for you, I will come back and take you to be with me that you also may be where I am. (John 14:2-3)

6.3 Pentecost

We have already seen the first Pentecost in lesson 3. Perhaps now we better understand why it was that the Spirit was sent after the Lord

---

[44] *Jacob of Sarug's Homily on the Ascension of the Lord*, trans. and ed. Thomas Kollamparampil, Gorgias, Piscataway, 2010, 165-168, p. 24.

[45] In the Jewish tradition, only the High Priest could enter the most sacred part of the Temple, so too, only Jesus could go straight to the very side of God the Father.

[46] A "libation" is a sacrificial offering of liquid, often water or wine.

[47] *Jacob of Sarug's Homily on the Ascension of the Lord*, from 481-486, pp. 56 and 58.

had returned to His Father on the day of the Ascension. In the Syriac tradition, Pentecost, when the Holy Spirit descended on the heads of Our Lady and the apostles in tongues of fire, is related to what happens afterwards, when they go forth and teach to the assembled people speaking to them so that they (the apostles) could be understood not matter which language the hearer spoke. St Luke described it this way:

> Now there were staying in Jerusalem God-fearing Jews from every nation under heaven. When they heard this sound (of the apostles preaching), a crowd came together in bewilderment, because each one heard their own language being spoken. Utterly amazed, they asked: "Aren't all these who are speaking Galileans? Then how is it that each of us hears them in our native language? Parthians, Medes and Elamites; residents of Mesopotamia, Judea and Cappadocia, Pontus and Asia, Phrygia and Pamphylia, Egypt and the parts of Libya near Cyrene; visitors from Rome (both Jews and converts to Judaism); Cretans and Arabs—we hear them declaring the wonders of God in our own tongues!" Amazed and perplexed, they asked one another: "What does this mean?" Some, however, made fun of them and said: "They have had too much wine." (Acts 2:5-13)

I will not go on to quote what St Peter says in the passage following, but there can be no doubt at all that St Luke wishes us to understand that a miracle has taken place, that it involves *communication of the truth,* and that people were astonished and did not know what to make of it. As the Syriac tradition observes, and as we shall see when we come to the lesson on the Church, the Church is intended to bridge the gaps between all peoples, and preach them the Gospel in their own tongues. Our tradition also relates this descent of the Holy Spirit to the work which He performs in baptism.

6.4 The Holy Spirit

The Holy Spirit, the Third Person of the Most Holy Trinity, has always played a relatively large part in Maronite spirituality and piety. Although very little is said about Him in the New Testament, He is mentioned quite prominently in each and every celebration of the Divine Sacrifice, and is often invoked as *fire* and as *oil*, or more precisely, the power for change and for aiding life which is found in fire and oil. First of all, we need the warning which St Ephrem gives in his *Memra on Faith*:

> Father, Son and Holy Spirit can be reached only by Their names;
> do not look further, to Their Persons (*qnome*),
> just meditate on Their names.
> If you investigate the person of God, you will perish,
> but if you believe in the name, you will live.
> Let the name of the Father be a boundary to you,
> do not cross it and investigate His nature;
> Let the name of the Son be a wall to you,
> do not cross it and investigate His birth from the Father;
> let the name of the Spirit be a fence for you,
> do not enter inside for the purpose of prying into Him.[48]

Often, we find that what is said of the Holy Spirit is also said of the Lord, for example, when we are baptised we put on a "spiritual robe." This robe can be and is described as being the Holy Spirit and as being Christ. We pray in each baptism that at the end of our lives Christ will also be for us the imperishable robe (which will save our souls for eternal life although the body decays). The distinguishing point of Christian baptism is precisely that it is a baptism in the name of the Holy Trinity, so that the grace of the Holy Spirit is received in baptism.

---

[48] Sebastian Brock, *The Luminous Eye*, Cistercian, Kalamazoo, 1985, p.63. St Jerome records that he read, in a Greek translation, Ephrem's work *On the Holy Spirit*, and that: "… even in translation I could recognize the acuteness of his sublime genius." *On Illustrious Men*, trans. Thomas P. Halton, *Catholic University of America,* Washington D.C., 1999, §105, p. 149. Unfortunately, that work has been lost.

Thus John the Baptist states: "As for me, I baptise you with water for repentance, but He who is coming after me is mightier than I, and I am not fit to remove His sandals; He will baptize you with the Holy Spirit and fire" (Matthew 3:11). In the Book of Acts we read:

> ... Paul passed through the upper country and came to Ephesus, and found some disciples. He said to them: "Did you receive the Holy Spirit when you believed?" And they said to him: "No, we have not even heard whether there is a Holy Spirit." And he said: "Into what then were you baptized?" And they said: "Into John's baptism." Paul said: "John baptized with the baptism of repentance, telling the people to believe in Him who was coming after him, that is, in Jesus." When they heard this, they were baptized in the name of the Lord Jesus. And when Paul had laid his hands upon them, the Holy Spirit came on them, and they began speaking with tongues and prophesying. There were in all about twelve men. (Acts 19:1-7)

Note how when the Holy Spirit descends upon these people, they too can speak with tongues. This connects the baptism in the Spirit with the first Pentecost, but whereas that was a miracle worked for the Jews, this was a miracle for the Gentiles.[49]

It is usual today, based on Scripture, to speak of the Seven Gifts of the Holy Spirit. These are: wisdom, understanding, counsel, fortitude, knowledge, piety, and fear of the Lord (Isaiah 11:1-3 "... And a branch from his roots will bear fruit. The Spirit of the Lord will rest on Him, The spirit of wisdom and understanding, The spirit of counsel and strength, The spirit of knowledge and the fear of the Lord. And He will delight in the fear of the Lord ...").

---

[49] The incident in Acts 10 was also a Gentile miracle. Note especially: "While Peter was still speaking these words, the Holy Spirit came on all who heard the message. The circumcised believers who had come with Peter were astonished that the gift of the Holy Spirit had been poured out even on Gentiles. For they heard them speaking in tongues and praising God. Then Peter said: "Surely no one can stand in the way of their being baptized with water. They have received the Holy Spirit just as we have."

The twelve fruits which the Holy Spirit gives us are: charity, joy, peace, patience, kindness, goodness, generosity, gentleness, faithfulness, modesty, self-control, and chastity (Galatians 5:22-23).

As stated, in the Syriac tradition, the Holy Spirit becomes the spiritual robe which the faithful person puts on. Hence, Aphrahat states:

> [In the case of] the person who receives the Spirit from the waters [of baptism] but [then] grieves it, the Spirit departs from him before he dies and goes to its natural condition with Christ, and brings accusation against that person who grieved it. And when the time of the completion of the age comes, and the time of the resurrection draws near,[50] the Holy Spirit which has been kept in purity receives great power from its nature, comes before Christ, stands at the entrance of the graves where those who have kept it in purity are buried, and waits for the shout.[51] And when the watchers have opened the gates of heaven before the King, then the horns will sound and the trumpets will shout, and the Spirit that listens for the shout will hear and quickly open the tombs and raise up the bodies and that which was buried in them, and the Spirit will put on that glory which came with it. The Spirit will be within for the resurrection of the body, and the glory will be on the outside for the adornment of the body. The natural spirit will be swallowed up in the heavenly Spirit and the whole person will become spiritual, since his body is in the Spirit. Death will be swallowed up by life and the body will be swallowed up by the Spirit. And through the Spirit that person will fly to meet the King who will receive him with joy, and Christ will give thanks for the body which has guarded the Spirit in purity.[52]

There are many scriptural allusions here. For example, when Aphrahat states that the Spirit brings accusations, he is referring to the concept of the Spirit as the *Paraclete*, the Advocate, who will always

---

[50] That is, the end of the world at which time all shall rise from the dead for judgment.

[51] St Paul says that when Our Lord returns to judge the world, He will utter a loud command, and an archangel will speak out (1 Thessalonians 4:16).

[52] *The Demonstrations of Aphrahat, the Persian Sage,* trans. Adam Lehto: "Demonstration 6," §14, p. 193.

speak the truth before the Just Judge (who is Christ).

Then, in 1 Corinthians 6:19, St Paul teaches: "Do you not know that your body is a temple of the Holy Spirit who is in you, whom you have received from God? You are not your own ..." This idea of an intimate relation between our corporeal[53] bodies and the Spirit who dwells within, is developed by Aphrahat, together with what St Paul says later in that same letter, in chapter 15 about how, at the second coming (which is the Second Coming of the Lord to earth, but this time to judge): "...the perishable must clothe itself with the imperishable, and the mortal with immortality," and death shall be "swallowed up in victory" (1 Corinthians 15:53-54).

When we look at *typology*, you will better understand why the Syriac tradition can speak of the Holy Spirit of God and the spirit within our human bodies as if they were similar or even the same. But the point is, to put it simply, that *our* spirits are like reproductions based on the original or model of the Holy Spirit. This allows to see the Holy Spirit in every one we meet, not, of course, in His divinity and purity, but nonetheless, as the principle or source of earthly life and potentially as the principle of spiritual life.

The Holy Spirit becomes a spiritual robe: we put that robe on at baptism, and we strive to keep it until the moment of death, when, in that robe, we may be recognised and admitted into heaven.

6.5 The Parable of the Talents

This parable appears in both the Gospels of St Matthew and St Luke. It is fitting to deal with it here, because it relates to how the Lord realised that even the apostles needed the aid of the Holy Spirit and sent the Paraclete to them so that they could fulfil their potential and their mission. We shall take the version in St Matthew:

---

[53] "Corporal" means "made of flesh."

Again, it will be like a man going on a journey, who called his servants and entrusted his wealth to them. To one he gave five talents, to another two talents, and to another one talent, each according to his ability. Then he went on his journey. The man who had received five talents went at once and put his money to work and gained five talents more. So also, the one with two talents gained two more. But the man who had received one talent went off, dug a hole in the ground and hid his master's money.

After a long time the master of those servants returned and settled accounts with them. The man who had received five talents brought the other five. 'Master," he said: "you entrusted me with five talents. See, I have gained five more." "His master replied: "Well done, good and faithful servant! You have been faithful with a few things; I will put you in charge of many things. Come and share your master's happiness!' The man with two talents also came. 'Master," he said: "you entrusted me with two talents; see, I have gained two more." His master replied: "Well done, good and faithful servant! You have been faithful with a few things; I will put you in charge of many things. Come and share your master's happiness!'

Then the man who had received one talents came. 'Master," he said: "I knew that you are a hard man, harvesting where you have not sown and gathering where you have not scattered seed. So I was afraid and went out and hid your talent in the ground. See, here is what belongs to you."

His master replied: "You wicked, lazy servant! So you knew that I harvest where I have not sown and gather where I have not scattered seed? Well then, you should have put my money on deposit with the bankers, so that when I returned I would have received it back with interest. So take the talents from him and give it to the one who has ten bags. For whoever has will be given more, and they will have an abundance. Whoever does not have, even what they have will be taken from them. And throw that worthless servant outside, into the darkness, where there will be weeping and gnashing of teeth." (Matthew 25:14-30)

Questions for Contemplation

1. What talents has God given me?

2. What use have I made of those talents?

3. What steps can I take to make more use of them?

Lesson 7

The Catholic Church

7.1   Introduction

7.2   The Founding of the Church

7.3   The Mission of the Church

7.4   What the Church Is and what it Is not

7.5   The Universalism of the Church.

7.1   Introduction

There is a beautiful Maronite hymn called "The Church":

> Blessed are you, O Church, garden of the Beloved.
> From a mustard seed, the smallest of all seeds, you have grown.
> Your roots are in firm soil, sheltered from the winds.
> In your branches are the martyrs, their blood shed for the faith.
> The birds quench their thirst at this marvel.
> Psalms and prophecies fill your vast space.
> You are the land of the Spirit, the meeting place of the nations.
> Blessed are you, dwelling place of the guest, neighbour of the
> One who is near.

The Church is here compared to a garden, to the mustard tree of the parable set out below, to a country, and to a house. When we speak poetically, we can say that it is all of these things at once. The Parable of the Mustard Seed reads:

> The kingdom of heaven is like a mustard seed that someone took and sowed in his field; it is the smallest of all the seeds, but when it has grown it is the greatest of shrubs and becomes a tree,

so that the birds of the air come and make nests in its branches. (Matthew 13:31-32)

The birds may stand for individual human souls, for nations, or both. But the parable is about the both Kingdom of Heaven and the Church, for they are connected. Here on earth, we speak of the "Church Militant," meaning the church which has to struggle. But in heaven, the Church is also present as the "Church Triumphant," while the suffering souls in Purgatory are called "the Church Penitent" or the "Church Suffering."

We saw in the first lesson that the Church is the mystical body of Christ, which means that it is Christ in a way which we cannot fully understand. Then, in the second lesson, we learnt in the Nicene Creed, which we say in each Divine Sacrifice of the Mass, that: "We believe in one holy, Catholic, and Apostolic Church." This is the heart of what the Church is. Now we need to look at the founding of the Church.

7.2 The Founding of the Church

We have seen in the first lesson, the texts from the New Testament which demonstrate that Our Lord intended to found a Church. Of these, the most important is Matthew 16:18 "You are Peter and upon this rock I build my Church, and the gates of hell shall not prevail against it." We can add to this, from the Gospel of Saint Luke, that when the towns of Israel refused to listen to the disciples, Our Lord said: "The one who listens to you listens to Me, and the one who rejects you rejects Me; and he who rejects Me rejects the One who sent Me" (Luke 10:16). We may add to this Matthew 18:17: "If (someone with whom you have a dispute) refuses to hear even the Church, let him be to you as a heathen." We who are members of the modern Church are the direct descendants of the disciples, who put the structure of the present church in place, establishing churches in each city or town they could, and appointing bishops and priests.

The word "church" comes from a Greek phrase which means "the house of the Lord." *Kuriakos* in Greek means "belonging to the Lord." The two "k"s were shown in English as "ch"s, and so we came to have our word "church." So the church is really the house of the Lord, which explains why it means both the building and the people.

Now, in ancient Greek, the church was called the *ekklesia*, which is from where we derive our words like "ecclesiastic." That word *ekklesia* has to do with "being called out (from among others)." The members of the church, therefore, were those who had been called out from the world to join a new body. That body had to be set up. This process of setting up the Church is clearly shown in three epistles attributed to St Paul: 1 and 2 Timothy and Titus, which are therefore known as "the pastoral Epistles." 1 Timothy opens as follows:

> Paul, an apostle of Christ Jesus according to the commandment of God our Saviour, and of Christ Jesus, who is our hope, to Timothy, my true child in the faith: Grace, mercy and peace from God the Father and Christ Jesus our Lord. As I urged you upon my departure for Macedonia, remain on at Ephesus so that you may instruct certain men not to teach strange doctrines, nor to pay attention to myths and endless genealogies, which give rise to mere speculation rather than furthering the administration of God which is by faith. But the goal of our instruction is love from a pure heart and a good conscience and a sincere faith. For some men, straying from these things, have turned aside to fruitless discussion, wanting to be teachers of the Law, even though they do not understand either what they are saying or the matters about which they make confident assertions. (1 Timothy 1:1-7)

Then, in the Epistle to Titus, St Paul writes:

> For this reason I left you in Crete, that you would set in order what remains and appoint elders in every city as I directed you, namely, if any man is above reproach, the husband of one wife, having children who believe, not accused of dissipation or rebellion. For the overseer must be above reproach as God's steward, not self-willed, not quick-tempered, not addicted to wine, not

pugnacious, not fond of sordid gain, but hospitable, loving what is good, sensible, just, devout, self-controlled, holding fast the faithful word which is in accordance with the teaching, so that he will be able both to exhort in sound doctrine and to refute those who contradict. (Titus 1:5-9)

We can see from these alone that St Paul was above all concerned that the faith be handed on in an ordered manner, and that care be taken to have the revealed truth taught with love. The main features which emerge from this are:

1. The Church is charged to hand on the revealed faith, and not ideas which we have tampered with or fabricated.

2. The Church's obligation is to further the administration (*oikonomia*) of God. The "economy" of God includes looking after his creation and his faithful, as best we can. Appointing suitable elders is central.

3. Because that administration is furthered by faith, then the true belief is critical.

4. The teaching of the Church aims at inculcating a love which comes from (a) a pure heart, (b) a good conscience, and (c) a sincere faith.

5. We must not be pretentious self-appointed teachers.

Implicit in this is the commandment that we be responsible administrators of the sacraments. St Ignatius of Antioch, who was martyred by 117, wrote a letter to St Polycarp, the bishop of Smyrna in modern Turkey. As with St Paul's letters, which are addressed to the key people in the area, St Ignatius is concerned that Polycarp, the bishop, be himself holy:

I exhort you to press forward on your course, in the grace wherewith you are endued, and to exhort all men to gain salvation. … Care for unity, for there is nothing better. Help all men, as the Lord also helps you … Be diligent with unceasing prayer. Entreat for wisdom greater than you have. Be watchful and keep the spirit from slumbering. (1:2-3)

In addition to fighting untrue doctrines (3:1), Ignatius advises Polycarp:

> Let not the widows be neglected. Be yourself their protector after the Lord. … Do not be haughty to slaves, either men or women; yet do not let them be puffed up … Speak to my sisters that they love the Lord, and be content with their husbands in the flesh and in spirit. In the same way enjoin on my brothers in the name of Jesus Christ "to love their wives as the Lord loved the Church" (4:1 and 3; 5:1)

While Our Lord founded the Church, the establishment of the Church had to take place over time, and its establishment and maintenance are, indeed, never ended. The Church is always developing, just as a river may change its direction and its size in certain respects, while remaining the same river. But the point is that that development was commenced and authorised by the Lord. He sent out apostles and disciples. This is called the "commissioning" of the apostles – they were sent out with a mission. After the Ascension, the apostles took the leading role, and they inaugurated the system of deacons which has survived to today in order to look after the faithful:

> Now at this time while the disciples were increasing in number, a complaint arose on the part of the Hellenistic Jews against the native Hebrews, because their widows were being overlooked in the daily serving of food. So the twelve summoned the congregation of the disciples and said: "It is not desirable for us to neglect the word of God in order to serve tables. Therefore, brethren, select from among you seven men of good reputation, full of the Spirit and of wisdom, whom we may put in charge of this task. But we will devote ourselves to prayer and to the ministry of the word." The statement found approval with the whole congregation; and they chose Stephen, a man full of faith and of the Holy Spirit, and Philip, Prochorus, Nicanor, Timon, Parmenas and Nicolas, a proselyte from Antioch. And these they brought before the apostles; and after praying, they laid their hands on them. The word of God kept on spreading; and the number of

the disciples continued to increase greatly in Jerusalem, and a great many of the priests were becoming obedient to the faith. (Acts 6:1-7)

The Hebrew widows were looked after by an informal social system: their families and friends, for they had lived in Jerusalem all their lives, and were surrounded by their dearest. But the Hellenistic Jews, those who spoke Greek, had often moved to Jerusalem only in their old age. That is, a Jewish family might live somewhere in the Mediterranean and speak Greek, as their neighbours did. When the children grew up and left home, the parents might decide to retire to Jerusalem. And there the widows would be outside the support group for Hebrew speaking Jews, lacking any families to look after them. The Christians were helping these widows, but were evidently receiving complaints. So the apostles, who, while they were helping, were being stretched beyond their capacity, appointed deacons or "servitors" to care for these people.

7.3. The Mission of the Church

We have already mentioned in lesson 3 the first Pentecost. Here is the conclusion of that story: it recounts what St Peter said to the crowds after the descent of the Holy Spirit, and what the Church did.

> (The listeners) were pierced to the heart, and said to Peter and the rest of the apostles: "Brethren, what shall we do?" Peter said to them: "Repent, and each of you be baptized in the name of Jesus Christ for the forgiveness of your sins; and you will receive the gift of the Holy Spirit. For the promise is for you and your children and for all who are far off, as many as the Lord our God will call to Himself. And with many other words he solemnly testified and kept on exhorting them, saying: "Be saved from this perverse generation!" So then, those who had received his word were baptized; and that day there were added about three thousand souls. They were continually devoting themselves to

the apostles' teaching and to fellowship, to the breaking of bread and to prayer.

Everyone kept feeling a sense of awe; and many wonders and signs were taking place through the apostles. And all those who had believed were together and had all things in common; and they began selling their property and possessions and were sharing them with all, as anyone might have need. Day by day continuing with one mind in the temple, and breaking bread from house to house, they were taking their meals together with gladness and sincerity of heart, praising God and having favour with all the people. And the Lord was adding to their number day by day those who were being saved. (Acts 2:37-47)

Questions for Contemplation

1. From this, what can you say about the Church's mission?

2. Can you see yourself taking part in such work?

3. What seems to you valuable in what they feel and what they do?

Today, the mission of the Church develops along the same pattern: teaching the revealed truth comes first, then administering the sacraments and prayer (breaking the bread, i.e. the Eucharist, and also going to the Temple). Then, placing the divine dimension first, the social organisation falls into place. We can say that the pattern is to begin with the *aim*, and that will show what to do and how.

7.4   What the Church Is and what it Is not

We will commence with the liturgy for the Consecration of the Church. Significantly, this is where the entire liturgical calendar starts, in early November. This is appropriate, after all, because without the Church there would be no Christianity today. The Church has been the means of passing on the Lord's teaching and His sacraments to posterity. The Entrance Hymn shows how the Church succeeds to Israel and fulfils its promise while exceeding it as a global people given the fullness of the truth:

> Come and shine in purity at the altar of the Lord,
> where the priest stands in between God and all humanity.
> He takes what the people give and lifts it up, heavenward on high,
> And the Spirit, full of light, is called down to sanctify the cup and the bread.
> Great and awesome sacrifice!
> Sinners, come receive the flesh and blood of Christ for the pardon of your sins.
> In Jerusalem was built Solomon's great temple there,
> where You showed Your face on earth, merciful and loving One ...

The hymn goes on to compare the Church to the flock of Christ, reminding us of the parable of the Good Shepherd:

> "Amen, amen, I say to you, he who does not enter by the gate into the fold of the sheep, but climbs up some other way, he is a thief and a robber. But he who enters by the gate is a shepherd of the sheep. To him the gatekeeper opens, and the sheep hear his voice, and he calls his own sheep by name and leads them out. When he puts forth all his own, he goes ahead of them, and the sheep follow him because they know his voice. A stranger they simply will not follow, but will flee from him, because they do not know the voice of strangers." This figure of speech Jesus spoke to them, but they did not understand what those things were which He had been saying to them. So Jesus said to them again: "Amen, amen, I say to you, I am the door of the sheep. All who came before Me are thieves and robbers, but the sheep did not hear them. I am the door; if anyone enters through Me, he will be saved, and will go in and out and find pasture. The thief comes only to steal and kill and destroy; I came that they may have life, and have it abundantly."

> "I am the good shepherd; the good shepherd lays down His life for the sheep. He who is a hired hand, and not a shepherd, who is

not the owner of the sheep, sees the wolf coming, and leaves the sheep and flees, and the wolf snatches them and scatters them. He flees because he is a hired hand and is not concerned about the sheep. I am the good shepherd, and I know My own and My own know Me, even as the Father knows Me and I know the Father; and I lay down My life for the sheep. I have other sheep, which are not of this fold; I must bring them also, and they will hear My voice; and they will become one flock with one shepherd." (John 10:1-16)

This parable is referred to in the First Epistle (Letter) of St Peter:

Therefore, I exhort the elders among you, as your fellow elder and witness of the sufferings of Christ, and a partaker also of the glory that is to be revealed, shepherd the flock of God among you, exercising oversight not under compulsion, but voluntarily, according to the will of God; and not for sordid gain, but with eagerness; nor yet as lording it over those allotted to your charge, but proving to be examples to the flock. And when the Chief Shepherd appears, you will receive the unfading crown of glory. You younger men, likewise, be subject to your elders; and all of you, clothe yourselves with humility toward one another, for God is opposed to the proud, but gives grace to the humble. (1 Peter 5:1-15, the last words being adapted from Proverbs 3:34)

The Church can, then, be thought of as a flock, provided that Our Lord is understood to be the Shepherd. This relates to the four marks of the Church, being *one*, *holy*, *catholic* and *apostolic*, for Our Lord said, as we saw in John 10:16 above: "they will become one flock with one shepherd." The unity of the Catholic Church today is one of doctrine, worship and government (for we all have the Pope as the head of our Church). We know that Our Lord valued unity, for in addition to all the above, He said: "A kingdom divided against itself cannot stand" (Mark 3:24).

The next mark is *holiness*. This does not mean that everyone in and connected with the Church is completely holy. What it does means is, first, that the founder of the Church, Our Lord Jesus Christ, was holy (indeed, He is the embodiment of holiness). Second, that the Church teaches holy doctrines (which lead to God), and provides the means of leading a holy life. These doctrines show us how to imitate Christ in holiness, not that we can be the same as Christ, but that we can aim to follow His example as sincerely as possible, to the best of our individual abilities.

An essential part in this is played by the seven Sacraments, for they enable us to receive the grace of God by a sure means, provided that we participate in them with a clean heart and in a state of grace (being contrite or not in mortal sin). We explore the concept of mortal sin (sin which is the most serious sin) and that of venial sin (lesser sins which leave us wounded but not spiritually dead) in a future lesson.

Also significant in considering the holiness of the Church is the fact that she does produce holy saints, the martyrs not being least of these. Hence, the *qolo* of the Sunday of the Consecration of the Church says: "As I entered (the feast of the Church) I saw there prophets, martyrs and the just, the apostles with the priests, then Baptism and the Cross. On the altar there was placed Christ's own Body and His Blood for the pardon of all sins."

It is also part of the holiness of the Church that the gates of hell shall never prevail against her (Matthew 16:18, the "gates" probably means the armies, which would issue out of the gates). Hence we read in the Prayer of Forgiveness on the Sunday of the Consecration of the Church: "Let us glorify, honour and praise the Wise Builder who, by His grace and His divine providence,[54] and mercy, built the Church to be an invincible and secure fortress and a tower of salvation ... so that the gates of hell shall not prevail against her."

The Church is *catholic* in that it is "universal," which is what "catholic means. This word was first used of the Church by St Ignatius

---

[54] Divine providence is the foresight with which God establishes and maintains the world order.

of Antioch (which is further evidence of how important he is):

> See that you all follow the bishop, even as Jesus Christ does the Father, and the presbytery (i.e. the college of priests) as you would the apostles; and reverence the deacons, as being the institution of God. Let no man do anything connected with the Church without the bishop. Let that be deemed a proper Eucharist, which is administered either by the bishop, or by one to whom he has entrusted it. Wherever the bishop shall appear, there let the multitude of the people also be; even as wherever Jesus Christ is, there is the Catholic Church. (*Letter to the Symrnaeans,* 8)

Our Lord intended that the Church be catholic, for He commanded: "Go therefore and make disciples of all nations" (Matthew 28:19) and "Go into the whole world and preach the Gospel to every creature" (Mark 16:15), and to the apostles, He said: "You shall be witnesses for me in both Jerusalem and in Judaea and Samaria, and even to the very ends of the earth" (Acts 1:8). It is no accident that it was a bishop from Antioch, the spiritual home of the Maronite Church, who first saw the Church as being *catholic,* for Antioch was the base from which missionaries went out to every region they could reach, hence they were keenly aware of the international dimension of the faith.

Our Church is *apostolic* because Christ taught the apostles, and the bishops are the successors of the apostles in an unbroken historical chain. The role of the apostles was quite special and unique. Our Lord said to them: "You have not chosen me but I have chosen you" (John 15:16). He later said to them, after His resurrection: "As the Father has sent me, I also send you" (John 20:21). It is significant that He should say that He was sending them out just as the Father had sent Him. This points to the specialness of their charge. He granted them the power to baptise, teach, forgive sin and to govern, but most of all, to perform the Divine Sacrifice of the Mass (Matthew 18:18 and 28:19; Luke 10:16; John 20:23 and 1 Corinthians 11:24-25).

None of the above teachings lead to the following ideas, all of which are incorrect:

1. The Pope can never make any mistake.
2. All non-Catholics go to hell.
3. All Catholics go to heaven.

To state the matter very briefly concerning items 2 and 3, non-Catholics are judged by their consciences (Romans 1:19-20), and Catholics must keep the commandments to be saved.

7.5 The Universalism of the Church

If the Church has been entrusted by Our Lord with the truth about our relationship with God, and with the sacraments, then the Church not only has a great privilege, but even more importantly, a great responsibility. The epistles or letters which are in the New Testament show how the apostles in Jerusalem kept in contact with all the churches, from the start. Towards the end of his first letter, St Peter says: "The church that is in Babylon, elected together with you, salutes you ..." (1 Peter 5:13).

Jacob of Sarug ties this in with the story of the Tower of Babel. That story is told in the first book of the Bible, the Book of Genesis:

> And the earth was of one tongue, and of the same speech. And when they ... found a plain in the land of Shinar ... each one said to his neighbour: "Come, let us ... make a city and a tower, the top of which may reach to heaven" ... And the Lord came down to see the city and the tower ... And he said: "Behold, it is one people, and all have one tongue: and they have begun to do this, neither will they leave off from their designs, till they accomplish them in deed. Come, therefore, let us go down, that they may not understand one another's speech. And so the Lord scattered them from that place into all lands, and they ceased to build the city. And therefore its name was "Babel," because there the language of the whole earth was confounded: and the Lord scattered them abroad upon the face of all countries. (Genesis 11:1-9)

So, at the Tower of Babel, the people of the world wanted to reach heaven, but their languages were confused, and being unable to cooperate, they separated. Jacob of Sarug's point is that the Church *reverses the process, bringing the people of the world together so that they can reach heaven.* In his homily on Pentecost, Jacob links this to the story of the Apostles in the Upper Room on Pentecost, which we have already seen, and to St Peter's first letter:

> ... Peter ... called the beloved company of the apostolic group 'the Church-elect in Babel'
> He heard the tongues that were spoken in it (the apostolic group) abundantly,
> and he described it as 'babel' in which all the tongues had been divided.
> That Church-elect which is in Babel greets you (with) peace,
> as if one were to say 'she who sings in all tongues'. (81-86)[55]

The Church aims, then, to bring all people together in God, and to get them to heaven as the first Tower of Babel had aimed at doing in the Old Testament legend. Hence the Church tries to reach all people, and to accommodate their languages and cultures, so far as it can consistent with the truth and with the nature of the Sacraments.

---

[55] *Jacob of Sarug's Homily on the Holy Sunday of Pentecost,* trans. Thomas Kollamparampil, Gorgias, Piscataway NJ, 2010, 12.

Lesson 8

Virtue and Sin

8.1   Virtue and Sin

To understand what good behaviour is, we also need to understand what bad behaviour is. Good or bad, it is all behaviour. Virtue is intentionally done good behaviour, and sin is intentionally committed bad behaviour, i.e. behaviour against the Will and Law of God.

Virtue, or *goodness* is what pleases God, and sin is what offends Him. Virtue or sin, it is all a question of God's law. And God's law, of course, is intimately related to His love: it cannot be anything else. Because God is the "lover of all people," as the Maronite liturgy says time and again, virtue will naturally be something which is good for human beings, and sin will naturally be something which is bad for them. When we speak of "good" and "bad" in this context, we speak of them from the most important perspective of all, that of our immortal souls.

It is noteworthy that the Creed says nothing about what either sin or virtue actually is. All it says is: "We confess one Baptism for the forgiveness of sins …" It does not even refer to the other ways of receiving forgiveness of sins. The Creed was not drafted to settle the complete teaching of these subjects, it was more in order to clear up questions about who God, and especially Jesus, is and was.

Speaking pastorally, the point is that in considering our own selves, our virtues and our sins, we should try and maintain an impartial balance, not being too inclined in either direction, that is, not being too predisposed to see ourselves as either virtuous or sinful. Oddly enough, there are some people who have a sort of obsession with seeing themselves as sinful, and not just as being bad, but as being thoroughly evil. Very, very rarely is anyone evil through and through. But now for our teaching.

First, not one of us who has attained the age of reason, and is responsible for their actions, can have avoided sin. St John teaches:

> If we say that we have no sin, we are deceiving ourselves and the truth is not in us. If we confess our sins, He is faithful and righteous to forgive us our sins and to cleanse us from all unrighteousness. If we say that we have not sinned, we make Him a liar and His word is not in us. (1 John 1:8-10)

The Anaphora *Šarar*, one of the most distinctive Maronite Anaphoras (as we saw in lesson 5), says this in the prayer before the Peace:

> Lord, God, powerful one. You who in the abundance of your mercy examined our weaknesses, and raised we sinners who are your slaves even to the service of your greatness so that we might become servants of your holy altar. You, Lord, strengthen us with the force of your sanctifying spirit, and give us to rejoice and to call your most Holy Spirit to this offering presented for the forgiveness of our debts and for the salvation of our souls. Then we shall offer one another the holy kiss of peace. We will be enriched in your love, strengthened in your hope, and overwhelmed by your mercy. And so we shall offer worship to you now and forever.

This tells us that God's awareness of our weaknesses is an example of His mercy. How can this be, unless God has examined our weaknesses like a good physician who looks to *diagnose* us with a view to *healing* us? God is called a "physician" in St Ignatius of Antioch's letter to the *Ephesians* 7:2: "For there is one physician, both fleshly and spiritual, born and unborn, God come in the flesh, true life in death, from both Mary and God, first subject to suffering and then beyond suffering, Jesus Christ our Lord." This image is picked up in our liturgy:

> ... the creator of all ... appeared in the world as a physician and healed the sick in body and soul. ... O Christ our God, Physician of souls and bodies, in your plan of salvation, you had pity on the leper, who was outcast, and healed him by your word. ... Cleanse us and make us holy.[56]

Virtue must consist in serving God by becoming servants of His altar, but not only at His altar. We serve God throughout life, and in the world, because, if we worship God sincerely and rightly, all the other aspects of our life will fall into place. If we worship God in truth, and with love, we will want to know what God wants us to do, and we will try our very best to do it. Further, as we fall short, we should try to improve. Anyone who really loves God will hate sin because God hates it, and desire to be virtuous because God loves it.

Virtue is doing what is pleasing to God, and sin is doing what offends God. Few of us are so completely good that we can be called "virtuous," full stop. Few of us are so completely evil that we can be called "sinful," full stop. Most of us are somewhere in-between. Further, we do not have *complete control* over our actions or their consequences, but we are *responsible* for them. Our liturgy recognises this when it says: "Grant rest, O God, to the departed, and forgive the sins we have committed with or without full knowledge."[57]

The Arabic is even more challenging: it does not have the word "full," rather, it simply reads: "with or without knowledge." How can

---

[56] Taken from the *Hoosoye* for the feast of *The Healing of the Leper*.
[57] This is the penultimate prayer before the Fraction, Signing, Sprinkling, Mingling and Elevation.

one sin without knowledge? The short answer is that we can and should take responsibility whenever we find that have caused pain, suffering or sadness to others. For example, if you fling open a door, and hit someone whom you had not known was behind it, you would be sorry. You would think: "I wish I had not been in such a hurry to get through the door." Or even worse, if you are driving and an animal runs onto the road and you cannot avoid hitting it, you may regret not having driven a little more slowly, or not having had more of the road in your sights as you were driving.

So the idea of sinning without knowledge does make sense: bad things can happen through my negligence, thoughtlessness or haste. I wish to be in a position where bad things do not happen through me because of my inattention. I want to fill the spaces of my life with the grace of God and consciousness. It is useful to think of virtue and sin in terms of seven virtues:

1. Charity (or Love)
2. Faith
3. Hope
4. Prudence
5. Justice
6. Temperance
7. Courage (or Fortitude)

There is an alternative list, which is matched with the seven deadly sins:

	Sin	Virtue
1	Pride	Humility
2	Wrath (or Anger)	Patience
3	Envy	Kindness
4	Greed	Charity (or Generosity)
5	Lust	Chastity
6	Gluttony	Temperance
7	Sloth	Diligence

There is an overlap, for charity and temperance appear in both lists of virtues. Some questions of definition arise, for some of these are words which we either use very rarely or use loosely:

Prudence	Devising, choosing and preparing appropriate means for the attainment of any purpose or for avoiding any evil.
Temperance	Broadly considered, temperance is maintaining a moderation in activities. Speaking strictly, it is a habitual moderation in all activities, especially pleasures of eating, drinking and sex.
Fortitude	Broadly considered, fortitude is a steadiness of the will in doing good. Strictly speaking, it is a firmness which strengthens us in the face of obstacles to one's duty or fulfilling a virtue.
Charity	Love for God and humanity (because they are His children).
Sloth	Deliberate boredom or disgust with spiritual works and duties.

There is a specific example of pride which is called *blasphemy*. This is to speak disrespectfully about God and about sacred things. However, in modern life where mocking God and religion, and swearing, especially using the name of the Lord are so common, blasphemy has become a special issue of great importance. People often feel peer pressure to swear. But one should not swear, and in particular, one should not use the name of the Lord. As Aphrahat states: "… the one who swears falsely on God, to whom can he petition? How can he petition God of whom he is a lying servant, the God who is not established in him when he prays?"[58] If I call on the name of the Lord as a swear word, or to express dissatisfaction or impatience, God will not, of course, hear me. Can I really expect that if, without contrition, I call on His name for assistance, He will answer that as if nothing has happened? Or by abusing the name of God, do I not implicitly but

---

[58] *The Demonstrations*: "Demonstration 23: The Grapecluster," §63, p. 526.

unmistakeably align myself with the Enemy? I once had an example of a man who suffered what he believed were demonic visitations. He may well have been correct, for they ceased when he was blessed. The only sin we could find which may have opened the door to Satan was his improper use of the Holy Name. When we pondered it, it all fell into place. He had called on the Lord only to abuse the privilege. He had effectively said: "All that God means to me is a swear word." He had left the welcome mat out for the devil.

8.2 Sorrow and Remorse

Remorse, which comes from words meaning "bite intensively," is when our consciences pain us for having done or failed to do something, and we now regret this. Remorse can and should lead us to repentance, which is "sorrowing deeply." But the Greek word for "repentance" in the New Testament is *metanoia*, which means "change of mind." This is the fundamental meaning of repentance, for a repentance which does not lead to a change of our minds, hearts and attitudes, is not a repentance worth mentioning.

It is good to study words like this: it can help us see what is missing from our internal lives. An important related word is *contrition*, from a Latin root meaning "to grind." I feel contrition when I am sorry for sin because I detest it, and have formed a firm resolution not to sin in the future. This sorrow and resolution grind down the attraction for sin which exists within us all.

We can also distinguish *perfect contrition* (which springs from a pure love of God and a hatred of sin because it keeps us removed from him), from *imperfect contrition*. The latter is also known as *attrition*. I feel attrition when I am sorry for sin because I detest sin because it means that I am open to the punishment due to sin, or because by losing the love of God I am vulnerable to the assault of the devil. *Perfect contrition*, in other words, is positively motivated by love of

God, while the *imperfect* variety is motivated by fear. Although we should of course seek perfect contrition, even so, attrition is still good, and can, with grace, be perfected.

A very good way of ensuring that we feel contrition to the maximum extent for us, is to ponder on four facts:

(1)   The Church's teaching on sin is teaching of the Lord Himself. We know what sin is because Our Lord taught us. This means that in humility we accept the teaching.

(2)   Our Lord suffered in order to bring this teaching to us, and especially through His Passion and Crucifixion, He suffered to repair the damage caused by sin.

(3)   Sin causes us to forfeit divine grace, and become cruder, rougher, less sensitive, more likely to accept sin, and to commit even worse sins.

(4)   By our becoming less virtuous, and losing grace, we damage those around us – we cannot help them as we would wish to, and they are saddened to see us declining into sin.

This last matter for contemplation ties in with the teaching of Our Lord in the Golden Rule: "In everything, therefore, treat people the same way you want them to treat you, for this is the Law and the Prophets." (Matthew 7:12 and Luke 6:31). Ponder how you would like it if other people treated you the way you treat them.

8.3 Making an Examination of Conscience

There are many different ways of making an examination of conscience: what I have done well and what have I done wrong? The best way of all is to sensitise our consciences so that our consciences tell us as soon as we have started to do or think something wrong, and rebuke us if we actually do it, or omit to do what is right. Then, as a spiritual practice, it is very good to review our conscience each night, simply going over the events of the day. Also, it is good to plan the day each morning: where do I usually go wrong? What special challenges do I need to prepare for today?

Then, when it is appropriate, I go to the priest for confession. It is required that we do so once a year at least, during the Season of Easter. However, it is good to do this regularly. One might suggest once a month, or once each two weeks in order to keep the fire of contrition alive in me (see below). But it is a question of judgment, there is no right or wrong answer for all cases.

However, let me offer one warning. There is a method, which is fairly widely propagated, of using a whole list of sins, generally arranged under the Ten Commandments, to help me pinpoint my faults. If it is used from time to time, it can be useful. But as the regular form of examination of conscience, I have two main reservations.

First of all, it is not part of the Maronite tradition, and should not be allowed to displace it. That is, the Maronite tradition is based on conscience and personal discussion with a priest. Therefore, any system which has the tendency to replace the awakening of conscience with ticking a sheet of paper is questionable. In every single liturgy we pray: "Holy and immortal Lord, sanctify our minds and purify our consciences, that we may praise you with purity and listen to your Holy Scriptures." (The priest's prayer after the *Qadišat*). From experience, it can be said that people who use this method not only sometimes but often become fixated upon the list, and lose a *feeling* for what they have done beyond an all-consuming sense of guilt, so strong that it approaches despair.

Second, the lengthy screed[59] system insinuates a view of sin which almost reinstates the Law, and leads to scrupulosity. That is, right and wrong conduct is seen as being a question of whether I comply or do not comply with a great number of commands and prohibitions. These orders are set out at such length and in such terms that many people can

---

[59] A "screed" is a long speech or piece of writing.

hardly find anything they do which does not have some sinful aspect. This conduces to a person falling prey to either despair or to the obsessive problem of *scruples*: an exaggerated and unreasonable fear that one is in a state of sin.[60] One of the strange features of this is how the scrupulous penitent practically refuses, stubbornly, to entertain the thought that they might not be in a state of sin. It is, in fact, a form of self-obsession.

Of course there are commands and prohibitions, but these are not the whole of the concept of sin. As we saw in lesson 2, Our Lord boils the many commandments of the Law down to:

> The first of all the commandments is, Hear, O Israel; The Lord our God is one Lord: And you shall love the Lord your God with all your heart, and with all your soul, and with all your mind, and with all your strength: this is the first commandment. And the second is like it, namely, you shall love your neighbour as yourself. There is no other commandment greater than these. (Mark 12:28-31)

If love is the key, then hatred is a granite door without a keyhole, for in our hatred we see only what is opposed to love. As Jacob of Sarug states: "When people hate they hate even the gift of their adversary."[61] What he means is that hatred is so poisonous that it robs us of reason and of proper human gratitude. This is another clue to the life of virtue: if we are humble and grateful, and acknowledge our blessings, we are on the path to virtue and away from sin.

So remember love, fear hatred, its opposite, and cultivate the virtues of humility and gratitude which free us from sin, and bring us to virtue. Next to this, the value of lists is minimal. Please note: I do not say never to use lists or these documents called "examinations," but to use them sparingly, and as an aide to help prompt and develop our

---

[60] A "scruple" was a tiny stone was used as the smallest weight. Therefore: "scrupulous" came to mean "... overnice or meticulous in matters of right and wrong ... prone to hesitate or doubt." *Shorter Oxford Dictionary*.

[61] *Jacob of Sarug's Homilies on Praise at Table,* ed. and trans. Jeff W. Childers, Gorgias, Piscataway, 2016, Homily 146, line 73, p. 120.

consciences. The aim is to have an alert conscience which warns me so that I can eventually leave the lists alone, maybe reviewing them every now and then.

Our Lord taught a very deep story about virtue, sin, forgiveness and being forgiven, which is often called "the Parable of the Unforgiving Servant." It is worth pondering this, for the unforgiving servant lacked both humility and gratitude:

> Then came Peter unto Him and said: Lord, how often shall my brother offend against me, and I forgive him? Seven times? Jesus said to him: I say not seven times; but seventy times seven times. Therefore is the kingdom of heaven likened to a king, who would take an account of his servants. And when he had begun to take the account, one was brought to him, that owed him ten thousand talents. And as he had not wherewith to pay it, his lord commanded that he should be sold, and his wife and children and all that he had, and payment to be made. But that servant falling down, besought him, saying: Have patience with me, and I will pay you all. And the lord of that servant being moved with pity, let him go and forgave him the debt.
>
> But when that servant was gone out, he found one of his fellow servants that owed him an hundred pence: and laying hold of him, throttled him, saying: Pay what you owe. And his fellow servant falling down, besought him, saying: Have patience with me, and I will pay thee all. And he would not: but went and cast him into prison, till he paid the debt. Now his fellow servants seeing what was done, were very much grieved, and they came and told their lord all that was done. Then his lord called him; and said to him: You wicked servant, I forgave you all the debt, because you besought me: Should you not then have had compassion also on your fellow servant, even as I had compassion on you? And his lord being angry, delivered him to the torturers until he paid all the debt. So also shall my heavenly Father do to you, if you forgive not every one his brother from your hearts. (Matthew 18:21-35)

Questions for Contemplation

1. Do I ever have one standard for myself and another for other people? I need to be careful: no one is ever really unforgiving all the time, but sometimes we forgive some while being relentless with others. So the fact that I do what is good on one occasion does not mean that I always do so, and can afford to excuse my failings.

2. In this parable, the lord stands for God. Who then, do the fellow servants stand for?

3. If I have sometimes trouble seeing where I go wrong, can I learn to see myself by comparing myself with others?

8.4 The Sacraments of Forgiveness of Sins (Baptism, Eucharist, Anointing)

It is more accurate to speak of the sacraments (in the plural), rather than of the sacrament (in the singular) of forgiveness, because four sacraments by and of themselves are effective for the remission of sins: Baptism, the Eucharist, Reconciliation and the Anointing of the Sick. First of all, God is not limited to the sacraments: He can provide His grace as and when He pleases, although He has promised to provide grace through the sacraments when they are worthily received. It is known that fasting and acts of charity can lead to the forgiveness of sins, hence St Peter teaches: "Above all, keep fervent in your love for one another, because love covers a multitude of sins" (1 Peter 4:8). The Sacrament of the Eucharist likewise effect remission of sins, for as we pray in the liturgy before each and every communion:

> Make us worthy, O Lord God, so that our bodies may be sanctified by Your Holy Body and our souls purified by Your forgiving Blood. May our communion be for the forgiveness of our sins and for new life. ...

When the priest administers the Sacrament, he says to the communicants: "The Body and Blood of Our Lord Jesus Christ are given to you for the forgiveness of your sins and for eternal life." When he leaves the altar, and silently says the Farwell Prayer, he implores: "May the offering I have received from you be for the forgiveness of my sins ..."

We shall return to the Anointing of the Sick later, but it suffices to say now that it is based on the instruction of St James:

> Is anyone among you sick? Then he must call for the elders of the church and they are to pray over him, anointing him with oil in the name of the Lord; and the prayer offered in faith will restore the one who is sick, and the Lord will raise him up, and if he has committed sins, they will be forgiven him. Therefore, confess your sins to one another, and pray for one another so that you may be healed ..." (James 5:14-16a).

The word for "elders" here is *presbyterous*, the Greek word which came to be used to mean "priest," and from which the English "priest" is derived. So, St James is really speaking about calling the priests.

When it comes to the Sacrament of Confession, the beginning is the Gospel of St John, describing what happened after the Resurrection, and how Our Lord breathed upon the apostles, saying: "Receive the Holy Spirit. If you forgive the sins of any, their sins have been forgiven them; if you retain the sins of any, they have been retained." (John 20:22b-23) We studied this passage in lesson 6.

Over the course of time, the Church has adapted the rite (meaning the *form*) of the sacrament. Today, we usually begin with both the priest and the penitent making the Sign of the Cross. The following will be a typical exchange in the confessional:

Penitent: Bless me, Father, for I have sinned. It has been two weeks since my last confession. I have (*the penitent describes what he or she has done or failed to do*). For these, and for any sins I may have forgotten, I am truly contrite.

The priest may ask some questions to elucidate the state of the penitent at the relevant times, and hence how culpable he or she may be. The priest may also consider it pastorally prudent to explain something. The priest then gives the penitent a penance to perform (e.g. to say certain prayers or perform a certain act).

Penitent   O my God, I am very sorry that I have sinned against You, because You are so good, and with Your help I will not sin again.

Priest   In the name of Our Lord Jesus Christ and of His Holy Church, I absolve you of your sins. Go in peace with the blessing of the Holy Trinity, Father, Son and Holy Spirit. Amen.

Let us close this lesson with a meditation from St Jacob of Sarug. In his *memro*, or "verse homily" on the Sinful Woman, he says: "The confused sins of an evil world are traps for me." In Syriac, it is *H.To. he b.lee.le d.3ol.mo bee.šo h.waw lee fa.He*. The verb *H.To* has a root meaning of "to miss the mark." This is one aspect of sin: we are aiming for virtue, but we fail. This shows why sins can be called "confused": they stop us listening to our consciences and to the guidance of God. By turning us aside from our true aim: the beatific vision of God in heaven, we become confused and aimless. *We are purpose seeking missiles, made to seek virtue and avoid sin. When we pervert this, we become lost.*

Appendix: "Mortal" and "Venial" Sin

All sin is serious, because even the lesser sins accustom us to ignoring the law of God, and diminish the life of grace in our souls. Mortal sin involves an intrinsically grave matter, full knowledge of what I am doing, and full and free consent to doing it. This is derived from the biblical teaching that there are gradations of seriousness in sin. As St John says:

If anyone sees his brother committing a sin not leading to death, he shall ask and God will give life to him (if he is among those who have not committed any sin leading to death). There is a sin leading to death; I do not say that he should make request for this. All unrighteousness is sin, and there is a sin not leading to death. (1 John 5:16-17)

No given act – irrespective of the knowledge and consent of the actor – is always a mortal sin. By itself, an act of a certain type is not enough to make a mortal sin every time one does it. For example, murder is a *grave matter* and hence murder can be a mortal sin. But if I murder someone in self-defence, having intended only to inflict the minimum harm necessary to defend myself, that is one of the sins committed "without knowledge" which we speak of in the liturgy. This is why St John speaks of sins leading to death and sins not leading to death in his first epistle.

Lesson 9

Our Lady, The Blessed Virgin Mary

When we speak of "Our Lady," we mean "Mary," the daughter of Ss Joachim and Anna who became the Mother of Our Lord Jesus Christ. No one can be certain when she was born or when she died, but if we thought of her as having been born in or before 15 BC, that will probably not be too far out, and she had almost certainly been assumed into heaven by 70 AD (see below).

Our Lady is, beyond all question, the greatest human who walked the earth, or could. We can either exclude Our Lord from this statement as He was not only human but also divine, or else we could say that Mary is the greatest after Jesus Himself. It makes no difference: she is the purest of all creatures, for Our Lord was not a creature, He was the Creator. Yet, she was chosen to give birth to Him without any human conception. This was a signal distinction. Whereas we fell through our first mother, Eve, we were saved because Mary, the second Eve, cooperated with the plan of God.

But one thing must be made clear about Our Lady once for all: we do not worship her, rather we ask her to intercede for us to Jesus Christ Our Lord. This will be expanded and clarified in the lesson on prayer.

9.1 Our Lady in the New Testament

St Mark opened his Gospel, which was probably the earliest, with the baptism of the Lord. St Luke decided to go back to Jesus' birth, doubtless to shed light on who Our Lord was and what He had done.

> In the sixth month, the angel Gabriel was sent from God into a city of Galilee, called Nazareth, to a virgin espoused to a man whose name was Joseph, of the house of David; and the virgin's name was Mary. And the angel being come in, said unto her: "Hail, full of grace, the Lord is with you: blessed are you among women." She having heard, was troubled at his saying, and thought within herself what manner of salutation is this? The angel said to her: "Fear not, Mary, for you have found grace with God. Behold you shall conceive in your womb, and shall bring forth a son; and you shall call His name Jesus. He shall be great, and shall be called the Son of the most High; and the Lord God shall give unto Him the throne of David his father; and He shall reign in the house of Jacob for ever. And of his kingdom there shall be no end." Then Mary asked the angel: "How shall this be done, because I know not man?" The angel answering, said to her: "The Holy Spirit shall come upon you, and the power of the most High shall overshadow you. And therefore also the Holy which shall be born of you shall be called the Son of God." (Luke 1:26-35)

There was an ancient tradition that Mary as well as St Joseph, whom she married, were of the House of David, meaning that they were descendants of King David of ancient Israel, who made his capital in Jerusalem. Lord Hervey also believed that this was likely, not because of the tradition, but because Joseph would marry his cousin, there being few of the tribe of Judah living in his town of Nazareth.[62]

---

[62] Lord Arthur Hervey, *The Genealogies of Our Lord and Saviour Jesus Christ*, Macmillan, London, 1853, 57-58.

This would also explain why the elder Joseph would marry the much younger woman.

Next, the angel Gabriel's greeting to Our Lady: "full of grace," is not at all usual. It means that she was herself a person with a special gift of grace from God. If it was just a standard way of saying a respectful hello, why would she have been troubled? Note the terms of what the angel says to her: would she have understood that Jesus was not going to establish a kingdom on earth?

Clearly Mary believed that she was to become pregnant very soon if not immediately. That is the only basis on which her reply makes sense. It is also strongly suggestive that she was not intending to have marital relations with St Joseph. Gabriel's next sentences explain how she will conceive. The *overshadowing* is significant: in the ancient world it was believed that the shadow of a god could impregnate someone.[63]

> Mary ... went into the hill country with haste into a city of Judah. And she entered into the house of Zachary, and saluted Elizabeth. ... when Elizabeth heard the salutation of Mary, the infant leaped in her womb. And Elizabeth was filled with the Holy Spirit: and she cried out ... "Blessed art thou among women, and blessed is the fruit of your womb. And whence is this to me, that the mother of my Lord should come to me? For behold as soon as the voice of your salutation sounded in my ears, the infant in my womb leaped for joy. And blessed art thou that you have believed, because those things shall be accomplished that were spoken to you by the Lord."
>
> Then Mary said: "My soul magnifies the Lord. And my spirit has rejoiced in God my Saviour, because he has regarded the humility of his handmaid; for behold from henceforth all generations shall call me blessed. Because he that is mighty, has done great things to me; and holy is his name. His mercy is from generation unto generations, to them that fear him. He has showed

---

63   Pieter W. van der Horst, "Sex, Purity and Asceticism in the *Protoevangelium Jacobi*", *Neotestamentica*, 28/3, 1994-1995, 205-218.

might in his arm: he has scattered the proud in the conceit of their heart. He has put down the mighty from their seat, and has exalted the humble. He has filled the hungry with good things; and the rich he has sent empty away. He has received Israel his servant, being mindful of his mercy: As he spoke to our fathers, to Abraham and to his seed for ever." (Luke 1:39-55)

Before Elizabeth speaks, she is filled with the Holy Spirit. However, it is not said that the Holy Spirit descends upon Our Lady before she delivers her great hymn (known as the *Magnificat*). I think that this means that the Holy Spirit who has already overshadowed her has remained with her: she is permanently in the Spirit (as was Simeon: 2:25).

Questions for Contemplation

1. How do I think I might have reacted in Mary's place?

2. For whom was Mary concerned when she went to visit Elizabeth?

3. What was the role of the Holy Spirit in all of this amazing narrative?

We are entitled to ask many questions about the Magnificat: why this preference for the poor? Are all of the rich to be sent away empty? Casting down the proud is very clear; but would it be right to condemn someone just because of their wealth? The opinion of the Church has long been that this means *those who are attached to their wealth* i.e. the opposite of the "poor in spirit" who are to be blessed. This makes sense: financial standing is not necessarily correlated with virtue. Our Lady was not intending us to understand that every poor person was a saint. Similarly, although the *Magnificat* refers to "Israel" it is meant not in terms of the twelve physical tribes of Israel, but of the elect of God, the church (the proper Greek word for the church is *ekklesia*, which, as we have seen is similar in meaning to "elect").

Our Lady is the subject of other important stories in the New Testament, the presentation of Our Lord in the Temple, and the finding of Him in the Temple.[64]

St John depicts Our Lady as being present at the opening of Our Lord's public ministry, at the Wedding at Cana ("the first sign He performed," John 2:11) and also at the close of that ministry, when she stood at the foot of the Cross (John 19:25). By placing her at the commencement and the conclusion of the public ministry, St John implicitly associates her with all of the ministry.

Further, at the Crucifixion, Jesus said to his mother: "Woman, behold your son," and to "the disciple" who was present, he said: "Behold your mother" and, from that moment, John took her into his house (John 19:27). The morale of that story, as many have pointed out, is that to truly be the disciple of Jesus, one has to take Mary as one's mother. And she will take us as her children.

However, while Our Lady is mentioned as having been present at the first Pentecost, and the Syriac tradition has always understood that she was present at the Ascension of the Lord and that she lived with St John, nothing is said of her death in the New Testament. Yet, with all Catholics and Orthodox, we Maronites believe that upon her death she was assumed into heaven (this is called "the Assumption"). In the Book of Revelation we read:

> A great sign appeared in heaven: a woman clothed with the sun, with the moon under her feet and a crown of twelve stars on her head. She was pregnant and cried out in pain as she was about to give birth. Then another sign appeared in heaven: an enormous red dragon with seven heads and ten horns and seven crowns on its heads. Its tail swept a third of the stars out of the sky and flung them to the earth. The dragon stood in front of the woman

---

[64] I have written an article which argues against the view that Our Lady is the subject of criticism by the evangelist in the Gospel of St Mark: it is due for publication in a volume of papers in 2017, *The Virgin Mary at the Beginning of the Third Millennium*, edited by Kevin Wagner.

who was about to give birth, so that it might devour her child the moment he was born. She gave birth to a son, a male child, who "will rule all the nations with an iron sceptre."[65] And her child was snatched up to God and to his throne. The woman fled into the wilderness to a place prepared for her by God, where she might be taken care of for 1,260 days. (Revelation 12:1-6)

The woman is *both* the Mother of the Lord and the Mother of the Church. We only get into trouble with the interpretation if we try to determine whether she is one or the other. This story also represents a continuation of the story of Israel, showing how the Church is the new Israel.

9.2 Our Lady in the Maronite Mass

We begin with the Maronite Mass of *The Announcement to Mary*, the second Sunday of the Season of Announcement and Nativity. In the *Hoosoye*, we read, with minor corrections:

> Let us glorify, honour and praise the Father who sent Gabriel to Nazareth as a messenger; and to the Son, who dwelt in the Virgin Mary as the Good News; and to the Spirit, who sanctified her and accomplished this wondrous mystery ...
> Glory to you, Exalted One, for you chose to live among us. You are the power who dwelt in the pure Virgin Mary and appeared from her as God Incarnate. Today we cry out proclaiming:
> "Blessed are you, Mary, because the Son of God has chosen you as His mother."
> "Blessed are you, Mary. Because of you Adam has been freed!"
> "Blessed are you, Mary, because you are the glory of nations and the pride of all generations."

I have quoted so much of it for several reasons. First, the Church teaches what we find in the liturgy. The contents of the liturgy are not simply an advisory opinion. We are entitled to deduce from this prayer

---

[65] This is an allusion to Psalm 2:9 in the Old Testament where God the Father speaks to His son, the king.

that Church adores God, but only declares Mary to be blessed. There is a technical vocabulary for this (*worship* for God, *reverence* for the saints, and *great reverence* for Our Lady).

We can also find implied here the teaching of the virginal conception and birth, that she was the Mother of God, that she was the new Eve who undid the damage done by our first parents, and that the prophecies of the *Magnificat* (her great hymn) have been fulfilled. These ideas are found very fully developed in St Ephrem and the Syriac tradition.

In every Mass, we remember Our Lady in the Creed, when we say that Our Lord "was incarnate of the Virgin Mary, and became man." Then, in the Pre-Anaphora, there are two Marian hymns. The first comes before the prayer over the offerings:

The Lord reigns clothed in majesty, Halleluiah!
Our Lord Jesus said "I am the Bread of Life. From the Father I was sent
as Word without flesh to give new life.
Of the Virgin Mary I was born, taking flesh as man;
as good earth receives a seed, her womb received me.
Priestly hands now lift me high above the altars." Halleluiah! Our gifts,
Lord, receive.
Then, after the prayer over the offerings we say:
Halleluiah! Honour Mary Mother of Our Lord and God,
and with her remember all the righteous ones, prophets and apostles,
martyrs and the priests, and the children of the Church, from age to age.

This celebrates Our Lady's role in the conception of the Lord. The second hymn praises her role as Mother of the Church. Further, within the prayer over the offerings, she is also mentioned when the priest says: "As we remember Our Lord God and Saviour Jesus Christ ... we recall upon this offering all those who have pleased God from Adam to this day, especially Mary, the blessed Mother of God ..."

Then, in the anaphoras, Our Lady is always mentioned in the intercessions when we ask God to remember all those who have pleased him, especially Mary the Holy Mother of God, and to assist us through her prayers. Before the Institution Narrative, in the Anaphoras of the Twelve Apostles, St Peter, James, John Chrysostom and John Maroun, we pray:

> Holy, holy, holy are you ... For our salvation, your Only-Begotten Son became flesh of the pure Virgin Mary ... (from the Twelve).[66]

This mention is Christological first and foremost, although of course Our Lady has the great honour of being mentioned in a uniquely Christological context.

In the Anaphora of St James, Our Lady is also mentioned in the last prayer before the Final Blessing: "Grant protection to the living and bless them with hope, through the prayers of the Virgin Mary and all the saints, now and for ever."

So, Our Lady is mentioned quite prominently when the oblations are brought forward: that is, when what belongs to this world has been led to the altar to be offered to God. That is her role. Then, as we near the transubstantiation, her role is only incidental to that of the Lord, and in so far as she is one of the faithful. Indeed, during the intercessions, we pray for Our Lady, that the Lord remember her!

In addition, each Wednesday in Pentecost is the Mass of Our Lady. The opening prayer is reminiscent of the one in the Anaphora of St John Chrysostom: "Jesus Christ Our Lord, the Sun of Justice, you dawned from the Father before all ages and from Mary at the appointed hour." The *Hoosoye* refers to "the Exalted One who humbled himself and exalted the humble Virgin ..." It goes on to say:

> O Lord, through the prayers of your Mother,[67] keep away from

---

[66] Particularly beautiful is the unique commemoration in the Anaphora of St John Chrysostom: "In your mercy, you sent your Only Son into the world for our salvation. He dawned from the holy Virgin, like a ray of light from a bright cloud. ... He was born from a woman's womb, that we may be born again from a spiritual womb."

[67] It does not mean that Our Lord uses his mother's prayers as a sort of tool but that her prayers help us when we call on Him.

the earth and its people the devastation of wrath, and all dangers, dissension, war, famine, and epidemics. Have compassion on us, heal the sick, help the poor, save the oppressed. Grant rest to the faithful departed who have left us and gone to you, and make us worthy of a safe and peaceful death.

In addition, there is the role of Our Lady in the life of the Maronites. She is most famous now at as Our Lady of Lebanon, with her chief shrine at Harissa. In addition, Saydat Bishwat is very important.

9.3   Our Lady in the Letters of Ignatius of Antioch

St Ignatius of Antioch is counted as the third bishop of Antioch. The first bishop is traditionally said to have been St Peter, while the second was Bishop Evodius. He must have died by 117, when he was martyred, probably by being fed to the lions in Rome. There is a late tradition that he knew St John the Beloved, although the evidence is late, and may be wrong. He was very important in the Maronite tradition, and in fact there is a Maronite anaphora of St Ignatius! Of course he cannot have written it, but his letters could have inspired it.

Antioch was an extremely important city in early Christianity. In fact, in practical terms, it was second only to Jerusalem, and after the destruction of Jerusalem, was probably the most important centre of Christianity anywhere. It is where we were first known as Christians, and it was a centre of missionary activity. The respect shown to St Ignatius as he travelled to his martyrdom attests to the honour which the bishop of Antioch possessed.

Now let us look at St Ignatius of Antioch's references to Mary in his epistles:

> For there is one physician, both fleshly and spiritual, born and unborn, God come in the flesh, true life in death, from both Mary and God, first subject to suffering and then beyond suffering, Jesus Christ our Lord. *Ephesians* 7.2

For our God, Jesus Christ, was conceived by Mary according to the plan of God; he was from the seed of David, but also from the Holy Spirit. He was born and baptized, that he might cleanse the water by his suffering. *Ephesians* 18.2

The virginity of Mary and her giving birth escaped the notice of the ruler of this age; so too did the death of the Lord – three mysteries of a cry which were accomplished in the silence of God. *Ephesians* 19.1

And so, be deaf when someone speaks to you apart from Jesus Christ, who was born from the race of David and from Mary, who was truly born, both ate and drank, was truly persecuted at the time of Pontius Pilate, was truly crucified and died, while those in heaven and on earth looked on. *Trallians* 9.1

… he (Jesus Christ) was truly from the family of David according to the flesh, Son of God according to the will and power of God, truly born from a virgin, and baptized by John that all righteousness might be fulfilled by him. *Smyrnaeans* 1

The most significant idea here is the one saying how the virginity of Mary and her giving birth were unknown to the Devil. In both the story of the Temptation in Matthew 4 and in Luke 4, the Devil says: "*If* you are the Son of God." He did not at that point know. This idea is also found in *Ode of Solomon* 19.5 (below): "Then she gave the mixture to the world, while they did not know …" The "she" is the Holy Spirit.

9.4 Our Lady in the *Odes of Solomon*

These survive today in a Syriac text which can be dated to around 100. Of the 42 Odes, only 41 survive. They were once popular throughout the Christian world, and are known to have been used not only in Coptic, Greek and Syriac, but also Latin. These odes constitute the oldest surviving Christian hymnal. In hymn 19, we possess a beautiful meditation on Our Lady. It reads:

1 The cup of milk was offered to me, and I drank it in the sweetness of the Lord's kindness.
2 The Son is the cup,
   and the Father is he who was milked,
   and the Holy Spirit is she who milked him.
3 Because his breasts were full
   and it was undesirable that his milk should be released without purpose
4 The Holy Spirit opened his [the Father's] bosom
   and mixed the milk of the two breasts of the Father.
5 Then she gave the mixture to the world, while they did not know,
   and those who have received [it] are in the perfection of the right [hand].
6 The womb of the Virgin received [it],
   and she conceived and gave birth.
7 So the Virgin became a mother with great mercies,
8 She laboured and bore the Son, but without pain,
   because it did not occur without purpose.
9 She did not seek a midwife,
   because he allowed her to give life.
10 She bore with desire as a strong man,
   And she bore according to the manifestation,
   and she possessed with great power.
11 And she loved with salvation,
   and she guarded with kindness
   and she declared with greatness.
   Hallelujah.

Who is the "I" speaking in the first verse? Is it Our Lady, or is it someone else, perhaps a priest? Sometimes the person speaking in these hymns *is* a priest, but it can also be Our Lord, and it can also perhaps be anyone from the congregation. Returning to Ode 19, note how consistently the Holy Spirit is referred to as feminine. This is, perhaps, because in Syriac the word for "Spirit" is feminine (Syriac, like Arabic has genders for all of its words).

The reference in verse 3 to his breasts being full is, I believe, to the fullness of time which had come, when the prophecies were to be fulfilled. The next verse probably refers to Our Lord and the New Testaments. If so, this is the earliest writing to place Our Lord and the two Testaments together.

The reference to needing no midwife in verse 9 is because there was an ancient belief, indeed a very ancient belief, that Our Lady gave birth without any pain. This is doubtless because painful child-birth was a consequence of the sin of Adam and Eve, from which Our Lady was free.

9.5 Our Lady in the *Protevangelium of James*

This is one of the most important documents in the history of the early Church, especially in the Eastern Church. It is believed to come from somewhere between 100 and 150, but it (or its oldest parts) may be as early as 70 or 80. The initial name of the document was probably the *Genesis (Birth) of Mary*.

Although it is little known today, it seems that no book in the early Church was as important or widespread as this document except the New Testament. From it we know the name of Mary's parents (Joachim, or Youwakim and Anna), and that Our Lord was born in a cave outside Bethlehem.

It opens with the story of Joachim, and then goes to the birth of Mary, which is presented as a virginal conception. It would follow that the author believed in the teaching of the Immaculate Conception (that Our Lady was born without original sin).[68] From the age of three, we are told, Mary was placed in the Temple, and remained there until the age of 12, weaving the veil of the Temple. There is a deep typology here, because she continued weaving it although she had to leave the Temple, and once

---

[68] This is an important doctrine in the Church: it makes sense because the first Eve was created without original sin, and so too, was the second Eve. Yet, the choice to do good and cooperate with God's plan was Mary's free choice.

she had conceived the Lord, she finished the veil. In other words, Our Lord represented the veil (Hebrews 10:20 says that the Lord's flesh *was* the veil – presumably because it hid His divinity.) Further, the death of the Lord coincides with the rending of the veil of the Temple from top to bottom at the death of the Lord (Matthew 27:5). *Typologically*, the veil is the *antetype* of the *type* which is the body of the Lord.

Chapter 11 makes clear that the virginal conception will be a miracle caused by the *overshadowing* of Mary by the Holy Spirit. In the *Protevangelium*, the moment of the birth is quite exceptional:

> 18. And he (Joseph) found a cave there, and led her into it; and leaving his two sons beside her, he went out to seek a midwife in the district of Bethlehem. And I, Joseph, was walking, and was not walking; and I looked up into the sky, and saw the sky astonished; and I looked up to the pole of the heavens, and saw it standing, and the birds of the air keeping still. And I looked down upon the earth ... And those that were eating did not eat, and those that were rising did not carry it up, and those that were conveying anything to their mouths did not convey it; but the faces of all were looking upwards. And I saw the sheep walking, and the sheep stood still; and the shepherd raised his hand to strike them, and his hand remained up. And I looked upon the current of the river, and I saw the mouths of the kids resting on the water and not drinking, and all things in a moment were driven from their course.

They were driven from their course by the birth of the Saviour. It is an extraordinary piece of writing showing all of creation caught in suspension between actions! This document is also important because it shows how the early Church could take liberties with the biblical text in the interests not of fiction but of *typology*.

9.6 Our Lady in St Ephrem

We have met St Ephrem (c.306-373) before. In the fourth of his *Hymns on the Nativity*, it is said that the first to see the new lamb were the shepherds (123), and that it is significant that it was *shepherds* who first heard the news of the birth of the True Lamb (124). This lamb was born in winter when lambs are not usually born (121-2), which is fitting as his conception was not simply a natural one (126). There are many paradoxical statements in this hymn, e.g.:

> He was lofty but he sucked Mary's milk, and from his blessings all creation sucks. He is the Living Breast of living breath; by His life the dead were suckled, and they revived. ... As again He dwelt in his mother's womb, in His womb dwells all creation. Mute He was as a babe, yet He gave to all creation His commands. (from ll. 149-155).

St Ephrem follows the *Odes of Solomon* in seeing that Our Lord gave Mary the power to bear Him: "By power from Him Mary's womb became able to bear the One who bears all" (182). Ephrem also uses the imagery of the weaving of the body of the Lord which we saw in the *Protevangelium of James*: "He diminished his measurements corresponding to the garment. She wove it and clothed in it Him Who had made Himself small" (187-188).

Our Lady is being referred to here in connection with the mystery of the Lord. That is, she is mentioned rather than celebrated. However, in Hymn 8, this changes. St Ephrem mentions Sarah and Isaac, and Rachel who sought children (Genesis 30). Then he says:

> Blessed is Mary, for without her asking, You dwelt in her womb chastely O Gift who pours himself out upon his recipients. ... Blessed is Mary, who without vows and without prayer, in her virginity conceived and brought forth the Lord of all the sons of her companions who were and will be pure and just men, priests and kings (14 and 16).

In Hymn 25, Our Lady is praised for being worthy to become his mother, while the fact that she was "a needy girl" in a "small town" is contrasted with His greatness. But the climactic praise follows in stanzas 14 and 15:

> Blessed are you, also, Mary whose name is great and exalted

because of your child. Indeed you were able to say how much and how and where the Great One, who became small, dwelt in you. Blessed is your mouth that gave thanks but did not inquire and your tongue that praised and did not investigate. since His mother was awed by Him, although she bore Him, who is sufficient [to know] Him?

O you, woman that no man knows, how shall we see the son you have brought forth?

To say that Mary is the woman that no man knows is not merely to say that she is a virgin. Surely it means that she is a mystery to all people. There is also a pun in stanza 14. The word translated as "exalted" is *m.ra.yam* in Syriac. It has the same four consonants as the name *ma.r.yam*, which is her name.

However, the most important Marian hymn I have yet found in St Ephrem is 16 from the *Hymns on the Nativity*. The psychological insight and, one senses, the psychological truth in this is almost overwhelming:

> While I gave birth to you openly, your hidden power was not removed from me. You are within me, and you are outside of me, O mystifier of his mother. When I see your outward image before my eyes, your hidden image is portrayed in my mind. In your revealed image I saw Adam, but in your hidden one I saw your Father who is united with you. Have you shown your beauty in two images to me alone? Let bread and the mind portray you. Dwell in bread and in those who eat it. ... (2-4)

> A new utterance of prophecy seethes in me. What can I call you, a stranger to us, who was from us? Shall I call you son? Shall I call you brother? Shall I call you bridegroom? Shall I call you Lord, O [you] who brought forth his mother in another birth out of the water? For I am your sister from the House of David, who is a second father. Again, I am mother because of your conception, and bride am I because of your chastity. Handmaiden and daughter of blood and water am I who you redeemed and baptised.

St Ephrem is saying that Our Lady in and of herself was changed by bearing the Lord. When this is proposed, it seems obvious, but who today states it? That Our Lord mystified his mother (i.e. made her wonder) also seems plain. It makes sense of the New Testament statements about how Our Lady pondered what she had seen. And how beautiful a thing it is to be mystified by the Lord.

St Ephrem has Our Lady say that she sees in the Lord both Adam and the Father. My understanding of this is that she sees in Him all of humanity, the very essence of what it is to be a human being, and she also sees in Him the essence of the divinity. She understands that the Father has worked through the Lord, and that Adam has been redeemed in Him. But there is no right or wrong answer to this.

It states that the Lord "baptised" Our Lady by entering her womb: a new statement so far as I am aware. She also refers to herself as being of the House of David, which St Ignatius of Antioch and the *Protevangelium of James* also affirm, although this is not in the New Testament.

9.7 Mary as a "Type"

In number 25 from his *Hymns on Virginity*, St Ephrem writes:

> You Lord, they saw while observing another. Your mother saw you in your disciple,[69] and he saw you in your mother. O, the seers who at every moment see you, Lord, in a mirror manifest a type (*Tupso*) so that we too in one another may see you, Saviour. (9)

The Syriac word for a mirror is *maH.zee.to*. The Syriac concept is not only a looking glass in which you see your own reflection, but more a sort of magic mirror or telescope in which you see other things as well. It is the ability to penetrate beneath material surfaces and to see the spiritual reality beneath. That is, the Lord is like a magic mirror: we see all things in Him, and we can see Him in other things, too, not least in our brethren (as St Matthew states in the parable of chapter 21:35-

---

69 This is St John, the beloved disciple according to the tradition.

46). Our Lady is included in this, for we can see in her the Lord Jesus Christ whom she bore, and in her Son, we see her. When we ponder the story of Our Lady, we should ask: "Where am I in this? What would I have done? Do I see her in other women? Do I see her in people who do the will of God? Do I try to be like her, so that people may see her or her Son in me?

I suggest that the concepts of *type* and *antetype* are best understood as referring to Our Lord. He is the type, and everything identified with him or something from his life, including the sacraments, is an antetype (so the flood of Noah and the crossing through the Red Sea are antetypes of the type which is baptism).

This is not the same as a symbol (*razo*): a symbol is something which is a sign for something else. There is no identity, and it does not necessarily relate to Our Lord. So St Ephrem can say that Our Lady is a symbol of the eye (*b-raz 3ayno*). She is a symbol of the eye because the eye was thought to have light inside it, and she bore Our Lord who is the True Light. But in number 37 of his *Hymns on the Church*, Ephrem writes:

> It is clear that Mary is 'the land' that receives the source of light. Through her it has illumined the whole world which, with its inhabitants, had grown dark through Eve, the source of all misfortunes. Mary and Eve in their symbols resemble a body, one of whose eyes is blind and darkened, while the other is bright and clear, providing light for the whole. The world, you see, has two eyes fixed in it: Eve was its left eye, blind; while the right eye, bright, is Mary. (3-4)

Again, Our Lady has to be understood as the new Eve. In the first of his *Hymns on Mary*, written for the Feast of the Congratulations of Our Lady (26 December, the very day after Christmas), he repeats the idea that she maintained her perpetual virginity, and wonders how she had milk with which to feed the Lord, although she was a virgin. This hymn is a great celebration of her, calling upon all virgins, Adam, the priests, the patriarchs and the prophets to rejoice in her. Important for we Maronites is the second of these hymns: "She is a ship bearing a cargo of treasures, bringing to the poor the riches of heaven. From her the dead too have been enriched, for it is Life that she bore" (5). This reappears in our incense prayer for the deceased (something similar is also found in St Ephrem's seventh hymn). In the same hymn it is said that she has redeemed all women from insults and shame: "They are no longer subject to blame," and also that, married women find joy in her (10-11).

We cannot pursue this and the many other aspects of Mariology (the study of Our Lady) here, but there are even connections to be drawn between Our Lady and the Eucharist. We should conceive new life through the Eucharist, as Our Lady did. The sacrament of the Eucharist is, in Maronite theology, a second Incarnation of the Lord. Hence, Joseph the Visionary, an eighth century Syriac mystic addresses the Eucharistic Lord as follows:

> May I receive You, not into the stomach which belongs to the body's limbs, but into the womb of my mind, so that You may be conceived there, as in the womb of the Virgin. And may You thus be revealed in me through spiritual works and good deeds that re pleasing to your will.[70]

---

[70] In Sebastian Brock, *The Syriac Fathers on Prayer and the Spiritual Life*, Cistercian Studies, Kalamazoo, 1987 p. 360.

Lesson 10

Prayer and Eastern Spirituality

10.1 Introduction

We worship God, meaning that we reverentially acknowledge God, and God alone, to be the all-good all-powerful Creator and Sustainer of everything which exists, the source of goodness, the embodiment of truth and beauty.

God in Himself is holiness. Any prayer addressed to Him, to the extent that it is sincere, comes to share in His Holiness, for it expresses the relationship of a soul to its Creator. Prayer therefore will not only result from a certain love of God, which may be weaker or stronger, but it will deepen our love for Him because it brings us closer to Him. Prayer not only *seeks*, it also *effects*. Prayer is a work.

The reverential acknowledgement which is proper to prayer is not merely a question of our minds alone, but just as much of our hearts. It involves a willing orientation of the whole person, from the deepest to the most superficial parts of our personalities, upwards to God.

This worship of God is the highest activity any human being is capable of. Worship, prayer, and a life wherein we seek virtue should all come together as one life, one course of conduct. Each of these actions is related to and is strengthened (or weakened) by the other.

Worship is not just a matter of saying "We adore you" and singing. It is a movement of the soul in humble love towards God who is our ultimate good, and in whom we find all life and all which lives: for "Christ is all and in all" (Colossians 3:11). We find a beautiful example of worship in the Gospel of St John:

> So when it was evening on that day, the first day of the week, and when the doors were shut where the disciples were, for fear of the Jews, Jesus came and stood in their midst and said to them: "Peace be with you." And when He had said this, He showed them both His hands and His side. The disciples then rejoiced when they saw the Lord. So Jesus said to them again: "Peace be with you; as the Father has sent Me, I also send you." And when He had said this, He breathed on them and said to them: "Receive the Holy Spirit. If you forgive the sins of any, their sins have been forgiven them; if you retain the sins of any, they have been retained."
>
> But Thomas, one of the twelve … was not with them when Jesus came. So the other disciples said to him: "We have seen the Lord!" But he said to them: "Unless I see in His hands the imprint of the nails, and put my finger into the place of the nails, and put my hand into His side, I will not believe." After eight days His disciples were again inside, and Thomas with them. Jesus came, the doors having been shut, and stood in their midst and said: "Peace be with you." Then He said to Thomas: "Reach here with your finger, and see My hands; and reach here your hand and put it into My side; and do not be unbelieving, but believing." Thomas answered and said to Him: "My Lord and my God!" Jesus said to him: "Because you have seen Me, have you believed? Blessed are they who did not see, and yet believed." (John 20:19-29)

Questions for Contemplation

1. What is the significance of Our Lord's giving the apostles the Holy Spirit, and the power to forgive sins?

2. When does Thomas realise that Jesus is God?

3. Am I one of those who has not seen yet believed? How can I strengthen my belief?

10.2 Worship and Prayer

Our liturgy expresses our very identity. It should even express our being. Perhaps one can truly say that whether we know it or not, how we participate in the liturgy does in fact express our being. Prayer should not be only the occupation of a few moments: we need to work at it, constantly. How constantly will vary from person to person over their lives. Sometimes we find that we can pray easily and with great fervour. On other occasions, our desire to pray will apparently disappear: we will wonder why, but may not be sure.

Also, the way that we pray can vary over a period of time. When we were children we often identified praying with repeating a set of words we had learnt. As we grew older we heard an older person extemporise[71] words, or we may even have invented our own. The fact that we can find our own words for prayer comes to some people as a revelation, and to others as a sad duty forced upon them. I think that at different times we need both extemporised prayer and prayer according to set words. This way, we remain part of the Christian tradition, using ideas and concepts which have proven their value over time. We not infrequently find in these older prayers some gem of wisdom which we could not have lighted upon ourselves.

While speaking of prayer with words, absolutely fundamental to the Christian teaching on prayer is the lesson given by Our Lord. St

---

[71]   Make up on the spot.

Matthew tells us that Our Lord taught:

> "And when you pray, do not be like the hypocrites, for they love to pray standing in the synagogues and on the street corners to be seen by others. Amen, I tell you, they have received their reward in full. But when you pray, go into your room, close the door and pray to your Father, who is unseen. Then your Father, who sees what is done in secret, will reward you. And when you pray, do not keep on babbling like pagans,[72] for they think they will be heard because of their many words. Do not be like them, for your Father knows what you need before you ask him. This, then, is how you should pray:

> 'Our Father in heaven, hallowed be your name, your kingdom come, your will be done, on earth as it is in heaven. Give us today our daily bread. And forgive us our debts, as we also have forgiven our debtors. And lead us not into temptation, but deliver us from the evil one." (Matthew 6:5-13)

Note that Our Lord is not speaking about praying in the liturgy: He is referring to how one prays as an individual (even if one is in a place like a church or a synagogue when praying). The Lord states, first, do not draw attention to yourself, or put yourself where you will attract attention. Rather, pray in secret: it is an internal matter between yourself and God.

Secondly, Our Lord taught us not to use too many words. Perhaps the Lord meant that we should not get lost in words. Rather, we should intend the thoughts and words with which we pray. And intend them not only in our hearts but also in our lives: to say one thing but to deliberately do another is to be a hypocrite. Our Lord always condemned hypocrisy.

Therefore, we should try to reflect the God whom we worship in our prayer, and to reflect the spirit of our prayer in our lives.

Third, this is a *manner* of praying, for He said "pray like this." Other

---

[72] People who believed in a multitude of gods. Often these gods practised immorality (even by pagan standards).

forms of words can be used, but always in that structure: addressing God, praising Him, His goodness and His will, and then coming to ourselves in relation to others, and seeking salvation from the devil.[73]

What prayer means to you will change through your life. It will never stop changing. Prayer is a major part of one's vocation, whether one becomes a member of clergy or remains a lay person. In so far as offering prayer is a priestly task, we are all priests. When Psalm 139:5 says of God that He has laid His hand upon me, this can mean, in Syriac, not only that He loves and cares for me, but also that He has ordained me a priest, for in Syriac "to lay on hands" means "to ordain a priest." Since Psalm 139 is believed to be the words of Adam (not that we think Adam wrote this Psalm, but that the Psalmist spoke in his name), it ties in with the Syriac tradition (found in Jacob of Sarug) that "Adam was created as a priest, with a vocation to stand before God on behalf of the whole creation."[74]

Similarly, most translations of Genesis 2:15 read that God put Adam into the Garden of Eden "to cultivate it and to keep it." Now the word "to cultivate" is the verb *3abad*, which in Hebrew and Syriac means not only "to do, to make" but also "to serve, to worship." So it is open to say that God created Adam in order to worship and to keep the Paradise into which he was born.

The desire to worship is, therefore, an expression of desiring to live with God. Who worships in the fullness of the faith, worships in the presence of God. As Aphrahat said: "When a man sweeps clean his

---

[73] With the "Our Father," there are at least two questions of translation: first and clearest of all, although the English says "save us from evil," it could well mean "save us from the Evil One," that is, the devil. Second, the word "daily" bread, could in fact mean "supernatural" bread. The arguments for each of these alternative translations has had adherents.

[74] Baby Varghese, *West Syrian Liturgical Theology*, Ashgate, Hants, 2004, p.8.

soul in the name of Christ, Christ dwells in him ..."[75] And there is a community dimension to this, for as Our Lord taught: "...where two or three gather together in My name, there am I with them" (Matthew 18:20).

The prayer of one person is one thing, and it is a great matter. The prayer of a group of the faithful is another phenomenon: through it we express not only our relation to God but also to His children. When we are in the presence of prayerful attention, we can sense it, and it helps us, if we ourselves have that a taste of that attention stirring in us.

We could hardly do better than to end this section with this thought from John the Solitary. He lived in the first half of the fifth century, and so was an older contemporary of St Maroun:

> At the beginning of your prayer, have it in mind to say in God's presence: "Holy, holy, holy, Lord Almighty, with whose glory both heaven and earth are filled." Then be mindful of whatever is appropriate in your prayer, which should always include remembering God's Church, petitions for the weak and afflicted, entreaty for those who have gone astray, compassion for sinners, forgiveness of those who have done wrong.[76]

10.3 An Ancient Maronite Text on Prayer

In the Divine Sacrifice of the Mass, we keep repeating: "Let us glorify, honour and praise ..." and "... we shall thank and praise you," and similar sentiments. These little formulas are often called "doxologies," meaning "words of glorification." They are important because they keep bringing us back to the purpose of the Divine Sacrifice, the praise and

---

[75] Aphrahat, Demonstration IV: "On Prayer," in Sebastian Brock, *The Syriac Fathers on Prayer and the Spiritual Life*, Cistercian, Kalamazoo, 1987, 15-16. It must be borne in mind when reading this excellent book, that many if not most of the writers were monks writing for other monks. What they say is applicable to us all, but the standards and efforts required will be more fully met within the monastic life.

[76] John the Solitary: "Letter to Hesychius," 66, in Brock, *The Syriac Fathers on Prayer*, 96.

glory of God, included within which is thanksgiving. The distribution of the Eucharist to the faithful forms the climax of this ceremony.

The Maronite teaching on prayer is identical to that of the Universal Catholic Church. However, we emphasize certain aspects of the faith, and we de-emphasize others (e.g. in our Divine Sacrifice of the Mass we often ask for forgiveness of our sins, and we often mention the second coming of the Lord, we say less about what we might call "social justice" than some other churches do). Let us take one specifically Maronite example of a treatise on prayer, with a distinctive emphasis upon standing facing the East, having good attention, and preserving chastity. This is from a text from about 600, written in Syriac:[77]

1. We should pray in faith, without letting our minds be in doubt or be lacking in a firm trust in our God. This is what Our Lord Himself teaches us when He says "All that you shall ask in prayer in my name, having faith, you shall receive."[78] Potent (powerful) indeed is the prayer which is offered from a pure heart in faith. For this reason we should persevere in prayer, my brethren, and not weary of it. ...

3. We define prayer, then, as the means of escape from misfortunes, the delivery from all that can cause hurt, the key to the gates of heaven, converse and encounter with God.

4. Petition is a request for the things that are lacking from what is requisite.

5. Supplication, then, my beloved, is a profound form of the same thing.

6. Thanksgiving is the expression of gratitude for what has been given.

---

[77] Published by Sebastian Brock: "An Early Maronite text on Prayer," *Parole de l'Orient*, 13 (1986) 79-94. Much of this text is drawn from other sources, but it is the text as a whole, and the selection of the material which matters. It is not absolutely certain that the prayer is Maronite, but Brock thinks it most likely, and has no better suggestion.

[78] Matthew 21:22 with John 15:16.

7. … The holy Basil[79] teaches us … "… this is the reason why our gaze is directed eastwards when we stand in prayer: it is so that our eyes may gaze in the direction of Paradise, and in this way we may seek for our original abode which we lost when our forefather Adam transgressed the commandment. Few people are aware of this, for it corresponds to what is written: "Paradise is in the East, and its planter is God."[80]

(The author then quotes Our Lord, St James and St Paul on prayer)

11. The holy Gregory,[81] the brother of Basil the Great, also teaches us as follows in his *Exposition of the Lord's Prayer*: "If prayer takes place prior to taking care of (one's) affairs, then sin is unable to find any entrance into the soul." "The same is the case if someone is going on a journey, or is going off in war, or is going to get married." "If he does everything accompanied by prayer his course will go well."

12. From the fact of our praying it so happens to us that we are with God, and whoever is with God is well away from the Adversary.[82] Prayer thus preserves chastity, it beats down anger, it drowns pride, it gets rid of resentment, it destroys envy, it causes evil to vanish, it reforms wicked ways." "Prayer is the seal of virginity, the firm basis of marriage, the armour of those who travel, the protection of those who are asleep, the source of confidence for those who are awake." In brief: "prayer is talking to and encountering God."

13. The blessed teacher Mar Jacob[83] says: "Prayer reveals the profundities of the Divine … from it one can clearly espy what is hidden, by it the soul can approach and speak with God, it raises up the mind so that it reaches the Majesty …

14. … When we arise from our beds let our mouths not utter anything else before we have given praise and thanks to God. Just as

---

[79] St Basil the Great (329-379). This is adapted from Basil's *Treatise on the Holy Spirit*, 27.
[80] This is adapted from Genesis 2:8.
[81] St Gregory of Nyssa (335-395) who was indeed the brother of St Basil.
[82] The devil.
[83] St Jacob of Sarug (451-521).

buildings which are constructed with dressed beams do not collapse all of a sudden, even if fierce gales buffet against them, so it is with us: provided we gird our way of life and our actions with prayers all the days of our lives, we will not suddenly fall.

15. ... Hang up this armour on the walls of your house, over your bed, and over your table; and when you are leaving home, make the sign of the cross on your forehead and give mental thanks to God; then, clothed in this armour, you can walk out in the street with a firm trust in God and with thankfulness of heart. And when you get back home, draw close to the presence of your Lord many times over in prayer. When you are about to eat and drink, do not break bread or drink a cup of anything without first singing it with the cross and hallowing it with prayer. And when you have had sufficient, give praise and thanks to him whose good things you have enjoyed.

16. At the time when you stand before your Lord in prayer, do not start off in a languid fashion, otherwise you will perform your entire prayer in a lax and lazy way. Rather, when you stand (in prayer) sign yourself with the cross, collect your thoughts together and prepare yourself in readiness. Concentrate on Him to who you are praying, and take care that your thought does not depart from Him until your prayer has reached its conclusion. At the very beginning of your prayer compel yourself so that your tears flow and your mind is filled with "suffering." In this way your whole prayer will prove advantageous. For any prayer in which reflection on God and mental contemplation is not mingled is a mere weariness of the flesh.

Take care that your mind does not wander off during the time of prayer as it thinks about empty matters: in that case, instead of arousing the Judge to reconciliation, you will stir Him to anger ... You are full of fear before the world's judges, but in God's presence you show contempt: if someone is not aware of where he is standing and what he is saying, how can he suppose that he is offering up prayer? ... Your Lord is speaking with you, so do not wander off: His chosen angels surround you, so do not be perturbed ... Rather, take refuge in trust in your Lord and start off on the road of prayer confidently, turning aside neither to the right nor to the left: then all of a sudden you will arrive at the place of tranquillity which is exempt from any element of fear, and the offering of your prayer will be accepted, as was Abel's, your mind being attentive and aware; whereas the Adversary who opposes you is put to shame, for he becomes fearful of you during your time of prayer, seeing that the words of your mouth correspond to the will of God.

18. Being aware of all this, my beloved, we urge and advise you that we should not pray as if it was some ordinary thing, but when we pray we should do so with divine love, for without love prayers and supplications are not acceptable to God.

Notice that in section 16, the author says: "take care that your thought does not depart from Him," not "take care that your words do not depart ..." for thought is prior to words. Further, not all prayer involves words. I can have a thought or a feeling which is a prayer. St Ephrem writes: "... prayer and petition can both be conceived in the mind and brought to birth in silence, without using the voice."[84]

Such a wordless state of being even has a duration which one can sense: one just knows that the moment of prayer has not yet finished, the interior statement has not been completed, and yet I might not be able to explain what I am saying.

10.4 Thoughts on Prayer

From this we can see that prayer is a conscious turning of the attention to God. The Syriac tradition placed great importance on *attention* and *awareness*. When the attention moves upwards, heart and mind are animated and raised aloft, as one. Prayer involves, therefore, a lifting of our souls so that, from that higher perspective, it becomes aware of the divine presence. The divine presence is here and now, but it is also at the same time beyond all here and now. We become more

---

[84]   Ephrem: "Hymns on Faith," 20, in S. Brock, *The Syriac Fathers on Prayer*, 33.

or less sensitive to it depending upon our state. Now our state does, to some extent, depend upon external conditions. But *not* completely. Being out in nature, and being able to take in the impressions of the sky, trees, mountains, sea, river, fields, bird song, farm-lands and flowers can raise my spirits and even induce me to think of God. Who has not looked at the heaving of the sea and been reminded of the power of God, or considered the way the mountains arise and not thought of how God supports all the earth? But if I am depressed, none of this helps me at all. There has to be a meeting of the spirit within and the Spirit without.

Some times are better for prayer than others. The best time is "now." The worst times are "later on": "if only yesterday," and "I don't have time." I can turn to prayer whenever I am reminded of it. Sometimes the prayer will be the subject of my complete concentration: e.g. I am sitting quietly at home, or kneeling in church, or standing before a statue. At those moments, prayer will be the foremost activity in my mind and heart; it will be in the foreground. But maybe I am doing something risky, or maybe I am disturbed, or I am speaking to people. Prayer can then proceed in the background, as it were. Yet how much better it would be if, even then, prayer was in the foreground, and I trusted to God to find the words I would speak, and to lead my hands to do what He wills me to perform. Perhaps I do not have the leisure to take out my rosary and say a decade. But I can always stop where I am for one half of a second, collect myself., turn towards God, acknowledge His greatness and my weakness, and call on Him to help.

Prayer can involve petition: seeking something from God. There is nothing wrong with this, but remember that God does not promise to give us material things, only grace, and grace is a spiritual gift. In the "Our Father" see what the petitions are: that God's name be hallowed, that His Kingdom come and so on. What we seek for ourselves in that prayer is our daily supernatural bread, forgiveness of sins (as we forgive others), freedom from temptation and from the devil. There is no mention of material goods or job prospects. However, if one does pray for a car and does not receive it, you can nonetheless be granted the grace to deal with your disappointment. It is then up to you to use that grace.

But prayer does not only involve petition: it can also be pure thanksgiving. It can be pure worship. It can just be talking to God, telling him what has happened and how you feel about it. St Isaac of Nineveh said: "Every kind of prayer that there is consists in asking, or petition, or praise, or thanks."[85]

The Syriac tradition places some emphasis on the preparation of the heart, sometimes encouraging the use of pictures. Hence, Evagrius writes: "Prayer that does not have mingled into it the thought of God and interior vision is a weariness of the flesh. … a single word said with an attentive mind is better than a thousand when the mind is far away."[86]

10.5 Morning Prayer

Morning is a natural symbol of life. Every day, God speaks to us through natural symbols. Each and every morning is an *antetype* of Easter morning when Our Lord rose from the dead. In the same way, each sunset tells us that each life is fated to find its natural end, until it arrives in eternity. Through His natural symbols of day and night, God tells us that each life must know both a beginning and an end. Each morning announces a fresh start to life, and to our lives. The dawn tells us to arise and praise God for He is good, and His creation is intrinsically good. The sun is a natural symbol of how God stands high over the ever-changing world.

Morning is a perfect time to make an unconditional offering to

---

[85]   Isaac of Nineveh: "Discourse 22," in Brock, *The Syriac Fathers on Prayer*, 254.
[86]   Evagrius: "Admonition of Prayer," in S. Brock, *The Syriac Fathers on Prayer*, 71.

God of the day and whatever it may bring. We should pray that we may worthily commence the day and honourably live it out. We do not know what will happen to us, but as it must occur in accordance with His laws, we cannot reject it: we must live and work through it.

Further, the very fact of being alive in the morning calls us to thank God for having preserved us through the night, and for the gift of another day, a present greater than all the treasure any of the rulers of this world could offer. *Ashraqa n-nouru* ("the light has arisen") is an ancient Syriac hymn, now set to music as an Arabic language hymn, which we can pray at dawn with the monks and priests who say it as part of their Divine Office. It is in the appendix.

10.6 Evening Prayer

Evening prayer is one of the most beautiful achievements of the Church. It is good before we go to sleep to kneel by the side of our beds, or sit on a chair. But whatever you do, take some special posture, do not just lie down in bed. Then spend at least five minutes preparing ourselves for the night. One can choose one of the prayers attached to the end of this paper, or any others from a good Catholic book. It is also good to examine one's day: what did I do when I arose? What did I do at 9.00am? At 10.00am? At each hour of the day? And so on. How was I in that meeting, or during that class? What did I do well and what did I do badly? Where can I improve?

There is a very common snare: some will say that they are not worthy to pray, or too distracted to pray. This is not and never can be true. As soon as you have the wish, you are able, and we are always worthy enough to ask God to make us more so. Remember that, as was said above, prayer not only seeks, it also effects. St Isaac of Nineveh writes:

> You should not wait until you are cleansed of wandering thoughts
> before you desire to pray; such distraction is not banished from

the mind except by assiduous prayer entailing much labour. If you only begin on prayer when you see that your mind has become perfect and exalted above all recollection of the world, then you will never pray.[87]

10.7 Veneration of Our Lady and the Saints

We only worship God. But from love of Him, we honour or venerate the saints. We render to Our Lady a veneration which is greater than that offered to any other saint, although she is only a saint, not God.

When we "pray" to Our Lady and the saints, it is not as if we believe that they have the power to grant our prayers. They do not. But they *hear* our prayers because God allows them to. Then, they have the power to *join in our prayers* to God. When the saints share in our prayers to God, we call this *intercession.* By that we mean that the saints add their prayers to ours. But be clear: it is only God who has the power to do anything by way of granting prayers.

One can think of it like this: if a child wants their father to do something, the child often goes to their mother and asks the father on the child's behalf. The father knows that the child is making the request, but his wife is also making it, and so he is more likely to grant it. It is the same sort of principle when we seek the intercession of Our Lady and the saints. God knows that we are praying to Him, but now our prayer is joined with Our Lady's. History shows us that the prayers of the saints are often heard: almost every modern saint has been supported by good evidence of two or more miracles.

Part of the reason for the confusion about to whom Catholics pray is that the original sense of the English word "pray" was not restricted to praying to God or some divine figure in other religions, but rather of *asking earnestly* (with some seriousness). It was once a far more widely

---

[87]   Isaac of Nineveh, from *Centuries of Knowledge*, 4.34, in Brock, *The Syriac Fathers on Prayer*, 264.

used term than it is now. People might say: "Pray tell …," meaning that they wanted some information. So, in olden days, when we asked Our Lady to pray for us to the Lord, it was immediately understood that we were asking Her to earnestly ask Her Son for us.

Let us close with this very deep thought:

> The purpose of prayer is for us to acquire love of God, for in prayer can be discovered all sorts of reasons for loving God.
>
> Love of God proceeds from conversing with Him. This conversation of prayer comes about through stillness, and stillness comes with the stripping away of the self.[88]

---

[88] Isaac of Nineveh, from "Discourse 63," in Brock, *The Syriac Fathers on Prayer*, 250.

Lesson 11

Sacred Scripture and the Maronite Faith

11.1 Introduction

The Bible is not a book like any other. If you compare a novel with a cookbook, and either of these with a political manifesto, you can see clearly that different books have to be read in different ways. You cannot just take one the way you take the other: with the novel you suspend disbelief so that you can enter the imaginative world which is painted within it. You take the cookbook as a more or less authoritative guide to preparing something to serve and eat, while with the manifesto you are more critical, knowing that someone is trying to convince you of something to do with the ordering of society.

The Bible falls into a very small category, that of ancient sacred books, or "Scripture" (what is written). It contains history, but it is history for a spiritual purpose. It contains poetry which is neither really fact nor fiction, but prayer, such as the Psalms. It also contains many passages where prophets declare what God desires, commands, and has revealed of the future, but not in the straightforward manner of a weather forecast, for example. The church, which put together and authorises the Bible, says that it is to be read with reverence, with love, and with a sense of wonder. We should not place ourselves above it as judges, but rather, we should approach it in humility and gratitude.

As St Ephrem says:

> ... we leave behind in it (Scripture) far more than we take from it, like thirsty people drinking from a fountain.
>
> The facets of His word are more numerous than the faces of those who learn from it. God depicted His word with so many beauties, so that each of those who learn from it can examine that aspect of it which he likes. And God has hidden within His word all sorts of treasures, so that each of us can be enriched by it from whatever aspect he meditates on. ...
>
> Anyone who encounters Scripture should not suppose that the single one of its riches which he has found is the only one to exist; rather he should realise that he himself is only capable of discovering that one out of the many riches that exist in it. ... Let the fountain vanquish you thirst, your thirst should not vanquish the fountain.[89]

Sacred Scripture is fundamental to our worship, not in that we worship the Bible, but in that its spirit pervades us during worship, and that those who composed the liturgy drew abundantly upon its words, its poetry, its stories and its teachings. The extent to which the words of Scripture are drawn upon either directly or indirectly, and more often indeed, *indirectly*, means that it is the atmosphere in which we breathe the liturgy. The use of indirect allusion more than direct quotation is significant: it shows that the liturgy is not just Scripture put into dramatic form, but something new, drawing upon its treasures. The use of allusions rather than quotations also respects the unique nature of Scripture: it is not to be cut and pasted, but rather meditated upon.

---

[89] St Ephrem, quoted in Sebastian Brock, *The Luminous Eye*, revised edition, Cistercian, Kalamazoo, 1992, 50-51.

When there are direct readings from Scripture, this is formally marked out from the rest of the liturgy, and the fact of a reading from Scripture is clearly brought to people's attention with introductory chants. So the Liturgy of the Word, the first part of the Divine Sacrifice of the Mass, leads up to a reading from one of the Epistles (letters of the apostles), and reaches its climax when the priest proclaims the Gospel of the Lord.

11.2 The Bible as a Whole

The very word "Bible" comes from a Greek word which means "book." The Bible is *the book.* It is a compilation of seventy-two smaller books. Bound together, they form one volume (the Bible) in two parts (the Old Testament and the New Testament). The Gospel of St John, for example, was originally an entire book in itself, although today we read it as one of the four gospels. The four gospels are themselves part of the larger volume we call the "New Testament."

The Greek word which we have translated as "testament" is *diathēkē.* The meanings of the noun *diathēkē* are "last will and testament," as well as "covenant." "Covenant" is the word used in the Old Testament for the promises made by God to His people Israel.

Today, by the "Old Testament," we mean the 46 books revealed by God to the Jews before the birth of the Lord, and written over hundreds of years. The Old Testament used by Our Lord and the first Christians was in two forms. The first form of the Old Testament, is the 39 Hebrew books (used in Palestine) which is today accepted in Judaism and in Protestantism. [90] The second form, based on a translation of these books, plus some seven other books (some of which were translated from Hebrew and some of which were written in Greek, and which originated in Alexandria in Egypt, is known as the "Septuagint." This

---

[90]   Richard Marius, *Luther*, Quartet, London, 1975, 163. Luther wanted to remove the Book of Esther from the Old Testament although it was a Hebrew book: see his comments in *Martin Luther's Table Talk*, trans. William Hazlitt, Christian Heritage, republished 2003 (no original date given), Fearn Great Britain, 102.

is sometimes referred to by the abbreviation "LXX."[91] To speak of "the Old Testament" is to use a distinctively Christian terminology. For Judaism, the "Bible" is only the 39 books they retained.

It seems that the Lord also used both forms: the Hebrew and the Greek. The reason for Judaism's choice of the Hebrew form, to the exclusion of the Greek, has never, I believe, been satisfactorily explained, for the records are incomplete, but I have seen suggestions that it may even have been influenced by the Christian use of the Greek Old Testament. The answer to the question of which collection we Catholics accept as the revealed Old Testament is clear: it is the 46 books of the LXX.

By the New Testament, we mean the 27 books all written within about 70 years from the death of the Lord, and telling us:

1. What Our Lord said and did (the four Gospels of Ss Matthew, Mark, Luke and John).
2. What the apostles, especially Ss Peter and Paul, said and did (the Acts of the Apostles).
3. What the apostles said to certain churches and individuals (the epistles or letters).
4. What God revealed to St John (the Apocalypse).

There is only one form of the New Testament in use, with 27 books, although certain persons have questioned parts of it (e.g. Luther placed the books of Hebrews, James, Jude and Revelation in an appendix at the back of his translation).[92]

---

91 "LXX" is the Latin way of writing "seventy." "Septuagint" means "seventy." The legend was that the Hebrew Bible was translated into Greek by seventy-two scholars. The books they rejected, but which the Christians kept, were: the Books of Tobit, Judith, Wisdom of Solomon, ben Sira (also known as "Ecclesiasticus" because it was so popular in the church, *ekklesia* = church); Baruch, 1 and 2 Maccabees; and some passages within other books. Some Orthodox Churches have more than 46 books in their Old Testament.

92 See http://www.bible-researcher.com/antilegomena.html, accessed 3 February 2017.

Books, in ancient times, were generally presented as *scrolls*, and sometimes but far more rarely, as *codices* (the singular of this word is *codex*). A codex is the form of the modern book: pages are bound at the spine. The scroll was made of a length of either papyrus (a plant from which something like paper was made), or parchment (animal hide), which would be rolled up, and often had rollers at each edge to help manage it. A scroll could, but did not need to have, separate pages, which were each written on a separate length of material. Then, to make the scroll, all the pages were put together in order, either from the top down to the bottom, or alongside one another.

In collections of scrolls, each book was usually kept separately. Sometimes, if a number of books were short, they could be placed on the same scroll, e.g. the "Twelve Prophets" from the Old Testament were all written on just one scroll.

It is quite possible that the books of the New Testament were originally circulated as scrolls or even as letters on papyrus. It is quite certain that the letters originally were genuinely letters, and were copied and sent from church to church. Further, the ancient historians record that St Mark's Gospel was the first of the Gospels to be written. Then the other three were written, but many other gospels were written which the Church excluded.

Without the Church, how would we today be able to tell what was authentic and what was not?

The short answer is that we could not, for in the ancient world, and even today, there is considerable controversy. The discovery of an entire library of manuscripts including, amongst other books, *alternative* Gospels and apocalypses has revived this question. This library, found at Nag Hammadi in Egypt in the mid-twentieth century, has been called "Gnostic," but not all of its documents fit that label, and the very word "Gnostic" is hard to define with any precision.

But the point is that, as a result of that find, scholars are clearer than ever that the make-up of the New Testament was for a long time fluid. The list of books which went into the New Testament (what is called "the canon") was not settled for several hundred years, and when it was settled, it was by people who were part of the Great Church (what we call today the Catholic and Orthodox Churches). If the list of the canon had to be worked out by each individual or community, the idea of a "Christian bible" would collapse, and there would be multiple "bibles."

By about 300, there was a broad consensus as to what was accepted as worthy to be read in churches. However, this consensus was not complete, and there existed grey areas where people knew, for example, that the four Gospels we use today could be read, but they also had some other books of which they were were not so sure. For example, and this is an important one, Bishop Serapion of Antioch (c.191-211) went to a church in Syria where there was an argument about whether the *Gospel of Peter* could be read in the church. At first, he said, it would be better to read it than to let the issue split the community. But when he realised that the so-called Gospel supported heretical ideas (teachings contrary to the truth), he banned it.[93] It is worth thinking about this: within two hundred years of the death of the Lord, there were be questions about the revealed nature of the *Gospel of Peter*, and these were only settled by the authority of the bishop. Our Lord did not say what would be in the Bible: none of the New Testament had even been written when He died? How could the make-up of the Bible ever have been settled without the Church? As the story of Bishop Serapion shows, the Bible was the Church's book, and it used it as an an authoritative text, but a living human being in authority was needed to allow or disallow the text.

Early in Church history, it seems, the Gospels circulated as one book, the Acts of the Apostles together with the letters of James,

---

[93] Eusebius, *Ecclesiastical History*, 6.12. I used the edition by J.E.L. Oulton, Loeb Classical Library, 1932, vol. II, p. 41 (reprinted 1980).

Peter, John and Jude circulated as another book, the Pauline epistles as another, and the Book of Revelation, likewise. But the oldest known copy of the Bible, the Codex Sinaiticus, probably from the 4th century, has two additional documents we no longer consider part of it. It has all 27 books of the New Testament plus the *Letter of Barnabas* and the *Shepherd of Hermas*. This is but part of the evidence that the ancient Christians were certain about the four gospels, and most of the letters of Paul and the Acts and Revelation, but were uncertain about what other books could be included. The Church had to decide this. It was not until the last half of the fourth century that any finality emerged in practice: and when it did the Christian Bible always included, in its Old Testament, *all* the LXX books.

Further, so far as is known, all the collections of the New Testament as a whole were made in the form of codices, as mentioned above. A *codex* can be opened at any page, and, of course, closed at once. With a scroll, you have to always open it at the same place, then unroll it to get to where you want to be, and then roll it back up again. It was a unique practice to write books in a codex: codices were usually used as workmen's notebooks. That the Christians immediately started to use codices suggests that a decision was made somewhere centrally that Christians would distinguish their Scripture from all other literature by using codices.[94]

The Bible is the most important of all books to Christians: it is our *Sacred Scripture*. We read from it in each and every Mass, and each time we read the Divine Office. At each Mass, straight after the *Qadišat* , the priest says: "Holy and immortal Lord, purify our minds and sanctify our consciences so that we may praise you with purity and listen to your Holy Scriptures." This tells us three things:

1. It is critical to be in a state of purity when we listen to the

---

[94] It may also have meant that many Christians were workmen. This point has been made by many scholars, not least, by David Trobisch, *The First Edition of the New Testament*, Oxford University Press, Oxford, 2000.

Scriptures.
2. We listen to Scripture not only with our ears and minds, but also with our *consciences*.
3. The reading of Scripture is related to the praising of God.

Of course the conscience does not listen, in any literal way, but it participates in the act of listening, because we desire to read the Scripture only out of love for God and to learn His Word. We do not listen for ulterior or superficial motives: e.g. to acquire information to support us in a position we believe and wish to take as true, but to learn from it what position we should hold to be true. This must be kept firmly in mind: so many people abuse the Bible in this way that a word of warning must be given. People have scanned the Bible looking for codes, for the date of the End of the World, or to found their own religions. All this is a misuse if not an abuse of Scripture.

The other matter which people find strange is the connection between listening to Scripture and worship. They are not two entirely different activities: all reading of Scripture with a Christian spirit is worship, but not all worship is reading Scripture. The Bible is so readily available to us today, and in so many formats (such as on our phones) that it is almost impossible to remember and to feel, each time we read, it, that this is not an ordinary book, but rather Sacred Scripture. Really, reading Scripture should be a subset of worshipping and understanding God.

Perhaps for this reason, it is part of the Maronite tradition that Scripture be read out aloud and the people listen to it. One absorbs the material very differently when one hears it, as opposed to reading it. When one reads something, it is easy to proceed on automatic pilot: the eyes pass over the page, but the head does not take it in. The same is possible when one hears: but it is harder, because the very act of listening calls our attention. Also, when we read we always hear our own voice inside our head. But when we listen, we see how someone else would read, where they put the emphasis, how they bring the meaning out. Their interpretation may be quite new to us.

To be able to read Scripture out aloud and to read it well, that is, to *proclaim* it, is quite an art, and a valuable one, too.

Another interesting question is that of *revelation*, meaning what is revealed to us by God. The truths which have been revealed to us are often beyond our human minds, e.g. the doctrine of the Trinity, and everything to do with the nature of the soul and life after death. There are two types of revelation: public and private. The public revelation began with Adam and Eve, our first parents. It closed with the last apostle. Private revelation has come and continues to come to certain individuals: but no one else is required to believe it. The Church may say that a private revelation is approved, and that it contains nothing contrary to faith or morals, but this is not the same as saying that any of the faithful *must* believe it as true (the same way that the contents of the Creed and what is taught in the liturgy must be firmly held).

When we say that God is the author of Scripture, we do not mean that He dictated the words to the writers: rather, we mean that they were inspired by Him. This means that, working with the language they knew and all their mental and emotional equipment, the writers of Scripture put down what the Holy Spirit prompted them to say. Being human vessels for a divine teaching, they were striving to express in words something which can hardly be put into words. Not infrequently, the result is a certain ambiguity. Readers and interpreters of the Bible are forever disputing what this or that passage means. This is why the Church is needed to provide authoritative interpretations in cases where the difference really matters.

11.3 The Old Testament

The "Old Testament" is the first part of the Christian scriptures. The use of the word "Old" tells you that there must be something "New" to compare with it. Further, it seems that the Christians had chosen the books which they would recognise as scripture (that is, as officially recognised holy books) before the Jews did (although this is not entirely clear, for there is a lack of evidence at important points).

As stated, the first Christians chose to read their Old Testament in Greek, the LXX. The Old Testament is extremely important as showing how the religion of the ancient Jews continued to develop right up until the time of the Lord. Indeed, the later books which are retained only in the LXX show how intensely Israel was being prepared for his coming. I shall take just one example: it is known that among the ancient Jews there was no clear concept of what was involved in the afterlife: the general idea was that the deceased all went to a place called *Sheol* (an underworld). The teaching of heaven and hell was not known among them with any clarity. However, the doctrine did start to appear in little flashes here and there, and then, towards the very end of this period, in a book written only a little before the birth of Our Lord, 2 Maccabees, it is written: "It is a holy and wholesome thought to pray for the dead that they may be loosed from sins" (2 Maccabees 12:46). This valuable book is retained within the LXX, and so is read by Catholics and our Orthodox brethren, but it is not in Protestant Bibles.

11.4 The New Testament

We have already read and discussed much material from the New Testament, especially from the Gospels and the Book of Acts. The question for us now is the relationship between the Old and the New Testaments. Jacob of Sarug discussed this by making reference to the veil over the face of Moses. That veil is mentioned in the Book of Exodus, describing how the Lord would allow Moses to approach, and would speak with him:

> When Moses came down from Mount Sinai with the two tablets of the covenant law in his hands, he was not aware that his face was radiant because he had spoken with the Lord. When Aaron and all the Israelites saw Moses, his face was radiant, and they

were afraid to come near him. But Moses called to them; so Aaron and all the leaders of the community came back to him, and he spoke to them. Afterward all the Israelites came near him, and he gave them all the commands the Lord had given him on Mount Sinai. When Moses finished speaking to them, he put a veil over his face. But whenever he entered the Lord's presence to speak with him, he removed the veil until he came out. And when he came out and told the Israelites what he had been commanded, they saw that his face was radiant. Then Moses would put the veil back over his face until he went in to speak with the Lord. (Exodus 34:29-35)

Using this story to make his point, Jacob wrote:

Jesus is a radiant light in the Scriptures, and so
a veil is thrown over Him so that He might be hidden from the sight of spectators.
That veil of Moses openly cries out to the entire world
that the words in the Scriptures are likewise veiled:
Moses is the model of all that is uttered in prophecy,
providing a type (*Toofso*) for the veiled character of the Old Testament.
That veil was removed only with Our Lord
in whom all mysteries were explained to the entire world.[95]

This "veil" and its lifting by the life of Christ is illustrated by the narrative, in Acts 8, of St Philip and the Ethiopian eunuch who was reading how the Book of Isaiah (in the Old Testament) describes someone whose life is taken "like a sheep to the slaughter." He asks St Philip: "Tell me, please, who is the prophet talking about, himself or someone else?" (Acts 8:34). St Philip then explains that it is Jesus. That is, with the veil over the Old Testament, one cannot know who is being referred to except some "suffering servant." But interpreting the Old Testament in light of Our Lord's life, we understand that Isaiah was prophetically referring to the Lord.

---

[95] *Jacob of Sarug's Homily on the Veil on Moses' Face*, trans. and ed. Sebastian Brock, Gorgias, Piscataway, 2009, 69-76, pp. 18 and 20.

11.5 The Bible and Tradition

My own definition, for what it is worth, is that *tradition is the eternal unity of the truth faith, including both teaching and practice, connected in time with the past and the future, and connected in eternity with God Himself who embodies the truth.*

This definition has the virtues, I would say, of highlighting first, that tradition is not ours for us to play with and change around as we like; second that we have a triple responsibility, to receive it in obedience from the past, to maintain it diligently in the present, and to transmit it in fidelity[96] to the future.

"Tradition" is passed down to us with the intention that we pass it on, and with the understanding that it is of more than merely temporary value. Holy Scripture is part of that tradition, maybe even the single largest portion.

But Christ Himself is the most fundamental aspect of the tradition, and the very fact that Christ Himself is still alive, in heaven, and reigns over the universe, shows that "tradition" is more than simply some sort of historical record or chain of testimony, although it includes that.

Our Lord contrasted the commandments of God with the traditions of men, saying: "You have let go of the commands of God and are holding on to human traditions" (Mark 7:8). In doing so, He was referring to adulterating[97] the sacred tradition I am speaking of with our own ideas and wishes, that is, He was condemning not passing on the eternal tradition as we received it.

St Paul told the churches to hold on to the traditions. He wrote in 2 Thessalonians 2:15: "So then, brothers and sisters, stand firm and hold fast to the traditions we passed on to you, whether by word of mouth or by letter"; and in 3:6: "In the name of the Lord Jesus Christ, we

---

[96] "Fidelity" is "loyalty" or "faithfulness."
[97] "Adulterating" is "making something poorer by adding an extraneous substance," in this case, mingling what is divine with what is human.

command you, brothers and sisters, to keep away from every believer who is idle and disruptive and does not live according to the tradition you received from us." Clearly, the traditions were partly written and partly oral, and taught how to live. But they were to be retained as a living treasure: it was not simply a question of referring to books, although they have their place. Further, we know from St Paul's writings that the tradition included what we today term the Divine Sacrifice of the Mass (see 1 Corinthians 11).

Without any derogation to the importance of the Bible, the second part of the tradition, the basic teachings of the Church, are needed to interpret it. That is, great as Holy Scripture is, it is not always possible to understand it with any certainty, and some important parts of the Christian teaching are either not to be found in it at all, or are quite unclear. For example, the doctrine of the Trinity is nowhere clearly stated in the Bible, although it can be deduced from it. Infant baptism is nowhere clearly recommended in the New Testament (although some of the households who were baptised may have included children). It is the task and office of the Church to interpret Scripture where serious questions are to be decided.

But more significantly: *the Bible does not tell you which books go into the Bible.* If I said that the letter of St Jude, for example, did not belong in it, how could you tell whether it does or not? In fact, Luther rejected the Letter of St James because it contradicted his teaching, yet Lutherans all accept it today. That was the right thing to do, because if you start throwing out books because you do not agree with them, the process would never stop. But the real issue is deeper: the fact that the Church set the canon of the Bible, shows that the Church's authority is prior. After all, Our Lord founded a Church (Matthew 16:18). He never founded a printing press.

In addition, the teaching of the Fathers (see below), and human reason have to be used when interpreting Scripture and the Church's official declarations. The teaching accepted by the Church, especially in its liturgy, passes on the content of the faith. There is much material in the Bible, but it is of varying value, and often needs interpretation. Some people make entire sects out of allowing an undue importance to prophecies of the end times, despite the clear warning of the Lord that we know not when that final hour will be (Matthew 24:36 and 25:13). But the Church, aware of the need to interpret the whole of Scripture in accordance with its context in sacred history, does not fall for this trap.[98]

The "basic teachings of the Church" which I call the second stream of the Tradition are mainly to be found in or inferred from the teachings of the Fathers of the Church. While different people have different ideas on who were Fathers of the Church, the following writers are among the most significant:

St Clement of Rome (first century)
St Ignatius of Antioch (died by 117)
St Ephrem the Syrian (306-373)
St Basil of Caesarea (329-379)
St Gregory of Nazianzus (329-390)
St Gregory of Nyssa (335-395)
St Jerome (347-420)
St John Chrysostom (349-407)
St Augustine (354-430)
Jacob of Sarug (c.451-521)
St Gregory the Great (540–604)
St Isidore of Seville (560-636). St Isidore is often considered the last of the Fathers of the Church.

So, the clearest way of thinking about it is to say that the Bible is part of the tradition of the Church. While it is arguably the single

---

[98] I briefly mentioned in lesson 5 that there are some matters, such as the Fall, which are not directly referred to by the Lord, yet are fully part of the tradition, and are essential in explaining who Our Lord was, why He came among us, and what He did. This does not mean that Our Lord never referred to these matters, only that the evangelists did not record them. This further illustrates the importance of the oral tradition, and the necessity to be open to the rational and orderly development of doctrine, into which Blessed John Henry Newman had the unique insights which he set out in his *Essay on the Development of Christian Doctrine* (1845).

most important part of that tradition, it cannot be properly understood and interpreted without the rest of the tradition. Indeed, without the tradition of the Church we would not even know which books belong to the Bible.

The only reliable interpreter of the Bible is the body which brought the Bible into being, and decided what would go into it: the Church.

11.6 Reading the Bible: The Book of Revelation chapters 21 and 22

The final two chapters of this book are, for me, the greatest in all literature.

> Then I saw a new heaven and a new earth. The former heaven and the former earth had passed away, and the sea was no more. I also saw the holy city, a new Jerusalem, coming down out of heaven from God, prepared as a bride adorned for her husband. I heard a loud voice from the throne saying: "Behold, God's dwelling is with the human race. He will dwell with them and they will be his people and God himself will always be with them. He will wipe every tear from their eyes, and there shall be no more death or mourning, wailing or pain, for the old order has passed away."
>
> The one who sat on the throne said: "Behold, I make all things new!" Then he said: "Write these words down, for they are trustworthy and true." He said to me: "They are accomplished. I am the Alpha and the Omega, the beginning and the end. To the thirsty I will give a gift from the spring of life-giving water. The victor will inherit these gifts, and I shall be his God, and he will be my son." (Revelation 21:1-7)

Apart from the sheer beauty of this material, what is its value? At the least, it is a comfort to anyone going through difficult times. Remember, this is said to be a revelation which Our Lord himself granted to John, the Beloved Disciple after His death.

> Then the angel showed me the river of life-giving water, sparkling like crystal, flowing from the throne of God and of the Lamb

down the middle of its street. On either side of the river grew the tree of life that produces fruit twelve times a year, once each month; the leaves of the trees serve as medicine for the nations. Nothing accursed will be found there anymore. The throne of God and of the Lamb will be in it, and his servants will worship him. They will look upon his face, and his name will be on their foreheads. Night will be no more, nor will they need light from lamp or sun, for the Lord God shall give them light, and they shall reign forever and ever. And he said to me: "These words are trustworthy and true, and the Lord, the God of prophetic spirits, sent his angel to show his servants what must happen soon. Behold, I am coming soon. Blessed is the one who keeps the prophetic message of this book."

It is I, John, who heard and saw these things, and when I heard and saw them I fell down to worship at the feet of the angel who showed them to me. But he said to me: "Don't! I am a fellow servant of yours and of your brothers the prophets and of those who keep the message of this book. Worship God." Then he said to me: "Do not seal up the prophetic words of this book, for the appointed time is near. Let the wicked still act wickedly, and the filthy still be filthy. The righteous must still do right, and the holy still be holy. Behold, I am coming soon. I bring with me the recompense I will give to each according to his deeds. I am the Alpha and the Omega, the first and the last, the beginning and the end. Blessed are they who wash their robes so as to have the right to the tree of life and enter the city through its gates. Outside are the dogs, the sorcerers, the unchaste, the murderers, the idol-worshipers, and all who love and practice deceit. I, Jesus, sent my angel to give you this testimony for the churches. I am the root and offspring of David, the bright morning star." The Spirit and the bride say: "Come." Let the hearer say: "Come." Let the one who thirsts come forward, and the one who wants it receive the gift of life-giving water. I warn everyone who hears the prophetic words in this book: if anyone adds to them, God will add to him the plagues described in this book, and if anyone takes away from the words in this prophetic book, God will take away his share in the tree of life and in the holy city described in this book.

The one who gives this testimony says: "Yes, I am coming soon." Amen! Come, Lord Jesus! The grace of the Lord Jesus be with all. (Revelation 22:1-21)

As we saw in lesson 4, it was a characteristic of Our Lord that he would use the word "Amen" when speaking, and that in Revelation 3:14 Jesus calls Himself "The Amen." In our Maronite liturgy, we pronounce the word in a distinctive way, with two long vowels.

Note, also, how Revelation places an emphasis on how we must keep the commandments, and teaches that we will be rewarded in accordance with our obedience.

The passage has a lot to say about new creation, and even the new Jerusalem. It gives a beautiful description of the heavenly Jerusalem: see Revelation 21:9-27. But the entire Book is about new creation. It is about the totality of creation and history, life and eternal life. Revelation is a book about *everything*.

Why does Our Lord so often say in this book that he is the "Alpha and the Omega"? Alpha and omega being the first and last letters of the Greek alphabet, this signifies that he is the beginning and the end of *everything which has meaning*.

The Book of Revelation is important partly because it is the summation of the entire Bible. If you can take its main themes, you have the key to the entirety of the Bible. The main themes are:

1. Jesus Christ is God.
2. He sends His messages to the Churches.
3. He warns that world will end among great tribulation.
4. At the end of the world we will be judged.
5. The criterion by which we are judged is whether we kept His commandments.
6. The righteous will enjoy the vision of God in heaven (the *beatific vision*)

Questions for Contemplation:

1. How do you find that this passage from the Book of Revelation speaks to you? Does it touch your feeling, or only reach your mind?

2. Do different parts of it strike you in different ways? If so, how?

3. What, in your own words, would you say is the deep message here?

Lesson 12

Sacred History and Typology

12.1   Sacred History

12.2   Typology

12.3   Applying Typology to Sacred History

12.1 Sacred History

Not all history is sacred history: for example, the list of the kings of Scotland may be of great interest, but it has only the remotest connection with God. On the other hand, the life of Our Lord is the life of God on earth, so it is the essence, indeed the *centre* of sacred history. The life of the Lord is therefore, as we shall see, the foundation of *typology*, for *typology* is seeing the eternal pattern within history.

The story of sacred history commences with the creation, which is painted with grandeur in the Book of Genesis. That book, the first in the Old Testament and hence in the Bible begins:

> In the beginning God created the heavens and the earth. Now the earth was formless and empty, darkness was over the surface of the deep, and the Spirit of God was hovering over the waters. God said: "Let there be light," and there was light. God saw that the light was good, and he separated the light from the darkness. God called the light "day," and the darkness he called "night." And there was evening, and there was morning—the first day. (Genesis 1:1-5)

The story of the creation is unfolded, and reaches a climax with the fashioning of humanity, when God created the first man and woman, Adam and Eve. In a very important verse, Genesis tells us:

> So God created mankind in his own image, in the image of God he created them; male and female he created them. (Genesis 1:27)

Among the works of creation were the Garden of Eden. Genesis tells us that:

> The Lord God took the man and put him in the Garden of Eden to work it and take care of it. And the Lord God commanded the man: "You are free to eat from any tree in the garden; but you must not eat from the tree of the knowledge of good and evil, for when you eat from it you will certainly die." (Genesis 2:15-17)

However, the devil, in the form of a serpent, tempted our first parents, and they ate from the tree of knowledge of good and evil. So God expelled them from the garden, and made them subject to sickness and death. This is called "the Fall," as was mentioned in lesson 5. As a result of the Fall, human nature is wounded. We were made to be able to rationally control our emotions and actions, but now, our will-power is too weak to allow us to exercise full control. One can think about it like this: if a couple have a seaside mansion, a Rolls Royce and tons of money, but then gamble it away, the children will be left with nothing, despite the fact that they children have done nothing wrong. Adam and Eve did that by allowing, through their own free will, sin to enter the world. After this catastrophe, God addressed the devil as follows:

> So the Lord God said to the serpent: "Because you have done this, Cursed are you above all livestock and all wild animals! You will crawl on your belly and you will eat dust all the days of your life. And I will put enmity between you and the woman, and between your offspring and hers; he will crush your head, and you will strike his heel." (Genesis 3:14-15)

This is often referred to as the *Protevangelium* (sometimes *Protoevangelium*) or "first Gospel." The "woman" spoken of is understood to be a prophecy of Mary, and her "offspring" is Our Lord Jesus Christ, while the striking of the heel is the devil's persecution of Our Lord. But the Lord's victory in the Resurrection is also prophesied. This could easily be taken purely literally as referring to the only woman then alive (Eve), and to her children stepping on snakes and snakes biting people's heels. But while that may apply, the woman Eve is *typologically* (or: "according to the pattern of") Mary, and Jesus is the model for all humanity in their war against the devil.

After this, various events occurred on earth, one of which we looked at in lesson 7, the Tower of Babel. To this age, called the "primeval history," belongs the story of the Flood. Of course, the Flood did not happen as told in that story, but in this part of the Book of Genesis, some of the stories are legendary. In the Flood legend, God decided to cause a great flood to cover the earth, because people were so sinful. But Noah, being a just and good man, the Lord warned him to build a huge boat (the ark) and so save his family and some of the animals of the earth. When the flood came, the ark was lifted on the waters, and so Noah and the crew were saved.

We move into more solid history when we come to Abraham. Our Lord referred to Abraham on several occasions (e.g. Matthew 8:11 and 22:32; John 8:56). Chapter 12 of the Book of Genesis tells how God called Abraham to go into a new and Promised Land, where He would make Abraham the father of a great nation. That new country is present day Israel and Palestine, and the people were the Hebrew or Jewish people. Genesis then tells many stories of Abraham, his son Isaac, his grandson Jacob and Jacob's children.

But the important point to remember is that Abraham represents a new beginning. After the "primeval history" and the great Flood, comes a new start when God calls Abraham out of the midst of a pagan people. Abraham's great-grandchildren were made slaves in Egypt, until one of these people, a man named Moses, was called and helped by God to free the Israelites. The many families who had gone into Egypt left it as a people. After many years of wandering in the desert, their children entered Israel, the Promised Land. Eventually, these Israelites chose a king, the second of whom was King David, who established a kingdom ruled from the holy city of Jerusalem.

David was succeeded by King Solomon, who built a magnificent Temple of the Lord in Jerusalem, and was famous for his wisdom. Many of the Psalms (sacred hymns) are attributed to David, and three of the books of the Old Testament are associated with the name of Solomon, although his exact role, if any, in writing the books, is disputed. There is a fourth book, found in the LXX but not the Hebrew Bible, called "Wisdom" or "The Wisdom of Solomon" which was certainly not written by him, yet is a most profound work. After Solomon's death, the Kingdom of Israel split into two: Judah in the south based on Jerusalem, and Israel in the north. The people of Israel were later carried into exile by the Assyrians, and appear to have been lost to history. While the population of Judah was later conquered by the Babylonians, and the Temple destroyed, and many of their elite were taken into exile, the majority of the people seem to have been left in the land, although precise figures are not available.

When King Cyrus of the Medes conquered the Babylonians, he allowed the Jews to return to Israel. Some remained in Babylon, which was a major metropolis, probably the greatest in the world at that time. Those who returned eventually rebuilt the Temple, called "the Second Temple." Just before the birth of the Lord, this was completely rebuilt by King Herod. Our Lord was descended from the children of King David, and is believed to have been entitled to the throne of Israel.

The Gospel of St Matthew tells this sacred history as follows:

> This is the genealogy of Jesus the Messiah the son of David, the son of Abraham: Abraham was the father of Isaac, Isaac the father of Jacob, Jacob the father of Judah and his brothers … (I omit some generations here) and Jesse the father of King David. David was the father of Solomon, whose mother had

been Uriah's wife … and Josiah the father of Jeconiah and his brothers at the time of the exile to Babylon. After the exile to Babylon … Matthan the father of Jacob, and Jacob the father of Joseph, the husband of Mary, and Mary was the mother of Jesus who is called the Messiah. Thus there were fourteen generations in all from Abraham to David, fourteen from David to the exile to Babylon, and fourteen from the exile to the Messiah. (from Matthew 1:1-17)

We see key junctions in sacred history: first, the statement that Jesus was the Messiah (which is the Hebrew word the Greeks translated at "Christ," both words meaning "anointed," for the king was anointed with oil). Note that He is called the "son of David" and David is called the "son of Abraham" even though they were not sons in the strict sense of the word, but rather descendants. The Semitic languages can use the word "son" to describe a person who fulfils the life-mission of another. Even in English such a usage would be understood. The "son" follows in the footsteps of his father.

We now have the outline of sacred history. We can proceed to *types* and *typology*, and then apply that to sacred history.

12.2 Typology

"Typology" is based on "types." Types are patterns. Typology can use symbols, but a symbol is not a pattern. A symbol says that, for example, a bird stands for the soul. But if the relationship was typological, then we would be saying that the bird *is the* soul, and that of course would be absurd. A symbol is a human use of images. A type is a divine pattern, the mould in which the universe was formed.

When we come to Maronite spirituality, a type is specifically something which, represents what Jesus Christ did, or caused to be done. When that type is found earlier in sacred history, or even later in human history, it is called an *antetype* (a *pre*-type), sometimes spelled *anti*-type, but I think the other spelling is better, as *anti* suggests opposition.[99] People often call "types" what I would call "antetypes." I think it is better to be consistent, and restrict "types" to Our Lord and His actions.

When we place side by side a type (e.g. the baptism of Our Lord in the Jordan River) with an antetype (the Flood in which Noah and his family were saved by the ark) we can see a pattern: in this case it is *salvation connected with water.*[100]

BDAG (which is the leading dictionary for New Testament Greek) defines an *antítupos* as:

> *antítupos, -on*   1. *pertaining to that which correspond to something else*, adj. *corresponding to* ... something that has gone before ... the salvation of Noah and family via water ... which supported the ark, is the *túpos* for the salutary function of the water of baptism 1 Pt 3:21.

This last reference "1 Pt 3:21" is to the First Letter of St Peter, which provides an excellent example of typology. St Peter says about Noah's flood and the saving of a few people by means of the ark:

> This *prefigured* baptism, which saves you now. It is not a removal of dirt from the body but an appeal to God for a clear conscience, through the resurrection of Jesus Christ, who is at the right hand of God, with angels, authorities and powers subject to him (1 Peter 3:21-22, my italics).

When this translation has St Peter say that Noah's flood and the ark *prefigured* baptism, it is rendering the Greek *antitupos*: "before

---

[99]   In Greek, which this root comes from, *anti* is often translated as "opposite," although basically, it means "in front of." For this reason, the mountains you cross before entering Lebanon from Syria are called the "Antelebanon," and the Fathers who wrote before the Council of Nicaea, the Antenicene Fathers. To be *in front of* someone is often to be *in opposition.*

[100]   The noun "type" comes from a Greek word *túpos*, which means "*a blow*," and then "*the effect of a blow, the print* or *impress of a seal.*" It also took the sense of "*a figure, image statue ... the type* or *model* of a thing ...." Liddell and Scott, *An Intermediate Greek-English Lexicon*, 824. This explains how *antítupos* comes to mean "*corresponding* as the stamp to the die ..". *An Intermediate Greek-English Lexicon*, 82. The "die" here is the mould used in metal-working.

the type." So baptism is the type, and the salvation of the ark is the antetype. Further, St Ephrem also sees the ark as an antetype of the Church (because types are patterns, the types, just like patterns, can have more than one application); the dove which brings Noah the olive leaf is an antetype of both the Holy Spirit and of the anointing of the Messiah (with chrism made from olive oil).[101] Ephrem says: "Christ has many facets, and the oil acts as a mirror to them all: from whatever angle I look at the oil, Christ looks out at me from within it."[102]

Christ is in eternity, above history, even though He entered into history. He can therefore be found all throughout history, just as a light which is on a mountaintop can be seen from all sides of the mountain. The Church, being part of God's plan, and existing in heaven with Him, is also, in that way, above history, and can be patterned in history.

The Baptism of Our Lord took place on a day in history, but it is also an eternal reality, and is the fundamental pattern of all subsequent baptisms. The *suffering* of Our Lord did actually occur in ancient Israel, but it is also an eternal fact, and all suffering can be seen as being based on its pattern: if we but join our suffering to it, and accept to suffer for love of God when suffering is unavoidable, we are united to His suffering. The Resurrection of Our Lord took place in history. But it is also an eternal reality. It is the pattern which shall be repeated when everyone who is raised from the dead arises.

So too, when the Old Testament Book of Isaiah speaks about a "Suffering Servant" of God, Jesus is the type, while the Suffering Servant is one of many antetypes of Jesus. When the Old Testament Book of Exodus mentions a lamb which is sacrificed so that the people might escape death, Jesus is once more the type, while the lamb is one of many antetypes of Jesus. Then, when in the Book of Revelation we

---

[101] S. Brock, *The Luminous Eye: The Spiritual World Vision of Saint Ephrem the Syrian*, 1985, p.58.

[102] Hymn on Virginity, 7, cited in Brock, *The Luminous Eye*, p. 59. Similarly, I often find that when one contemplates the life in nature, one cannot but think of the Creator of all life, and to make a feeling connection at the same time.

read the following, we know that this once more is Jesus himself:

> And I saw ... a Lamb standing, as if slain, having seven horns and seven eyes, which are the seven Spirits of God, sent out into all the earth. And He came and took the book out of the right hand of Him who sat on the throne. When He had taken the book, the four living creatures and the twenty-four elders fell down before the Lamb, each one holding a harp and golden bowls full of incense, which are the prayers of the saints. And they sang a new song, saying: "Worthy are You to take the book and to break its seals; for You were slain, and purchased for God with Your blood men from every tribe and tongue and people and nation. ... Then I looked, and I heard the voice of many angels around the throne and the living creatures and the elders ... saying with a loud voice: "Worthy is the Lamb that was slain to receive power and riches and wisdom and might and honour and glory and blessing." And every created thing which is in heaven and on the earth and under the earth and on the sea, and all things in them, I heard saying: "To Him who sits on the throne, and to the Lamb, be blessing and honour and glory and dominion forever and ever." (from Revelation 5)

When the Book of Revelation speaks of a woman in the sky clothed with the sun, Our Lady is the type, and the sign of the woman mentioned in Revelation is an antetype. The water of creation is an antetype of the water in which Our Lord was baptised, and of the water which flowed from His side on the cross.

Questions for Contemplation

1. Do you think that the writer of Revelation means us to understand that these events took place, or that he saw them as in a vision?

2. If they were seen in a vision, can they nonetheless have meaning?

3. What might that meaning or meanings be?

In Romans 5:14, it is said that Adam was a type of Christ, who was to come. But I would say that Adam was an *antetype*, because, more frequently in the Christian tradition, a *type* represents either what Jesus Christ did or something from His life. As stated, the ancient usage of these terms was not always consistent. I think that we should forge a consistent vocabulary with a defined range of meaning.

As we see a little further below in more detail, the Syriac tradition has a wonderful way of putting this: the antetype is there called the *Teloneeto* or "shadowing." The reality which is Christ is the true figure, and what we see in the world is a shadow cast from that figure.[103]

In the Maronite tradition, which uses the Syriac writers, practically every appearance of water in the Old Testament where it has a salvific value is an antetype of baptism. So, the waters of creation over which the Spirit hovers in Genesis 1 can be related to the waters of baptism which He sanctifies. Even the crossing of Moses and the Twelve Tribes through Red Sea is an antetype of baptism. Thus St Paul says:

> I do not want you to be unaware, brothers, that our ancestors were all under the cloud, and all passed through the sea, and all of them were baptised into Moses, in the cloud and in the sea. All ate the same spiritual food, and all drank the same spiritual drink, for they drank from a spiritual rock that followed them, and the rock was the Christ (1 Corinthians 10:1-4).

A network of meaning is created by following these types. For example, the flow of blood and water from the side of the Lord on the Cross is symbolically related to the water of baptism. It is often said that it *is* the water of baptism, even we know full well that the waters are different. But *they are one and the same* in that they are related to our salvation. These symbols can even link baptism and the death and resurrection of the Lord: "You were buried with Him in baptism, in which you were also raised with Him through faith in the power of

---

[103] This will remind some of Plato's "Simile of the Cave" in book VII of the *Republic*.

God, who raised Him from the dead. (Colossians 2:12)

The existence of antetypes shows that God is the Lord of history, that He has a constant purpose, and has always been attentive to His people. It means that although certain things happened to certain specific people in the past, they still have significance for all people at all times and places. A person can thus create their own network of meaning, discovering new connections. The one fact or picture can be related in several ways (as the burial of the Lord can be related to baptism as well as to Jonah in the belly of the great fish).

It can be seen that the logic of types includes within itself a sort of philosophy of history. It also relates to *revelation* because through the types we are shown the workings and the nature of God in a way which a mere lecture, never could. Sebastian Brock, in a study of St Ephrem, who found antetypes in nature as well as in the Bible, states:

> The purpose of the types and symbols available in Nature and Scripture is ... to entice humanity back from its fallen state by offering innumerable glimpses of the divine reality; through these instances of divine self-revelation humanity is offered the opportunity of growth in spiritual awareness: "Lord, you bent down and put on humanity's types so that humanity might grow through your self-abasement."[104]

That nature is made up of antetypes is a huge topic. When Psalm 19:1 says: "The heavens shew forth the glory of God, and the firmament declares the work of his hands," it is saying that the brilliance and artistry of the creation are antetypes of the brilliance and artistry of God. A concrete example of a type connected with nature is the Cross: a bird, in order to fly, has to open its wings in the form of the Cross![105] The Cross is the *type* and the bird taking flight is an *antetype*, from which we learn that humanity, like the bird, must open the wings of faith to fly upwards. McVey says that:

---

[104] S. Brock, *The Luminous Eye*, 1985, p.54.
[105] S. Brock, *The Luminous Eye*, p.59.

Ephrem's poetry is based upon a vision of the world as a vast system of symbols or mysteries. No person, no thing or event in the world exists without a mysterious relation to the whole. History and nature constitute the warp and woof of reality. To divorce an individual from its context in either direction would destroy the handiwork of God in time and space. Each moment of life is governed by the Lord of life and is an opportunity to see oneself and the community in relation to that Lord. So not only the events described in scripture but all historical events must have profound religious significance ...

Nature, too, is replete with intimations of the presence of God. In creating the world God deliberately presented us not only with examples of beauty and order but also with symbols that allude more richly to the identity of their Creator.

> In every place, if you look, His symbol is there.
> And when you read, you will find his prototypes.
> For by him were created all creatures,
> and he imprinted His symbols upon His possessions.
> When he created the world,
> He gazed at it and adorned it with His images.
> Streams of His symbols opened, flowed and poured forth
> His symbols on its members (*Hymn on Virginity* 20.12).

... to attempt to understand Christ without knowing about the Passover would be to deprive oneself of the depth and richness of meaning placed in human history by God himself. Yet conversely, in Ephrem's view, to stop with the Passover Lamb rather than interpreting it as a symbol of Christ would mean missing the fullness of God's revelation and accepting a truncating version of the meaning of history.[106]

12.3 Applying Typology to Sacred History

I have said that the *type* which is what Jesus did or what was associated with Him is logically and spiritually prior. That is the

---

[106]   K. McVey, *Ephrem the Syrian*, Paulist Press, NY, 1989, 41-43.

basis of the pattern. This can clearly be the case for everything which happens after the time of Our Lord, but it is also mystically the case for what happened before His life on earth, for He is in eternity and above and beyond all time. Thus it is that Jacob of Sarug, noting that Moses fasted for forty days (Exodus 34:28), and after him Elijah fasted forty days (1 Kings 19:8), and after him Our Lord fasted forty days (as we saw in lesson 5), states that rather than Our Lord following them, they were following Him, even if they lived first:

> Toward the mountain of the Lord, Horeb, did he (Elijah) set his face,
> And went on while fasting for Moses' forty, in order to reach his (Moses') spot.
> The prototype (*Teloneeto*) of Our Lord's fast settled upon him ...
> The days came and went day after day, in order to prefigure (*nSooroon*) –
> This number, for that amount had already been established –
> Those forty that the Son rested while travelling,
> That even Moses himself had prefigured (*rošem*) when he fasted.
> Our Lord did not Himself undertake to travel in the footsteps of His prophets;
> They anticipated Him and prefigured (*Sor*) His images with their actions.[107]

The word *rošem* comes from a root *ršam* meaning "to engrave, inscribe, draw, delineate, ordain, make the sign of the cross." The noun *ršom* means "signing with the sign of the cross; indicating, foreshadowing." So, from meaning to *engrave* and *trace out*, it came to specifically refer to tracing the Cross on my body, a shadow of the Cross of Christ.

The word *Teloneeto* is literally a "shadowing," so it is as if what Our Lord was to do in the future already existed in eternity or above time, and cast a shadow into time. It is like someone coming down a mountain with the sun behind him: his shadow falls on the valley

[107] *Jacob of Sarug's Homilies on Elijah*, trans. Stephen A. Kaufman, Gorgias, Piscataway, 2009, Hymn "On Elijah when he Fled from Jezebel," lines 173-175 and 179-184, p. 134.

before he does. The words *nSooroon* and *Sor* are from a root *Swr* meaning "to form, fashion, paint" and also "to represent, show forth, signify, typify." The dictionary offers this as an example of the use of the word: *seblto zqeefeh d-forooqan Sort*: "Jacob's *ladder typified Our Saviour's Cross*."[108] This refers to the dream Jacob had where he saw a ladder between heaven and earth:

> He had a dream in which he saw a stairway resting on the earth, with its top reaching to heaven, and the angels of God were ascending and descending on it. There above it stood the Lord, and he said: "I am the Lord, the God of your father Abraham and the God of Isaac ... All peoples on earth will be blessed through you and your offspring. I am with you and will watch over you wherever you go, and I will bring you back to this land. I will not leave you until I have done what I have promised you." When Jacob awoke from his sleep, he thought: "Surely the Lord is in this place, and I was not aware of it." He was afraid and said: "How awesome is this place! This is none other than the house of God; this is the gate of heaven" (Genesis 28:12-17).

What this all means is that our small histories can not only draw inspiration from the great history of God, but more, that they are united in some mystical way, as shadows thrown from the reality of God. In an odd way, this is perhaps related to ideas found in mysticism from India to Plato, but it does not deny the reality of the world (as the Hindu doctrine of *maya* may), or say that knowledge of the world is impossible (as Plato's theory of the forms does). Rather, the reality of the world is *guaranteed* by its connection with the divine (even if a person's individual knowledge is not), and the world is knowable in principle because God has made us so that we can obtain knowledge of it.

The topic is a huge one, and there is far more typology in the New Testament than I have hinted at. For those who desire to learn more, there are four good books available:

---

[108] R. Payne Smith *A Compendious Syriac Dictionary*, Eisenbrauns, Winona Lake, 1998 (first ed. Oxford University Press, Oxford, 1903) 476.

Jean Danielou, *From Shadows to Reality: Studies in the Biblical Theology of the Fathers*, Burns & Oates, London, 1960

Leonhard Goppelt, *Typos: The Typological Interpretation of the Old Testament in the New*, William B. Eerdmans, Grand Rapids, 1982 (original published in German in 1939)

Richard M. Davidson, *Typology in Scripture*, Andrews University, Berrien Springs, 1981

Kees den Biesen, *Simple and Bold" Ephrem's Art of Symbolic Thought*, Gorgias, Piscataway, 2006

However, I shall leave the last word in this chapter to Cardinal Daniélou, who did a great deal of significant research on the Early Church. After examining typology in the ancient Church, and the different ways it developed and the various forms it took, he concluded:

> ... over and above all these diversities and deviations, we meet an agreement of all schools upon the fundamental types. This proves that we are face to face with something that is part and parcel of the deposit of Revelation.[109]

---

[109] Danielou, *From Shadows to Reality*, 288.

Lesson 13

The Teaching of the Lord

13.1 The Sermon on the Mount

This famous sermon opens in the Gospel of Matthew, 5:1-2: "When Jesus saw the crowds, He went up on the mountain; and after He sat down, His disciples came to Him. He opened His mouth and began to teach them, saying ..." It then goes on, through to the end of chapter 7, telling us what Our Lord said on that occasion. The first teaching He gives is called "the Beatitudes," because the key word in this text is "blessed," and the Latin word for that is "beatus." It reads:

Blessed are the poor in spirit, for theirs is the kingdom of heaven. Blessed are those who mourn, for they shall be comforted. Blessed are the meek,[110] for they shall inherit the earth. Blessed are those who hunger and thirst for righteousness, for they shall be satisfied. Blessed are the merciful, for they shall receive mercy. Blessed are the pure in heart, for they shall see God. Blessed are the peacemakers, for they shall be called sons of God. Blessed are those who have been persecuted for the sake of righteousness, for theirs is the kingdom of heaven. Blessed are you when people insult you and persecute you, and falsely say all kinds of evil against you because of Me. Rejoice and be glad, for your reward in heaven is great; for in the same way they persecuted the prophets who were before you. (Matthew 5:3-12)

There are eight groups: (1) the poor in spirit; (2) those who mourn; (3) the meek; (4) those who desire righteousness; (5) the merciful; (6) the pure in heart; (7) the peacemakers: and (8) those who have been persecuted for righteousness' sake. Eight groups of people: seven being the number of completion, the eighth takes us up to more than completion, it raises us to abundance, to overflowing. The first seven categories could almost be expected whenever speaking about humanity, but the eighth category relates specifically to those who follow the Lord and are attacked because of their devotion to the ways of God (which is what "righteousness" means).

To be clear, the first seven categories relate to all the world. They are complete in themselves. But then an eighth or "super" class is added: the Christian who is persecuted for the Kingdom of God.

---

[110] Some translate the Greek word *praos* as "gentle." It can mean that. Although many people today not know the meaning of the word "meek," that is only a reason to teach them this useful term. The word means "gentle, soft, humble, indulgent." It has the nuance of being the sort of person who might have a right to say or do something, but out of compassion, does not. That is, I have a right or a priority, but I do not insist on it. This seems to exactly fit Our Lord's meaning: those who have considerately given way to others will be rewarded with more than they have foregone: they will receive all the earth.

Now consider what each group will find through the justice of God:

(1) The poor in spirit *receive* the Kingdom of Heaven.

(2) Those who mourn *receive* comfort.

(3) The meek *receive* the earth.

(4) Those who desire righteousness *receive* satisfaction.

(5) The merciful *receive* mercy.

(6) The pure in heart *receive* the vision of God.

(7) The peacemakers *receive* the title of being sons of God.

(8) Those who have been persecuted for righteousness' sake *receive* a great reward in heaven.

Because "the Kingdom of Heaven" is St Matthew's way of speaking of the "Kingdom of God," we can say that four of the Beatitudes offer good people the reward of being united with God. These are the poor in spirit (meaning those who are humble and unassuming, those who lack pride); plus the pure in heart, meaning those who do not have suspicion, and who do not look for bad motives in people. The other categories are all straightforward.

The Beatitudes display mutual ethics: it is mutuality when the Lord says: "the Father Himself loves you, because you have loved me and have believed that I came from the Father" (John 16:27). Later in this Sermon, we have the famous "Golden Rule": "In everything, therefore, treat people the same way you want them to treat you, for this is the Law and the Prophets." (Matthew 7:12 and Luke 6:31).

This mutuality is also found in the "Our Father" (also known as "the Lord's Prayer"), which is itself in the Sermon on the Mount: *forgive us our trespasses as we forgive those who trespass against us*. It is found also when Our Lord says, for example: "The measure with which you measure will be measured out to you ..." (Mark 4:24). I think a case can be made that this mutuality in ethics is related to the *symmetry* and *balance* which we find in many of the Lord's sayings, e.g. He said to fishermen (Simon and Andrew): "Come after me, and I will make you fishers of men" (Matthew 4:19 and Mark 1:17). We see it also when He reverses the form of certain ideas to reveal the truth by that very reversal:

- "The Sabbath was made for man, not man for the Sabbath" (Mark 2:27).

- "Nothing that enters one from outside can defile that person; but the things that come from within are what defile" (Mark 7:15).

  Sometimes, Our Lord uses these rhetorical devices to state matters in a very striking way which is not meant to be absolutely and literally true, such as in the following passages:

- "Follow me, and let the dead bury their dead," from Matthew 8:21-22 does not mean that we should not bury the dead, but rather, that the service of God is the first priority.

- "I did not come to call the righteous but sinners" in Matthew 9:13 cannot mean that the Lord does not want the righteous to follow him! But He is emphasising His special concern for those who are lost (as He does in the Parable of the Lost Sheep.)

- "If anyone comes to Me and does not hate his father and mother and wife and children and brothers and sisters — yes, even his own life — he cannot be My disciple," (Luke 14:26). This needs understanding, for Our Lord cared about His mother enough to make her the mother of St John, so that she would be cared for after His crucifixion.

Therefore, when we read the Beatitudes, we may take delight not only in the way that Our Lord expresses Himself, but draw the wider lesson that whenever we suffer anything, that suffering will be reversed, if only we make our suffering one for the greater glory of God. We do this by making our own the prayer which He said: "... My Father, if it is possible, let this cup pass from Me. Yet not as I will, but as You will" (Matthew 26:39).

13.2 Discipleship

Part of the reason that the Sermon on the Mount is so important is because it teaches us what it means to be disciples of the Lord, and of course all good things come from that:

> You are the salt of the earth; but if the salt has become tasteless, how can it be made salty again? It is no longer good for anything, except to be thrown out and trampled underfoot … Do not think that I came to abolish the Law or the Prophets; I did not come to abolish but to fulfil. For truly I say to you, until heaven and earth pass away, not the smallest letter or stroke shall pass from the Law until all is accomplished. … Unless your righteousness surpasses that of the scribes and Pharisees, you will not enter the kingdom of heaven. (from Matthew 5:13-20)

The teaching on salt means that we have to be mix with people, and to do what we can to spread the truths God has taught us throughout the world. Salt, after all, is a seasoning: a little bit of it in a meal brings out the flavour. But if we do not retain what we have received from God, that is, if we do not make use of our talents (see lesson 6), then we will be worse off than we were beforehand, for we will not have met our responsibilities. We can even say that if we allow ourselves to lose our "saltiness," we will have betrayed the Lord. We are meant to become individuals: attempts to force children (or anyone else) into a preconceived mould is wrong.

When Our Lord says that He did not come to abolish the Jewish religion (that is the law of Moses and the prophets to the ancient Israelites) but to *fulfil* them, He is referring to Himself. He is the fulfilment of everything which had been promised to Israel. The time when "all is accomplished" is His own death and resurrection. More was being demanded of his followers, hence the last sentence: we have to be better than what has gone before. It was good, but not good enough.

13.3 Surpassing the Previous Dispensation: Our Attitudes

A "dispensation" is a religious system. Our Lord did not repeal but rather included and surpassed the Jewish dispensation. He taught:

> You have heard that the ancients were told: "You shall not commit murder' ... But I say to you that everyone who is angry with his brother shall be guilty before the court; and whoever says to his brother: "You good-for-nothing," shall be guilty before the supreme court; and whoever says: "You fool," shall be guilty enough to go into the fiery hell. ...
>
> You have heard that it was said: "You shall not commit adultery'; but I say to you that everyone who looks at a woman with lust for her has already committed adultery with her in his heart. ...
>
> It was said: "Whoever sends his wife away, let him give her a certificate of divorce'; but I say to you that everyone who divorces his wife, except for the reason of unchastity, makes her commit adultery; and whoever marries a divorced woman commits adultery.
>
> Again, you have heard that the ancients were told: "You shall not make false vows, but shall fulfil your vows to the Lord." But I say to you, make no oath at all, either by heaven, for it is the throne of God, or by the earth, for it is the footstool of His feet, or by Jerusalem, for it is the city of the great king. ... But let your statement be: "Yes, yes' or 'No, no'; anything beyond these is of evil.
>
> You have heard that it was said: "An eye for an eye, and a tooth for a tooth." But I say to you, do not resist an evil person; but whoever slaps you on your right cheek, turn the other to him also. ...
>
> You have heard that it was said: "You shall love your neighbour and hate your enemy." But I say to you, love your enemies and pray for those who persecute you, so that you may be sons of your Father who is in heaven; for He causes His sun to rise on the evil and the good, and sends rain on the righteous and the unrighteous. For if you love those who love you, what reward

do you have? ... If you greet only your brothers, what more are you doing than others? Do not even the Gentiles do the same? Therefore you are to be perfect, as your heavenly Father is perfect. (from Matthew 5:21-48).

Although the Jews had the highest moral codes of antiquity, Our Lord is clearly raising the moral demands to an even more exalted level. Let us take the areas He spoke of:

- Anger.
- Lust.
- Divorce (only for *porneia* which is not "unchastity" but marrying close relations).
- Swearing (in the sense of making oaths).
- Revenge.
- Love, especially love of enemies.
- Perfection.

Although one might be able to see how bad lust is, Our Lord taught that not only behaviour but also thought is important. That is, attitudes determine how we will act. [111] Our attitudes connect us to the world outside: as soon as something happens to us, or comes into our sight or knowledge, we *interpret it according to our pre-existing attitudes*, and these determine how we will react to it. This is why so often, indeed *too often*, we react not to what is happening or to what people do, but rather, to the past. Frequently, it has been my experience that X does something, and in me an instantaneous reaction takes place: "This person always does this, and I am fed up with it." Then, if I find out that my view was wrong, I feel remorse for having exploded. But even if I was right, I often feel remorse because my reaction is an *over-reaction*, out of all proportion to what the person has done. We usually over-react like this because this angry thing in us makes us want to punish them for all that they have done, and to change them so that they never do it again. *Anger is often a manipulation device.*

---

[111] Our attitudes are a series of thoughts and feelings, invoked together, which have the same outlook.

Similarly, when it comes to lust, what we feel is stronger than it might have been, because we have been preparing the ground, getting ourselves worked up, as it were, by what we have been thinking about. This is part of the reason that pornography is so dangerous: it changes the landscape of the mind, and makes us think of abnormal physical relationships as being desirable, guilt- and consequence-free, usual behaviour for everyone and bringing happiness. Our sexual appetites are more controllable than we realise, but we place a lot of emotional capital in sex, and often the sex act serves extraneous purposes of dealing with anxiety, sadness and frustration. If we could manage those feelings in more constructive fashions, our appetite for sexual release would be much weaker: if we had meaningful, God-centred lives, our lusts would be controllable.

Finally, the ban on swearing does not apply to when one takes an oath in court or for the purposes of justice (e.g. swearing allegiance to a country). But we should not otherwise swear. It is particularly serious to use the name of the Lord when swearing, because if I disrespect His name, I am aligning myself with the hellish.

13.4 Prayer and Openness

When Our Lord says: "Beware of practicing your righteousness before men to be noticed by them; otherwise you have no reward with your Father who is in heaven," (Matthew 6:1) he is referring both to prayer and to public activities. He then speaks about actions and prayers:

> So when you give to the poor, do not sound a trumpet before you, as the hypocrites do in the synagogues and in the streets, so that they may be honoured by men. Amen I say to you, they have their reward in full. But when you give to the poor, do not let your left hand know what your right hand is doing, so that your giving will be in secret; and your Father who sees what is done in secret will reward you.

> When you pray, you are not to be like the hypocrites; for they love
> to stand and pray in the synagogues and on the street corners so
> that they may be seen by men. Amen, I say to you, they have their
> reward in full. But you, when you pray, go into your inner room,
> close your door and pray to your Father who is in secret, and your
> Father who sees what is done in secret will reward you. ... "Pray,
> then, in this way: 'Our Father who is in heaven *etc.* ... For if
> you forgive others for their transgressions, your heavenly Father
> will also forgive you. But if you do not forgive others, then your
> Father will not forgive your transgressions. (from Matthew 6)

This shows us how the virtues are related together: one can almost
say that to have one virtue must possess all of them, at least to some
degree. Thus, even when we are doing good works, we should do so
without any vanity, because if we do, our intention is impure. In other
words, the "good works" would be good only for appearance's sake,
but our *intention* in what we do is all-important, and so it would not in
fact be a virtuous act.

The logic of what Our Lord says here is quite significant: "Amen,
I say to you, they (the hypocrites) have their reward in full (because
they took their reward in vanity and display)." The same logic applies
to anything done for low or selfish motives: the very selfishness of the
action is its own reward. But when we act selflessly, and not for reward, it
is then that God Himself repays us. Yet, we cannot expect to act seeking
a reward from God: *the motive must be unconditional love.*

It is very difficult to be able to act from such motives, even perhaps
impossible. But it is quite possible to *wish* to act from such motives.
And if that is all we can muster, then so be it. We must not give in to
the temptation to say: "My motive is not pure, therefore I shall not
act." Rather, we must say: "My motive is not yet fully pure, but I shall
ask God to cleanse my heart." Then, with time, our motives may be
purified. We should not worry because our motives are not yet pure:
we can pray that they be purified, and trust to God that with time they
shall become cleaner.

Then, what does it mean to say: "But when you give to the poor, do not let your left hand know what your right hand is doing"? Of course, our hands know nothing, so is it just a nonsense? It means not to *identify* with our charitable actions. To identify, in this sense, means to imagine that because I have given something in charity, I am therefore a good person. I may be a good person, but it is not for me to judge. Perhaps when God judges me he will tell that I have not done enough, and that what I did give was calculated to be easy for me. I should act out of love, unconditional love, not taking credit for what I have done or expecting a reward from other people. This ties in with reference to the hypocrites who already have their reward: they certainly did let their left hand know what their right hand was doing – and they let everyone else see it.

Note, once more, the mutuality and symmetry in what Our Lord goes on to say about prayer.

13.5 Trust and Anxiety

A little later on in the Sermon, Our Lord teaches:

> … do not be worried about your life, as to what you will eat or what you will drink; nor for your body, as to what you will put on. Is not life more than food, and the body more than clothing? Look at the birds of the air, that they do not sow, nor reap nor gather into barns, and yet your heavenly Father feeds them. Are you not worth much more than they? And who of you by being worried can add a single hour to his life? … You of little faith! Do not worry then, saying: "What will we eat?' or 'What will we drink?' or 'What will we wear for clothing?' For the Gentiles eagerly seek all these things; for your heavenly Father knows that you need all these things. But seek first His kingdom and His righteousness, and all these things will be added to you. So do not worry about tomorrow; for tomorrow will care for itself. Each day has enough trouble of its own. (from Matthew 6:25-34)

The wisdom of this saying: " … who of you by being worried can add a single hour to his life?" is amazing. And yet we don't put it into practice. One has to think about it, and see where we are worrying unnecessarily, and then to apply this saying. Our fears and anxieties are there to make us both aware of a problem and desirous to end it. The anxiety is meant to stimulate us to action. Fear of a snake, for example, will make us leap up and run. If we didn't have that fear, we could spend so much time weighing up the yes and the no, that we could be bit, poisoned and dead, before we made a decision. But when our anxiety has made us aware that there is an issue, it has done its work. At that moment we should simply: "… seek first His kingdom and His righteousness …" and then everything we *need* (as opposed to *want*) will come to us in its turn, because we have put our priorities first.

As with other sayings which we have seen above, this is not to be taken completely literally, meaning never to worry about what we will eat or wear tomorrow. It means, once more, to have our priorities right, and then to act in obedience to the laws and wishes of God.

13.6 Judging Others

Our Lord then expands on the prayer in the "Our Father" that we should forgive others our trespasses, by going to the very foundation of our attitude to others:

> Do not judge so that you will not be judged. For in the way you judge, you will be judged; and by your standard of measure, it will be measured to you. Why do you look at the speck that is in your brother's eye, but do not notice the log that is in your own eye? … You hypocrite, first take the log out of your own eye, and then you will see clearly to take the speck out of your brother's eye. (Matthew 7:1-3 and 5)

This is clear. It is, however, interesting that we cannot excuse and indulge ourselves on the basis of what other people do or have not done. The point is that we should not judge others, but rather attend to ourselves. Clear as this is, we find that the inner lives of some people are almost consumed with judging others. We do not *say* that we are judging, on the contrary, we abjure the very idea. But we then go on to criticise, often in uncompromising terms. Our criticisms are based on judgments.

13.7 Prayer and Reward

This passage has a twin in St Luke. Here, St Matthew writes that Jesus said:

> Ask, and it will be given to you; seek, and you will find; knock, and it will be opened to you. For everyone who asks receives, and he who seeks finds, and to him who knocks it will be opened. Or what man is there among you who, when his son asks for a loaf, will give him a stone? Or if he asks for a fish, he will not give him a snake, will he? If you then, being evil, know how to give good gifts to your children, how much more will your Father who is in heaven give what is good to those who ask Him! (Matthew 7:7-11)

St Luke has a variant:

> So I say to you, ask, and it will be given to you; seek, and you will find; knock, and it will be opened to you. For everyone who asks, receives; and he who seeks, finds; and to him who knocks, it will be opened. Now suppose one of you fathers is asked by his son for a fish; he will not give him a snake instead of a fish, will he? Or if he is asked for an egg, he will not give him a scorpion, will he? If you then, being evil, know how to give good gifts to your children, how much more will your heavenly Father give the Holy Spirit to those who ask Him? (Luke 11:9-13)

I think that all of these images may well be based on Christ. Following Martin Hengel, I think the likeliest theory is that St Luke wrote before St Matthew.[112] His images are of someone seeking a fish and an egg, and not being offered a snake or a scorpion. St Matthew

---

[112] Martin Hengel, *The Four Gospels and the One Gospel of Jesus Christ*, Trinity Press International, Harrisburg, 2000.

changes these images to seeking a loaf and then a fish, and not being offered a stone and a stone. It does seem odd.

But in each case, I suggest, the "fish" is Our Lord Himself, for the Greek word *ikhthus* meaning "fish" was used as a acrostic code for the words "Jesus Christ, Son of God, Saviour" (that is, the letters of the word *ikhthus* are the first letters of the words which spell out "Jesus Christ, Son of God, Saviour"). I suggest that the egg stands for "life" and the scorpion for "death," and the "bread" for the Eucharistic bread, the bread of life, and the "stone" for death.

If this is so, then this is a way of saying that *God promises to give us Our Lord Jesus Christ in the Eucharist and eternal life*. That is, this passage does not mean that Our Lord has promised to give us whatever we *want*. He offers us what we *need*. It is a promise that we shall have spiritual blessings.

13.8 The Golden Rule

There then follows, in one marvellous sentence, the greatest rule of moral conduct every given: "In everything, therefore, treat people the same way you want them to treat you, for this is the Law and the Prophets." (Matthew 7:12) This relates to *charity* and *love*. Charity is best understood as the third in a series of the almost miraculously beautiful gifts of faith, hope and charity. These three virtues are known as the "theological virtues" because they relate directly to God, being faith in God, hope in His promises, and love for Him.[113] They are found together in a letter of St Paul:

> If I speak with the tongues of men, and of angels, and have not charity, I am become as sounding brass, or a tinkling cymbal. And if I should have prophecy and should know all mysteries, and all knowledge, and if I should have all faith, so that I could remove mountains, and have not charity, I am nothing. And if I should

---

[113] "Theos" is the Greek word for "God."

distribute all my goods to feed the poor, and if I should deliver my body to be burned, and have not charity, it profits me nothing.

Charity is patient, is kind: charity envies not, deals not perversely; is not puffed up; is not ambitious, seeks not her own, is not provoked to anger, thinks no evil; rejoices not in iniquity, but rejoices with the truth; bears all things, believes all things, hopes all things, endures all things.

Charity never falls away: whether prophecies shall be made void, or tongues shall cease, or knowledge shall be destroyed. For we know in part, and we prophesy in part. But when that which is perfect is come, that which is in part shall be done away. When I was a child, I spoke as a child, I understood as a child, I thought as a child. But, when I became a man, I put away the things of a child. We see now through a glass in a dark manner; but then face to face. Now I know in part; but then I shall know even as I am known.

And now there remain *faith, hope, and charity*, these three: but the greatest of these is charity. (1 Corinthians 13: italics added)

The Greek word translated here as "charity" is *agape*, which has a meaning of "the quality of warm regard for and interest in another person," and is often translated as "love."[114] Because "love" can often be taken as a purely internal emotion, whereas "charity" has the sense of a love which acts outwardly, it seems to me to the preferable translation.

13.9 Faith

In the Epistle to the Hebrews we read:

Now faith is the substance of things to be hoped for, the evidence of things that appear not. For by this the ancients obtained a testimony. By faith we understand that the world was framed by the word of God; that from invisible things visible things might be made. (Hebrews 11:1-3)

---

[114] *BDAG*, 6.

This tells us that faith and hope are related, and that faith is related to the *present*, while hope is more *future* looking. Further, it shows that we can understand and believe certain things through faith, especially where the evidence for them would seem to be lacking.

But faith is not a question of bare belief: it has to be accepted as a factor in our lives. St James wrote:

> What good is it, my brothers and sisters, if someone claims to have faith but has no deeds? Can such faith save them? Suppose a brother or a sister is without clothes and daily food. If one of you says to them: "Go in peace; keep warm and well fed," but does nothing about their physical needs, what good is it? In the same way, faith by itself, if it is not accompanied by action, is dead.
>
> But someone will say: "You have faith; I have deeds." Show me your faith without deeds, and I will show you my faith by my deeds. You believe that there is one God. Good! Even the demons believe that – and shudder. ... You see (from the story of Abraham) that a person is considered righteous by what they do and not by faith alone. ... As the body without the spirit is dead, so faith without deeds is dead. (James 2:14-19, 24 and 26)

St Ignatius of Antioch has the same idea as St James, and links faith to charity and love (*agape*):

> This is the beginning and end of life: faith is the beginning, love is the end. And the two together in unity are God; all other things that lead to nobility of character follow. No one who professes faith sins, not does anyone hate after acquiring love. The tree is known by its fruit; so those who profess to belong to Christ will be seen by what they do. For the deed is not a matter of professing in the present but of being found in the power of faith at the end. (*Ephesians*, 14)[115]

Our faith provides us with the security of certainty. One does not have to continually revisit one's first principles, and go over the same

---

[115] Ignatius of Antioch: "Letter to the Ephesians," in *The Apostolic Fathers*, vol. I, ed. and trans. Bart D. Ehrman, Loeb Classical Library, Harvard University, Cambridge, Mass, 2003, pp. 233-235.

ground again and again. The truth has a greater effect on us when it is held with faith than when it is held as a hypothesis, let alone when one doubts. Hence St James wrote:

> ...when you ask (God for something), you must believe and not doubt, because the one who doubts is like a wave of the sea, blown and tossed by the wind. That person should not expect to receive anything from the Lord. Such a person is double-minded and unstable in all they do. (James 1:6-8)

St Ephrem picks up this idea of the necessity of having a certain faith, held without division or doubt in one's mind, and relates it not only to prayer but also to how faith changes our very being:

> Inner prayer cleanses troubled thoughts.
> Faith cleanses external senses.
> One person who is indeed divided,
> Let him be gathered, Lord, and become one before you![116]

13.10   Hope

The way that hope is described by some commentators, it is hard not to see it as simply being faith in the future, specifically in the Second Coming, the resurrection of the dead and in the forgiveness of sins ("Hope is looking forward with confidence to a future good").[117] The relationship between faith and hope is real, as saw above, when we read from Hebrews 11. Yet, we should be able to distinguish it from faith.

Our hope is surely based on our faith, for without that faith, there would be nothing to believe in. However, hope does more work in us than simply give us stronger belief in our faith. I can have faith that God has a divine plan for salvation, and yet despair that I will be included in it.

---

[116] Ephrem: "Hymn on Faith 20," 20.17, in *St Ephrem the Syrian: The Hymns on Faith*, Catholic University of America, Washington D.C., 2015, p. 156.

[117] For example, Seung Ai Yang: "Hope" in *The New Interpreter's Dictionary of the Bible*, vol. 2, Abingdon, Nashville, 2007, 885-889.

The feeling that salvation is possible for me – not that it is certain – but that it is *possible* for me, is my hope. It is possible to say that faith is more intellectual and hope is more a matter of feeling. That is really to say that our faith tells us what God has done and promised (hence the Creed opens "We believe"), while my hope assures me of the real chance of persevering to obtain what has been promised.

This should not be understood in an individualist way, that is, denying the dimension of hope we share with others. Our hope is a "common hope," St Ignatius of Antioch tells us, even with the prophets of the Old Testament, for Jesus Christ was their expectation.[118] In other words, just as our faith and love bind us together, so too should our hope.

Hope includes a feeling of assurance, providing us with the strength to persevere and not lose our faith, no matter how dark circumstances seem. Faith can suffer vicissitudes,[119] for example, the apostles were despondent after they had laid Christ in his tomb, but, as St Ephrem states: "their faith was raised up with you."[120]

This is the approach which St Ephrem takes in his *Commentary on Genesis*. He tells the story of how God had promised to Abraham that he would have children, although his wife Sarah had been barren, and Abraham believed it. This was faith (Genesis 15:1-6). But, when he came to be 99 years old, and his wife 90, and they still had no child: "Abraham fell facedown; he laughed and said to himself: "Will a son be born to a man a hundred years old? Will Sarah bear a child at the age of ninety?" (Genesis 17:17). This was a lack of hope. It could also be considered a lack of faith, because we could say that he no longer believed. But people are mixed, and as St Ephrem understands this story, and this is surely the correct understanding, Abraham intellectually still

---

[118] Ignatius of Antioch: "Letter to the Philadelphians" 5 in *The Apostolic Fathers*, vol. I, ed. and trans. Bart D. Ehrman, pp. 287-289.

[119] A "vicissitude" is a change of circumstances or fortune.

[120] Ephrem: "The Homily on the Lord," 10.1, in *St Ephrem the Syrian: Selected Prose Works*, trans. Edward G. Mathews, Jr and Joseph P. Amar, (The Fathers of the Church 91), Catholic University of America, Washington D.C., 1994, p. 287.

believed, that was faith. But in his feeling he despaired that he would ever see it.[121]

That hope was seen as a source of strength emerges clearly from the *Odes of Solomon*:

> As honey drips from the honeycomb of bees,
> And milk flows from the woman who loves her children,
> So also is my hope upon Thee, O my God.[122]

That is, just as the honey and the milk naturally come forth to the bees and the children, so too does hope flow forth from God to the faithful one. And it flows from God right now. Although hope has a future reference, it is a present good, because it brings patience, the knowledge that things will not always be as they are now, and the strength to persevere until the good will be established. We may have hopes for the future, but they are present hopes with present effects.

13.11   Charity

As we have seen: "charity" and "love" are English words with meanings which overlap in some respects. But the reality behind them is sublime. The word "love" has become over-used, and cheapened. Traders and advertising people have debased the word, which is very sad, because what it represents is the highest. The great Christian teacher of love is St John, who wrote:

> For this is the message you heard from the beginning: We should love one another. ... Do not be surprised, my brothers and sisters, if the world hates you. We know that we have passed from death to life, because we love each other. Anyone who does not love remains in death. Anyone who hates a brother is a murderer, and you know that no murderer has eternal life residing in him. This is how we know what love is: Jesus Christ laid down his life

---

[121] Ephrem: "Commentary on Genesis," 14.2 and 3, in *St Ephrem the Syrian: Selected Prose Works*, pp. 156-157.

[122] Ode 40:1, trans. James H. Charlesworth, p. 138.

for us. And we ought to lay down our lives for our brothers. If anyone has material possessions and sees a brother in need but has no pity on them, how can the love of God be in that person? Dear children, let us not love with words or speech but with actions and in truth. (1 John 3:11, 13-18)

Time and again the themes which St John mentions here relate to what we have seen elsewhere: the great commandment of Our Lord to love God and our neighbour as ourselves; the statement that no greater love has a man than this that he lays down his life for his friend (John 15:13), and the need to put our love and our faith into practice through practically helping people (James 2:16-17). This shows the consistency of the Christian faith as taught by the apostles. St John returns to love in the next chapter, revealing the great mystery that God actually *is* love:

Dear friends, let us love one another, for love comes from God. Everyone who loves has been born of God and knows God. Whoever does not love does not know God, because God is love. This is how God showed His love among us: He sent His one and only Son into the world that we might live through Him. This is love: not that we loved God, but that He loved us and sent His Son as an atoning sacrifice for our sins. Dear friends, since God so loved us, we also ought to love one another. No one has ever seen God; but if we love one another, God lives in us and His love is made complete in us.

This is how we know that we live in Him and He in us: He has given us of His Spirit. And we have seen and testify that the Father has sent His Son to be the Saviour of the world. If anyone acknowledges that Jesus is the Son of God, God lives in them and they in God. And so we know and rely on the love God has for us. God is love. Whoever lives in love lives in God, and God in them. This is how love is made complete among us so that we will have confidence on the day of judgment: In this world we are like Jesus.

There is no fear in love. But perfect love drives out fear, because fear has to do with punishment. The one who fears is not made perfect in love.

> We love because He first loved us. Whoever claims to love God yet hates his brother is a liar. For whoever does not love their brother, whom they have seen, cannot love God, whom they have not seen. And He has given us this command: Anyone who loves God must also love their brother. (1 John 4:7-21)

There is so much in this short passage that a book would not exhaust it, but let us simply note three points: first, that God *is* love (*agape*) is insisted upon, and from this we can deduce that any genuine love we show others is God working through us. In loving, we approach to God. The more complete our love, the more complete our godliness.

Second, that perfect love casts out fear. If we are complete in love, we shall be free of worry and anxiety. Love is the complete answer to our concerns: but not love of this person or of that person although they all count. Rather, the love of God living in us is this perfect love.

Third, and finally at this stage, the point which was so important in the Syriac tradition, that love is not something we do (at last not in the ordinary sense), but that it is something we receive, and by receiving it, we are ourselves changed. Ode 3 of the *Odes of Solomon* states: "For I should not have known how to love the Lord, if He had not loved me. Who is able to distinguish love, except him who is loved? I love the Beloved, my soul loves Him, and where His rest is, there also am I."[123]

13.12   The Good Samaritan

This parable is found only in the Gospel of St Luke. It is critical to take it with the passage immediately preceding where Our Lord is asked what one must do to inherit eternal life:

> On one occasion an expert in the law stood up to test Jesus. "Teacher," he asked: "what must I do to inherit eternal life?" "What is written in the Law?" he replied. "How do you read it?"

---

[123] Ode 3:3-5, based on the translation of James H. Charlesworth, with minor amendments, p. 19.

He (the lawyer) answered: " 'Love the Lord your God with all your heart and with all your soul and with all your strength and with all your mind' ; and: "Love your neighbour as yourself. "

"You have answered correctly," Jesus replied. "Do this and you will live." But he (the lawyer) wanted to justify himself, so he asked Jesus: "And who is my neighbour?"

In reply Jesus said: "A man was going down from Jerusalem to Jericho, when he was attacked by robbers. They stripped him of his clothes, beat him and went away, leaving him half dead. A priest happened to be going down the same road, and when he saw the man, he passed by on the other side. So too, a Levite,[124] when he came to the place and saw him, passed by on the other side. But a Samaritan,[125] as he travelled, came where the man was; and when he saw him, he took pity on him. He went to him and bandaged his wounds, pouring on oil and wine. Then he put the man on his own donkey, brought him to an inn and took care of him. The next day he took out two denarii and gave them to the innkeeper. 'Look after him," he said: "and when I return, I will reimburse you for any extra expense you may have." Which of these three do you think was a neighbour to the man who fell into the hands of robbers?"

The expert in the law replied: "The one who had mercy on him." Jesus told him: "Go and do likewise." (Luke 10:25-37)

This parable is often misunderstood. It is not saying that *everyone* is my neighbour right now – but that they potentially are. To be a "neighbour" literally means to be "near." How can I be near someone if I am closed to him? Neither does Our Lord ask who *the robbed man was neighbour to*. Our Lord was teaching that I can become a person's neighbour when I have compassion on him.

---

[124] The Levites were from a tribe which was dedicated to assisting the priests.

[125] The Samaritans were very close to the Jews, religiously and culturally, but there were – and are – differences, and there was mutual distrust and often hostility between Jews and Samaritans.

Questions for Contemplation

1. What does this parable say about true and false faith?

2. In what could the man who was robbed and left for dead have any hope?

3. In my own words, how does this parable answer the question Our Lord was asked at the start?

Lesson 14
The Ten Commandments:
The Worship of God

1. The Ten Commandments (introduction)

2. The First Commandment

3. The Second Commandment

4. The Third Commandment

If this introduction to the Maronite Catholic faith has one theme, it is the worship of God as a whole of life vocation. The worship of God is inseparable from loving Him in serving Him and serving Him in loving Him, not only in church but also in the world, in ourselves and in others. God is first. God is fundamental. We are to order our aims, our thoughts, feelings, actions and omissions, our entire lives to Him.

In this, we are aided by the specifically Syriac method of *typology*, in which we learn to see the patterns of the life of Christ and His sacraments everywhere in reality. To study typology but then not turn to the world to search for God's patterns in it, to sense His greater beauty through its lesser beauty, would be like studying books on swimming but never getting into the water.

The spiritual source of our Maronite Catholic existence is found in the Divine Sacrifice of the Mass, the Sacrament of the Eucharist, where Our Lord offers Himself to His Father, on the altar, through the ministry of the priest. The Maronite liturgy, as we shall soon enough see, is modelled on the Divine Liturgy in heaven; it is an ascent from earth to heaven, wherein we meet the descending power of the Holy Spirit and the condescension[126] of Our Lord Jesus.

We now examine how the way was prepared for the incarnation of Our Lord, and how the ancient Hebrews were given the Ten Commandments. After a brief introduction, we focus here on the first three which concern the worship of God: this is always first.

1. The Ten Commandments

First of all, it should be noted that the Hebrew phrase which we translate as "the Ten Commandments" actually means "the Ten Words," (*asereth had-devarim*). As in English and Hebrew alike, a "word" can refer to a single term or to a larger communication. Hence, in the New Testament we read: "Let us see this word that is come to pass, which the Lord has shown to us" (Luke 2:15). By calling the relevant message a "word" we indicate both its coherence around one concept, and its conciseness. This explains how Judaism counts the initial declaration: "I am the Lord your God ...," to be the *first* commandment of the Ten, although it commands nothing except, implicitly, the acknowledgment of God.

The Ten Commandments are part of the Jewish Law, and this is part of the *covenant* with God. Several covenants are referred to in the Old Testament, so we call this one the "Mosaic covenant" because it was given through Moses during the period when Israel was wandering in the desert on their return to the Promised Land (see section 12.1). The relationship between Israel and God is defined by that covenant. In the Christian covenant, established by Our Lord, a major part of the covenant is that God adopts us as His children (a concept also known in the Old Testament, but not so prominently).

---

[126] "Condescension" in this context literally means how Our Lord comes down to our level.

The Law of Judaism was given at Sinai. As Tigay states:

> The momentous encounter with God at Sinai is, for Judaism, the defining moment in Jewish history, the moment when God came down on earth and spoke to all Jews, present and future, giving them his rules for life ... These laws ... became the basis of all Judaism ... it became the duty of every Jew, not just an intellectual elite, to study them.[127]

Exodus 20:1-17 records the first occasion the Ten Commandments were given.[128] It reads as follows:

> Then God spoke all these words: "I am the LORD your God, who brought you out of the land of Egypt, out of the house of slavery. You shall not have other gods beside me.[129] You shall not make for yourself an idol or a likeness of anything in the heavens above or on the earth below or in the waters beneath the earth; you shall not bow down before them or serve them. For I, the LORD, your God, am a jealous God, inflicting punishment for their ancestors' wickedness on the children of those who hate me, down to the third and fourth generation; but showing love down to the thousandth generation of those who love me and keep my commandments.
>
> You shall not invoke the name of the LORD, your God, in vain.[130] For the LORD will not leave unpunished anyone who invokes his name in vain. Remember the Sabbath day—keep it holy.[131] Six days you may labour and do all your work, but the seventh day is a Sabbath of the LORD your God. You shall not do any work, either you, your son or your daughter, your male or female slave, your work animal, or the resident alien within your gates. For in six days the LORD made the heavens and the earth, the sea and all that is in them; but on the seventh day he rested. That is why

---

[127] Jeffrey Tigay, *Jewish Study Bible,* second edition, Oxford University Press, Oxford, 1999, 206.

[128] It is not clear how they are to be divided. The version in Deuteronomy 5:6-21 is just a little bit different, especially in relation to the Sabbath. However, the differences are not significant

[129] First commandment.

[130] Second commandment.

[131] Third commandment.

the LORD has blessed the Sabbath day and made it holy.
Honour your father and your mother,[132] that you may have a long
life in the land the LORD your God is giving you.
You shall not kill.[133]
You shall not commit adultery.[134]
You shall not steal.[135]
You shall not bear false witness against your neighbour.[136]
You shall not covet your neighbour's house.[137] You shall not
covet your neighbour's wife, his male or female slave, his ox or
donkey, or anything that belongs to your neighbour.[138]

A certain amount of commentary has been included in the Bible,
particularly around the first three commandments. This is because the
most important of the commandments are those which relate to God.
This makes sense: God is the basis of any sound morality. Any other
possible basis for morality is subjective, meaning that it depends upon
the viewpoint of the person concerned. If our moral teachings have not
been mandated by God, what reason can I possibly give for not only
following the moral commandments but also for believing them?

Political parties have many ideals, but they can always change them
by a vote of the members of the party. Philosophical associations can have
their principles, too, but they are not bound to them: as soon as they change
their mind they can change their principles. The Church is not like that,
because our faith is based on revelation: i.e. God speaking to humanity.

The Ten Commandments are usually understood as applying to
many types of behaviour which are not explicitly covered. That is, they
reach to behaviour which is *implicitly* included. The two matters which
are positively enjoined upon us are to worship God alone and to honour
one's parents. These commandments still speak to us today.

---

[132] Fourth commandment.
[133] Fifth commandment.
[134] Sixth commandment.
[135] Seventh commandment.
[136] Eighth commandment.
[137] Ninth commandment.
[138] Tenth commandment.

2.   First Commandment: I am the LORD your God ... you shall not have other gods beside me.

For Christians, this means to worship God as He is, in the Holy Trinity (for the Jews of the Old Testament, the commandment would likewise have meant to worship God with a knowledge of Him corresponding to the extent that He had revealed Himself, an extent which, at that time, did not include the Trinity). A true worship will be both truly exterior and truly interior. That is, it will have both a public and a private dimension. What we do exteriorly will often arouse and strengthen our interior devotion. *Both* are the best way to worship God: with body and with soul. We are to worship God with our *entire* being. When we worship God publicly, by coming to church, or attending processions and so on, we also give good examples to other people, and we show our unity with the Church of God. When we pray, or attend church activities, we need the right disposition in our souls. This means that we should pray with fervour and reverence. This always requires humility. At times we worship with joy, and at times in sadness, or with more neutral feelings, but always our internal disposition should be one of humble reverence for the Lord.

When worshipping, we should also avoid singularity and exaggeration. "Singularity" is "the quality or fact of being one in number or kind," and comes to mean not only being distinctive, but also being odd. Anything which would draw attention to ourselves in an extreme manner should be avoided. For example, if I go to church, I should not wear dress which attracts attention, especially not by way of immodesty. We are there to praise God, and to celebrate a liturgy, not to distract others from this. Similarly, we should not make unnecessary noise during the Divine Sacrifice of the Mass. It is selfish and inconsiderate to drive to or from churches in revved up cars.

This principle of circumspection[139] applies to religious activities

---

[139] To be "circumspect" is to exercise caution and be considerate of others before acting. It comes from a Latin verb meaning "to look around."

outside the church, as well. If I am sitting in a restaurant, it is a good thing to make the Sign of the Cross before I eat my food. But it is best done seated, and without large movements to attract attention. It actually gives a good example to others. People notice it as a sign of sincerity. But to stand or to utter a lengthy prayer and pray with head bowed and hands clasped would be singularity: recall what we saw in lesson 10, about how Our Lord said not to seek to draw attention to ourselves when we pray.

People will notice us. That is unavoidable, and is, in any event part of life. But we do not seek to distract others who are trying to concentrate on the liturgy, or to satisfy our vanity by making heads turn. People will favourably notice a well-dressed and well-behaved person. That sets a good example. When we think of the First Commandment, we should also remember that Our Lord said: "... Everyone who acknowledges me before others I will acknowledge before my heavenly Father. But whoever denies me before others, I will deny before my heavenly Father" (Matthew 10:32)

It is also good to venerate sacred representations: these include statues and icons, and other sacred art. In this respect, Christianity has superseded the ancient prohibition on depictions of God, for a good reason: through His Incarnation, God became flesh. This veneration is another way of strengthening our internal devotion, and if the art has been well fashioned, it can have a significant and positive effect upon us. The culture which surrounds us reflects back to us our values, and forms us. The most important sacred representation of all is the crucifix: it is a sign not only of Our Lord but also of our redemption, and so must be especially venerated. We do not pray to the crucifix, of course, but to Our Lord Jesus Christ, who is represented by it. It used to be a rule, and effectively still is in the Maronite Church, that no sacrament can be administered and no liturgy held without the presence of the crucifix. It is still a good custom to place a crucifix in the hands of the dying.

Sins against religiosity are forbidden, too, by the First

Commandment. These are usually stated to be superstition, sacrilege, idolatry and simony. These are all sins against the sacred, that is, those things which pertain to or belong to God.

This commandment is also significant for the question of sacred art. For us, in this world, sacred art serves as a sort of bridge between the earthly and the heavenly. Sacred art is not distinguished by its subject so much as by its content and the being of the artist, or to be more precise, how the artist's being is manifested in the art. Much of what passes for "modern sacred art" is modern but has nothing sacred about it. If one asks what constitutes sacred art, the starting point, in the authentic Maronite tradition, is the same as the Orthodox one: that is, it must be traditional. This does not mean to blindly imitate, but to reverently follow. This immediately dismisses striking innovation and the expression of romanticism, sentimentality and personality. However, it is a large topic, and we do not have time to exhaustively deal with it here.

Opposed to sound religious practices is superstition. "Superstition" means "unreasoning awe or fear of something unknown, mysterious or imaginary, especially in connection with religion." It can also mean "an irrational religious belief or practice founded upon fear or ignorance."[140] But in the Church, we understand "superstition" as "attributing to a creature a power that belongs to God alone." It includes using magic and spells, believing in "lucky" rabbits' feet, fortune-telling and astrology. It extends to seeing omens everywhere, and signs from God in all sorts of accidents. These can vary from major to minor sins: major superstitious sins would include participating in séances attempting to raise the spirits of the dead, and minor examples would be believing in lucky and unlucky numbers.

"Sacrilege" is "stealing or misappropriating what is consecrated to God's service," and also "any outrage on consecrated persons

---

[140] *Shorter Oxford Dictionary*, 2194.

or things, and the violation of any sacred obligation."[141] A thing is consecrated when it is committed to the service of God. This can include everything from a person such as a priest or a nun all the way through to altar vessels, and to churches and graveyards, for these have been consecrated to religious purposes.

Sometimes people tell what we call a "pious fable," e.g. that angels took Our Lady's house from Palestine to Italy. There is nothing wrong with these as long as we do not try and make money or derive some other personal advantage from them. But we should never ourselves make them up. Although they can help some people to feel the faith as something almost tangible, yet there is enough reality and truth in the faith. They are not needed, and because they are liable to be exploded and expose the faith to ridicule, they should be allowed to die out.

Idolatry is when one pays to a creature the worship due to God alone as the Supreme Being. When Christianity was founded, Christians were put to death for refusing to burn incense on the altars of the gods (including the emperor, who was treated as a god). They went to their deaths for refusing to give to false gods and to human beings the honours due to God only.

Simony is buying and selling sacred or spiritual things and possessions. Today the faithful must be especially careful of being deceived by people who purport to sell relics. Relics of the saints must not be sold, for they are not commercial items. Apart from the fact that those who purport to sell them are invariably frauds, even if they had authentic relics, it is wrong to reward them for their sin by paying for those relics. If no one bought supposed relics, this sacrilegious trade would immediately die out.

Here is a story about sacrilege and idolatry from the Book of Daniel in the Old Testament. It is so striking that it has given rise to the famous phrase "(reading or seeing) the writing on the wall," meaning "knowing that your doom is upon you":

---

[141] *Shorter Oxford Dictionary*, 1871.

King Belshazzar gave a great banquet for a thousand of his nobles, with whom he drank. Under the influence of the wine, he ordered the gold and silver vessels which Nebuchadnezzar, his father, had taken from the temple in Jerusalem, to be brought in so that the king, his nobles, his consorts, and his concubines might drink from them. When the gold vessels taken from the temple, the house of God in Jerusalem, had been brought in, and while the king, his nobles, his consorts, and his concubines were drinking wine from them, they praised their gods of gold and silver, bronze and iron, wood and stone.

Suddenly, opposite the lampstand, the fingers of a human hand appeared, writing on the plaster of the wall in the king's palace. When the king saw the hand that wrote, his face became pale; his thoughts terrified him, his hip joints shook, and his knees knocked. The king shouted for the enchanters, Chaldeans, and diviners to be brought in. "Whoever reads this writing and tells me what it means," he said to the wise men of Babylon: "shall be clothed in purple, wear a chain of gold around his neck, and be third in governing the kingdom."

But though all the king's wise men came in, none of them could either read the writing or tell the king what it meant. Then King Belshazzar was greatly terrified; his face became pale, and his nobles were thrown into confusion. ...

Then Daniel was brought into the presence of the king. The king asked him: "Are you the Daniel, one of the Jewish exiles, whom my father, the king, brought from Judah? I have heard that the spirit of the gods is in you, that you have shown brilliant insight and extraordinary wisdom. ... I have heard that you can give interpretations and solve problems. Now, if you are able to read the writing and tell me what it means, you shall be clothed in purple, wear a chain of gold around your neck, and be third in governing the kingdom."

Daniel answered the king: "You may keep your gifts, or give your presents to someone else; but the writing I will read for the king, and tell what it means. ... You ... Belshazzar have not humbled your heart ... you have rebelled against the Lord of heaven. You had the vessels of his temple brought before you, so that you and your nobles, your consorts and your concubines, might drink wine from them; and you praised the gods of silver and gold, bronze and iron, wood and stone, that neither see nor hear nor have intelligence. But the God in whose hand is your very breath and the whole course of your life, you did not glorify. By him was the hand sent, and the writing set down. This is the writing that was inscribed: MENE, MENE, TEKEL, and PARSIN. These words mean: MENE, God has numbered your kingdom and put an end to it; TEKEL, you have been weighed on the scales and found wanting; PERES, your kingdom has been divided and given to the Medes and Persians."

Then by order of Belshazzar they clothed Daniel in purple, with a chain of gold around his neck, and proclaimed him third in governing the kingdom. That very night Belshazzar, the Chaldean king, was slain (from Daniel 5)

Questions for Contemplation

1. Do I have a sense of the sacred?
2. Do I ever take the sacred for granted, or treat it without respect?
3. Do I take time out of the day to acknowledge and worship God?

It is also against the First Commandment (in the sense that it is against the love of God), either *to presume* or *to despair.* These seem to be opposite vices, but in fact they are both sins against hope. "Presumption" is trusting too much in God's support and mercy, while despair is trusting too little in it.

Another example of presumption is committing a sin in the belief that God will forgive me. This includes, of course, committing a sin in the confident belief that I can go to confession and have it forgiven.

Part of the salutary (healthy) value of not presuming upon the mercy of God is avoiding the occasions of sin. Avoiding the occasion of sin is avoiding those situations wherein we sin, and those people who lead us into sin. For example, if certain so-called friends offer me drugs, then staying away from those people is avoiding the occasion of sin. If I sin because every time I go to the club I get drunk, or because I gamble, or both, then avoiding the club is necessary for me to lead a virtuous life.

Despair, on the other hand, is losing all hope that God can save my soul or will give me the necessary help should I seek it. That is, it is losing hope of eternal salvation or of the means of obtaining redemption. The way to overcome despair is, of course, to be sincerely repentant, and to trust that God is satisfied with that true repentance or *contrition*. I feel contrition when I am sorry for sin because I detest it, and have formed a firm resolution not to sin in the future. This sorrow and resolution grind down the attraction for sin which exists within us all.

Related to despair is *sloth*, which is a laziness in loving God and in loving or aiding one's neighbour. It is a form of selfishness of a very mean variety, because it is simply a selfish refusal to bother oneself to take a loving or even a rational action which is in one's own best interests. It includes having correct priorities, so that one is doing what one should be doing, putting the most important duties first. Otherwise, one could avoid going to church, or caring for the sick because one was doing the gardening.

It is also sloth if I do not perform my duty to God and man. I should perform it out of love. It is only laziness which has taught us to think of duties as being irksome. Children love being given responsibility, and the chance to show what they can do. We can recover that enthusiasm simply by reasoning correctly: duties are privileges given to those who are responsible enough to be trusted. We can offer up the performance of our duties to God.

Another sin against faith in God is *giving scandal*: injuring our neighbour by causing or tempting him to sin. It can include giving a bad example. This is particularly important with children, because children are especially vulnerable to bad examples. I can offer as an example which both gave scandal, and promoted superstition in a crass form, the peddling of a voice recording as being St Charbel's voice miraculously becoming manifest on someone's telephone. This sort of novelty can be dismissed out of hand: if God wanted to work a miracle there are many more edifying ones than a telephone message offering platitudes in modern Lebanese.

3.   The Second Commandment: You shall not take the name of the Lord your God in vain.

This is often taken to mean that one should not swear or make a false oath using the name of the Lord. This is not wrong, but the Commandment is, however, primarily directed against irreverent speech. A person who really understands this virtue, understands and feels how sacrilegious it is for people to swear or even express surprise, anger or displeasure by using the name of the Lord.

In his Epistle to the Philippians, St Paul wrote: "… God greatly exalted him (Jesus) and bestowed on him the name that is above every name, that at the name of Jesus every knee should bend, of those in heaven and on earth and under the earth, and every tongue confess that Jesus Christ is Lord, to the glory of God the Father" (2:9-11).

Cursing is especially forbidden: it is calling evil down upon someone or something. However, this is not to say that one can really do harm by cursing, or cause satanic powers to act. This is nonsense. It is the evil intention which constitutes the sin in cursing. Even in a natural sense, cursing indicates a lack of self-control. From a religious point of view it is even worse: cursing is against the will of God, because He seeks goodness, and to change people by improving them where possible.

There is a story of a priest in ancient Rome who was asked to curse someone's enemy. He refused, saying: "I became a priest to bless not to curse," or words to that effect.

Beyond misusing the name of God, which is profanity, there is a sin of blasphemy: *expressing contempt for God* and for holy people or things.

An *oath* is calling upon God to witness the truth of what we are saying. It is permissible if and only if three conditions are present:

1. We have a good and weighty reason for making the oath.
2. We believe that what we will say is true.
3. It will not cause us to do evil.

A simple oath is when one person makes an oath to another. But a solemn oath is when the oath is confirmed as true before an ecclesiastical or a civil authority. It should only be made for a good purpose, for example, to confirm in a court of law that we are telling the truth. This is a proper use of the oath, because it is part of helping justice to be done. Of course, we must absolutely tell the truth under oath. To ask God to witness a lie is to commit the grievous sin of *perjury*. In fact, the Hebrew wording of this Commandment (*lašow*), while often translated "in vain," actually means "falsely" as a comparison of this phrase elsewhere in relevant contexts demonstrates. Oaths of blind obedience are bad when made to a bad authority, e.g. to a secret society.

A promise made under oath ceases to bind if the person to whom it was given relaxes it (that is, allows a departure from the oath), if the object becomes sinful or useless, or substantially changes (e.g. I promise to stay home but then the house catches fire), or the reason for the oath ceases to exist (e.g. I promise to go to the church for a ceremony, but it is cancelled), or the oath is annulled, dispensed or commuted (changed) by lawful authority.

An example of an oath wrongfully made is when King Herod promised to give Salome whatever she asked for. She asked for the head of John the Baptist on a platter. It was wrong to keep his oath:

> Herodias's own daughter came in and performed a dance that delighted Herod and his guests. The king said to the girl: "Ask of me whatever you wish and I will grant it to you." He even swore [many things] to her: "I will grant you whatever you ask of me, even to half of my kingdom." She went out and said to her mother: "What shall I ask for?" She replied: "The head of John the Baptist." The girl hurried back to the king's presence and made her request: "I want you to give me at once on a platter the head of John the Baptist." The king was deeply distressed, but because of his oaths and the guests he did not wish to break his word to her. (Mark 6:22-26)

It is not a sin if I give evidence in a court of law in a country like Australia, where the government rules by law. The courts are there to administer justice, and I can only cooperate with them. Very often, people mistakenly think that a guilty person is innocent, and *vice versa*. The best policy is to allow the court to hear all the admissible evidence and then decide.

Related to the *oath* is the concept of a *vow*. A vow is a deliberate promise made to God, by which one binds oneself to do something or to refrain from some act. To make a vow to God is a serious matter, and should be entered only with the permission of a priest or a bishop, because to fail to fulfil a vow is a sin. *People often confuse a pious promise and a vow.* They are two quite different things, and it leads to needless anxiety to treat a promise with the solemnity which only a vow merits. If I ask St Charbel to help me in the exams, and in return I will visit his Church, this is really only a promise, although it is a serious one. It is not a vow: a vow can only be made to God. A vow is the most solemn promise it is possible for us to make, and so it should only concern most grave matters: e.g. the health of a child who is seriously ill.

As with oaths, a priest can always commute, annul or dispense with a vow. Sometimes people make rash promises,[142] or make them under compulsion. Neither vows nor oaths are valid unless made voluntarily. If either of them turns out not to be feasible, see a priest to have them commuted or annulled altogether. Not only is it a sin not to fulfil a vow, it is also a sin to needlessly postpone fulfilling it. A vow made and fulfilled is especially good because one makes a gift both of the binding of one's will, and of the promised action, to God.

4.   The Third Commandment: Keep Holy the Sabbath

The "Sabbath" is Saturday, the seventh day. Sunday, on the other hand, is the first day of the week, and was so, even in Our Lord's time. The Sunday observance of Christianity goes back to Sunday being the day of the Resurrection, not to the third Commandment. The Jewish Sabbath is not our Christian Sunday. However, in establishing the Christian Sabbath and its rules, the Church has wisely taken over some of this Commandment, but adapted it to the needs and, one might say, the genius of Christianity.

Note that this Commandment is not in the form of a prohibition ("Thou shalt not"), but in the form of an injunction: "You shall ..." It is a question of finding some impulse within to meet the challenge, for the keeping sacred is not to be a matter of pretence or play-acting.

The reason given by the Book of Exodus for keeping the seventh day holy is first and foremost *to remember that God created the universe in six days*. That He hallowed the seventh day by resting upon it is reason why we should likewise keep it holy by resting. Here we again see that to keep something "holy" is to associate it with God. However, the fundamental rationale for this Commandment is that on this day we would recall the Creation. But it is also mentioned later, in Exodus 23:12, that the Sabbath holiday (literally, *holy*-day) also allows us, our

---

[142] A "rash promise" is one made without due consideration for what is entailed in the promise and its consequences.

servants and our animals to rest and be refreshed, and in 31:16, that it is a covenant (and hence, we assume, was to remind them of that covenant).

It is also implied in Exodus that the Sabbath day of rest is to be used for God's purposes, hence one can praise and worship Him, even visit holy sites and sing psalms. But, in Old Testament times, one was forbidden to gather food or fuel, to light a fire, or to engage in business or agricultural activities.

The Lord Himself taught us that this Commandment was but imperfectly understood. St Mark tells us the following story of Our Lord:

> One Sabbath Jesus was going through the grain fields, and as his disciples walked along, they began to pick some heads of grain. The Pharisees said to him: "Look, why are they doing what is unlawful on the Sabbath?" He answered: "Have you never read what David did when he and his companions were hungry and in need? In the days of Abiathar the high priest, he entered the house of God and ate the consecrated bread, which is lawful only for priests to eat. And he also gave some to his companions." Then he said to them: "The Sabbath was made for man, not man for the Sabbath. So the Son of Man is Lord even of the Sabbath." (Mark 2:23-28)

Therefore, the Lord was able to change the Sabbath rules. It is uncertain what Our Lord mandated about the Sabbath and Sunday. However, two modern scholars have concluded that the first Christians probably began assembling for worship on the Lord's Day (Sunday), and did not initially replace the Sabbath, but rather transformed the Sabbath from a day of rest to a day of the memorial of the Creation. The idea of a day of rest seems to have actually disappeared from early Christianity. Rather, at first, Sunday was for praising God, and only later, did it became a day of compulsory rest.[143]

---

[143] Paul Bradshaw and Maxwell E. Johnson, *The Origins of Feasts, Fasts and Seasons in Early Christianity*, Liturgical Press, Collegeville, 2011, 1-28.

We are enjoined and encouraged, therefore, to rest from servile labour on Sunday if possible (that is, not to engage in corporeal work for wages or profit). That does not mean that if we have a business not to open it on Sunday: that is a question of discretion. But we might not need to work in it. Neither does it mean that students should not study. Further, what is necessary (e.g. repairing a roof through which rain is pouring) is always permissible.

But even in those instances, we should strive to the utmost not to allow these duties and undertakings to prevent us from fulfilling our Sunday obligation. The one thing we absolutely must do on Sunday (or the vigil, where that is available), unless impeded, is attend the Divine Sacrifice of the Mass. We are not obliged to receive the Eucharist, although we must receive it at least once a during the Season of the Resurrection.

Then, in addition, we should try and perform good and pious actions on Sunday, not make demands on others. We should aim to spend some quiet time in religious reading and contemplation. Every Sunday should remain us of the fundamentals of our faith, and of the glory of the Resurrection, hence on Easter Sunday, the *qolo* of the liturgy reads:

> On this day creation sings, giving praise with hymns of joy,
> for the Son of God arose from the darkness of the tomb,
> and reigns in majesty upon His throne. Mighty Lord of Hosts!
> We the holy faithful ones on the altar see Our Lord …

Lesson 15

The Ten Commandments: Social Virtue

15.1 The Fourth Commandment: Honour your Father and your Mother

The commandment to "honour" (*kabbed*) is not the same as the commandment to love. God commands us to honour Him (e.g. in Exodus 14:4), so there is a certain analogy between what is due to God and to one's parents: after all, God created us and our parents bore us, and God is called our Father.

One might think that such a commandment is unnecessary if one's parents are lovable, and futile if they are not. But we must dig deeper. First, this commandment was always interpreted as meaning that there is a duty to care for the elderly in one's extended family. That is, it was not understood to be restricted to caring for one's biological mother and father. On this basis, the full text of the commandment ("Honour your father and your mother, that you may have a long life in the land the Lord your God is giving you") could be taken to mean that by caring for the elderly, they will live long lives in their own country. But the Hebrew says *honour your father and your mother*, masculine singular, in order that *your days*, again masculine singular, may be long in the land which God *gives you*, masculine singular. In other words, it is saying that by honouring one's parents one will be given long life together with the land. God will reward those who respect their parents.

In the context of this commandment, to "honour" includes not striking or cursing one's parents (Exodus 21:15 and 17). It would also include providing for them, especially if they are in need, and also discharging their duties where there is occasion to do so (e.g. if one has siblings dependent upon one's parents, and one's parents can no longer provide for them, then one should do one's best to supply their needs).

There are other rules in the Old Testament relating to parents, but they are in some respects obsolete (e.g. to take disobedient sons to the elders at the gate of the town to have them stoned to death, Deuteronomy 21:18-21). These laws have not survived Christianity, if indeed they were ever really practised.

For us, the model relationship to one's parents is that of Jesus to Mary and Joseph. As St Luke wrote of the boy Jesus: "Then he went down to Nazareth with them and was obedient to them. But his mother treasured all these things in her heart. And Jesus grew in wisdom and stature, and in favour with God and man" (Luke 2:51-52). However, when He had his divine work to do, He placed that first (Luke 2:49 and Mark 3:31-35).

St Paul repeats this commandment with some commentary:

> Children, obey your parents in the Lord, for this is right. "Honour your father and mother," which is the first commandment with

a promise: "so that it may go well with you and that you may enjoy long life on the earth." Fathers, do not exasperate[144] your children; instead, bring them up in the training and instruction of the Lord. (Ephesians 6:1-4)

In other words, the obligations are mutual. Parents are required to give their children all that is needful and good for their bodily and spiritual welfare. This includes nourishment, clothing, lodging, protection from hot and cold, medical aid and medicine, education including vocational training, and opportunities for play and recreation. The parents' responsibilities are personal, and can only be delegated where there is real need. These goods should not be less than the child's station in life would require.

Neither is it required for children to act without knowing the reasons their parents want something: however, the amount of explanation the children can require depends on their age and maturity. Certainly, we do not have to obey our parents if they ask or even command us to do something immoral or illegal. Further, one does not have to procure one's parents' consent before choosing a vocation (i.e. marrying or becoming a cleric). The Church has always recognised that in these two situations, the child has the right to decide for himself (this is the right to autonomy). It is positively a sin for parents to coerce their children in these respects.

Perhaps, however, the highest duty which we owe to our parents has been left unstated: the duty of praying for them, and providing for their spiritual needs. For example, when one's parents are sick, one should call in a priest to administer the sacraments, and when they die, give them a decent Christian funeral service and burial.

It can be hard to *love* our parents if our relationship was fraught with pain. But if we pray for them out of a sense of duty, and with the humility to accept that we are all weak, we can come to sincerely

---

[144] To "exasperate" is to cause significant irritation, a feeling of "when will this end?"

pray for them, and eventually love will appear as our understanding grows, and we acquire a better perspective on the past. We all have a love for our parents somewhere in our hearts, but it can be covered up by a history of conflicts. However, as one's response in times of crisis often shows, these are ultimately superficial. The love we have for our families is part of our essence, and cannot be plucked out.

15.2 The Fifth Commandment: You shall not kill.

No one is allowed to kill, except where there is a specific authority (e.g. in self-defence, or in a just war). God is the author of life. That must be respected. An innocent life may never be taken. When one does act in self-defence, one must act proportionately, to the best of one's judgment and ability (e.g. if someone was trying to knock my hat off my head, it would be disproportionate to shoot him; but if he was attempting rape, shooting could be reasonable, although we should, if possible, check rather than maim, and maim rather than kill.

This commandment against murder was greatly expanded by Our Lord in the Sermon on the Mount:

> "You have heard that it was said to the people long ago: "You shall not murder, and anyone who murders will be subject to judgment." But I tell you that anyone who is angry with a brother will be subject to judgment. Again, anyone who says to a brother: "Raka,"[145] is answerable to the court. And anyone who says: "'You fool!" will be in danger of the fire of hell." (Matthew 5:21-22)

The Ten Commandments possess a certain power which is based, in part, on their brevity. But Our Lord was quite clearly going beyond them. Thus He said: "You have heard that it was said to the people long ago ... But I tell you ..."

So when we Christians read the Old Testament, we should also remember that Our Lord has perfected the ethical commandments, and

---

[145] "raka" or "raqa" is an Aramaic word which has the sense of "empty (head)" or "blockhead."

that the Old has to be read in the light of the New Testament. As the Church applies the principles of the faith to new situations, it applies the fundamental rules in ways not previously considered. This is the true development of tradition.

There are psychological principles which can be used to help us get the better of our anger: many of these are dealt with in spiritual works such as the *Philokalia*, and other monastic literature. We cannot enter into that important topic here, for this book is devoted to the outline of the faith. However, it can be said that in struggling with anger or any negative emotion, or any sinful tendency, the following are critical:

A. Grace. Without the grace of God nothing can be done. For this we must pray and often perform penance and mortification. Central to these efforts are the sacraments: each of them has a role to play, but for ongoing improvement, regular confession and reception of the Eucharist are essential.

B. The right attitude. It is critical not to fall into one of three traps: over-confidence, under-confidence, and diffidence or apathy. We should not over-estimate our ability to change. If you try and weed a large garden in twenty minutes you will fail. You must choose one area, clear that, and as conditions allow, move on to others, while all the time checking that the first has not become reinfested. The best attitude to have is the optimistic one that change for the better is possible, for God does not demand anything beyond our powers. He asks us to *strive in the way of holiness*, and all of us can do that.

C. To cease justifying or excusing our failures. We must not be too quick to say that our anger is righteous anger: that is a rare commodity. Related to this, we should reflect that anger is never a long-term solution. Anger achieves nothing but causing opposition and resentment. Why think it will help now? Try a new way. As Our Lord said:

"You have heard that it was said: "Eye for eye, and tooth for tooth." But I tell you, do not resist an evil person. If anyone slaps you on the right cheek, turn to them the other cheek also. And if anyone wants to sue you and take your shirt, hand over your coat as well. If anyone forces you to go one mile, go with them two miles." (Matthew 5:38-41)

15.3 The Sixth Commandment: You shall not commit adultery.

To commit adultery (to have sexual knowledge of a person married to someone else) is to interfere with the relationship of the man and woman whom God has placed together. We shall return to sexual matters later in the course.

15.4 The Seventh Commandment: You shall not steal.

In Old Testament thought, an act of theft is an act against the person who owns the property. I am not sure, however, that it was not also thought of as being against God. That is our teaching. We do not only respect other people's property for the owner's sake, but for God's. Sometimes people say: "They won't miss it if I take it". But that stealing is a sin, and it is not up to me to decide what other people would or would not miss. Stealing includes stealing from work, although, strangely, some people seem to forget this. Even if an employer is unfair, no one has licence to steal from him. It is also stealing to take advantage of another's mistake. All we need to do to see this is to reflect on how we would feel if we made a mistake and someone else took advantage of us.

Equally, it is sinful to cheat someone of their rightful wages; in fact, this is a particularly serious form of theft, because one allows another to labour and then cheats him of his due reward. All sorts of exploitation are covered by this: workers should be given fair wages, rather than the very least that an employer can get away with.

15.5 The Eighth Commandment: You shall not bear false witness against your neighbour.

"False witness" means telling lies in legal proceedings. This is worse than simply lying and harming one's neighbour, because the community is concerned to make sure that its courts deliver justice. A question arises as to who one's "neighbour" is here, but we answer it by saying that in Christianity no false witness is ever allowed against anyone.

Is it ever permissible to lie? Yes, it is. First, it is permissible to lie when you have a duty to do so: for example, if someone seeks my friend's address in order to kill him as he opens his door, I should not only give him the wrong address, I should make it as far away in the wrong direction as feasible.

Second, there may be cases where the other person has no right to the truth, the question they ask is personal, and I have sufficient reason to wish to keep my secret. Consider this passage from the Gospel of St John:

> After this, Jesus went around in Galilee. He did not want to go about in Judea because the Jewish leaders there were looking for a way to kill Him. But when the Jewish Festival of Tabernacles was near, Jesus' brothers said to Him: "Leave Galilee and go to Judea, so that Your disciples there may see the works You do. No one who wants to become a public figure acts in secret. Since You are doing these things, show Yourself to the world." For even His own brothers did not believe in Him.

> Therefore Jesus told them: "My time is not yet here; for you any time will do. The world cannot hate you, but it hates Me because I testify that its works are evil. You go to the festival. I am not going up to this festival, because My time has not yet fully come." After He had said this, He stayed in Galilee. However, after His brothers had left for the festival, He went also, not publicly, but in secret. (John 7:1-9)

Questions for Contemplation

1. What does this tell us about Jesus' attitude to His mission?

2. When do you think Jesus' cousins (called here his brothers) would have understood that Jesus was unique?

3. Does this mean that lying can be permitted in some instances not because it is good in itself, but because there is a higher good?

15.6 The Ninth Commandment: You shall not covet your neighbour's house.

The Hebrew concept of "coveting" is more than just wanting, it is taking pleasure in something, and – some say – trying to get it. We shall not go far wrong if we distinguish this from stealing by saying that this commandment prohibits jealousy and envy. In modern usage, the two words are little differentiated, if at all. Originally, "jealousy" simply meant being zealous, but we can think of these sins as follows: I am envious if I dislike the fact that someone else is or has something. An envious person can be satisfied by destroying his rival. I am jealous if I have something, and am fearful of losing it, or I lack something or some quality and I wish to possess it. Consider this story of King Solomon:

> Now two prostitutes came to the king and stood before him (Solomon). One of them said: "Pardon me, my lord. This woman and I live in the same house, and I had a baby while she was there with me. The third day after my child was born, this woman also had a baby. We were alone; there was no one in the house but the two of us. During the night this woman's son died because she lay on him. So she got up in the middle of the night and took my son from my side while I your servant was asleep. She put him by her breast and put her dead son by my breast. The next morning, I got up to nurse my son, and he was dead! But when I looked at him closely in the morning light, I saw that it wasn't the son I had borne."

242

The other woman said: "No! The living one is my son; the dead one is yours." But the first one insisted: "No! The dead one is yours; the living one is mine." And so they argued before the king.

The king said: "This one says: "My son is alive and your son is dead," while that one says: "No! Your son is dead and mine is alive." " Then the king said: "Bring me a sword." So they brought a sword for the king. He then gave an order: "Cut the living child in two and give half to one and half to the other."

The woman whose son was alive was deeply moved out of love for her son and said to the king: "Please, my lord, give her the living baby! Don't kill him!" But the other said: "Neither I nor you shall have him. Cut him in two!" Then the king gave his ruling: "Give the living baby to the first woman. Do not kill him; she is his mother." (1 Kings 3:16-27)

The second woman was jealous: she wanted the other woman's child. But she was also envious: if the other woman lost her child too, she would be satisfied. This story also shows the extreme evil of these sins.

15.7 The Tenth Commandment: You shall not covet your neighbour's wife ... or anything that belongs to your neighbour.

What we have said above about stealing and jealousy is sufficient to deal with coveting what your neighbour owns. We shall discuss sexual questions later on.

15.8 The Church's Social Teaching

The Church has always had a powerful social teaching, but of course, the social teaching was adapted to the society in which the Church found itself. If one reflects for but a moment, one can see how natural this is. The religious principles may be the same, e.g. fairness and justice, but they will be applied very differently in a feudal society of seven hundred years ago from how they will be applied in a modern industrial society. For example, *wage justice* will not be an issue in feudal society: the lord would be responsible for ensuring fairness to his people, but he did not pay them wages as we understand them. Questions of environmental concern were quite minimal in pre-industrial societies when humans were incapable of doing very much damage to the natural world. Questions of tolerance were quite different in a society when all people were Catholic. The noble aim of an entire country being dedicated to God and following a law entirely based on His Word might then be feasible. Today it is not, at least not to the same degree. This is a sad change, but still, we certainly do not have to depart so far from the ideal of Christian law as we have in most countries of the world today.

However the situation in the Middle East and with the Maronite Church was rather more complicated, yet in many ways, simpler. It was more complicated in that the Patriarchal Domain (that is, the geographical heart in the Middle East) of our Maronite Church was either threatened by or under the domination of foreign powers throughout the entirety of its history. The political and religious life of the people was a constant struggle, and often a hostile one, with these foreign powers. This had two effects: it limited the political independence of the Maronites, but it also bound the people more tightly to the Church. Many if not most families had someone in the monastery, the presbytery or the convent. They looked to the Church for ongoing stability and guidance. Where there was education it was Church-provided education.

Also, people invariably lived in small villages or moderate sized towns. With the possible exceptions of Damascus and Aleppo. there were no cities to be compared to the many major centres of Europe. This meant that the people were closer together, custom had greater power, and the local church was absolutely fundamental in people's lives. Even the feudal lords who ran the towns worked closely with the Church, often being made subdeacons. Sometimes the lords had their way at the expense of the Church, sometimes it was the other way around, and perhaps more frequently, distinctions between the two were apparent rather than real.

Therefore, the major developments in social teaching within the Latin Church at the end of the nineteenth century were watched by Maronite intellectuals, but not immediately applied. After all, the social, economic and labour conditions in the Middle East were very different from those in Europe. The Middle East was basically feudal with a command economy run by the Turkish authorities, while in Europe there were nation states which were enduring massive conflicts between the political establishment and various labour groups, inspired by or allied with ideologically driven revolutionaries.

But the Church, including the Maronite Church, has now expounded a social teaching which commences with God's plan of salvation for us. It will consider the human person and human rights, basing these on the truth that man was made in the image of God (as we saw in lesson 12), and that from this we can deduce the innate dignity of man.

Because we all share this dignity, we should seek the "common good," which means the goal of allowing all people, justly, to develop their human and spiritual potentials. This will deal with many questions such as the just wage and fair labour conditions, and reasonable returns for investment. The massive internationalisation of the world in the last hundred years has necessitated serious thinking to update the Church's teaching, but always in conformity with the perennial truths of the faith.

In lesson 23, we shall consider, in a little more depth, what the Church has to say on safeguarding the environment and some other issues.

Lesson 16
The Sacraments:
Baptism and Chrismation

16.1   Baptism

16.2   Chrismation.

There are three Sacraments of Initiation, that is, of "formal introduction" and "instruction in the elements" of the faith. These are Baptism, Chrismation (also known as Confirmation) and the Eucharist.

16.1 Baptism: Introduction

The first fact is that we baptise those who wish to become Christian in obedience to the command of the Lord Himself. The second is that our baptisms are united, typologically, with the baptism of the Lord. That is, our baptisms are the baptism of the Lord in a mystical sense which we cannot fully understand.[146] We shall see the relevant passages as we work through the liturgy, because they are included in the readings for this sacrament.

Our starting point must be the liturgy of Baptism itself, for as we have mentioned, the Church teaches authoritatively through its liturgies. The first version of this liturgy was probably written by

---

[146] Maxwell E. Johnson, *The Rites of Christian Initiation*, revised and expanded edition, Liturgical Press, Collegeville, 2007, 290.

Jacob of Sarug.[147] It has been modified, but even so, in some respects it contains the most ancient material of any Syriac baptismal rite.[148] The latest version of the Baptism liturgy commences by gathering at the font the candidate, the candidate's sponsors, and, if the candidate is young, its parents and any others who wish to attend.

The font was originally *outside* the church, so that once the candidate was baptised, the candidate made the journey from the font *into* the church, and was presented at its altar. Now the font is simply placed where it is considered practicable. But it should always be somewhere which allows a *movement* from the font to the altar. For this reason, it is best if the font is either at the back of the church, or, if the church is large enough, off to the side. It is not desirable that the entire ceremony take place at the altar, but if this does occur, it is neither fatal to the efficacy of the ceremony or sacrilegious.

Together with the movement from the font to the altar, which we shall see later, there is also a movement or change from *ordinary* clothes to the *white robe* of baptism. Indeed, the very word *candidate* comes from the Latin word "candidatus" meaning "made white," because the candidate for office, and for baptism, would wear a white robe.

16.1(a)   The Opening Prayer of the Baptism Ritual

The rite commences with the sign of the Cross, made in the traditional Maronite way *"Glory be to the Father and to the Son and to the Holy Spirit now and forever."* That is, we open by glorifying, rather than by invoking the *name* of the Trinity. The first prayer, spoken by the celebrant, reads:

---

[147] Johnson, *The Rites of Christian Initiation*, 273. Spinks shows that there is a great similarity of ideas between the Maronite rite and Jacob's writings on baptism. He concludes: "Though any direct link between Jacob and the Maronite baptismal rite is impossible to demonstrate, the ascription of the rite to Jacob is certainly appropriate." Bryan D. Spinks, *Early and Medieval Rituals and Theologies of Baptism*, Ashgate, Aldershot, 2006, 91-92.

[148] Johnson, *The Rites of Christian Initiation*, 291. Spinks, *Early and Medieval Rituals*, 92.

Lord God, You commissioned Your holy apostles to baptise the world with fire and Spirit. Enable us to celebrate this spiritual service of holy baptism for (N.), *(for adults only:* who seeks Baptism); that having been adorned with the gift of the Holy Spirit, he/she may glorify and thank You, Your blessed Father, and Your living Holy Spirit, now and forever.

The reference to the "commissioning" of the apostles, is to when the Lord appeared to his apostles after his Resurrection:

But the eleven disciples proceeded to Galilee, to the mountain which Jesus had designated. When they saw Him, they worshiped Him; but some were doubtful. And Jesus came up and spoke to them, saying: "All authority has been given to Me in heaven and on earth. "Go therefore and make disciples of all the nations, baptizing them in the name of the Father and the Son and the Holy Spirit, teaching them to observe all that I commanded you; and lo, I am with you always, even to the end of the age." (Matthew 28:16-20)

We say "adorned" with the gift of the Holy Spirit, because one of the ideas behind Maronite baptism is that humanity originally wore a garment of light, a sign of the sanctity of their bodies and souls. But when Adam and Eve sinned, they lost this covering robe, which is how they knew that they were naked. Baptism restores this garment of light to our souls, which gives added point to the white which the candidates wear or are changed into. The final prayer asks that Our Lord Himself may be our vestment of light when we come to leave the world.

16.1(b)   Psalm 51

This penitential psalm is much-favoured in the Maronite tradition. It used to be in practically all our rites and liturgies. It is the only psalm which has been retained in both the funeral services, that is, the services for a man and for a woman. We do not use the entire psalm in the baptism liturgy, but only this selection:

From Psalm 51 [50]: 1-2, 5, 7, 9-10a, 11

Cong: (*antiphonally*)

* Have mercy on me, O God, according to Your merciful love;
   according to Your great compassion blot out my transgressions.

**Wash me completely from my iniquity, and cleanse me of my sin.

* See, I was born guilty,

a sinner when my mother conceived me.

**Cleanse me with hyssop, and I shall be clean;

wash me, and I shall be whiter than snow.

* Turn Your face away from my sins,

and blot out all my guilt.

**Create in me a clean heart, O God,

and do not take Your holy spirit from me.

*/** Glory be to the Father, and to the Son, and to the Holy Spirit,
   now and forever.

"Hyssop" is a plant which grows in the Near East and has medicinal and antiseptic properties. It may possibly be what we now call oregano, thyme, marjoram caper, or a combination of them, but it is not clear which. Hyssop is often referred to in the baptism rite.

This is an excellent psalm for baptism, because it focusses us on virtue and vice, and on the desire to abandon sin. It also stresses the importance of a pure heart, that is, the internal aspect of repentance.

16.1(c)　　Prayer of Forgiveness

Cel: Let us honour, glorify and praise Him who sanctifies holy things
    and exalts the services of the Sacraments; to the High Priest, who
    Himself once taught us the way of purification in the waters of the
    Jordan and led us on the path of life, to purify us from our sins.
    To the Good One is due glory and honour at this holy baptism
    and all the days of our lives and forever.

Cong: Amen.

This is the *froemion* (or "introduction") from the Incense Prayer, which is really a series of several sub-prayers and a hymn. In Syriac, it is known as the *Hoosoye*, which literally means "the atonements." This series of prayers is accompanied by incense, and is distinctive of the Syriac-language Churches. This prayer and the one afterwards are not reserved to the priest. The reference to the Jordan is to Our Lord's baptism in the Jordan. This was the first Epiphany. We shall return to it later. The next prayer in this series is called the *sedro* (or "order").

> **Cel:** O God, out of Your love You became man, and, in a manner beyond understanding, were born in the flesh of the Holy Virgin to present all people to Your Father for adoption, making them His children by water and the Spirit.
>
> You form infants in the womb, yet You willed to become an infant, to renew, through new birth from the spiritual womb of baptism, the image of Adam which had grown old and corrupted by sin.
>
> Although You had no need to do so, in Your compassion you came and were baptised to sanctify the waters of the Jordan.
>
> Son of Majesty, You bowed your head before John the Baptist, while the Father called out from on high: "This is My Son, the Beloved, with whom I am well pleased!"
>
> The Holy Spirit came down and hovered over Your head in the form of a dove, and the spiritual powers stood in fear and trembling.
>
> Lord, let Your merciful right hand rest upon (N.), this son/daughter of Your grace, who has been prepared for holy baptism. Sanctify, purify, and cleanse him/her with Your forgiving hyssop. Bless and protect Your people and Your inheritance.
>
> You have clothed us with the robe of glory by Your divine Baptism, and have marked us with the seal of the holy and life-giving Spirit, calling us to be spiritual children through holy baptism, a second birth. So also, Lord, by Your almighty power, enable us to meet You with the confidence of beloved children, that we may glorify and give thanks to You, to Your Father, and to Your Holy Spirit, now and forever.
>
> **Cong:** Amen.

In addition to themes we have already seen, this makes reference to the virginal conception of Our Lord. The waters of baptism are considered to be a new womb in which we are reborn, this time being born of the Spirit (as to which, see the Gospel readings below.) It is just this theme of Baptism as rebirth, and therefore a new womb, which is what makes this text so ancient.[149]

Next comes a hymn called the *qolo* which is part of the series called the *Hoosoye* or "Incense Prayers." It can be sung by all the congregation:

> Alleluia!
> On this day the cherubim are filled with wonder;
> For the priest baptises and anoints with chrism with his right hand.
> He, though dust, invokes the Spirit, Lord of fiery ranks.
> Then the Spirit answers him and grants what he desires.
> He brings back the dead to life and gives the world hope.
> Alleluia! We praise Christ our King!

The idea here is that baptism is a form of resurrection, because the one who was dead in sin now lives in the grace of God. The final part of the *Hoosoye* is the *3etro* prayer. This is reserved to the priest.

> **Cel:** Holy One, You sanctify Your saints, and they proclaim Your holiness. Sanctify our bodies and souls to be dwelling places for Your divinity through the descent and action of Your Holy Spirit. Cleanse our hearts with the hyssop of Your compassion. Enlighten our feeble minds and rescue our thoughts from the worldly anxieties, that we may adore, give thanks, and praise Your mercy toward us: Father, Son, and Holy Spirit, now and forever.

16.1(d)   The *Qadišat*

This is also found in our Divine Sacrifice of the Mass. It originated in the East, probably in Antioch, in the fifth century. It is a much loved part of the Maronite tradition. It is one of the ancient portions which was retained in the Latin Good Friday ceremony, in Greek and Latin

---

[149] Johnson, *The Rites of Christian Initiation*, 291. Spinks, *Early and Medieval Rituals*, 92-93.

translation beginning *Hagios o theos*, which equals *Sanctus Deus*, which is our *Qadišat aloho*.

> *Qadišat Aloho, Qadišat hayeltono, Qadišat lomoyuto.*
> *Itraham 3aleyin* (x3)
> Holy are you, God. Holy are you, Strong One, Holy are you, Immortal One.
> Have mercy on us.

As with the Divine Sacrifice of the Mass, the response varies in the liturgical seasons.

> Christmas: Msheeho deteeled men bat Daweed. Itraham 3aleyin.[150]
> Epiphany: Msheeho det3amed men Youhanon. Itraham 3aleyin.[151]
> Easter: Msheeho dqom men bet meeteh. Itraham 3aleyin.[152]

16.1(e)   The Epistle

One of the three following epistles is chosen:

> When the goodness and loving kindness of God our saviour appeared, He saved us, not because of any works of righteousness that we had done, but according to His mercy, through the water of rebirth and renewal by the Holy Spirit. This Spirit He poured out on us richly through Jesus Christ our Saviour, so that, having been justified by His grace, we might become heirs according to the hope of eternal life. (Titus 3:4-7)

It is clear from this that baptism is regarded as essential for justification, and so for eternal life. As we shall see, our confidence in this respect comes from the Lord Himself. The second choice is from another letter attributed to St Paul:

> Therefore I, the prisoner of the Lord, implore you to walk in a manner worthy of the calling with which you have been called,

---

[150] Christ, born from the daughter of David. Have mercy on us.
[151] Christ, baptized by John. Have mercy on us.
[152] Christ, risen from the dead. Have mercy on us.

> with all humility and gentleness, with patience, showing tolerance for one another in love, being diligent to preserve the unity of the Spirit in the bond of peace. There is one body and one Spirit, just as also you were called in one hope of your calling; one Lord, one faith, one baptism, one God and Father of all who is over all and through all and in all. But to each one of us grace was given according to the measure of Christ's gift. (Ephesians 4:1-7)

The *oneness* of Baptism referred to here is a critical issue, for the early church insisted that by having the same essential form of baptism we showed our divine unity (this is a feature of the Creed which we saw in lesson 1). This does not mean that the baptismal rite has to be identical in all Churches, only that the form and content be the same in the essentials. What is essential is what is mentioned in the Gospels of St Matthew and St John: that the candidate be baptised with water in the name of the Persons of the Trinity. The third choice is from the First Letter of St Peter:

> But sanctify Christ as Lord in your hearts, always being ready to make a defence to everyone who asks you to give an account for the hope that is in you, yet with gentleness and reverence; and keep a good conscience so that in the thing in which you are slandered, those who revile your good behaviour in Christ will be put to shame. For it is better, if God should will it so, that you suffer for doing what is right rather than for doing what is wrong. For Christ also died for sins once for all, the just for the unjust, so that He might bring us to God, having been put to death in the flesh, but made alive in the spirit; in which also He went and made proclamation to the spirits now in prison, who once were disobedient, when the patience of God kept waiting in the days of Noah, during the construction of the ark, in which a few, that is, eight persons, were brought safely through the water. Corresponding to that, baptism now saves you—not the removal of dirt from the flesh, but an appeal to God for a good conscience—through the resurrection of Jesus Christ. (1 Peter 3:15-21)

We dealt with this passage in lesson 12. We can add to that that St

Ephrem also sees the ark as an antetype of the Church (the types can have more than one application); the dove which brings Noah the olive leaf is an antetype of the Holy Spirit and the anointing (with a chrism from olive oil) of the Messiah. Ephrem says: "Christ has many facets, and the oil acts as a mirror to them all: from whatever angle I look at the oil, Christ looks out at me from within it." So, links are made between baptism and other events in sacred history.

16.1(f)   The Gospels

The first Gospel available for baptism services is from St Mark:

> The beginning of the good news of Jesus Christ, the Son of God. As it is written in the prophet Isaiah: "See, I am sending my messenger ahead of you, who will prepare your way; the voice of one crying out in the wilderness: "Prepare the way of the Lord, make His paths straight,"

> John the baptizer appeared in the wilderness, proclaiming a baptism of repentance for the forgiveness of sins. And people from the whole Judean countryside and all the people of Jerusalem went out to him, and were baptised by him in the river Jordan, confessing their sins. Now John was clothed with camel's hair, with a leather belt around his waist, and he ate locusts and wild honey. He proclaimed: "The one who is more powerful than I is coming after me; I am not worthy to stoop down and untie the thong of his sandals. I have baptised you with water; but he will baptize you with the Holy Spirit."

> In those days Jesus came from Nazareth of Galilee and was baptised by John in the Jordan. And just as He was coming up out of the water, He saw the heavens torn apart and the Spirit descending like a dove on Him. And a voice came from heaven: "You are My Son, the Beloved; with You I am well pleased." (Mark 1:1-11)

Questions for Contemplation

1. What is the relation between Our Lord and John the Baptist?
2. What sort of character does John the Baptist appear to you to have been?
3. What is the role of the Holy Spirit in this account?

This "John the Baptizer" is also known as "John the Baptist." The second reading possible at baptisms (Matthew 3:13-17) adds little to this which is relevant to us now. They all describe the Baptism of the Lord, which is the *type* while our baptisms are the *antetype*, sharing in the reality of the first Epiphany. The word "epiphany" (Greek *epiphaneia*) means "manifestation" or "visible surface." It is a beautiful term because the baptism of each child is the first public moment when its immortal soul is the subject of a liturgy, and the white robes into which the child is changed serve as a visible sign of its cleansed and purified soul.

The third possible reading is the story from the Gospel of St John 3:1-6 about Nicodemus. It makes the additional point that Our Lord said that we must be born of water and spirit to be able to see and enter the Kingdom of God.

16.1(g)   The Simple Proclamation

This short series of exchanges and replies is often omitted, but it is nonetheless intrinsically interesting. In the course of it, the cantor says: "You (Jesus Christ) came into the world and made baptism to be like a mother bearing forth her children, for everlasting life. ...You sanctified the waters of the Jordan and all the waters when You were baptised . You promised us the kingdom and new life to all who receive Baptism and profess You Lord for evermore."

The application of maternal imagery to baptism, one of the

operations of the Holy Spirit is worth noting, because in the original Syriac tradition the Holy Spirit was referred to by a feminine pronoun. This was not because God was thought to be female: in fact, He is beyond gender. But it was because the Syriac word for "spirit" is female. Although this is a very ancient authentic Christian tradition, it was later changed.[153]

16.1(h) Sealing with the Cross

The most important part of this part of the ceremony is when the priest says:

> In the name of God the almighty Father, who created all things, and whose name is "I Am who I Am"; in the name of the glorious one, the Son of God, who became man and humbled the dominion of the evil one, and urged by his love accepted the wood of the cross and death to save Adam and his children from the slavery of sin;
>
> *(The celebrant places the Cross on the head of the candidate for baptism, saying):*
>
> I sign and seal this lamb, who has come here to become a dwelling place of the Holy Spirit, in the name of the Father, + and of the Son, + and of the Holy Spirit +.

1(i) Renunciation of Satan and Affirmation of the Faith

At this point, the celebrant turns the face of the candidate toward the West (or at least opposite the Altar), to renounce Satan. The godparents and the parents repeat after him: "I renounce you, Satan and all your teachings, and all that is from you." Baptism is the most powerful form of exorcism.

All then turn to face toward the East (the Altar), to proclaim their

---

[153] Johnson, *The Rites of Christian Initiation*, 292..

faith in God. The godparents and the parents repeat after the celebrant: "I believe in You, God the Father, and in Your Son, Our Lord Jesus Christ, and in Your living and Holy Spirit, and in all the teachings of the one, holy, catholic, and apostolic Church." The full Creed is then said.

1(j) Consecration of the Baptismal Water

If the water has already been blessed, this blessing is omitted, but it is full of grandeur and depth. The celebrant opens by praying:

> Glory be to you, Eternal One. Your hidden command supports the universe which your glorious wisdom created. Your miraculous power is visible to your servants in the beauty of your creation, which has no being or existence without You. To You, Lord God, glorious in Your beauty, concealed in the riches of Your nature, but visible in Your wonders, we offer our supplication and prayer. In Your compassion, You receive the penitent, work wonders, and have desired to give us life through Your incomparable love. You sent Your only Son, eternally begotten from You, for our salvation. Even when He descended into the womb of the Virgin to be born in the flesh, He did not leave you. He came to us, and yet He remained with you. He was baptised in the Jordan River, though He had no need for baptism.

> He sanctified baptism for us, and made of it a pure and miraculous womb. By His will, Your will, and the will of the Holy Spirit, He descended into the world in three ways: dwelling in a human womb, in the womb of Baptism, and in the mansions of Sheol.

Inspired by the action of Our Lord in John 20:22-23, when He breathed on the apostles and gave them the power to forgive sins, the priest then breathes on the water in the form of a Cross, saying:

> God the Father, look upon this water placed before You in this humble vessel. May Your Holy Spirit dwell in it. May He fill it with invincible strength. May He bless it, + sanctify it, + and make it + like the water that flowed from the side of Your only

Son on the Cross, cleansing and purifying all those who are baptised in it. May they put on the garment of righteousness, be adorned with heavenly vesture, and be girded with the shield of faith against the arrows of the Evil One. May those who are baptised in this water rise up cleansed, sanctified and wearing the armour of salvation. They will glorify You, Father, your Son and Your Holy Spirit, now and forever.

The celebrant places his thumb in chrism and then mixes it into the water, and "signs" the water in the names of the Persons of the Trinity. He finally prays: "Blessed are you, O glorious Trinity. You have sanctified this water by your power, that it may be a new womb giving birth to spiritual children. To you be glory forever."

This talk about making the water in the font "like" the water which flowed from the side of the Lord is probably based on a Maronite prayer for blessing water in which the water is blessed to *be* the water of creation, the water in which the Lord was baptised, and the water which flowed from His side on the Cross. That is, it is more than a question of being *like* something, it is a question of *being* it. Really, if only we ponder it, we can recognise in all water the water of creation.

1(k) Anointing with Holy Oil on the Forehead

The celebrant then prepares the candidate for baptism by making the sign of the Cross on the candidate's forehead with the baptismal oil, saying:

> (N.) is signed as a lamb in the flock of Christ, with the living oil of divine anointing, in the name of the Father, + and of the Son, + and of the Holy Spirit, + for eternal life.

This is not the baptism itself, but for ages it has preceded it, and seems to show that the different parts of the baptismal liturgy, including the chrismations, before and after, were considered to form one integrated whole.

1(k) The Baptism Proper

I quote from the ceremony itself:

> Baptism is then bestowed, either by pouring the sanctified water on the child's head, or by immersing him/her in the font of sanctified baptismal water. If the water is poured over the child's forehead, it is poured three times. If baptism is by immersion, it is done as follows: the godparent lowers the child into the baptismal font so that the sanctified water covers him/her to the waist. The celebrant holds him/her with his left hand, and with his right hand he three times takes some water from the holy font and pours it over the head of the child and his entire body. Instead of being immersed, adults are baptised by the celebrant's pouring sanctified water on their heads three times, saying:

> **Cel:** "(N.) is baptised, a lamb in the flock of Christ, in the name of the Father + and of the Son + and of the Holy Spirit + for eternal life."

> The godparents or parents lift the newly baptised from the baptismal font and dries their body. The parents now clothe them with the white garment of baptism, while the celebrant says:

> "Behold, you have put on the living Father; you have received Christ the Son; you have adorned yourself with the Holy Spirit; and you have accepted the robe of glory which Adam had taken off."

I have already explained this imagery. Note that we do not say "I baptise", but rather that the child is baptised, meaning that God is the actor. There now follows Chrismation, which is the sacrament known as "Confirmation" in the Latin Church.

16.2 Chrismation

First of all, it is just an accident of history that in the Latin Church, Confirmation (what we call "Chrismation") is not administered together with Baptism. In fact, although the very earliest history is a little unclear, Baptism, Chrismation and the Eucharist were once administered together in both the Eastern *and the* Western Churches. Being administered together, it was not so much a question of *baptising* candidates for the faith, as it was of *initiating* them.[154] As mentioned above, both the pre- and post-baptismal anointings were considered part of one coherent and inter-related ritual. Clear signs of this are still present even in the new Maronite baptismal liturgy.

At one point in the West, however, the administration of Baptism, Chrismation and the Eucharist were all separated out, and spoken of as being different sacraments. On one theory, the baptism service grew too long to be united with that for confirmation. Another theory is that the bishop had to administer both baptism and confirmation, and because in France he had huge parishes, he allowed priests to administer baptism.[155] This thesis does not sound satisfactory to me. I am not sure if anyone knows with certainty why the two were separated out. But separated they were, and still are throughout much of the Latin Church. In the Orthodox Churches, the three Sacraments of Imitation are generally first administered together, which is the original Maronite tradition, too. However, it should be borne in mind that when these traditions were being formed, infant baptism was not the rule, even for children born into Christian families. This had the result that those being initiated into all three sacraments were already adults, or at least very often young adults.[156] This separation of the administration of the sacraments had a predictable result:

---

[154] The history of Christian initiation is dealt with at some length in Johnson *The Rites of Christian Initiation*. For Johnson's conclusions, that an integrated rite of initiation including Baptism, Chrismation and the Eucharist are part of the historical Western tradition, and not only the living Eastern tradition, see especially 304-307.

[155] See Johnson, *The Rites of Christian Initiation*, 247-252.

[156] See Johnson, *The Rites of Christian Initiation*, 36, 45. Newman's comments on the prevalence of adult baptism in the Early Church are still the most eloquent statements on the topic known to me: *An Essay on the Development of Christian Doctrine*, edition of 1878, reprinted Christian Classics, Westminster MD, 1968, 127-129. Infant baptism was controversial when it was introduced: see Johnson, *The Rites of Christian Initiation*, 89-90.

Either as "separated" from baptism and first communion, or as an *addition* to baptism and first communion outside of Rome, confirmation will become a rite and sacrament in search of a theological meaning and interpretation ... Since no one could (or would) deny that baptism itself "gave" the Holy Spirit, medieval theologians struggled to find the appropriate language to distinguish and clarify what was now seen as "two" gifts of the Holy Spirit in Christian initiation.[157]

That being so, what is the difference between the two sacraments of Baptism and Chrismation? One theory is that Chrismation is specifically designed so that the one baptised has the ability and the courage to spread the Christian faith. On this view, Baptism is the entry to the faith, and Chrismation is to do with the sharing of it, that is, with evangelisation. There have also been theories put forward about Baptism bringing innocence but Chrismation being for adulthood in the faith, and also that Chrismation brings the fullness of sanctity.

However, when it comes to the Eastern Churches, there is also a theory that searching for distinctions is misguided. The original Eastern concept of the Sacraments is not the same as that which was developed in the West, which limits the sacraments to seven different rites. Interestingly, the Western Church has started to move in the direction of the Eastern idea that the Church itself and its actions are sacraments, or more precisely, *mysteries*.[158]

Liturgically, the main difference between them is that *that part of the historical initiation rite which deals just with Baptism* is centred on Our Lord's baptism in the Jordan River by John the Baptist, while fully acknowledging the presence and the operation of the Father and the Holy Spirit. However, *that part of what was historically the initiation rite which deals just with Chrismation* is focussed on the Holy Spirit and His work in completing and strengthening the results of the Son's work. So while it is a simplification, it might not be an undue or unfair

---

[157] Johnson, *The Rites of Christian Initiation*, 252-253.
[158] Johnson, *The Rites of Christian Initiation*, 299.

simplification to see Baptism and Chrismation as two sacraments so closely related as to form one united reality, in which the emphasis moves from Our Lord Jesus Christ and the Father (and the mystery of adoption as children of God) to the Holy Spirit (and the mystery of His ongoing work in us).

It is known that in the ancient Church there was a ceremony of laying-on of hands which was associated with baptism and the reception of the Holy Spirit. There are traces of this is Acts 8 and 19, and Hebrews 6. However, how it was ordinarily administered, and in particular whether it was ideally separated from Baptism in the Apostolic Church are not known.

Our modern Maronite Rite of Chrismation is set out in the next section. Where a Maronite child has been baptised according to Latin rite, and not received either Chrismation or Confirmation, that child can receive just that part of the Maronite Rite of Chrismation (even if historically speaking it is more accurate to think of this as being one part of the initiation ritual).

2(a) Invocation of the Holy Spirit

Cel: *(places his right hand on the head of the candidate, saying):* Living Father, may Your living Holy Spirit descend upon the head of Your servant (N.) and dwell in him/ her. May he/she be signed with Your name, and the name of Your only Son, and of Your living Spirit, the comforter and forgiver of sins. May the body and soul of Your servant, who has been signed with You, be sanctified. May his/her conscience be confirmed in Your knowledge and may his/her mind be filled with faith in You, that he/she may glorify You, Your Christ, and Your living Holy Spirit, now and forever.

2(b) The Anointing with Chrism

Cel: *(Dips his right thumb in the Chrism and with it he signs the forehead of the newly baptised in the form of a Cross, three times,* *saying):* With the Chrism of Christ our God, the sweet fragrance of the true faith, the seal and fullness of the grace of the Holy Spirit, this servant of God (N.) is sealed in the name of the Father + and of the Son + and of the Holy Spirit +.

Cel: *(signing the newly confirmed with the Cross, says):* Confirm, Lord, this Your servant in holiness of soul and body. Perfect him/her with the gift of the Holy Spirit. Strengthen his/her soul in the way of Your life-giving commandments, that he/she may be worthy to enjoy the grace of adoption and the inheritance of Your heavenly kingdom. Father, Son, and Holy Spirit, to You be glory forever.

That is the text. Now the candidate has been both baptised and confirmed.

2(c) Procession with the Newly Confirmed and Baptised

The instructions read:

Bells or "nawaqees" are rung joyfully for the newly baptised. In procession, everyone returns from the baptismal font to the front of the altar, the priest censing and leading the way. One of the godparents holds the newly baptised along with the hand cross. They process up to three times around the church, carrying candles, usually singing the "Ya Oumallah." Then, when we reach the altar, the priest says:

Your new child in the Spirit, now worships You, Lord. The poor one who has become rich, the dead one who has risen, gives thanks to You. Perfect him/her, Lord, with Your gift. Give him/her a share in Your Church, that his/her tongue may sing thanks to You, and that with a radiant face he/she may call upon You saying:

Then we say the "Our Father," The Lord's Prayer. A final prayer includes all the themes from the ceremony:

Lord Jesus Christ Our God, You grant forgiveness of sins to those who have been born by water and Spirit from baptism and chrism. Enlighten the heart of Your servant who has been baptised. As You have enabled him/her to be a child of Your grace, keep him/her secure as one of Your treasured children, by Your mercy.

Be pleased with him/her, that having been purified in the waters of Your holy covenant, he/she may be among those who are a royal priesthood, a holy nation, a redeemed people, a blessed community. Then, when he/she shall lay aside the visible garment of this body, grant that he/she may not lay You aside, Christ, the hidden and invisible garment; but be for him/her a new and imperishable garment.

For You have compassion and save all who come to You, our Lord and God. To You be glory and thanks, to Your Father and to Your Holy Spirit, forever.

The most important part of this is how the prayers unite the whole course of our lives in the one thought: Christ is the invisible robe of light.[159] As we have put Him on in baptism, may we be clothed in Him when the end comes.

---

[159] As mentioned, the robe of light can also be considered as the "Holy Spirit."

Lesson 17

The Eucharist

17.1 Introduction

A full understanding of the Sacrament of the Eucharist requires the context of the Divine Sacrifice of the Mass, for the Sacrament is always prepared and consecrated in the Mass, even if it is sometimes distributed outside the Mass. However, in this lesson, we shall take the Eucharist alone.

The "Eucharist" or thanksgiving, can be understood in at least two ways: first, as the actual particle of transubstantiated bread which is distributed at communion, what in Arabic is called the *birshān*. Before it has been consecrated it is only named *qurbān*, the "offering." These words come from Syriac. "Offering" or "oblation" is clear enough, but *biršān* is less obvious. The word comes from a root meaning "to raise to power": "to constitute (as king, emperor, etc.)." In other words, what was offered to God has been accepted and raised to power, it has been constituted as Jesus Christ Our Lord.

A second meaning of the word "Eucharist" is "the Divine Sacrifice of the Mass" in which the climax and the very reason for the celebration is the consecration of the *qurbān* of bread, wine and water as the *biršān*, Our Lord Jesus Christ Himself.[160] That is, the species of bread, water and wine are changed into Our Lord in His full humanity and divinity. The term "transubstantiation" is often used.[161] There is no doubt that the species do change in the Mass, and become Our Lord Himself: it has no meaning without this. The priest prays, time and again, for the Holy Spirit: "to make it the life-giving bread" (from the Anaphora of the Twelve Apostles). This is what the Maronite church unequivocally teaches.

17.2 Historical Foundation

The fact is that the Church has always said that Our Lord Himself instituted the Sacrament of the Eucharist at the Last Supper on Holy Thursday, the evening before He died. This is now under challenge from scholars, but the tradition of the Church is most unlikely to change.[162]

St Mark records the Last Supper in terms similar to those we find in the Gospels of Ss Matthew and Luke:

> While they were eating, He took some bread, and having blessed, He broke it, and gave it to them, and said: "Take it; this is My body." And when He had taken a cup and given thanks, He gave it to them, and they all drank from it. And He said to them: "This is My blood of the covenant, which is poured out for many. Amen, I say to you, I will never again drink of the fruit of the vine until that day when I drink it new in the kingdom of God." (Mark 14:22-25)

The last Gospel to be written was that of St John. His account of the

---

[160] It is said that He is present "in His body, blood, soul and divinity." This definition is a late one, taken from the Latin Church. The early sources do not speak like this. However, not to use the phrase at least once could suggest that it is denied: and that is not the case.

[161] Despite the present trend away from it, I would contend that the word "transubstantiation" is a very good one for the Eucharist.

[162] I have myself written an academic article criticising the modern challenge. Joseph Azize: "The Institution of the Eucharist in the Gospel of John, the Didache and Ignatius of Antioch," *Universitas*, 504, 5 (2016), 3-35.

Last Supper is quite lengthy. He does not give the words of consecration (which we call the "Institution Narrative"), but he gives a lot of other important material. With St John, we need to begin with chapter 6 and the feeding of the five thousand. The early Church saw this feeding as relevant to the Eucharist. It was not perceived as being the *same* as the Eucharist, but it was believed to be *analogous*, meaning "partially similar, parallel." Then Our Lord said to the crowd something which refers to the Eucharist:

> "Amen, amen, I say to you, it is not Moses who has given you the bread out of heaven, but it is My Father who gives you the true bread out of heaven. For the bread of God is that which comes down out of heaven, and gives life to the world ... I am the bread of life; he who comes to Me will not hunger, and he who believes in Me will never thirst." ...

> Therefore the Jews were grumbling about Him, because He said: "I am the bread that came down out of heaven." They were saying: "Is not this Jesus, the son of Joseph, whose father and mother we know? How does He now say: "I have come down out of heaven'? Jesus answered and said to them: "Do not grumble among yourselves. ... I am the bread of life. Your fathers ate the manna in the wilderness, and they died. This is the bread which comes down out of heaven, so that one may eat of it and not die. I am the living bread that came down out of heaven; if anyone eats of this bread, he will live forever; and the bread also which I will give for the life of the world is My flesh."

> Then the Jews began to argue with one another, saying: "How can this man give us His flesh to eat?" So Jesus said to them: "Amen, amen, I say to you, unless you eat the flesh of the Son of Man and drink His blood, you have no life in yourselves. He who eats My flesh and drinks My blood has eternal life, and I will raise him up on the last day. For My flesh is true food, and My blood is true drink. He who eats My flesh and drinks My blood abides in Me, and I in him. As the living Father sent Me, and I live because of the Father, so he who eats Me, he also will live because of Me. This is the bread which came down out of

heaven; not as the fathers ate and died; he who eats this bread will live forever." (from John 6)

Our Lord was not speaking figuratively. He was speaking about the Eucharist, and saying, as clearly as possible, that we would have to eat His flesh and drink His blood. This is clear, because, when many of the disciples said that it was a hard teaching, Our Lord did not tell them that He was only speaking metaphorically. No, he insisted, rather, that what He was saying is "spirit and life" (John 6:60-63).

St Paul sets out the teaching of the Last Supper in 1 Corinthians 11:23-26. This is quite a good set of testimonies. On the basis that the New Testament was completed by 100 A.D., although it may have been earlier, there is good evidence that Our Lord commanded the disciples to regularly commemorate what He did at the Last Supper. St Paul's testimony is clearly of special importance: if all we had was the Gospel accounts, then you could say that they merely related what Our Lord had said, and you might not understand that He intended us to take His words as an ongoing commandment to continue commemorating Him. You could even be forgiven for thinking that only the bread and wine before Him were His blood and flesh. But St Paul's testimony makes that argument completely untenable. Paul's Letter to the Corinthians shows that the entire Church took the events of the Last Supper as instituting the Eucharist according to the principles we use today.

St Paul was also concerned with how people received the Eucharist:

> So then, whoever eats the bread or drinks the cup of the Lord in an unworthy manner will be guilty of sinning against the body and blood of the Lord. Everyone ought to examine themselves before they eat of the bread and drink from the cup. For those who eat and drink without discerning the body of Christ eat and drink judgment on themselves. (1 Corinthians 11:27-29)

Questions for Contemplation

1. What would be an "unworthy manner" of receiving the Eucharist?

2. What sort of examination may St Paul have had in mind here?

3. How can making a bad communion be a "judgment" on myself?

This still applies: while the Eucharist works for the forgiveness of sins, there is a question of degree. If I am in not in a state of grace, that is, if I have a mortal sin on my soul, I cannot approach the Eucharist. Otherwise, if I am only in venial sin, then taking the Eucharist with contrition works the forgiveness of those sins. We shall see this again when we come to the Divine Sacrifice of the Mass, but the Eucharist is given for forgiveness: all we have to do is to receive it worthily.

People are sometimes confused by this: if we are in sin, the Eucharist works absolution, but if too much sin, then we consume it to our detriment? How can this be?

The Lord is merciful to those who have sinned and are contrite. But if the sin is a very serious one then they must first approach the Sacrament of Confession to obtain their penance and absolution, because mortal sin is inimical to having any grace in one's soul, and it would be wrong to accept the Lord without some grace. One might think of going to the gym if you're tired: if you're a bit tired, going will wake you up. If you're too tired, you can hurt yourself.

Although it is not to be found in the New Testament, the requirement of the Church that each Christian receive the Eucharist at least once a year during the Season of the Resurrection has been adopted by the Maronite Church as being edifying, and consistent with good sense and policy. This is not to be confused with attending the Sunday celebration of the Divine Sacrifice of the Mass. That obligation remains even if one does not receive the Eucharist. There was once a concern among priests that people were attending Mass but not sufficiently receiving the Eucharist. If anything, the greater danger today is that people are attending Mass but not sufficiently preparing for communion. The ideal is to attend and make a good preparation, and that being so, then receive the Eucharist.

17.3 St Ignatius of Antioch

St Ignatius is a most important witness to the Eucharist since he was martyred during the reign of the Emperor Trajan (98-117), and therefore is the earliest named author to witness to the importance of the Eucharist to the Church. Further, because of his role as the third bishop of Antioch (St Peter being the first, and Evodius the second), he is seminal for the development of the Eucharist in our Maronite tradition.

St Ignatius wrote seven epistles: those to the Ephesians, Magnesians, Trallians, Romans, Philadelphians, the Smyrnaeans and to Bishop Polycarp.

In all of his epistles, St Ignatius is concerned for the unity of the Church. He is famous, indeed, for being the earliest clear witness to the three-fold hierarchy of bishop, priest and deacon.[163] This is the basis of the unity of the church, which is a *sacramental* unity. He writes:

> Be careful therefore to use one Eucharist (for there is one flesh of Our Lord Jesus Christ, and one cup for union with His blood, one altar, as there is one bishop with the presbytery and the deacons my fellow servants), in order that whatever you do you may do it according to God. (*Philadelphians* 4.1)

In another epistle, he says: "Let no man be deceived: unless a man be within the sanctuary he lacks the bread of God ..." (*Ephesians* 5:2). The bishop and the priest are the centre of the gathering in which the

---

[163] See my article: "Ignatius of Antioch on the Ecclesiastical Hierarchy: Logic and Methodology," *Phronema*, 30(2), 2015, 105-136.

community unites in "breaking one bread, which is the medicine of immortality, the antidote that we should not die, but live for ever in Christ." (*Ephesians* 20.2).[164] This would appear to be the basis of the Maronite tradition that Jesus is the "Good Physician," something we still say in our Mass today.

There are some other references to the Eucharist in St Ignatius (e.g. that he desires the bread of God, which is the flesh of Jesus Christ, and also for drink he desires his blood, which is "incorruptible love," *Romans* 7.3 and likewise *Smyrnaeans* 7.1).

The references to the unity of the Church are also significant, because Ignatius is known to have seen the Church as being one catholic whole – in fact, he is the first writer known to have used the word "Catholic" for the Church:

> Wherever the bishop appears let the congregation be present; just as wherever Jesus Christ is, there is the Catholic Church. It is not lawful either to baptise or to hold an *agape* (Eucharistic gathering) without the bishop ... (*Smyrnaeans* 8.2).

Taken as a whole, these references show us a sacramental view of the Eucharist, going far beyond mere table-fellowship. If it was only a question of coming together for a meal, how could the host be the medicine of immortality? And what of the references to it as being the body and blood of Our Lord? This cannot be merely coincidence, for just these words are used in the Synoptic Gospels. It seems to me that St Ignatius not only points to a Eucharist which is thought of as described in the Gospels and in St Paul, but to a tradition wherein it is the mark of the universal Church that the Eucharist is celebrated by the faithful who see themselves as one people for whom the ecclesiastical hierarchy is a sign of unity.

---

[164] So too, but for the reference to the medicine of immortality, see *Smyrnaeans* 8.1 and 2. The same epistle at 12.2 uses the flesh and blood of the Lord to greet Christians.

17.4.   St Ephrem

That the Eucharist is for the forgiveness of sins and for eternal life features prominently in St Ephrem, thus in Hymn 1 of the *Hymns on the Unleavened Bread*, he writes:

> Even though Adam killed the life within his body,
> there was within [his body] a type (*Toofso*) of the body that has perfected all.
> Behold, [through that body] the just are perfected and their sins are forgiven![165]

Adam killed himself through sin, but our bodies are antetypes of the type which is the Body of the Lord, which is given to us in the Eucharist, and through that we are forgiven and perfected. Here we see St Ephrem's typological thinking as being a form of logic: because there is this connection of types, there is a connection in the physical world – the type has an influence upon the antetypes. Typology is also a way of thinking because one can use it to investigate: the antetypes in the world exhibit the type (although not necessarily in a pure form), and the type shows us the potentialities inherent in the antetypes.

Of the Last Supper, Ephrem writes:

> He broke the bread with his hands as a symbol for the sacrifice of his body.
> He mixed the cup with his hands as a symbol for the sacrifice of his blood.
> He sacrificed and offered himself, the priest of our atonement.
> He clothed himself in the priesthood of Melchizedek, his type (*Toofseh*) ...[166]

For Ephrem, the connection with the Last Supper is absolutely real, hence he says of the apostles: "Between lamb and lamb stand the

---

[165] Hymn 1, *Ephrem the Syrian's Hymns on the Unleavened Bread*, trans. J. Edward Walters, Gorgias, Piscataway, 2012, §10.

[166] Hymn 2, *Ephrem the Syrian's Hymns on the Unleavened Bread*, §7 and 8a. The imagery of our prayer "O Lord, you are the pleasing Oblation" may well have been taken from this hymn, or else the two may share a source, so many are the parallels between the two.

disciples, they ate the pascal lamb and the true lamb."[167] They ate the pascal lamb at that supper and then were given the Lord's body (the true lamb). Ephrem draws out a paradox: the lamb (of God) ate the (pascal) lamb, and so:

> ... the symbol hastened to enter the belly of truth.
> For all the types (*Toofse*) in the Holy of Holies
> dwelt and anticipated the one who fulfils all.
> And when the symbols saw the true lamb,
> they tore the curtain and stepped out to meet him.
> They were all entirely based on and established for Him;
> for they all proclaimed everything about Him everywhere.
> For in Him the symbols (*roze*) and types (*Toofse*) were fulfilled,
> as He sealed it: "Behold all is fulfilled."[168]

This makes reference to the fact that in the Temple in Jerusalem, the Holy of Holies was the most sacred space. It was veiled from the rest of the Temple, and the High Priest alone could enter it, and even he could only do so but once a year to offer sacrifice and incense on the solemn feast of Yom Kippur (the Day of Atonement). The Book of Hebrews gives the Christian understanding of it as follows:

> Behind the second curtain was a room called the Most Holy Place, which had the golden altar of incense and the gold-covered ark of the covenant. This ark contained the gold jar of manna, Aaron's staff that had budded, and the stone tablets of the covenant. Above the ark were the cherubim of the Glory, overshadowing the atonement cover. ... When everything had been arranged like this, the priests entered regularly into the outer room to carry on their ministry. But only the high priest entered the inner room, and that only once a year, and never without blood, which he offered for himself and for the sins the people had committed in ignorance (Hebrews 9:3-7).

When Our Lord was on the Cross, on that first Good Friday, when

---

[167] Hymn 6, *Ephrem the Syrian's Hymns on the Unleavened Bread*, §1.
[168] Hymn 6, *Ephrem the Syrian's Hymns on the Unleavened Bread*, §10b-14. I have slightly corrected the translation in the last verse, where it was a little free.

He was ready to die, He said: "It is finished" (*tetelestai*). Further, St Matthew tells us, at the moment of His death: "… the curtain of the temple was torn in two from top to bottom."[169]

This all goes to show that the ultimate reality is found in Our Lord, and in the most holy Sacrament of the Eucharist ("the lamb of the type was without blemish").[170] History is centred on the Lord and the Eucharist.

Further, wherever we are, the Eucharist in which we participate is mystically united with all such sacrifices. St Paul said: "Is not the cup of thanksgiving for which we give thanks a participation in the blood of Christ? And is not the bread that we break a participation in the body of Christ? Because there is one loaf, we, who are many, are one body, for we all share the one loaf" (1 Corinthians 10:16-17). This idea is taken by St Ephrem who sees significance in the consideration that when He performed the miracles of the feeding of the multitudes, Our Lord broke twelve loaves of bread in all, but at the Last Supper, He broke but one: "… the symbol of the body, the Only-begotten [born] of Mary."[171]

17.5 Jacob of Sarug

St Ephrem's insight that to penetrate the secret of types is to penetrate the secret of God in history and the world, and so to come closer to reality, was taken up by Jacob of Sarug, who wrote in his homilies on partaking of the Eucharist:

> Come to prayer and bring along your whole self (*taw laSlooto wayto Koolok neete 3amoK*),
> do not let your mind stay in the market with the business.
> If you are here, let your inner person,

---

[169] See John 19:30 and Matthew 27:51.

[170] Hymn 9, *Ephrem the Syrian's Hymns on the Unleavened Bread*, §24. The translation has "typological lamb," while the Syriac has "the lamb of the type" (*emar Toofso*).

[171] Cited in Robert Murray, *Symbols of Church and Kingdom*, Gorgias, Piscataway, 2004, pp. 76-77 (first published 1957 and revised in 1977).

also be here inside the gate of the crowned one.
Why is your mind out roaming after affairs,
So that when you are here you are not here but there?
… Stand to pray a collected, unified and true man.[172]

In other words, while we receive from the Eucharist, we must also prepare for it. Jacob advises us to speak to our souls (as it were), reminding ourselves that we are sick and wounded, and that now the time to approach the medicine of the Eucharist has come.[173] At this time, the doors of heaven are open, and our petitions can be heard.[174] He continues:

This is the time when the Son of God
is immolated and set upon the table for sinners to forgive them.
This is the time when the gates and curtains permit
the sacrifice to come in and the mercy to go out for sinners.[175]

Having prepared for the Eucharist, and then having received it, the question is how shall we live? A pearl is kept with great care in a treasured casket. So too, the body and blood of the Saviour, which are the pearls of life, must be received in a cleansed and purified container: our bodies.[176] In the *Hoosoye* (from the Liturgy of the Word), and during the Liturgy of the Eucharist there are rites of confession within the Divine Liturgy itself, which are capable of the remission of what we refer to as *venial* or *lesser* sins. Therefore, although many people may not wish to approach the Eucharist with any unconfessed sins on their consciences, this caution is not necessary except in the grave case of *mortal* sins.

---

[172] *Jacob of Sarug's Homily on the Partaking of the Holy Mysteries*, trans. Amir Harrak, Gorgias, Piscataway, 2013, 89-94 and 99.

[173] *Jacob of Sarug's Homily on the Partaking of the Holy Mysteries*, 279-284.

[174] *Jacob of Sarug's Homily on the Partaking of the Holy Mysteries*, 285-286.

[175] *Jacob of Sarug's Homily on the Partaking of the Holy Mysteries*, 289-292.

[176] Tanios Bou Mansour, *La Théologie de Jacques de Saroug*, Kaslik, vil. I, 1993, p. 293.

Lesson 18

The Divine Sacrifice of the Mass

18.1 The Divine Sacrifice of the Mass

The Maronite Divine Sacrifice of the Mass is a supernatural event in which we are privileged to be allowed to participate. It is essentially a Mystery or Sacrament of "Eucharist."

There is a lot of elasticity in the terms that are used for the liturgy. One and the same word can often be used in different ways. The word "Mass" is English, but originally it was Latin. The celebrations of non-Latin Catholics are often not called "Masses," but "Divine Liturgies." However, other terms can be used. The Arabic word *qaddaas* (pronounced *addās* in Lebanese) means something like "the holy matters." The Syriac word *qoorbono* means "the offering," and is the Syriac version of the Greek word *anaphora*, which is used both for the Mass and for the Liturgy of the Eucharist.

The Divine Liturgy is also the highest form of worship possible for humans, and worship is the highest form of human activity. The Divine Liturgy is adoration and it is prayer; and also thanksgiving and praise. The Mass unites all those within the parish, diocese and the church (whether on earth, in Purgatory or in heaven). It operates therefore, as a factor to unite us with each other and with all the Church. The Mass includes all of these purposes even when celebrated by one priest alone, but the Maronite liturgy is written as the service of a community, and assumes the presence of a congregation.

In the Syriac tradition, Adam was seen as being the first priest, and he was created not only: "to cultivate and care for the Garden of Eden" (Genesis 2:15) but to *worship* and to care for it (the Hebrew word used for "cultivate" also means "worship"). Psalm 139:5, which can be taken as referring to Adam, speaks of hands being laid on. Because that phrase also means "ordain" in Syriac, it too points to Adam's being a priest.

We must not lose sight of the central reality of *worship*, even if this big picture is made up of smaller pictures. For example, the Divine Liturgy is also an excellent means of instruction. Without knowing it, we absorb spirituality and teaching through the Mass. We hear the Epistle and Gospel, we hear the words of the prayers, and something sinks in. We hear the music and the chants, and without knowing it, we start to acquire the attitude they embody. If we are in sympathy with our faith, these words and chants will evoke a sense of reverence in us. Many people have remarked how great an impact it made on them when they were merely passing by a church, to hear the sound of singing from a distance. Repetition has a tremendous value because it fashions strong links between the intellect and the feeling. However, variety is also needed, and the Divine Liturgy of the Catholic and Orthodox Churches are masterpieces of the balance of repetition and novelty, the familiar and the fresh, the traditional and the contemporary.

From the liturgical action as a whole, we also absorb a *sense* of what it means to be a Maronite. The way the priest and the servers move, the way the liturgy is chanted, the gestures of the hands, often with the hand-cross, the altar, crucifixes, icons, statues, candles, all the furnishings of the church play a part in creating a sense of the sacred. The architects of the traditional churches in Lebanon understood this well.

The old churches have few windows, and these are often high up (such a window is called a *Tāqah*) allowing in beams rather than streams of light, which touch a space rather than illuminate the whole. This produces a world of shadows and shafts of light. The churches were designed to be darker than other buildings, so that the altar would be illuminated by the two candles which stand beside it (not on it, the Maronite altar should only have the essentials and should never be used as a shelf), and by the light which comes in from the windows above it. When the sun comes in through those high windows, it seems to be the finger of God. The three windows close together above and behind the altar, when struck by the morning sun, produce one burst of light from three nodes, thus making a natural symbol of the Trinity. An example of this is found on the front cover illustration, which is from *kneeseh Mar Mama* (the church of St Mama) in Ehden, dating from the ninth century AD, making it the oldest continually used church in all of the Middle East.

Absolutely fundamental to this is the orientation of the church to the East, so that when the sun rises in the East, it rises above the altar, and its rays can enter the windows above the altar. It is noticeable that old churches in Lebanon all face East; it is only new churches which seem designed to face in any direction but. So basic is this feature that all Maronite churches must have been built to face East with three windows above the altar. Varghese studied the evidence and concluded that:

> The eschatological dimension of the liturgy is permanently marked in the ordo, in the prayer towards the East, a custom that

goes back to the beginning of the second century. ... Since the time of the expulsion, all children of Adam and Eve look back to their former home, the Paradise in the East, with a deep sense of spiritual nostalgia. We turn to the East in order to remind ourselves that we have to turn to God our Creator and to return to the joyful communion with God and with the entire creation as experienced by Adam and Eve before their Fall. The eastward orientation is an act of repentance. It stands for hope and homecoming.[177]

This exemplifies the architectural tradition of the whole Syriac Church. A Syriac hymn on the church at Edessa, c.540 reads:

(1) [Thou], divine Being, who dwells in the holy Temple,
the glory of which, in turn, [derives] from your doing so,
Give me the grace of the Holy Spirit;
that I may speak [worthily] of the church of Urwhāy.
... (3) clearly represented in it are the mysteries
both of thy Being and of thy divine dispensation;
and whoever looks at it;
is filled with wonder at what he sees ...
(13) the sanctuary, too, is illumined by one equal light;
which is admitted to it by way of three windows
and this proclaims to us the mystery of the Trinity;
of Father, Son and Holy Ghost.[178]

In addition to all of this, there is a progression in the Maronite Divine Liturgy. When we enter the church for Mass, we are leaving earth and approaching the threshold of heaven. As Fr Varghese says: "The architecture reveals that, in the liturgy, heaven and the earth stand face to face."[179] The progress of the Mass is our progress in ascending the mountain of God: this is implicit in the liturgy, as we shall see, but the association of worship and ascending His holy mountain is ancient, and was noted in the Psalms:

---

[177] Baby Varghese, *West Syrian Liturgical Theology*, Ashgate, Aldershot, 2004, 109.

[178] Richard Maitland Bradfield, *A Syrian Archive: Being a study of the early churches and convents on the limestone massif, north Syria, AD. 324-451, and of their consequences in the far West (to c.540)*, published by the author at Derby, 2010, 174-176.

[179] Varghese, *West Syrian Liturgical Theology*, 165.

Who may ascend the mountain of the Lord?
Who may stand in his holy place?
The one who has clean hands and a pure heart,
who does not trust in an idol
or swear by a false god.[180]

There is prevalent a folk-belief that the low doorways of the old churches in Lebanon were to stop the Turks riding in on horseback and cutting off people's heads. This is not so: the churches had low doorways when we were at peace, long before the Turks arrived. The low doorways were for the express purpose of making a person bow his head in humility. Further, the darkness of the Church, which is not a complete darkness, adds to the sense that here we are in a different realm: even the atmosphere is different, and space is bent, folding in upon the altar. The rays of the sun enter through high windows so as to fall just upon the altar, nowhere else. Candles are lit and their naturally flickering light provides a very different type of illumination from electric lighting. It is not so easy to read by this light, but it touches the feeling in a deeper way.

Fr Anthony Salim is, in my view, correct in principle when he writes: "Undoubtedly, the chief characteristic of the Syriac Church is its sense of awe and wonder before the Divine Mystery. ... there is a wonderful balance of dreadful majesty and loving compassion, of abasement and exaltation."[181] Of course, we sometimes fall short, but we should strive to improve our churches, our services and the level of our understanding.

As Catholics we believe that God wills to be worshipped according to the rite of the Eucharist, which we call the Divine Liturgy. This is a

---

[180] Psalm 24:3-4.
[181] Anthony Salim, *Captivated by your Teachings*, Tucson (2002) 242.

fact of history: it is the teaching of the Church.[182] The word "liturgy" only entered the English language recently. It is originally Greek. In its Eastern usage it only ever refers to the Divine Liturgy, the solemn Eucharistic assembly of the Church. In the West, today, the word "liturgy" refers to any cultic action.[183]

Second, we believe, as all Catholics and Orthodox believe, that the Divine Liturgy also involves a sacrifice. It is the sacrifice of Calvary offered upon the altars of every church. It is the bread and wine becoming, quite literally and objectively, and not merely subjectively, Our Lord Jesus Christ, in his body, blood, soul and divinity. The Eucharistic sacrifice is known in the Latin Church as a Sacrament, but in the Maronite Church as a "mystery" or "secret." This is probably because the supernatural aspect of the Mysteries remains hidden. Incidentally, this ties in with the theological emphasis in the Maronite tradition on the hiddenness of God.

18.2 The Scheme of the Mass

We commence with the Liturgy of the Word (or *synaxis*) wherein we hear the word of God, and we offer Him our praise and prayers. Then, after the Liturgy of the Word, we have the pre-Anaphora (during which the oblations are brought up), and then the Liturgy of the Eucharist (or the *anaphora*) where the priest ascends and enters the threshold of heaven, and the congregation join the angelic hosts as the divine sacrifice is offered at the altar, and the Holy Spirit descends upon us

---

[182] No Christian doubted this until Luther separated out the Scriptures from the tradition which had created, preserved and transmitted them. He set Scripture over and against the rest of the tradition. Luther believed that he could tell what was Scripture and what was not, and worse, that he knew "Christ" so well that he could change or dispense with Scripture. Today's Lutherans have a canon which they accept by reason of tradition. Interestingly, this canon is different from Luther's: he did not accept the Book of Revelation, and although he stated that he had not dispensed with the Epistle of St James, in practice he did.

[183] A.G. Martimort, ed., *Principles of the Liturgy*, vol. 1, by I.H. Dalmais, P.M. Gy, P. Jounel and A.G. Martimort, 1986, 8-9.

and upon our offerings.

There are many indications of this ritual of journeying in the Divine Liturgy, and there were even more markers of the transition from one part of the liturgy to the other. For example, when the priest enters the church for the Liturgy of the Word, he goes up to the sanctuary (the raised part of the church where we find the altar, the lecterns and the chairs that the clergy take). But it is only when the Liturgy of the Eucharist commences that the priest goes up to the altar. This is reflected in the chants which the priest intones. When he enters for the Liturgy of the Word, he prays:

l-baitokh aloho 3elet
I have entered your house, O God

But when, after the Liturgy of the Word, he goes up the altar, he humbly declares:

itelwot madbHe daloho walwot
I have come to the altar of God.

Note that the word *3elet* is related to the Arabic root *3aalee*, meaning "high." It does mean to enter, but it also has the association of going up, that is, ascending the mountain of the Lord.

At the old church at Saydit Elige, where the famous icon of Our Lady as a young woman holding the Holy Infant was discovered beneath a more modern painting, one can see how when people entered the church there was a raised platform just inside the entrance, on the left hand side. This was called the *bema*. The Maronite *bema* is different from the Orthodox one. This *bema* is where the Liturgy of the Word was proclaimed.[184] After that, the people would all follow the priest forward, approaching the sanctuary and the altar.

---

[184] The *bema* is of ancient importance, being prominent even in the church at Dura-Europas, destroyed in 256: Allan Doig, *Liturgy and Architecture*, Ashgate, Farnham, Surrey, 2008, 12-13.

We can distinguish various sections of the Liturgy. The first and most obvious division is between the Service of the Word with which the Liturgy opens and the Anaphora (Service of the Eucharist) which comprises its second half. We can consider the Mass to have four parts if we include the introductions to the Service of the Word and the Anaphora.[185] It can be even further broken down into the following main sections:[186]

1 Introductory Rites
Entrance Chant

Opening Prayers

Hoosoye: the Prayer of Atonement, including the *proemion* or first praises, the *sedro* or prayer, the *qolo* or hymn and the *3etro* or incense prayer.

Trisagion (the Thrice-Holy, or *Qadišat Aloho* etc.)[187]

2 Service of the Word
Psalm of the Readings or *mazmooro*

Epistle

Alleluia and chant or *fetgomo* or procession with the scriptures

Gospel

Homily

3 Pre-anaphora
Creed

Approach to the altar

Transfer Procession of the Offerings

Incensing of the Offerings

---

[185] As Fr Salim does, see pp.242-3.

[186] My scheme but partly modifies Fr Salim's, at pp.244-5.

[187] This could also be considered as the first part of the Service of the Word.

4 Eucharistic Prayer: Consecration, Anamnesis and Epiclesis

Rite of Peace
Eucharistic Prayer, including:
Narrative of the Institution of the Eucharist
Memorial of the Son's Plan (Anamnesis)
Invocation of the Holy Spirit (Epiclesis)
(Intercessions)
Lord's Prayer
Communion Rite
Blessing and Dismissal

In Part 4, the Rite of Peace through to the Institution Narrative is addressed to the Father, then the Eucharistic Prayer is addressed to the Son. After a section in which we remember what the Son did (the "anamnesis" or "remembering"), we come to the "Epiclesis" or "invocation", which is addressed to the Holy Spirit.

The Maronite Divine Liturgy possesses five features which make it somewhat distinctive:

1. The *Epiclesis* or invocation of the Holy Spirit over the gifts.
2. The frequent reference to repentance.
3. The role of Mary in the Liturgy.
4. The reiterated mention of the Second Coming of the Lord.
5. There are no Old Testament readings as such, but there is more place given in the Liturgy of the Word for prayerful formulations which make use of both of the Testaments.[188]

18.3 The Liturgy of the Word

The Maronite Entrance Chant sets the theme for the liturgical celebration. It is the start of the Mass. Any paraliturgical activities such

---

[188] There is evidence that the Maronite Liturgy once had Old Testament readings, but that they had disappeared by the 17th century: King (1948) 275.

as censing an icon should be conducted separately from it. Often the celebrant does not cense the icon himself, but has an assistant priest or deacon do so, specifically to indicate that it is not a part of the Mass.

The Entrance Chant is not "an opening hymn" designed to set the stage or produce a mood. It is an intrinsic part of the liturgy, providing content. For example, the entrance chant from the Mass for Saturdays in Pentecost, when we commemorate the Faithful Departed, reads:

> From Your throne above, Lord, You came to earth
> to redeem our mortal race defiled by sin.
> Grant that when we die we may join the saints
> in Your dwellings of pure light and give You praise. ...
> Blessed are the ones who depart this world
> with God's graces as a lamp to light the way.
> Life, with all its pain, passes like the night.
> Lord, your saints for ever sing Your praise on high.

As stated, what is now the access to the altar at the commencement of the service, was originally an access to the church building and *not* to the steps of the altar. When the Liturgy of the Word and its homily were complete, *then* the priest would continue the ascent of the Mountain of the Lord. Only now would he pray at the foot of the altar, and then he would go *behind* the altar, where the bishop's seat symbolised the throne of God the Father. The Maronite Liturgy of the Word would be celebrated from the *bema*, and when that was removed, from the side of the altar, so that the priest was profile to the people. To be face on is to be too directly in the line of sight. That is reserved for the holy mysteries and the altar. In line with this logic, the Liturgy of the Eucharist would be celebrated from behind the altar, with the priest's actions visible to the people. But the emphasis was on the altar, which prevented a good view of the priest.

From one point of view, the role of the people is not essential, as the Mass can be performed without the people. But so far as I can see, this is never contemplated in the Syriac tradition. I may have missed something, but the ancient Syriac documents do not seem to me to ever envisage a private Mass. Indeed, Narsai says that the people "seal" the ministry of the priest with "Amen" on various occasions. He adds:

> With Amen the people subscribe with the priest, and take part
> with him by their prayers and by their word (i.e. Amen).[189]

Returning to the Liturgy of the Word, the "Opening Prayers" commence with an invocation of the Most Holy Trinity, and then a prayer to Our Lord. He may be named as "Jesus Christ" or referred to obliquely as "God the Word." Sometimes others can be associated with Him, as in the Opening Prayer for the Circumcision:

> Lord Jesus, at the beginning of this new year, we celebrate the
> feast of your circumcision, when you were given the name Jesus
> … We ask you through the intercession of the great Saints Basil
> and Gregory …[190]

Then follows the blessing of the incense and a suite of prayers and a hymn which we call the *Hoosoye*. This is a Syriac word. In the singular: "Hoosoyo" it means "atonement," but in the plural "the atonements" it refers to this section of the liturgy. The *Hoosoye* is unique to the Syriac liturgy. It is made up of these parts:

1. The *proemion* or first praises.

2. The *sedro* or prayer (*sedro* means "order," but it comes to mean a prayer in which the opening of each line is in alphabetical order, e.g. the first line begins with *aleph*, the second line with *beta*, etc.).

   3. The *qolo* or hymn.
   4. The *3etro* or incense prayer.

When the *Hoosoye* were first put together, the incense would be

---

[189] *The Liturgical Homilies of Narsai*, R. Hugh Connolly, Cambridge University Press, Cambridge, 1909, 8. I am aware that there is a question of the degree to which we can assume that *everything* Narsai says is directly applicable to the Maronite liturgy. However, where it is possible to check, I have found the liturgy he describes and the ancient Maronite liturgy very close if not identical.

[190] These are St Basil the Great and St Gregory of Nazianzus.

lit and burnt at the time of the *3etro* as a symbol of both our prayers ascending to heaven, and of our sins being consumed as the incense grains are consumed by the burning of the charcoal. The connection of prayer and incense is as ancient as the Old Testament:

> I call to you, Lord, come quickly to me; hear me when I call to You.
> May my prayer be set before You like incense;
> may the lifting up of my hands be like the evening sacrifice.
> (Psalm 141:1-2)

Careful directions were given for its composition from four ingredients (Exodus 30:34), directions attributed to God Himself. The Syriac tradition, which added salt to the incense, and held salt to be composed of water and earth, saw in the burning of incense, a symbol of the four elements (air, earth, fire and water), and therefore, an offering which sent up to heaven elements of the entire creation.[191]

The *Hoosoye* is one of the great examples of how important *repentance* is in our liturgy and our tradition. I deal with this theme further below.

Another important aspect of the *Hoosoye* is how the *proemion* and the *sedro* offer opportunities for melismatic or elaborate chant. They can be spoken, or they can be delivered in a simple recitation on one or two notes. Many people are deeply affected by an experienced cantor who brings to these prayers not a performance but his own faith. When chanted in the traditional fashion, these chants unmistakeably mark the liturgy as being a Syriac liturgy.

Then comes the Trisagion (*Qadišat Aloho, Qadišat Hayeltono, Qadišat Lo-Moyouto*, which we saw in lesson 16). This chant was introduced into the liturgy at some point in the fourth century, possibly in Antioch. It is related to the chants we shall see later in the Liturgy of the Word, and is but another example of the importance of the heavenly vision of Isaiah chapter 6, when the prophet saw the angels singing

---

[191] Varghese, *West Syrian Liturgical Theology*, 157. Varghese ties in other biblical traditions on incense, at 156-157.

"Holy, holy, holy" in the presence of the Lord. This chant is a reminder that what we are doing is replicating the divine liturgy.

Then follows a psalm preparing us for the readings. It is not one of the Old Testament psalms, yet it is a psalm from the Syriac tradition, for the Syriac and Hebrew traditions were very close, and more psalms were written than only the 150 in the Old Testament.[192]

It seems that we did originally have Old Testament readings, for Jacob of Sarug refers to the reading of the prophets.[193] Today, we have only Epistle and Gospel readings.[194] The Gospel reading is followed by a sermon explaining and applying the Gospel. Then the Creed is said by all people. Oddly enough, the Creed was probably introduced into the liturgy by Arians (heretics who had a different view of the faith from that of the orthodox Christians). But it was seen at once that it was a good idea, and the recital of the creed is given pride of place by Narsai (c.399-502) in his liturgical homily 17.[195]

18.4 The Liturgy of the Eucharist

Now comes the second approach, the ascension to the altar. The priest kisses the altar, also attested by Narsai, who states of this that: "He kisses with love and affection the holy altar, and trusts to receive sanctification through his lips." [196]

In the preparation for the Institution Narrative, we have a Rite of Peace, and then the Eucharistic Prayer commences with the Pauline salutation. In 2 Corinthians 13:14, St Paul wrote: "May the grace of

---

[192] In the time of St John Chrysostom (died 407, a contemporary of St Maroun), Christians in Antioch would attend Jewish services in significant numbers, a practice which St John reproved: D.S. Wallace-Hadrill, *Christian Antioch*, Cambridge University Press, Cambridge, 1982, 18-19.

[193] *Jacob of Sarug's Homily on the Partaking of the Holy Mysteries*, 133-134.

[194] It is possible that the introduction and extension of the *Hoosoye* pushed the Old Testament reading out.

[195] *The Liturgical Homilies of Narsai*, 6.

[196] *The Liturgical Homilies of Narsai*, 7.

the Lord Jesus Christ, and the love of God, and the fellowship of the Holy Spirit be with you all." We reproduce that prayer at this point, but change the order to read Father, Son and then Holy Spirit:

> The love of God the Father, and the grace of the only-begotten Son, and the communion and indwelling of the Holy Spirit be with you, my brothers and sisters for ever.

Then the priest prays: "Let us lift up our thoughts, our minds and our hearts," to which the people respond: "Indeed they are before You, O God." The English, possibly under the influence of the Latin, mistranslates *innahā ladayka yā Allāh* as "We lift them up to the Lord." However, it literally means: "Indeed, they are before You, O God." The overall purpose of the Divine Liturgy is to *raise* us from earth to heaven. The "raising" of our faculties shows that we are approaching the Heavenly Throne. Quispel writes:

> The priest says: *Dominus vobiscum:* "The Lord *is* with you," thus affirming that God is present among the faithful through his Spirit. In antiquity the whole congregation answered: *Et cum spiritu tuo*: "And with thy spirit," alluding to the special charism of the priest, which was thought to be enhanced by this acclamation. Thereupon the priest exclaims: *sursum corda*: "Lift up your hearts." The congregation answers: *Habemus ad Dominum:* "We have lifted them up to the Lord." Thereby the faithful affirm that they have ascended here and now to heaven, where Christ reigns in eternal glory.[197]

The Maronite prayer makes this point even clearer than the Latin one. There is an ancient Syriac version in which, for ordinary celebrations, the response is: "To you, God of Abraham, Isaac and Israel, O glorious king." This shows that in the Syriac tradition at least, "God" is probably preferable here to "Lord." But the theology behind this is shown even more starkly on feast days, when the priest says:

> Above in the heavenly heights, in the respectful place of glory,

---

[197] G. Quispel: "The Asclepius," *Gnosis and Hermeticism*, ed. Roelof van den Broek and Wouter J. Hanegraaff, 69.

where does not cease the waving of the wings of the Cherubim, the hallelujahs and the pleasant chanting of hymns of Seraphim, let there be your minds.[198]

Further, from the same liturgy when the priest says: "Peace be with you," the people do not respond: "And also with you," or even "And with your spirit," but rather: "With you and with your spirit."[199] Narsai seems to relate this prayer to when the "priest asks for hidden power with (divine) help, that he may be performing his gift according to his desire …"[200] A little later, Narsai adds:

The people answer the priest lovingly and say: "with thee, O priest, and with that priestly spirit of thine." They call "spirit" not that soul which is in the priest, but the Spirit which the priest received by the laying on of hands. By the laying on of hands the priest receives the power of the Spirit that thereby he may be able to perform the divine Mysteries. That grace that the people call the "Spirit" of the priest, and they pray that he may attain peace with it, and it with him. This makes known that even the priest stands in need of prayer, and it is necessary that the whole Church should intercede for him. Therefore she (the Church) cries out that he may gain peace with his Spirit, that through his peace the peace of all her children may be increased …[201]

This would all seem to show that Quispel was correct in his understanding of the liturgy as an act of heaven taking place upon the earth, and the priest as being an intermediary between the two realms in a unique way.

After these prayers, but before continuing further, there was silence.

---

[198] Jacob Vadakkel, *The East Syrian Anaphora of Mar Theodore of Mopsuestia*, Oriental Institute of Religious Studies, India, Vadavathoor, 1989, 82. A rather similar prayer is attested by Narsai in the sixth century AD: *The Liturgical Homilies of Narsai*, 11-12. Gabriele Winkler says that this is "echoing … the previous tradition that humans are *lifted up* before witnessing the Sanctus." See her article "The Sanctus" in *Prayer and Spirituality in the Early Church*, vol. 3, ed. Bronwen Neil and ors, St Pauls, Strathfield NSW, 2003, 111-133, 129.

[199] Vadakkel, *The East Syrian Anaphora*, 79.

[200] *The Liturgical Homilies of Narsai*, 8.

[201] *The Liturgical Homilies of Narsai*, 8-9.

As Narsai said:

> All the ecclesiastical body now observes silence, and all set themselves to pray earnestly in their hearts. The priests are still and the deacon stands in silence, the whole people is quiet and still, subdued and calm. The altar stands crowned with beauty and splendour, and upon it the Gospel of life and the adorable wood (i.e. the Cross). The mysteries are set in order, the censers are smoking, the lamps are shining, and the deacons are hovering and brandishing (fans) in likeness of watchers. Deep silence and peaceful calm settles on that place ...[202]

The deacons take the role of angels (the watchers), especially by their gentle movement of the fans. This is no longer to be found in our liturgy, but the spirit can still be present.

The liturgy advances to the chant "Holy, holy, holy." As we saw, this was foreshadowed in the *Qadišat Aloho*. Further, it will be alluded to in the prayer before communion: "Holy (things) for the holy." It is based on the vision of the Temple in Jerusalem in Isaiah 6:

> In the year that King Uzziah died, I saw the Lord, high and exalted, seated on a throne; and the train of His robe filled the temple. Above Him were seraphim, each with six wings: With two wings they covered their faces, with two they covered their feet, and with two they were flying. And they were calling to one another:
>
> "Holy, holy, holy is the Lord Almighty;
>
> the whole earth is full of His glory."
>
> At the sound of their voices the doorposts and thresholds shook and the temple was filled with smoke. "Woe to me!" I cried. "I am ruined! For I am a man of unclean lips, and I live among a people of unclean lips, and my eyes have seen the King, the Lord Almighty." Then one of the seraphim flew to me with a live coal in his hand, which he had taken with tongs from the altar. With it he touched my mouth and said: "See, this has touched your lips; your guilt is taken away and your sin atoned for."

---

[202] *The Liturgical Homilies of Narsai*, 12.

Then I heard the voice of the Lord saying: "Whom shall I send?
And who will go for us?" And I said: "Here am I. Send me!"
(Isaiah 6:1-8)

This has the significant implication that by using this prayer we are
at the least drawing a connection with, and more likely recreating the
situation which Isaiah saw in the Temple. We are not only evoking the
presence of God, we are pointing to it as a mystical reality.

18.5 The Institution Narrative

While I was training for the priesthood, I analysed 30 different
anaphoras, most of them Syriac. All of them had the following
features:

> I. *They all make the Eucharist a memorial of the Last Supper.*
> They all assume knowledge of the Gospel story, and unite us with
> it in time, place and purpose.

> II. *They make a statement of Jesus' holiness, and what was done
> with and spoken over the two elements, bread and the chalice in
> which wine and water are mixed.*

Interestingly, many of the anaphoras mention Jesus looking up, and
acknowledging his Father; and His promise of eternal life. These two
features were imported from John 17:1-3.

Also, fully 23 out of 30 of the anaphoras I researched refer to the
mix of wine and water in the chalice, either explicitly stating that
Jesus mixed it, or simply averting to the fact of the mixture. Yet, this
item is not found in the four accounts of the Last Supper. This must
be a tradition of the church, and being found in so many anaphoras,
must antedate the fracturing of Christendom in the East in the wake of
the Councils Ephesus (431) and Chalcedon (451), for nowhere in the
New Testament is Jesus said to have mixed wine and water at the Last
Supper. However, it does accord with the early interpretation of John
19:34 as eucharistic: "But one of the soldiers with a spear opened his

side, and immediately there came out blood and water."

Running through these 30 examples of the words of consecration, with all their individual differences, there is one recognizable framework:

1. A statement of Jesus' purpose at the time of the Last Supper.

2. A statement of when this Supper occurred.

3. A brief description of Jesus' state of holiness is often included here just before telling us what Jesus did and said.

4. Jesus then takes and handles the bread. This includes a distribution of the bread to the disciples, who are more often than not described in broad terms as being both apostles and disciples.

5. Jesus then speaks. The text is invariably identical or almost identical to: "Take, eat it, this is my body which is broken and given for you and for many, for the remission of sins and for eternal life." This tells us both what the bread comprises, and what the purpose of the solemn drama is: the remission of sins and eternal life for many. This closes the first part.

6. A statement usually follows of when Jesus directed his attention to the chalice.

7. Jesus then takes and handles the chalice. As with the bread, the chalice is distributed.

8. Jesus then speaks, saying both what the chalice comprises, and that the purpose of the solemnity is the remission of sins and eternal life for many.

18.6   The Epiclesis

This is that section of the Liturgy which comes after the Institution Narrative and the Memorial of the Son's Plan. It involves the participation of the celebrant, the cantor, and the people, too, and calls upon the priest to make some unique gestures.[203] It includes within

---

[203] This interplay between celebrant, cantor and congregation may, not unfairly, be seen as a Trinitarian element in the Liturgy. Reality is, in a sense, Trinitarian as it comes from the Trinity.

itself a penitential element. It commences with the cantor's prayer:

> How awesome is this hour, O my beloved, in which the Holy
> Spirit will descend, and will overshadow this Eucharist which
> is prepared for our atonement. As we stand praying, saying, in
> divine fear ...[204]

The celebrant bows, then, standing upright, thrice flutters his hands, as if reproducing the activity of a dove. The celebrant then kneels, his head and hands visible from behind the altar, and prays in the words of Elijah's famous invocation on Mount Carmel: "Hear us, O Lord, Hear us, O Lord, Hear us, O Lord. May He come, my Lord, your living and holy spirit." The people respond *"Kyrie eleison, Kyrie eleison, Kyrie eleison"* (Lord have mercy). All of this is to be explained, theologically, by *typology*. This sacrifice (the earthly antetype) *is* the sacrifice of the Lord (the eternal type).[205]

The celebrant kisses the altar, signs the offerings with the Cross, and prays that the Holy Spirit may come down and cause the bread to be the Body of Christ, and the mixture of wine and water to be the Blood of Christ. To each petition, the people respond "Amen" ("may it be made firm/true") and then the celebrant prays for forgiveness, healing, strengthening of conscience, and pure lives.

There is no question except that the bread and mixture of wine and water become the body and blood of Our Lord. It cannot be argued that the transformation takes place only "for us." The Maronite Liturgy clearly speaks of an objective and real change. One cannot twist these words without intellectual dishonesty.

---

[204] I translated this and the next passage directly from the Syriac because the Arabic is a mistranslation, and the English follows the Arabic.

[205] The *kyrie eleison* was introduced into Eucharistic liturgies, both Eastern and Western. Its "earliest use seems to have been as a response to communal prayers." Andrew B. McGowan, *Ancient Christian Worship*, Baker, Grand Rapids, 2014, 212.

18.7 Repentance

The number of references to repentance in the Maronite Mass is quite unusual. The incense prayer at the opening of the Mass known as the *Hoosoye* is the centre-piece of what we might call the "rite of contrition."

Further references to sin, and the pleas for forgiveness which consciousness of sin naturally evokes, are found throughout the Mass. Another significant "rite of contrition" is found in the same section as the Our Father (the Lord's Prayer). This is fitting, because the Our Father seeks forgiveness of our sins. The reconciliation rite proper begins at the words "Bow your heads before the God of mercy, before his forgiving altar". It reaches its conclusion when the priest blesses the people, saying:

> Lord, bless your faithful people who bow before you. Deliver us from all harm and make us worthy to share in these Divine Mysteries, with purity and holiness, that through them we may be forgiven and made holy ... The grace of the Most Holy Trinity, eternal and consubstantial, be with you, my brothers and sisters, for ever.

In true Syriac fashion, the priest does not say *I absolve you*, but rather prays that we be forgiven and made holy and so on, because the doer is always God.

18.8 Symbolism of the Mass

There are different types of symbolism. There is a straightforward one-on-one substitution, as, for example, the Cross is a symbol of Jesus, who was crucified on it. The ashes which are placed on our foreheads on Ash Monday are a symbol of the inevitability of our death: "Remember that you are dust and unto dust you shall return."

There is also a form of direct symbolism, which is a little more complex. The *3etro* prayer from Hosanna Sunday, describes Christ as being "the pure fragrance pleasing to the Father ...". Christ is not a symbol of the incense. But by saying that He is the fragrance, it tells us that the rising clouds symbolize the Son who offers Himself as a pure and sweet-smelling sacrifice to the Father.

Symbols are not like codes where one thing stands for another. For example, there is a code where each letter stands for the one before it. If I want to write AMEN in that code, I will write BNFO. Symbols are fluid, and melt and merge depending on what seems to be appropriate. So, one week, the incense is a symbol of Jesus. But in the service for Passion Week, when we pray that God never allow us to be separated from him, the incense symbolizes us and our prayers. We pray: "O Lord, accept the incense of your Church whom you have redeemed by your sufferings. Be pleased by the fragrance of your flock ...".

Symbols do not even need to be in words: they can be constituted by actions. For example, we stand when the priest chants the words of consecration in Syriac. Why? what does this symbolize? First, it is a symbol of the resurrection, when the dead shall be called from their graves and resting places, to stand before the dread judge. Second, standing is a symbol of stability. Before the consecration, the Anaphora refers to the second coming, and in the words of consecration themselves, twice speaking of eternal life. Immediately after those words, the priest chants:

> Do this in memory of me. Whenever you eat this bread and drink from this cup, you proclaim my death and resurrection until I come again.

The congregation then responds:

> We commemorate your death, O Lord. We profess your resurrection. We await your second coming.

Shortly afterwards, in the *epiclesis* (or invocation of the Holy Spirit), the deacon chants:

> How awe-inspiring is this hour, my loved ones, for in it the Holy
> Spirit stirs. He descends and hovers over this Eucharist laid down
> here for our pardon. We stand praying in stillness and in fear.[206]

Note that in the last sentence it is specifically stated that we are *standing*. No argument that standing during this most sacred part of the Mass is not the authentic Maronite tradition can possibly succeed.[207]

Only the righteous can stand when the Lord appears as Himself, hence when he says "I AM" before the soldiers, they fall to the ground (John 18:6). In Luke 21:36 we are told: "… keep watch at all times, and pray that you may have the strength to escape all that is about to happen and to stand before the Son of Man." And so on. If we know that standing symbolizes this, then it means more to us. We understand why the Maronites stand rather than kneel. If we are attentive to the words of the 3etro, the smell of the incense does more than simply stir us to pleasant idyllic memories.

This may be a good place to mention that when something is *blessed* we ask God to protect it, to impart his holiness to it. But when we *consecrate* it, it is actually set aside the holy service. Unless it is de-consecrated, it can never be used for secular purposes again. Thus if I bless bread, I may eat it in any circumstance of life, lunch, a party, anything. But if it is consecrated, it can only be consumed in the service of God, and that effectively means that only the communion offerings are consecrated.

It is also necessary to mention another type of symbolism, the *symbolism of action*. The priest says, when he leaves the altar, in the older form of words:

> Remain in peace, O holy altar. Will it be possible for me to
> return to thee in peace? … and being acquitted of my debts, not

---

[206] I have translated this directly from the Syriac. It is not the same as the English translation used in the Missal, because that is based on the Arabic, although it does not follow it exactly.

[207] From pastoral care for the flock, we do not prohibit kneeling.

confounded when I appear before the throne of Christ, on the Day of Judgment. Remain in peace, O holy altar. I do not know whether I will ever again return to thee, to celebrate the Most Holy Sacrifice.

By performing the action of bowing and kissing, and saying these words, the priest thereby enacts something which has a symbolic meaning for the whole of his life: that we never know when our last moment will come, and so should strive to live in as holy a manner as possible.

Questions for Contemplation

1. Does the idea of making a worthy reception of the Eucharist, which St Paul mentioned and which we quoted in the last lesson, now mean more to you?
2. How has this lesson deepened your understanding of the Divine Sacrifice of the Mass, if at all?
3. What is the role of the congregation in the Mass?

Lesson 19

The Liturgical Calendar

19.1   The Framework of the Calendar

19.2   The Maronite Liturgical Calendar

19.3   The Haemorrhaging Woman

19.1 The Framework of the Calendar

As we shall see, the very concept of a sacred calendar is based on more than simply a collection of anniversaries. It is consistent with, and maybe even fully understandable only with, an understanding of types, for sacred time is the replaying in worldly time of the eternal pattern. That is, what we see in the world are shadows or antetypes cast from the eternal reality, the type.

The sacred or liturgical calendar is a human invention, but we use what was divinely revealed to us in putting it together. There are at least three different ways of marking the passing of time in the calendar. First, and most obviously, we use a solar calendar for some feasts (e.g. 25 December for Christmas, 15 August for the Assumption and 8 May for St John the Apostle), but a combined lunar and solar calendar to obtain the date of Easter, and therefore, to calculate the dates of all the other seasons of the year with the exception of the Seasons of Holy Cross and the Announcing. In the Latin calendar, because they don't have the Season of the Cross, all their seasons, but for Advent, are worked out by reference to Easter. (The date of Easter uses a *combined* lunar and solar calendar because it is only allowed to occur once every solar year). This is not inherently typological.

The second thing, is that while we use the *week* as a liturgical period, we also use periods of greater than a week. For example, we have Sunday Mass every Sunday. Therefore, we can legitimately say that the week is a basic unit of our liturgical calendars. But we also have *seasons*, and these, too, are basic units of our calendar. It is here that typology is needed for full comprehension. The seven Maronite seasons are:

1. Nativity
2. Epiphany
3. Great Lent
4. The Week of Suffering
5. Resurrection
6. Pentecost
7. The Holy Cross

Then, in addition to these seasons, there are five weeks of feasts which don't really fit into any of them, although some people count the first two in the Season of Announcement. These are the feasts of *The Consecration of the Church* and of *The Renewal of the Church*. It happens that these are often celebrated together on one and the same Sunday, and the Mass for them is identical except that when we celebrate the first, we refer only to the consecration of the Church, while on the second, we speak only of the renewal of the Church. When they are observed on one and the same Sunday, we mention the consecration *and* renewal of the Church. The other three weeks are those of commemoration, which I mention when we come to the Epiphany. Really, they are not part of the Epiphany. They should, in my opinion, be an eighth season. They are in fact treated that way, although not acknowledged as such.

Further, the calendar of saints' feast days, what is called the *sanctoral calendar* or *cycle*, cuts across the seasons. It follows the solar year, and is made up of many commemorations of the saints, e.g. St Maroun on 9 February each year. A feast will sometimes fall on a Sunday, but

Sunday takes precedence, although the saint can be remembered on that Sunday. That is, the cycle of Sundays is liturgically more fundamental than the sanctoral cycle, but the sanctoral cycle can be used to give added depth to a given Sunday.

There is good reason to believe that, originally, after the Easter season, the Maronite calendar had commemorations of the Old Testament saints, then of the Apostles and first Christian saints, and then of other saints. This is still visible to a small extent, although it has become somewhat obscured. So, in May there are the feasts of Ss Jeremiah (1 May) and Isaiah the Prophet (9 May); and in June, the feasts of the Four Evangelists (2 June), St Barnabas (10 June), St Bartholomew (11 June), St Jude, a.k.a. Leba (19 June), the birth of St John the Baptist (24 June), Ss Peter and Paul (29 June) and the feast of the Twelve Apostles (30 June)

Together with these feasts, we also have a series of *lectionary readings*. These are selected by the Church, and provide us with readings from the Epistles (including the *Acts of the Apostles* and the *Apocalypse*), and from the Gospels. The readings are chosen to complement or go with the liturgical celebration of the day. The way the Maronite readings have been chosen, the epistle readings tend to be longer than those of the gospels during the week, but it is the opposite on Sundays, when the gospel readings are longer. This allows the faithful to hear more of the New Testament.

Each of the liturgical Seasons has its own distinctive texts and hymns for the *Liturgy of the Word*. Some of them also have special rites or ceremonies: e.g. the blessing of waters on the Epiphany and on Pentecost. The *Anaphora* or *Liturgy of the Eucharist* does not change: we only select these from the anaphoras which have been authorised by Bkerké. While each different Liturgy of the Word has unique texts, especially the *Hoosoye*, they all follow the same format.

Altogether, then, in the Liturgy of the Word for each Mass and each

Season, we have an ever-changing panorama. As it revolves through the year, we hear different texts and we respond in slightly different ways. But there is also a basic similarity of purpose and prayer, reflected in the style and content. However, what is the heart of all this? In a word, it is Our Lord Himself.

The first season, that of the Nativity, deals with the announcement that the Messiah would be born, and his eventual birth on Christmas Day. The Maronite calendar then passes to the events of His childhood and, but 12 days later, on 6 January, we celebrate His baptism in the Jordan River. After the Epiphany, a short season, we have three weeks of commemoration of the deceased as a preparation for Lent.

During Lent, we take various events from the life of the Lord, particularly where they have to do with miracles of healing, for during this period we reflect that it is we ourselves who need to be cured of our sins. Finally, as Lent comes to a close, we recall the events which led up to the death of the Lord, such as Palm Sunday, and finally the week of sufferings, His passion, death and Resurrection. We then celebrate the events after that event, conquering death, until finally, after 40 days, we celebrate his Ascension into heaven. Nine days later we come to Pentecost, and after about four months of remembering what He had done during His life on earth, we have the Season of the Cross, when we celebrate the recovery of the true Cross, and recall that Our Lord is to return at the end of time to judge the world.

In this way, the liturgical calendar *teaches* by *liturgical re-enactment* of the whole divine plan of salvation over the twelve months of the year. Through the reading of the Gospels, we learning by *hearing*. This aspect of "hearing" the teaching, that is, the liturgy and the scripture readings is very important in the Maronite Church. It is not only a question of reading and studying for oneself: one absorbs differently when one listens, and the state and condition in which one hears can make a very great difference. Sometimes things penetrate when we hear them proclaimed aloud although we may have read them a thousand times. There are very many aspects to this, but one is that when we read we are also listening to our own voices in our heads during the act of reading. We read the way we have always read. But when someone else reads they bring a different experience to it, and sometimes that can bring us a fresh perspective.

As we grow older, we relive the feasts we have already experienced, but differently. One only has to consider how Christmas changes for us, imperceptibly, over time. But with that change there is also continuity. Feasts may acquire new memories: perhaps I was married, or ordained near a particular feast. That will never be forgotten. Or perhaps someone whom I love was then buried. I may have favourite days such as, for example, the Transfiguration. A specific feast of Our Lady may remind me of something I went through. In a funny way, we start to *personalise* the calendar, without ever intending to do so.

Now because Our Lord abides in eternity, above time, then this very fact of His centrality to the calendar is the basis of its typology. Recall that typology is based on the life of the Lord as type (or model) and its echoes in the world are antetypes (or reproductions from the model). Thus the original baptism of the Lord in about the year 30 is the type, and the Feast of the Epiphany which we celebrate each year is the antetype. Each Season shares something of the spiritual nature of the type.

19.2 The Maronite Liturgical Calendar

This brings us then to the Maronite calendar itself and its seven seasons. I cannot go into each of these Seasons or feasts in any detail. An entire new book would be needed for that. Sometimes, however, I make some comments because the knowledge may be hard to find.

1. The Season of the Nativity

A. The Feast of the Church.

The Maronite liturgical year opens with the feast of the Church, in November. Traditionally, there was one single Office for "Sunday of the Sanctification of the Church," which would be repeated if there were a second Sunday before the other compulsory Sundays, known as "Sunday of the Renewal of the Church." The fact of one ancient feast which sometimes would be celebrated on two consecutive Sundays is seen as a sign of its antiquity. The mood for these two Sundays is one of celebration.

B. The Season of the Nativity properly so-called.

The "Season or Cycle of Christmas" comprises the following Sundays or feasts:

i.   Sunday of the Announcement to Zechariah
ii.   Sunday of the Announcement to Mary
iii. Sunday of the Visitation of the Virgin to Elizabeth
iv.   Sunday of the Birth of John the Baptist
v.   Sunday of the Revelation to St Joseph
vi.   Genealogy Sunday (the Sunday before Christmas)
vii. Christmas
viii. Sunday of the Presentation of the Lord in the Temple (the first Sunday after Christmas)
ix.   The Circumcision of Our Lord, New Year's Day (for some years now, World Peace Day).

The proper attitude for this Season is one of joyful anticipation.

2. The Season of the Epiphany (DenHo)

The second season of the Maronite liturgical year is the Epiphany (DenHo). The feast of the Epiphany has anciently possessed a distinctive important and antique ceremony: "the blessing of the waters." In this season we recall the baptism of the Lord. This is one of two Seasons of the Holy Spirit, the other being Pentecost. It is a time of watching Our Lord manifest, and perhaps more a sense of wonder and anticipation than of outright joy.

Three Sundays precede Lent and are tacked on to the end of this season, although, as stated, I believe they should be recognised as an eighth and separate season:

i.   the Sunday of Priests (deceased priests),
ii. the Sunday of the Just (the equivalent of All Saints Day); and
iii. the Sunday of the Deceased (the equivalent of All Souls Day).

The mood in these seasons is of prayer and beseeching God.

3. Great Lent (Sawmō)

Lent is the period of preparation for Easter. It is a time for penance and mortification, which takes its character from the memory of Our Lord's Temptation in the Wilderness (see lesson 5). There are seven Sundays in the Maronite Lent:

First Sunday: The Entry to Lent, the Wedding at Cana
Second Sunday: Sunday of the Leper
Third Sunday: Sunday of the Haemorrhaging Woman
Fourth Sunday: Sunday of the Prodigal Son
Fifth Sunday: Sunday of the Paralytic
Sixth Sunday: Sunday of the Man Born Blind
Seventh Sunday: Palm Sunday, with its paraliturgy of the blessing
    of palms.

4. Holy Week

The first of the rites is the Arrival at Port on the vigil of Holy Monday, that is, Sunday evening. This is, I suspect, based on Phoenician celebrations thanking the gods for safely coming into the harbour. The ancient sailors would play music and offer praises to their deities.

As certain Phoenician elements such as the anchor (very commonly used in religious contexts in ancient Phoenicia) were taken into the Maronite faith, it is not impossible that this idea, too, was imported from them. The travel we have undertaken is the journey through Lent. We have now come through that, and are ready to remember, with great solemnity, the Lord's last week on earth.

There is a Rite of the Lamp on "Job Wednesday," or to use the Hebrew and Arabic name "Ayoub Wednesday" (Holy Wednesday). The rite involves candles, oil and dough.

We have the consecration of Myron and the Washing of Feet with a Eucharistic celebration on Holy Thursday (Thursday of the Mysteries). This seems to be very Latinised.

The Mass of the Presanctified and the Burial of Our Lord take place on Good Friday (Great Friday).

Holy Saturday or the Saturday of Light has no Mass, but a liturgy of forgiveness of sin (the Rite of Pardon). Fasting is obligatory on this day, the only Saturday when it is required.

5. The Season of the Resurrection

Easter Sunday, the Sunday of the Resurrection, is the centre of the faith. Besides that feast, we should note:

- The Rite of Peace on Easter Evening.
- The Week of the Neophytes (*al-Hawareyeen*, learners or catechumens)[208], which immediately follows the feast of the Resurrection.
- New Sunday, or "Thomas Sunday," the eighth day.
- The Ascension.
- Pentecost Sunday, when we celebrate the rite of genuflection, the meaning of which is still being discussed.

---

[208] This is a Syriac word meaning "the ones in white." This is because the catechumens wore white at the time of their reception into the Church.

The mood is of course one of great joy, hence in this season no one is required to fast.

6.   Pentecost

Unlike the Latin Church, we have no "ordinary time," although the Kaslik lectionary seems to have attempted to make one by joining Pentecost and the Season of the Cross together. I am not sure whether this is an ancient usage, or an imitation of the Latin Church. I am not in favour of obscuring or sidelining the very useful and beneficial Season of the Cross, so entirely different from Pentecost in mood.

In the Season of Pentecost, there fall the feasts of Ss Peter and Paul (29 June), the Transfiguration (6 August), the Assumption (15 August), and the Nativity of the Virgin (8 September).

7.   The Exaltation of the Cross (14 September)

This Feast was established for the recapture, in 628, by the Emperor Heraclius of the Cross which the Persians had stolen in 614. However, on this day we also commemorate the finding of the Cross by St Helena in 326, and the subsequent dedication of the Church of the Holy Sepulchre.

19.3 The Haemorrhaging Woman

This is the text we take on the Third Sunday of Lent:

> A large crowd followed and pressed around Jesus. And a woman was there who had been subject to bleeding for twelve years. She had suffered a great deal under the care of many doctors and had spent all she had, yet instead of getting better she grew worse. When she heard about Jesus, she came up behind him in the crowd and touched his cloak, because she thought: "If I just

touch his clothes, I will be healed." Immediately her bleeding stopped and she felt in her body that she was freed from her suffering.

At once Jesus realized that power had gone out from him. He turned around in the crowd and asked: "Who touched my clothes?"

"You see the people crowding against you," his disciples answered: "and yet you can ask: "Who touched me?' "

But Jesus kept looking around to see who had done it. Then the woman, knowing what had happened to her, came and fell at his feet and, trembling with fear, told him the whole truth. He said to her: "Daughter, your faith has healed you. Go in peace and be freed from your suffering." (Mark 5:24b-34)

Questions for Contemplation

1. In what did the woman's faith show itself?

2. Why do you think that Jesus spoke to the apostles and to the woman in the way that He did?

3. What does this story tell us about the spiritual efforts we can make in Lent?

Lesson 20
The Sacrament of Marriage
(Crowning)

20.1 The Christian Concept of Marriage

20.2 Betrothal

20.3 The rite of Crowning (or Marriage); (4) reflections on marriage; and (5) Sexuality

20.1 The Christian Concept of Marriage

Marriage is one of the sacraments of the Church. That is, it is something which is done in a liturgy which is both a sign of grace, and a channel for the grace of God. It is considered to be one of the *sacraments of vocation*. The two sacraments of vocation are *Holy Orders* and *Marriage* (also known as "Crowning" because the man and woman are crowned during the liturgy). By Holy Orders, men become priests, and by Crowning, men and women become husband and wife.

That marriage is a sacrament of the Church may be inferred from the earliest mention of it in ancient Christian literature, St Ignatius of Antioch's *Letter to Polycarp*, wherein he says: "But it is right for both men and women who marry, to form their union with the approval of the bishop, that their marriage may be according to God, and not after their own lust." (5)

So this is perhaps the first thing: *marriage is or can be an ordering of the lives of two people, and through them the family they raise, according to God.* By marriage they come closer to God and confirm their thoughts, words, acts and omissions to His Will. St Ignatius teaches us that marriage is not just a regulated form of lust, but rather a way of life in which many other aspects find a dignified and regulated place.

First, let us consider the Gospels. The Gospel of Matthew opens with a list of the forefathers and sometimes the foremothers of the Lord, which shows the importance of the married state and its product: children. For example, it mentions: "Eleazar the father of Matthan, and Matthan the father of Jacob. Jacob was the father of Joseph the husband of Mary, by whom Jesus was born, who is called the Messiah." (Matthew 1:15b-16)

So the relationship of Joseph to Mary is considered to be worth reporting. To the evangelist, the marriage was a fact he could not omit. This shows how even in working the miracle of the virginal conception, God desired to include marriage, for, although Mary *conceived* of the Holy Spirit, she was *betrothed* to Joseph at the time. St Matthew tells us: "… an angel of the Lord appeared to (Joseph) in a dream, saying: "Joseph, son of David, do not be afraid to take Mary as your wife; for the Child who has been conceived in her is of the Holy Spirit." … And Joseph awoke from his sleep and did as the angel of the Lord commanded him, and took Mary as his wife …" (Matthew 20b and 24).

In the Gospel of Matthew, the Sermon on the Mount, Our Lord says:

> You have heard that it was said: "You shall not commit adultery'; but I say to you that everyone who looks at a woman with lust for her has already committed adultery with her in his heart … It was said: "Whoever sends his wife away, let him give her a certificate of divorce'; but I say to you that everyone who divorces his wife, except for the reason of unchastity, makes her commit adultery; and whoever marries a divorced woman commits adultery. (Matthew 5:27-28 and 31-32).

There is controversy about one element here, the word translated "unchastity" or sometimes "fornication." To cut a long story short: "unchastity" or "fornication" in this context mean marriage to a sibling or a parent, a child, an uncle or an aunt. In other words, the marriage bond was sacred unless you had married someone the law forbade you to marry because you were too closely related.

20.2 Betrothal

The betrothal (more commonly called "engagement") marks a serious commitment between the man and woman. It is not binding in the sense that they are not obliged to continue to Crowning. They can discontinue the betrothal. But they are obliged to honour it in that they should be honest with one another to a heightened degree. It is a sign that the parties are relying upon each other to be open and truthful: to be especially charitable and loving, to consider themselves as virtually committed to each other to the exclusion of any other man or woman.

The betrothal ceremony, being, in modern terms, a *sacramental* rather than a *sacrament* (that is, a sign of a pious desire for blessing rather than an actual channel of grace instituted by Our Lord), the rite has some flexibility. So many more religious and legal consequences follow from Crowning that the marriage ceremony is not flexible. However, neither should any approved form of the betrothal be lightly changed. The present draft betrothal ceremony commences with Psalm 36:

> * Your mercy, Lord, reaches to heaven, Your truth to the clouds.
> ** Your justice is like God's mountains; like the great deep, Your justice.
> * How precious is Your mercy, O God!
> The children of Adam seek shelter in the shadow of your wings.
> ** They feast on the riches of Your house;
> for with You is the fountain of life, and in Your light we see light.

The celebrant asks the couple: "Do you N., and N., fully consent to exchange the betrothal of divine love with each other?"

They reply: "Yes, Father." The priest then declares: "I have not influenced your decision and those here present bear witness to this." When we come to the crowning ceremony, we shall see how the witnesses are much more important in that rite. The priest bestows on the couple-to-be a very solemn blessing:

> In Your name, Almighty Father, who rules all; in the name of Your beloved Son, who redeems all with His forgiving blood, shed on our behalf; in the name of the Holy Spirit, the Paraclete, who puts all things in order. We sign Your servants N. and N. who have come here together to make this betrothal before You. Shower upon them Your all-merciful grace. Grant them pardon of their faults, knowledge of Your commandments, obedience to Your laws, and understanding of Your wonders.
>
> As you bestow upon them these and other similar gifts, may Your harmony abide between them and Your peace stay with them. May your mercy descend upon them, and Your fear dwell in them.
>
> Likewise, You gave Your apostles the power to bind and loose,[209] and they, in turn, handed it on to us, through Your mercy.[210] Likewise, we also, through the power that comes from You, betroth these two children here present to each other, according to Your laws whose truth never deceives. We set before them the limits You established Yourself between the pure and the impure, between those who obey Your laws and those who disobey them.[211] Enrich them with all Your gifts, through the intercession of the prophets, apostles and blessed martyrs, and especially through the

---

[209] Matthew 18:18: ""Amen, I say to you, whatever you bind on earth shall have been bound in heaven; and whatever you loose on earth shall have been loosed in heaven."

[210] As we have seen in earlier lessons, the bishops of the modern Church are the successors of the apostles.

[211] This is probably drawn from the Old Testament Book of Job, chapter 14:1-5: "Man, who is born of woman, is short-lived and full of turmoil. ... You also open Your eyes on him and bring him into judgment with Yourself. Who can make the clean out of the unclean? No one! Since his days are determined, the number of his months is with You; and his limits You have set so that he cannot pass."

prayers of Our Blessed Lady, Mary, the Mother of God. Amen.

God sent his angel before Eliezer, the servant of Abraham, and by the well Eliezer betrothed Rebecca to Isaac, the son of his master.[212] May He send His grace upon this betrothal, and His mercy upon this couple and upon those who betroth them between them, reminding them of all good things. May it be a pledge of love, reminding them of all good things. May the harmony and peace of Our Lord God and Saviour Jesus Christ be with you.

Then follows a blessing of the rings:

O Lord, extend the right hand of Your Trinity and bless + these rings, which we give to Your servants. Sanctify + them by Your word and grant that they may wear them + in the sharing of their betrothal. May these rings be a wall of protection for their bodies, and shield them from all harm. May Your grace shine upon them and Your right hand, filled with mercy, bless them, so that in joy they may sing glory and thanks to You, for ever.

With the rings of your betrothal (engagement) may the right hand of Our Lord Jesus Christ descend upon you. May the blessing of His grace, which enriches the needy be bountiful in your lives. May these rings be a tower of protection for you. May they shield you from all harm. May you enter the heavenly kingdom and be counted among his blessed flock. O Lord our God, to You be glory, for ever.

This imagery recurs in the Crowning ceremony, and is discussed there.

It was a traditional part of the Maronite betrothal that the groom-to-be purchased new clothes for his wife, and had them blessed before she wore them, with this prayer:

---

[212] This story is found in Genesis 24: Abraham sends Eliezer to find a wife for his son Isaac, and he goes to Mesopotamia, where he providentially meets Rebecca at a well. There, she accepts his ring and bracelets, thereby betrothing Abraham's son Isaac, through a substitute (Eliezer). An angel is not explicitly mentioned in the story, only how well it went for Eliezer in a strange land, through the grace of God. This working out of God's good will is seen as executed by an invisible angel.

O God, by Your command, You established the world and all creation, and that the Ark of the Covenant be adorned with splendid ornaments. Now bless + these garments and those who will wear them, and give them many long years together in honour. May they wear them and rejoice in happiness. May they have the joy of preparing similar garments for their children and even more splendid ones for their children's children. May they shine forth in these garments; may they rejoice and exult in joyful celebrations ...

There follows a prayer from Psalm 118:27: "O Lord, bind our celebrations with chains, up to the horns of the altar." The corners of the ancient altars were shaped in the form of bull's horns, possibly because the great God of the Semites, El, was a bull-god.

There then follows the final prayer of the ceremony:

Almighty Lord God, in Your grace + bless our brother and sister. They have just had their betrothal blessed according to Your laws. Bless them with Your spiritual blessings and may they enjoy Your heavenly gifts. Make them and us worthy to stand blameless before the fearsome throne of Your majesty, so that, everywhere, we may glorify and thank You now and for ever.

20.3 The Crowning Liturgy

We best learn the meaning of Crowning by examining its liturgy. Let us recall that what the Church teaches in her liturgies, she teaches authoritatively. After an introductory prayer, the entire congregation recite Psalm 128:

* Blessed are all who fear the Lord, and walk in His ways!
** By the labour of your hands you shall eat. You will be blessed and prosper.
* Your wife like a fruitful vine in the heart of your house;
** Your children like shoots of the olive around your table.

* Indeed thus shall be blessed the man who fears the Lord.

We can see here the following elements:

1. The fear of the Lord is most important, because all the blessings follow from this. So always put God in first place, and in the last place, too! Then everything in between will be ruled by religion and the Spirit of God.

2. Next, it acknowledges the curse of Adam and Eve which we read of in the previous lesson (that they shall have to labour), but brings out of it a blessing. We must work, yes, and it is not easy, but from that work comes blessing and prosperity.

3. Finally, it is a good thing to have a wife who gives birth to children who grow up around the table. This is not merely an image thrown in because the Psalmist wanted to say something poetical. The children are at the table because the family eats together. They family is in one place, with one spirit. The children, like olive trees, grow and bear more children. The production and raising of children was always considered fundamental to the very purpose of marriage. But more than the actual children is the openness to having children, and the love of the man and woman together. If they cannot have physical children, yet they can have children of the spirit.

Shortly after, there comes the *Hoosoye* or incense prayer, which we have seen in many Masses. In a slightly revised translation to make it more accurate, it reads:

> Let us glorify, honour and praise the Heavenly Bridegroom, who betrothed the Church, the daughter of the nations, in His love. He purified and sanctified her by His cross, making her His glorious Bride. He invited prophets, apostles, martyrs, and saints to her wedding feast.
>
> Lord God, Creator and Perfector of all, you took the dust from

the earth into Your holy hands, and fashioned Adam in the image of your radiant majesty. In Your eternal mercy, You created our mother Eve from his rib. You said to them: "Be fruitful and multiply and fill the earth." You blessed the first patriarchs, the righteous and just, who were married in the spirit of righteousness, so that their descendants were blessed and multiplied. From them came forth the just, the priests, the kings, the prophets, apostles, martyrs, and saints.

Now we ask You, O Lord and Lover of all people, to bless this couple N. and N. Confirm them in faith, hope, and love. May their marriage be prosperous. Grant them the fruits of righteousness and blessed children. Assist them and enrich them with all good things. Keep them devoted to You all the days of their lives. May Your right hand rest upon them and Your life-giving cross protect them. May holy angels surround them, that with them …

There is a certain amount of teaching here. First, note that Jesus, the Heavenly Bridegroom, is said to have "betrothed the Church … in His love." This alludes to Our Lord's being the bridegroom in the Parable of the Ten Virgins which we studied in the previous lesson. It also relates to this passage from St Paul's Letter to the Ephesians:

Wives, be subject to your own husbands, as to the Lord. For the husband is the head of the wife, as Christ also is the head of the Church, He Himself being the Saviour of the body. But as the Church is subject to Christ, so also the wives ought to be to their husbands in everything. Husbands, love your wives, just as Christ also loved the Church and gave Himself up for her, so that He might sanctify her, having cleansed her by the washing of water with the word, that He might present to Himself the Church in all her glory, having no spot or wrinkle or any such thing; but that she would be holy and blameless. So husbands ought also to love their own wives as their own bodies. He who loves his own wife loves himself; for no one ever hated his own flesh, but nourishes and cherishes it, just as Christ also does the Church, because we are members of His body. For this reason a man shall leave his father and mother and shall be joined to his wife, and the two shall become one flesh. This mystery is great; but I am speaking with reference to Christ and the Church. Nevertheless, each individual among you also is to love his own wife even as himself, and the wife must see to it that she respects her husband. (Ephesians 5:22-33)

In the passage above, the prophets, apostles, martyrs, and saints *are* in fact the Church. All Christians were called "saints" or "holy ones" in the early days. Note that they are called to a "wedding banquet." Obviously, this must have been seen as an occasion of the very greatest joy. It helps us to understand, too, why marriage is a sacrament. It is an *antetype* of people coming together in a divinely sanctioned and upheld unity. The *type* to which it relates is the entry to the Kingdom of Heaven.

Unity is absolutely essential to so much in the faith, especially to lives spent as husband and wife. The gift of children adds a further dimension to this. Each child, in him- or herself, manifests the love of the father and mother, and the living providence of God.

The next paragraph of the rite is a reference to the creation story in the Book of Genesis, which we have already studied: God created Eve from Adam, and He commanded them to "go forth and multiply," that is, to have children. Having children is in itself a good thing. The other aspects of this prayer reinforce what we have already seen the Church saying of Crowning.

In the intercessions or prayers of the faithful, this prayer is mandated:

For all families, that they may live following the example of the Holy Family in Nazareth, bearing witness to the holy Gospel in their daily lives. We pray to the Lord.

Again, we are invited to take Jesus, Mary and Joseph, the Holy Family, as our example, and to bring this imitation of them into our daily lives.

The central part of the liturgy commences when the priest asks the groom and then the bride, about their intentions. The priest asks: "Beloved son N., do you take this servant of God, N., here present, to be your wife, according to the teachings of the holy Church?" He replies: "I do, Father." The priest then asks the bride exactly the same question.

When they have stated that this is their intention, the priest invites them in these words: "Proclaim your covenant before God and before the Church here present." The bride and groom join their right hands, place them on the Book of Gospels, and proclaim together:

> We who stand here before God, before this holy altar, Cross, and the pure Gospel, before the Church, and before you, Father, proclaim this our covenant. We promise to be faithful to it all the days of our lives. We ask God to help and bless us, that we may keep our promise. We ask you, Father, and all here present, to pray for us.

Marriage, from an Eastern theological perspective, is a covenant and not just a contract. We discussed the difference in lesson 5.4, when we considered the New Covenant which the Lord sealed with His blood. The Middle Eastern covenant was often an agreement between two lords to which they called their gods to witness. Related to this idea of the covenant being between kings, the crown which is placed upon the heads of the bridegroom and his bride, was initially placed on the king's head as a symbol of his city's walls. This tradition is so old that it goes back to when the king ruled over a city only. The crown, often in the form of the city walls, was placed upon his head to always remind him not only of his privilege, but also of his responsibility to care, guide and direct.

The covenant which the couple declare before the church, and the crowns which are placed upon their heads are to remind the man and woman that God is the indispensable third party in Christian marriage, and that they are now allowed to share in His work of creation as the responsible heads of a new family. Marriage is the perfect time to remind the faithful that privilege brings responsibility.

Because God witnesses the marriage covenant, it is an unlimited giving of each to each other. First, there must be no dishonesty or deception, because it is a *sacred* bond, God is a party to it. Next, the covenant is something which binds not just your money, goods or your services, but rather, it binds *you*: all of you, your very being. Could something be held back when God is a party? When He wishes to enter our house, who would not desire to open every door?

This gives us a perspective on birth and openness to bearing the children sent by God. What place can there be for contraception when God, the third party, has unified the couple, and even blessed them with the privilege of participating in the divine drama of creation? Whether children are conceived, how many and their condition, are matters for Him and the laws through which He works. Contraception is a human refusal to accept God's plan of and for creation. It is designed to thwart the creator's designs. It is an agreement between two people which changes the terms of the marriage covenant without consulting the third party who made it sacred.

In the next section of the ceremony, the priests blesses the couple:

> In the name of the Most Holy Trinity, Father, Son, and life-giving Spirit, we sign and seal + this bridal couple. By the authority given to us, and through the prayers of Mary, the Mother of God, the prophets, apostles, martyrs, Saint (the patron of the church), and all the saints, we bless the marriage of our son N. to our daughter N. by the hand of God and His Word. We bless it also by that covenant through which the sky (heavens) and the earth, the mountains and the hills, and the sea and the dry land were made; and by that covenant through which Sarah was joined to Abraham, Rebecca to Isaac, and Rachel to Jacob, so that they shall not separate from each other, all the days of their lives.

The references to the Old Testament figures are not merely there to add colour: they show that this new household stands in a venerable tradition. Once more, this is a tremendous privilege but also brings a corresponding responsibility.

The priest then blesses the rings:

> With these rings of your marriage, may the right hand of our Lord Jesus Christ rest upon you, + and may the blessing of His grace, that enriches all who are in need, abundantly descend upon you. May these rings be a wall of protection for you and a sign of unity and love between you all the days of your lives. O Lord our God, to You be glory, for ever.

The symbolism of the ring, then, is that it is an encircling wall. Like a wall, the love of the bride and groom, not allowing itself to be interfered with by any outside party at all, protects what is inside, and holds it together. For this reason it is a "sign of unity and love."

This is followed by a blessing of the crowns and the actual ceremony of crowning which gives the rite its name:

> May the Lord God, who crowned the earth with flowers of every kind; who adorned the sky with a multitude of lights, placing in it the sun, the moon, and the many stars; who fashioned the oceans as a crown for the earth; who crowned kings, priests, prophets, apostles, martyrs and saints: now stretch forth His merciful right hand, and bless + these crowns with His heavenly blessing; through the prayers of Mary, the Mother of God, and all the saints.

When the celebrant now flutters the crown three times over the head of the groom, this symbolises the descent of the Holy Spirit who hovers over the head of the groom. The priests says:

> The Lord crowns you with the crown of righteousness and adorns you with the gifts of the Holy Spirit.

The celebrant then places the crown on the groom's head, and stretches the Cross which he holds over the groom's head, calling him by name, and saying:

> N., may the Lord God, who crowned the holy fathers with the crown of righteousness and crowned the kings and made them great, be kind to you + and may His merciful right hand crown you, as He crowned Abraham, Isaac, and Jacob. As you have come to the holy Church asking for her blessings and assistance/guidance, may the Lord grant you the mercies of His grace and may He keep you and bless you, that you may live in happiness all the days of your life.

That does not add any new ideas to those which we have explored. But it interestingly bring together many of them, and in particular, that the groom is being likened to the kings. The blessing of the bride is notable for its suggesting that the marriage of the bride will *also* be a blessing for the church (thus adding another element to the spiritual dimension of marriage) and its mention of the intercession of Our Lady:

> N., may God, who crowned all the holy women, and blessed Sarah, Rebecca and Rachel, bless you + with His divine right hand. May He shower mercy upon you and exalt you with the crown of glory, that you may be a blessed vine in the holy Church, bearing spiritual fruits. May the Lord God grant you to rejoice always with your husband in peace and in love. May you bring forth blessed children pleasing to God, through the prayers of Mary, the Mother of God and all the saints.

Then the priest blesses the witnesses. In the days before registration, and centralised government records, it was important that there be living flesh and blood people who could attest to the ceremony, that the parties had freely consented, and how all had been done. Today it still has that value (after all, questions of consent and pressure cannot be decided by a notation in a registry), but perhaps we are more aware today that it is an important way of including family and friends, and through them the community, in the ceremony. Were it not like this, then we would require that witnesses be lawyers and detectives or other people with trained memories. The blessing of the witnesses reads:

> O King, whose crown is everlasting, whose reign neither ends

nor changes, and whose kingdom endures for ever; with Your divine grace and compassion, + bless these witnesses who attest to this crowning. Protect them by your victorious Cross and assist them in all things, so that they may merit from you the good reward when every person will be called to stand before you in judgment. May they go forth to meet you in joy having their lamps lit with good deeds. O Lord our God, to you be glory and thanks, for ever.

Soon after, there comes a blessing and the crowns are removed:

N., may God whose dwelling is in the heavens and whose dominion is over all the earth, bless you +. May He increase the fruits of your labour and may your home be secure as the dwelling place of King David. May your wife be precious in your eyes and like a pillar of light within your home so that you may rejoice in your blessings and you may enjoy the fruits of your work. May your children grow up before you like the sweetly fragrant cedars of Lebanon. May God grant you abundant wealth and all the good things that the earth produces, so that you may help those who call upon you in need. May you walk in the path of truth all the days of your life, raising glory and thanks to God, here and in the world to come, for ever.

May God, who sent His only Son, Our Lord Jesus Christ, who became flesh and saved all peoples by His Cross, + bless the groom N., the bride N., their witnesses and families. May He protect those here present by His victorious Cross. May the bride and groom live their married life in righteousness and may they reach the harbour of eternal life in the world to come.

The final blessing reiterates the main themes:

May God accompany you from His holy temple. May He guard your souls and bodies and be a wall of protection for you all the days of your lives. May the blessing of the Most Holy Trinity accompany all of you, Father +, Son +, and Holy Spirit +, the one God, to whom be glory, for ever.

20.4 Reflections on Marriage

Our Lord was never married. The only evidence is the New Testament and then, closest in time, the epistle of St Ignatius of Antioch to Polycarp in which he states:

> ... Tell my sisters to love the Lord and to be content with their husbands in body and soul. In like manner, exhort my brethren in the name of Jesus Christ to love their wives as the Lord loves the Church. If anyone is able to remain continent, to the honour of the Flesh of the Lord, let him persistently avoid boasting. ... For those of both sexes who contemplate marriage it is proper to enter the union with the sanction of the bishop; thus their marriage will be acceptable to the Lord and not just gratify lust. Let all things be done to the honour of God.[213]

We have seen some of this before, but it is worthwhile having the entire passage because as well as being evidence close in time that the Lord was celibate, it shows how ancient the tradition of Antioch is, and that it remains identical to what is taught today.

The celibacy of the Lord is significant because the *type* of marriage today cannot be His marriage to any woman, but rather, His marriage to the Church (see the passages from Ephesians 5 and Ignatius above), and the marriage of the bride and groom at Cana, which He blessed. This story is told only in the Gospel of St John, chapter 2:

> On the third day a wedding took place at Cana in Galilee. Jesus' mother was there, and Jesus and His disciples had also been invited to the wedding. When the wine was gone, Jesus' mother said to Him: "They have no more wine." "Woman, why do you involve Me?" Jesus replied. "My hour has not yet come."

> His mother said to the servants: "Do whatever He tells you." Nearby stood six stone water jars, the kind used by the Jews for ceremonial washing, each holding from twenty to thirty gallons.

---

[213] Translation found on the web, 14 February 2017, and checked with the Greek for accuracy: http://latter-rain.com/eccle/ignata.htm

Jesus said to the servants: "Fill the jars with water"; so they filled them to the brim. Then He told them: "Now draw some out and take it to the master of the banquet." They did so, and the master of the banquet tasted the water that had been turned into wine. He did not realize where it had come from, though the servants who had drawn the water knew. Then he called the bridegroom aside and said: "Everyone brings out the choice wine first and then the cheaper wine after the guests have had too much to drink; but you have saved the best till now."

What Jesus did here in Cana of Galilee was the first of the signs through which He revealed His glory; and His disciples believed in Him. (John 2:1-11)

This means that every marriage can be understood as a shadow of that marriage at Cana where Our Lord gave the best wine. No matter how good the reception, no matter whether you ride in a Rolls Royce or a horse and carriage, it is the gift of the Lord which comes at the end of it all and surpasses all else.

Every family can be seen as a shadow on earth of the Holy Family of Nazareth: not a perfect imitation, but having the possibility of becoming more like it, more infused with its spirit, reaching to that perfect model or type, so that our own may be purified.

Every child born in any family can be seen as an antetype of the type which is the Child Jesus. Every husband, typifies St Joseph, and every wife, Our Lady. Every family is an antetype of the Church. These are high ideals. They bring with them not only a great privilege, but also a serious responsibility.

Questions for Contemplation

1. What does this narrative tell us of the Lord's regard for marriage?

2. Is it significant that Our Lord acts as the behest of His Mother?

3. Could the wine be a symbol of another one of the sacraments? If so, which?

20.5 Sexuality

How then are we to understand human sexuality? Sexual differentiation is a feature of this world here on earth. There is no reason to think that the soul is either male or female. There is no marriage in heaven (Matthew 22:30), but we are raised body and soul. So it may well be that our differentiation into male and female continues into eternity. St Paul says that, for the baptised, there is "neither Jew nor Gentile, neither slave nor free, nor is there male and female, for you are all one in Christ Jesus" (Galatians 3:28). This does not mean that the differences do not exist, but that, compared to our oneness in the Lord, they count for nothing. Jesus Christ Our Lord was most definitely male. In His Godhood of course, he transcends the division into male and female. But the incarnation of the Second Person of the Trinity into history as a man cannot be denied, glossed over, or explained away as somehow culturally bound. It was God's choice, and a believer will respect that

Interestingly, since the Syriac word for "spirit" is feminine, the Holy Spirit was spoken of as female in some early Syriac texts. This was a beautiful tradition, and although it has passed, the memory of it reminds us that when we try to apply sexuality to the spiritual realm and to God, we are before a mystery, and that the best response is reverential respect.

It is often said that angels are not truly either male or female, although we of course speak of them as male because the Bible in almost every case when it mentions them does, and Scripture, too, should be respected.

Why then, are we divided into male and female on this earth? We cannot give any exhaustive answer, except to say that it appears to be the message of the Book of Genesis, which we saw in lessons 5 and 12, that God made us that way for procreation and for differentiation of personality. Male and female are needed for procreation, even if modern medical procedures mean that a man and a woman no longer have to come together, face to face, body to body. But medicine deals with human nature as it finds it: it does not create it.

It seems logical to think that the physical distinction makes possible a psychological and emotional differentiation which results in male and female being complementary, and facilitating their provision of companionship for each other as husband and wife (see Genesis 2:18: "The Lord God said: 'It is not good for the man to be alone. I will make a helper suitable for him'"" Here the Hebrew word *neged* literally means "in front of," and so: "corresponding," so that man and woman are before each other, suited for partnership although different).

This does not, however, apply to all people, only the great majority. First, some people, a very small number, are born with a condition where genitally, they are neither truly and completely male nor female. Second, some people seem by nature to be *asexual* not in gender, but in sexual desire. It is unclear whether this orientation is determined while within the womb, or as the person grows up. It is generally agreed that Our Lord was speaking of one of these two classes when He said:

> "Not everyone (can) accept this word, but only those to whom it has been given. For there are eunuchs who were born that way from their mothers' wombs, and there are eunuchs who have been made eunuchs by men, and there are those who make themselves eunuchs for the sake of the kingdom of heaven. Let he who can receive (this) receive (it)" (Matthew 19:11-12)

It may be that He was speaking of both, but the most likely interpretation is that He was saying that while some people are not born for marriage whether by psychology or biology, others are castrated, and yet others choose to remain celibate to obtain the Kingdom. There is little doubt that in the time of Our Lord, especially in Palestine, people were generally thought to be what we now call heterosexual by nature, and when they acted differently, this was thought to be the result of a conscious choice to depart from their inherit nature. Since Our Lord was speaking of people born asexual, then it must be that some people are intended to be that way. Perhaps Our Lord was suggesting that such people have a special affinity to the Kingdom of God. That is, being different from most others, God has a special role for them. The fact that these speculations are supported by a statement of the Lord, or appear to be, means that they cannot be lightly dismissed, even if that passage has not often received this interpretation, which does no violence at all to the text, but takes it quite literally.

There is now reasonable evidence for the view that more people are asexual than we have been aware, although our awareness is starting to change as people with an asexual predisposition are more likely to see themselves as being asexual.[214] This, in turn, is linked to the breakdown of the former belief that everyone was heterosexual by nature. However that may be, there can be little doubt that the great majority of people are (the evidence points to over 95% and perhaps closer to 98% of people being heterosexual).

Having no pronounced sexual identity of their own, asexuals are impressionable, and can be formed or conditioned to be attracted to people of either or both genders. On occasions, it seems, an unsatisfied love for one parent can dispose an asexual person to desire sexual congress with persons of that gender. In such instances, the sexual desire is a very concrete expression of the desire for emotional love. Because the seeds of this sort of development are planted while very young, the person is invariably unaware of the process, although they often recall for example, that one parent was dominating, and another distant. They will often be able to say that when they consider sexual

---

[214] Anthony F. Bogaert, *Understanding Asexuality*, Rowman & Littlefield, Lanham, 2012, chapter 4, "The Prevalence of Asexuality".

union with women, for example, they feel a repulsion which is related, distantly perhaps but nonetheless really, to a certain mother's suffocating emotionalism (which although not intended to be smothering, may be perceived that way by the child). It is as if wanting their mother to allow them space for their individuality, they will keep women from themselves sexually.

In everyone who feels a sex drive, the psychological component is immense. Implicit in the Church's call for self-discipline in sexual matters is the attitude that the sex drive is not as powerful as we are today taught to imagine, and that we can exercise more control over our carnal appetites than we might imagine. When one goes back even a little into history (for example into the world of Walter Scott and Jane Austen but two hundred years ago), one sees very clearly that most people expected themselves and others to be celibate outside of marriage, and so they did restrain themselves. These expectations were also linked to the conditions of life: committed marriage was the bedrock of society. It was a pillar of honour in everyone's life, and kept up morality in general. Further, the commitment of one man to one woman was related to the traditional roles of men and women: work was hard, and the rigid differentiation of male and female roles allowed specialisation in what people did, and that led to them acquiring expertise. Beyond even that, the differentiation of male and female roles gave people secure places. They did not need to negotiate every relationship. With those clear gender responsibilities also came clear rights. Sexuality was practically removed from the workplace. It was expected that groups of men working and living together would be celibate. Profligate men were looked down upon. The down side of carrying such a system into the modern world is that this unbending specification of gender roles is no longer needed to the same extent, and so individual likings and preferences may now be taken into account. This being the case, people who feel thwarted by these expectations will agitate for change.

However, the Church's teaching is based on the true nature of humanity, not on changeable incidents. The Church's teaching is as clear as it is demanding: sexual relations are for marriage, the commitment of one man and woman to the exclusion of all others for life. Having said this, all other sexual relations are excluded. The Lord raised marriage to a sacrament (and of course it is an antetype of the divine type of Our Lord to His Church, as St Paul implies in Ephesians 5:22-33) and wills that all sexual relations be restricted to marriage. That is, the powerful sexual impulse is to be used within marriage alone. No one is asked to deny or suppress their sexuality, but to understand it and to use it as a factor in their holistic development and progress towards heaven. Within marriage there can be a physical fulfilment. But we must not fall for the modern delusion that without physical sex life is some sort of farce.

If the Lord required celibacy, it is achievable. However, we have thrown away one of the most valuable aids in the struggle for self-control, the social belief that it is possible and that it is good.

Lesson 21

The Sacrament of Holy Orders

21.1 The Importance of Sacred Orders

21.2 What is the Priesthood?

21.3 The Service for the Ordination of a Priest

21.1 The Importance of Sacred Orders

Without sacred orders, there could be no Church. This is because the priest stands between God and humanity, mediating, and serving as a sort of a bridge. For this, the priest must lay himself down. The man who ministers as a priest does not have this quality of *mediumship* because of any personal qualities he may possess. It is, rather, the *priesthood within him*, which is a sharing in the priesthood of Christ, which has this function.

Jesus Christ is the type of the priesthood, and we who serve Him at the altar are antetypes or shadows of Him.

The priesthood was a central feature of Christian life from the very first days of the Church: hence in the first letter to Timothy, St Paul says:[215]

> (It is a true) saying: if a man desire the office of a bishop, he desires
> a good work. It behoves[216] therefore a bishop to be blameless, the
> husband of one wife, sober, prudent, of good behaviour, chaste,

---

[215] We examined other portions of these epistles in lesson 6.
[216] Is a duty for.

given to hospitality, a teacher, not given to wine, no striker, but modest, not quarrelsome, not covetous, but one that rules well his own house, having his children in subjection with all chastity. But if a man knows not how to rule his own house, how shall he take care of the church of God? Not a neophyte:[217] lest being puffed up with pride, he fall into the judgment of the devil. Moreover he must have a good testimony of them who are without: lest he fall into reproach and the snare of the devil.

Deacons in like manner (should be) chaste, not double tongued, not given to much wine, not greedy of filthy lucre:[218] holding the mystery of faith in a pure conscience. And let these also first be proved: and so let them minister, having no crime. The women in like manner chaste, not slanderers, but sober, faithful in all things. Let deacons be the husbands of one wife: who rule well their children, and their own houses. For they that have ministered well, shall purchase to themselves a good degree, and much confidence in the faith which is in Christ Jesus. (1 Timothy 3:1-13)

When this epistle was written, the threefold hierarchy of the Church was:

Apostles and *Prophets*
Episkopos or *Presbyteros* = Bishop or Priest
Diakonos = Deacon[219]

As the apostles had died, and the number of prophets thinned out, it became clear that some adjustment was needed if the hierarchy was to be preserved. What happened, then, was that the *episkopos* (whose title means "overseer") was separated out from the *presbyteros* (the "elder"), and placed above him in the hierarchy, whereas previously these had been alternative terms for one and the same function. It was

---

[217] Someone new to the faith.
[218] Money.
[219] Our words "bishop": "priest" and "deacon" come from these Greek words. I examine the question of the development of the ecclesiastical hierarchy in some detail, in my article "Ignatius of Antioch on the Ecclesiastical Hierarchy: Logic and Methodology," *Phronema*, 30(2), 2015, 105-136.

the death of the apostles which necessitated a shift to the hierarchy we have today:

Episkopos = Bishop
Presbyteros = Priest
Diakonos = Deacon

The earliest church documents also show the importance of the priesthood. The *Didache*, probably from before 100AD, states: "Appoint therefore for yourselves bishops and deacons worthy of the Lord, meek men, and not lovers of money, and truthful and approved ... for they also minister to you the ministry of the prophets and teachers" (15.1). In other words, the ministry of prophets was being taken over by bishops when this was written. As prophets disappeared from the world, their role was completely replaced by bishops.

That new world, the one in which we live, is described by St Ignatius of Antioch. In his letter to the Magnesians, he wrote: "Be zealous to do all things in harmony with God, with the bishop presiding in the place of God and the presbyters in the place of the Council of the Apostles, and the deacons, who are most dear to me, entrusted with the service of Jesus Christ" (6.1). Later in the same letter, he wrote: "Be diligent therefore to be confirmed in the ordinances of the Lord and the Apostles ... together with your revered bishop and with your presbytery, that aptly woven spiritual crown, and with the godly deacons" (13.1).

Later, St Ephrem would write:

Blessed is the priest who in the sanctuary
offers to the Father the Father's Child,
the fruit plucked from our tree,
although He is entirely from Majesty.[220]
Blessed are the consecrated hands that offer Him
and his lips wearied with kissing Him.[221]

---

[220] These two lines describe Our Lord as fully human and fully divine.
[221] St Ephrem, *Hymn on the Nativity*, stanza 16 (the edition of Kathleen McVey, pp.203-204.)

21.2 What is the Priesthood?

The priest is really a mediator between God and humanity. We see this in the Entrance Hymn from the Feast of the Consecration of the church, which states that the priest at the altar: "stands in between God and all humanity." In the liturgy for the Commemoration of Deceased Priests, the Entrance Hymn states:

> Yours is greater than all ranks.
> Not Michael, nor Gabriel, nor all their choirs have a rank so high."
> Priesthood guides us on the way to heaven's heights.
> … At the altar priests implore the heart of God,
> that He may forgive all sins.

The quotes in the first two lines are words attributed to Christ Himself, while the next lines are our own reflections on the priesthood. Later in the liturgy, the opening prayer reads: "They cared for your flock, served at your altars, and celebrated your Mysteries." The *Hoosoye* adds more details to this. It says of priests:

> They carried You in their hands, and they invited Your faithful people to Your banquet.[222] They proclaimed Your Word and Your Good News and they diligently cared for Your flock.

If we contemplate all this, we see that caring for the people of God and serving the sacraments are two sides of one work: doing the work of God in this world. The work of God involves first of all the service of the Sacraments, because the Word of God, Our Lord Himself, becomes present in the Eucharist. The teaching and the guidance which the priest dispenses both point to and serve the Sacraments, especially the Eucharist. Even the teaching of the Gospel and its message is subsidiary to the sacramental service.

---

[222] A reference to the parable of Luke 14:16-24: "A certain man made a great supper, and invited many …."

21.3 The Service for the Ordination of a Priest

We shall not set out all of this ceremony, but an examination of its main features, teaches us a great deal about the priesthood. Only a bishop can ordain a priest. Let us commence with the bishop's opening prayer:

> Support O Lord, with Your sublime and all powerful hand, Your holy Church which You have redeemed by Your precious blood. Grant her hope in You, to rejoice in Your salvation and to offer You a pure flock, now and for ever.

This points to the fact that salvation is the aim of all we are speaking of here. Salvation, of course, is being reunited with God. This is effected through the agency of the Church, and priests are central to the work of the church. In the *Hoosoye* of the liturgy, we read:

> O Merciful Lord, Our Master, and Lover of all people. The entire world is incapable of fully honouring and worshipping You. The angels and seraphim adore You, and the spiritual orders exalt You for Your many mercies. You willed to make glad our human nature when as a human You received heavenly praises. You completed us when You taught celestial rites to Your earthly apostles. The symbols which were traced out in the days of Moses have now, in You the Beloved Son, in Peter Simon the Head of the Apostles, and in Your Holy Church, been realised and perfected in their reality unto the end of time.

> We ask that You accept, in Your great mercy, these first fruits which we offer today to Your Majesty, Your servant (N.) whom You have called, that he may serve Your heavenly Mysteries and be a chaste priest, a good director, a spiritual custodian, a capable teacher, vigilant and industrious. May he be entrusted with the keys of Your heavenly kingdom to open the door of repentance for those who seek to return to You, and be present for those who offer their repentance. May he be firm in Your love and adorned with Your hope, resplendent with the ornament of sanctity and illuminated with purity.

> Eradicate from him, O Lord, all disposition to sin. Confirm him

in Your divine love, and Your hope, which is bliss. May he be orthodox in faith, and cleansed of soul and body; pure in spirit and noble in his actions. Make him worthy, in Your compassion, to be becomingly bold in working for the good. May he offer the service of Your Divine Mysteries in virtue of action and humility of conscience. May his life be totally redeemed and finally saved. May he find forgiveness for all transgressions in his pastoral work, through the grace and mercy of Your Only Begotten Son, Our Lord, Our God and Our Saviour, Jesus Christ. Glory and honour are due to You through Him, with Your living Holy Spirit, now and forever.

This text gives us an inkling of the greatness of the priesthood. No one and nothing in the entire universe is absolutely worthy to praise God. But, by the act of God Himself, we are made relatively or sufficiently worthy.

The references to the sketching out of symbols in the days of Moses take us back to *typology*. When God established the priesthood in the days of Moses, that priesthood took its truest meaning as a preparation for the priesthood of Our Lord. The lambs sacrificed by the priests were *antetypes* of Jesus the Lamb of God who sacrificed Himself for us, and is offered every day upon our altars by priests who work in the person of Christ. There are some sublime lines on this in St Ephrem's *Hymns on the Unleavened Bread*, wherein it is stated:

> He broke the bread with his hands as a symbol for the sacrifice of His body.
> He mixed the cup with his hands as a symbol for the sacrifice of His blood.
> He sacrificed and offered Himself, the priest of our atonement.
> He clothed himself in the priesthood of Melchizedek, his type ...[223]

The ideal character of the priest is unachievable for us, but the sincere striving for it is what is important: never giving up the struggle for holiness.

---

[223] The Syriac word is *Toofseh*. Hymn 2: 7-8a.

The Epistle read during this ceremony is a passage Saint Paul wrote to his disciple (Titus 1:1-9), which we have already seen.

The Gospel is preceded by this acclamation:

> Alleluia! Alleluia! The Lord has sworn and will not change His mind. You are a priest for ever.

This is taken from Psalm 110:4, the last part of which is quoted in the New Testament, in Hebrews 7:17. The Gospel of the ordination is John 21: 15-19:

> When they had finished breakfast, Jesus said to Simon Peter: 'Simon son of John, do you love me more than these?' He said to him: "Yes, Lord; you know that I love you." Jesus said to him: "Feed my lambs." A second time He said to him: "Simon son of John, do you love me?" He said to him: "Yes, Lord; you know that I love you." Jesus said to him: "Tend my sheep." He said to him the third time: "Simon son of John, do you love me?" Peter felt hurt because He said to him the third time: "Do you love me?" And he said to him: "Lord, you know everything; you know that I love you."
>
> Jesus said to him: "Feed my sheep. Amen, amen, I tell you, when you were younger, you used to fasten your own belt and to go wherever you wished. But when you grow old, you will stretch out your hands, and someone else will fasten a belt around you and take you where you do not wish to go." He said this to indicate the kind of death by which he would glorify God. After this He said to him: "Follow me."

This describes the priest's task, and also reminds us that the priesthood is a self-sacrifice. In the case of St Peter, it was so extreme a sacrifice that he gave up his life.

The ritual of Consecration to the Priesthood begins when:

> ... the bishop's assistant announces the name of the ordinand for ordination to the rank of priest, together with the name of the church or monastery where he will be incardinated. The ordinand

is presented. He places his hand in the bishop's, saying: *"Barekh Mor Aboun Reesh Kohneh."*

Three times bishop signs the ordinand on his forehead with the cross, and blesses him saying:

"May the Lord bless you among the priests of the Eparchy of Saint Maroun, Australia. May He keep you in the ranks of the holy fathers who kept the talent of the priesthood and deserved the heavenly reward. And I bless you in the name of the Father + and of the Son + and the Holy Spirit +.

To be incardinated means to be assigned to a specific parish. "Barekh Mor, Aboun Reesh Kohneh" means "A blessing (please), Lord, Father and Leader of Priests." The "talent" of priesthood refers to the parable of the talents, which we studied in lesson 8.

Then the ordinand presents to the bishop the following profession of faith, written in his own hand:

I, (N.), a deacon in the holy Maronite Antiochian Church, who is standing here before God and before His holy altar and His holy mysteries; and before our shepherd and Father, Mar (N.), our bishop; and in the presence of all the priests and the faithful people of God, renew now and for the rest of my life, my belief in One God: Father, Son and Holy Spirit, and in the one Holy Catholic and Apostolic Church.

And I declare that I am not worthy of this imposition of hands in which the Holy Spirit will raise me from the order of deacon to the order of priesthood.

I promise to be faithful to the Lord Jesus and to the teaching of His pure apostles and the holy fathers. And to the commandments of the Church, and her laws and holy Tradition. I give complete obedience to the church authorities: the holy Father, Pope of Rome, His Beatitude, Mar (N.) Boutros the Patriarch of Antioch,[224] and to Mar (N.) our Lord and shepherd.

---

[224] Every Maronite Patriarch takes the name "Boutros" or "Peter" on becoming Patriarch, adding it to another name, for Peter was the first bishop of Antioch, and the Patriarch follows in his steps.

I promise my faithful people to completely fulfil my priestly duties, to consecrate myself to God's service in the Holy Mysteries, to teaching and to ministering.

I ask God to give me the strength to fulfil all my promises and to confirm me in His holy service with your blessings for me, and with all your prayers on my behalf; through the intercession of Mary Mother of God, to whom I consecrate my priesthood, and Saint Joseph, Saint John, Saint Maroun and all the saints. Amen

The ordinand's sponsor now takes the ordinand by the hand, and presents him to the bishop:

We present to you ... this God-loving (N.), here present. May he receive from you the divine imposition of hands to elevate him from the Order of Deacon to the Order of Priesthood ...

May the divine grace, the heavenly gifts of Our Lord Jesus Christ which satisfy our needs, heal our illnesses, dress our wounds and bring forgiveness of our sins, be provided for all the children of our holy Church. She calls and selects candidates according to the divine will and the commandments of the Church, and now she chooses for God this servant of God, (N.), here present.

He submits his soul before this holy altar. His eyes are uplifted towards He who dwells on high, his heart seeks for Him, and his hands are outstretched towards the Lord of the priesthood. He is in expectation of the gift of Your compassion, to raise him from the rank of deacon to the rank of the priesthood. He has presented himself for the service of the altars of the Eparchy of Australia.

We now beseech You, O Lord, despite the poverty of those who present him to You. We pray and intercede for him, that your divine grace may descend upon him. We call out three times, saying: Forgive him, O Lord!

The answer made to this prayer is very interesting: "In peace we pray to the Lord." Usually, we simply say: "We pray to You O Lord," or something similar. This is the only example I know of where our state as we pray is mentioned. Of course, the prayer of a peaceful person will be different from that of a troubled one. But when one considers that "peace is the tranquillity of order," I think it is also a way of expressing that we are where we should be: we are in our right place when celebrating the ordaining of priests, and so we are at peace. It is also striking that "poverty" (or lack of absolute worthiness) and his need for forgiveness are mentioned.

Then follows the imposition of hands, which is absolutely central to the ceremony. In the Syriac tradition, the imposition of hands provides the entire ritual with its name.

The ordinand comes before the bishop, who removes his mitre, stands and uncovers the sacred Mysteries. He places his hands over the Holy Body, extends them, then joins them together, and touches the Holy Body. He moves his hands to the chalice, makes a sign over the Holy Body and the chalice, touches the chalice, and turns to the ordinand. He joins his hands, and places them upon the head of the ordinand. Three times, he places his hands upon the ordinand's shoulders.

The "Mysteries" referred to here are the chalice with the Holy Blood, and the paten bearing the Holy Body, for they have already been consecrated. Here, in this action, we see quite clearly, the bishop acting as *bridge* or *mediator* between God and humanity. This is practically definitive of what the priest should be, and of his service.

The bishop covers his right hand with a band of cloth and three times makes a sign upon the left hand of the ordinand, and upon his head and shoulders. The congregation sing *Kyrie eleison*.

"Kyrie eleison" is the Greek phrase: "Lord have mercy." Then follows "the first petition," a prayer which celebrates the depth of God's understanding and sight, and that God has chosen the ordinand rather than the ordinand choosing their own vocation (You did not choose me, but I chose you and appointed you so that you might go and bear fruit – fruit that will last – and so that whatever you ask in my name the Father will give you: John 15:16):

O great and wondrous Lord, Maker of all things, You have great power and inconceivable understanding. You know the secrets of our hearts and penetrate our inner most thoughts. All that has been done and is done is known to you. You are the one who knows the future, and choose in every generation for your divine service those who are pleasing in your sight. Elect, O Lord God, this your servant (N.) to the order of priesthood. Grant him to receive, without blemish and with unwavering faith, the great gift of your Spirit, that he may be worthy to serve the Gospel of Your Kingdom, and to stand before your holy altar and offer spiritual sacrifices, to renew your people with cleansing of the second birth, and to shine before all people, a lamp of the light of your only begotten Son, Who is co-equal to you in eternity. ...

For the second petition:

The bishop places his right hand on the ordinand, and his left hand on the holy Mysteries and proclaims:

"O great and wondrous Lord, you are generous in your gifts and know our innermost thoughts. In your grace, call your servant (N.) and elevate him from the Order of Diaconate to the Order of Priesthood. Enable him to perform good works, serve your altar in purity and follow your divine word. May he glorify your holy name in heaven as on earth and in the holy Church which we entrust this day to him. May he be worthy to joyfully greet you at your second coming and receive the reward of the good faithful servant. ...

The third petition adds nothing to what we have seen. Then the bishop anoints the ordinand's hands with holy myron (chrism). He places his hand over the candidate's head, and says this prayer:

Holy God, Father of Truth, you who pour out your holiness upon humanity, you are Lord. In the beginning, you made Adam in your mercy, and fashioned him in your image. You adorned him with all good qualities, and breathed into him the breath of life. You gave him Eden to dwell in, that he might be like a harp which sounds in tune with your glory. You gloriously clothed him so that he might be a great priest and pure minister in the service of your Godhead, and the celebration of your Holy Mysteries. But when Adam sinned and fell, transgressing your commandments, your majesty departed from him and he became estranged from his original service.

But you took pity on him, and sent your Beloved Son, the likeness of your Eternity, the image of your Splendour. He descended through His own good will, and tasted death in the body into which He was incarnated through the Ever-Virgin Mary. Your Son saved Adam from his own ignorance, and by the blood and water which flowed from His side, reinstated Adam in his first position and brought forgiveness for the entire world.

When He ascended from the Mount of Olives to you, Father, who had sent Him, He placed His sacred hands upon His holy apostles, and caused His hidden power to descend upon them and the priesthood. He sent His Holy Spirit to dwell within and to teach them, and they went out and made disciples of the nations and brought them back to God. The apostles instructed them in the true faith. They also established bishops, priests and deacons, making nine degrees within the Church, so that the clergy might be, as the heavenly ranks are, nine in number, linking together the four corners of the earth.

We, your poor and sinful servants, made by your holy hands, have received from your disciples the apostles, authority for the priesthood, although we are not worthy. We ask and we beseech that you extend your compassion to this your servant, (N.).

We have seen earlier, in lesson 14, the Syriac idea that Adam was created as a priest. This entire prayer has a lot of Adam imagery, showing that what happened to Adam prefigures what happens to all of humanity (or can, if we cooperate with God's plan for our salvation).

Jesus is described in Hebrews 1:3 as: "...the brightness of His (the Father's) glory, and the figure of His substance ..." This may well underlie the imagery here, for Hebrews is an epistle dedicated to the priesthood.

The third paragraph quoted here alludes to the belief that Our

Lord instituted the priesthood just before His Ascension into heaven. This probably fits into Matthew 28 better than any other part of the Gospels. The nine degrees of the church hierarchy depend upon certain dignities such as "archdeacon" which were instituted much later in the Church's history. The idea of having nine ranks of priest to match the nine ranks of angels is found in Patriarch El-Doueihy, the "Memory of the Maronites," who was Patriarch between 1670 and 1704. But it is older, and can be traced back to an ancient thinker known today as "the Pseudo-Dionysius."

Then: "… the bishop dips his thumb in the holy myron and anoints the palms of the ordinand with it, forming the sign of the cross from the ordinand's right thumb to the left wrist and from the left thumb to the right wrist, and then he joins the ordinand's hands, saying …" I omit the prayer as it basically calls down God's blessings on the candidate.

After this, the new priest is vested. There follows a procession:

> The bishop causes the new priest to bear upon his head a chalice in which the Holy Body immersed in the Sacred Blood has been placed. The chalice is covered in a large veil. The new priest holds it with both hands. Preceded by a large cross and candles, the new priest led by his sponsoring priest in a procession which goes amongst the congregation. The people bow their heads in humility before the Holy Eucharist.

The centrality of the Eucharist to the priestly vocation could not be made clearer. The closing prayer is an appropriate place to end this lesson.

> Blessed are you, O Lord God of all. You have adorned your Holy Church with diverse gifts, and exalted it. You called it to yourself from out of the world, through the new covenant of your Messiah. You established your Church first upon the Apostles, then upon prophets, teachers, ministers, those who exercise spiritual powers, and the pure bishops for the service of your holy altar.

> Perfect now, O Lord God, your grace and gifts, for us and for this

your slave, (N.), your new priest. Grant, that by the imposition of hands which he has today received from us, the Holy Spirit may descend upon him. In your mercy, make him worthy to serve you as priest, and to approach you with pure offerings, with vows, first offerings, and the fragrance of incense, pleasing to you and conformable to your lordly will. Bestow upon him, O Lord, the grace of your word and knowledgeable speech, that he may so preach as to admonish all those who have strayed from the truth.

May he always pray, petition and implore you on behalf of all the true and faithful, the children of the Holy Church. May he show concern for orphans, and care for widows. May he bring back to the fold those who have wandered, and comfort and hearten the lonely. May he keep your divine apostolic commandments all the days of his life, as he labours before you, rightly and properly.

In your eternal mercy, make us worthy to rejoice and be glad with him in your heavenly kingdom, through the prayers of Mary the Mother of God and all the saints.

The Maronite tradition was that on ordination a man would take a religious name. This is still observed, but only as a matter of choice, not of custom. It is, however, a beautiful one. It symbolises dying to the old life to live to the new. It gives the man a chance to take a new name for his new life, to leave behind what was worse for what is better.

21.4 The Lord Cleanses the Temple

This story is one of the few which is found in all four of the Gospels.

When it was almost time for the Jewish Passover, Jesus went up to Jerusalem. In the temple courts He found people selling cattle, sheep and doves, and others sitting at tables exchanging money. So He made a whip out of cords, and drove all from the temple courts, both sheep and cattle; He scattered the coins of the money changers and overturned their tables. To those who sold doves He said: "Get these out of here! Stop turning My

Father's house into a market!" His disciples remembered that it is written: "Zeal for your house will consume me."

The Jews then responded to Him: "What sign can you show us to prove your authority to do all this?" Jesus answered them: "Destroy this temple, and I will raise it again in three days." They replied: "It has taken forty-six years to build this temple, and you are going to raise it in three days?" But the temple He had spoken of was His body. After He was raised from the dead, His disciples recalled what He had said. Then they believed the scripture and the words that Jesus had spoken. (John 2:13-22)

Questions for Contemplation

1. Does this tell us anything about the sanctity of churches?
2. How serious a sin is it to trade in the House of God?
3. What did Jesus mean by His answer to the question about His authority to cleanse the Temple?

Lesson 22

The Sacrament of the Anointing of the Sick, and Funerals

We are weak and we are vulnerable. We suffer from deficiencies, limitations, and temptations. Not every weakness is a sin, and a tendency to unnecessary guilt can be as serious an impediment to the spiritual life as denying the reality of sin, although the latter is probably the more prevalent error today. Sin involves an offence to God: weakness does not, or at least not necessarily. Yet, both weakness and sin are the concern of the Church, tending as it does to each of the faithful in fullness as body and soul.

22.1 The Sacrament of Anointing

This sacrament brings us to the facts of sickness, suffering and death. These are with us now as the result of Original Sin. Like all facts of life, the Church addresses them. Every event within the pageant of life can be an opportunity to understand life and God, and to mature both as a person and as a soul (not that there is a rigid division between the two). But while spiritual development must always be accompanied by a greater psychological maturity, it does not always follow that the converse is true. After all, maturity can be completely worldly, and lacking in any supernatural dimension. It is precisely the supernatural aspect which differentiates the faith from a philosophy or a lifestyle.

First, original sin. We have mentioned this before. One of its consequences was that suffering and death entered the human world through it. The story is recounted in the Book of Genesis, the first book of the Old Testament, and as the Old Testament opens the Bible, it is the first book of the Bible. "Genesis" means "manner of birth": "origin" and "source" in Greek. It is an attempt to describe the contents of the Book. In Hebrew, it is called *berešeet*, meaning "in the beginning." It describes the creation of the world, as we saw in lesson 12. Then, on the sixth day, God created Adam, the first of humanity:

> Then God said: "Let Us make man in Our image, according to Our likeness; and let them rule over the fish of the sea and over the birds of the sky and over the cattle and over all the earth, and over every creeping thing that creeps on the earth." God created man in His own image, in the image of God He created him; male and female He created them. God blessed them; and God said to them: "Be fruitful and multiply, and fill the earth, and subdue it; and rule over the fish of the sea and over the birds of the sky and over every living thing that moves on the earth." Then God said: "Behold, I have given you every plant yielding seed that is on the surface of all the earth, and every tree which has fruit yielding seed; it shall be food for you; and to every beast of the earth and to every bird of the sky and to every thing that moves on the earth which has life, I have given every green plant for food"; and it was so. God saw all that He had made, and behold, it was very good. And there was evening and there was morning, the sixth day. (Genesis 1:26-31)

Note that when God looked upon His creation, it was "very good." This basic goodness has never left the heart of creation. God gave Adam work to do:

> Then the Lord God took the man and put him into the garden of Eden to cultivate it and keep it. The Lord God commanded the

man, saying: "From any tree of the garden you may eat freely; but from the tree of the knowledge of good and evil you shall not eat, for in the day that you eat from it you will surely die." (Gen. 2:15-17)

Then God created the first woman, Eve:

Then the Lord God said: "It is not good for the man to be alone; I will make him a helper suitable for him." .. So the Lord God caused a deep sleep to fall upon the man, and he slept; then He took one of his ribs and closed up the flesh at that place. The Lord God fashioned into a woman the rib which He had taken from the man, and brought her to the man. The man said: "This is now bone of my bones, and flesh of my flesh. She shall be called Woman, because she was taken out of Man." For this reason a man shall leave his father and his mother, and be joined to his wife; and they shall become one flesh. (Genesis 2:18, 21-24)

But all was not destined to be rosy. The devil tricked them into eating the fruit of the forbidden tree. This disobedience to God's command was the original sin. God disciplined them.

To the woman He (God) said: "I will greatly multiply your pain in childbirth, in pain you will bring forth children; yet your desire will be for your husband, and he will rule over you." Then to Adam He said: "Because you have listened to the voice of your wife, and have eaten from the tree about which I commanded you, saying: "You shall not eat from it'; Cursed is the ground because of you; in toil you will eat of it all the days of your life. Both thorns and thistles it shall grow for you; and you will eat the plants of the field. By the sweat of your face you will eat bread, till you return to the ground, because from it you were taken; for you are dust, and to dust you shall return." (Genesis 3:16-19)

So the fact of sin is what brought sickness and suffering into the world. But it does not follow that all suffering and sickness is now the result of sin. Many good innocent people suffer through no fault of their own, but because they share in the human condition. But God provided a remedy for all of this, only the remedy is in eternity.

A further result of the Fall is what we call "concupiscence," that is, the inability to overcome desire by rational direction alone. A person should be able to say: "This desire is wrong. I shall not entertain it." But as a result of the Fall, our wills are weak, and so sometimes we do something which is wrong although we know it is wrong and really do not wish to. As St Paul said:

> For that which I work, I understand not. For I do not that good which I will; but the evil which I hate, that I do. If then I do that which I will not, I consent to the law, that it is good. Now then it is no more I that do it, but sin that dwells in me. For I know that there dwells not in me, that is to say, in my flesh, that which is good. For to will, is present with me; but to accomplish that which is good, I find not. For the good which I will, I do not; but the evil which I will not, that I do. Now if I do that which I will not, it is no more I that do it, but sin that dwells in me (Romans 7:15-20)

Because sin had entered the world, God sent His Only Son to be incarnated among us and to bring goodness, and to teach us the way back to God. That is belief in God, following His commandments and that includes receiving the sacramental graces made available to us through the seven sacraments dispensed by true priests of the true Church. We have already met the sacraments of initiation (Baptism, Chrismation or Confirmation, and the Eucharist). Reconciliation and the Anointing of the Sick are the two sacraments of healing.

Before moving on, it is necessary to emphasise that the fact we suffer or become sick does not mean that we have sinned. Consider this:

> Now on the same occasion there were some present who reported to Him about the Galileans whose blood Pilate had mixed with their sacrifices. And Jesus said to them: "Do you suppose that these Galileans were greater sinners than all other Galileans because they suffered this fate? I tell you, no, but unless you repent, you will all likewise perish. Or do you suppose that those

eighteen on whom the tower in Siloam fell and killed them were worse culprits than all the men who live in Jerusalem? I tell you, no, but unless you repent, you will all likewise perish." (Luke 13:1-5)

In a similar manner, St John reports:

As He (Jesus) passed by, He saw a man blind from birth. And His disciples asked Him: "Rabbi, who sinned, this man or his parents, that he would be born blind?" Jesus answered: "It was neither that this man sinned, nor his parents; but it was so that the works of God might be displayed in him. (John 9:1-3)

In other words, the fact that we have suffered does not necessarily mean that we have sinned, but if we sin, we will suffer, in one way or another, and at one time or another. Also, one cannot see a person undergo some tragedy and then jump to the conclusion that this was the punishment of God. It is important to understand that suffering can have a healing role. When Our Lord spoke of "works of God .... Being displayed", He meant through healing.

Suffering can bring us to see that there is a problem (whether physical or psychological) and move us to take steps to rectify it. Indeed, the great salvation which Jesus made for us was brought about by His suffering: "Because his soul has laboured, he shall see and be filled: by his knowledge shall this my just servant justify many, and he shall bear their iniquities" (Isaiah 53:11). This is a prophecy concerning Our Lord: He was the Suffering Servant. He did not come to end our suffering at once, but rather, to share it.

The least well known of the Sacraments is probably Holy Anointing. Immediately there is a difficulty with it, in that people often hope that those to whom it is administered will be cured of their illness. This does sometimes happen. But sometimes it does not. Despite the fact that the ritual itself, and the Gospel of St Mark and the Epistle of St James both speak of the sick recovering, this does not always happen. Neither can the patient be blamed as lacking faith. It would be more correct if we prayed for that optimum of that degree of health which God wills for a person. Sometimes people will die. But we cannot really know when. We can, however, pray to the Lord to remit their suffering, and to grant us a happy life together, but we know that it must have a limit.

This sacrament is based on what Our Lord did and said, but the clearest testimony to it from the New Testament is that of the Epistle of St James, which is quoted below. Note, too, that the Risen Lord said of His apostles and disciples: "These signs will accompany those who have believed... they will lay hands on the sick, and they will recover" (Mark 16:17-18).

22.2 The Rite

The rite of this sacrament is often called "the Last Rite." The sacrament itself is often known as "Extreme Unction." However, the idea that it was reserved for those on the point of death, although current before Vatican II no longer prevails. The harder question of discretion now concerns not over-using it. Below I set out a legitimate form of Anointing, including in itself an extract from the Epistle of St James:

FORMULA FOR THE ANOINTING OF THE SICK

Priest: Glory be to the Father and to the Son and to the Holy Spirit, now and forever.

People: Our Father... Hail May...

The priest places a hand on head of sick person saying:

Priest: Holy Father, as I place my hand upon this Your servant, confident in your mercy, may he/she be renewed by the healing power of Your Son, Our Lord, Jesus Christ, the Good Physician, at whose touch lepers were cleansed, the blind given sight, the sick healed, and those burdened with suffering relieved of their infirmities.

People: Amen.

Priest: A reading from the Epistle of St James:

Is anyone among you suffering? Then he must pray. Is anyone cheerful? He is to sing praises. Is anyone among you sick? Let him bring in the priests of the church and they are to pray over him, anointing him with oil in the name of the Lord; and the prayer offered in faith will restore the one who is sick, and the Lord will raise him up, and if he has committed sins, they will be forgiven him. Therefore, confess your sins to one another, and pray for one another so that you may be healed. The effective prayer of a righteous man can accomplish much.

My brethren, if any among you strays from the truth and one turns him back, let him know that he who turns a sinner from the error of his way will save his soul from death and will cover a multitude of sins. (James 5:13-16; 19-20)

The priest continues: I ask you, O Lord, that Your hand, extended in mercy on this Your servant, may bring freedom from diseases, fevers, and afflictions, and that he/she may swiftly recover to praise You, Father, Son and Holy Spirit, now and forever.

The priest places his right thumb in the chrism and then anoints the head, mouth and heart of the sick person, making the sign of the Cross each time.

Priest: O Holy Father, who sent Your Son , Our Lord, Jesus Christ, to heal all sickness and to bring deliverance from death and evil, through the grace of Christ, Your Son may this holy anointing heal Your servant from every sickness of soul and body, and enable him/her, with Christ, to honour You and the Holy Spirit, now and forever.

People: Amen.

Priest: May the Lord God grant you a refreshing, quiet, and holy rest. Amen.

It can be seen from this that while it is a sacrament of preparation for death, as we do not know what God has in store for us, it is even more a sacrament of healing of soul and body. It does often happen, in a priest's experience, that people given this sacrament suddenly recover, sometimes even walking again. But it also happens that sometimes their bodies do not recover. We trust to God, however, that their souls have been made whole.

22.3 Funerals

As Holy Scripture states: "It is therefore a holy and wholesome thought to pray for the dead, that they may be loosed from sins" (2 Maccabees 12:46). As God can do all things, we ask Him to have mercy upon our dead. This is also good because every time we think of the faithful departed, we recall that they have passed from this world to the other, and will be in heaven, purgatory or hell. I shall dwell on this for but a moment, because there is prevalent in Protestant circles an idea, which I cannot call less than ridiculous, that it is somehow wrong to pray for the dead. Even if one puts aside what is said in the Book of Maccabees, there is still the evidence of St Paul himself, in his Second Epistle to St Timothy. St Paul wrote:

> May the Lord show mercy to the household of Onesiphorus, because he often refreshed me and was not ashamed of my chains. On the contrary, when he was in Rome, he searched hard for me until he found me. May the Lord grant that he will find mercy from the Lord on that day! You know very well in how many ways he helped me in Ephesus. (2 Timothy 1:16-18)

At the end of the letter, he wrote: "Greet Priscilla and Aquila and the household of Onesiphorus" (2 Timothy 4:19).

Not only does St Paul not mention Onesiphorus as alive, he speaks of what he did in the past tense (he often refreshed … was not ashamed … etc.). At the end, he sends his greetings to living people: Priscilla and Aquila and the household of Onesiphorus. Were Onesiphorus alive, it would be unthinkable that he did not name him. But just as powerfully, look at his prayer for Onesiphorus: "May the Lord grant that he will find mercy from the Lord on that day!" I cannot find a single example of where St Paul makes this prayer for someone living: but for someone deceased, it is the only reasonable prayer to make. Once more, we see the willingness of Protestants to ignore the clear words of Scripture in favour of their denomination's position on praying for the dead. As stated, it is good to remember the dead.[225]

Remembering the dead, we recall ourselves and our situation. Pondering the mystery of their fate, we can come to ponder the mystery of our own destiny: a destiny made by each action, omission, word and thought as we advance along the path of life.

Seeing how family and friends have come to their final end, we can see and perhaps deeply realise that we too will come to that common end, the "way of all earth" (I Kings 2:2). We should join to this a feeling of gratitude to God for allowing us the inestimable treasure of one more hour of life. Contemplating death, we contemplate the wonder of life.

As we think of those whom we knew, we think also of what they did well, what they did badly, and what they managed only in a mediocre or middling manner. This prompts us to think about ourselves: could I do better? Am I making the mistakes they did? Could I bring myself up to their best standards? Do I have something to learn from them?

We have two funeral services in our liturgy: for a man and for a woman. These provide prayers, psalms and hymns for the first part of the Divine Sacrifice of the Mass, the Liturgy of the Word. Both services open the same way, and close the same way: with the Anaphora (the Eucharistic Service) of the Divine Sacrifice of the Mass, some prayers for the dead, and the sprinkling of the coffin with holy water. Then the priest accompanies the body to the cemetery where it is buried with prayers.

Both funeral ceremonies open with a hymn from the Syriac: "Throw open your gates, O Jerusalem that our prayer might come to Christ's

---

[225] Incidentally, in so far as some Protestants argue that there is no Purgatory and that the deceased are either in heaven (where they do not need our prayers), or in hell (where our prayers will do them no good), then St Paul's praying for Onesiphorus tells against this view.

throne above." This alludes to the biblical image of heaven as being the celestial Jerusalem (Revelation 21:2, drawing from Ezekiel 40-48). The hymn asks Our Lady and the saints to pray for the deceased.

Funeral Ceremony for a Male

After the glorification of God, there is an opening prayer asking for mercy for the departed. Then comes an extract from Psalm 51, a prayer and a hymn. Since Psalm 51 is found in both the ceremonies (for a man and for a woman), and was used in almost all Maronite ceremonies, let us quote the relevant sections:

> Have mercy on me, O God, in Your kindness.
> In Your compassion blot out my offence.
> Wash me more and more from my guilt
> and cleanse me from my sin.
> Purify me and I shall be clean,
> Wash me, I shall be whiter than snow.
> Make me hear rejoicing and gladness
> that the bones You have crushed may revive.
> From my sins turn away Your face
> and blot out all my guilt.
> A pure heart create for me, O God,
> put a steadfast spirit within me.
> Do not cast me away from your presence,
> nor deprive me of Your Holy Spirit.

The second section of this service comprises Psalm 130 ("Out of the depths I cry to you, O Lord, Lord hear my voice!"), another prayer and a hymn. The second hymn refers to the deceased having shared the body and blood of the Lord, and being clothed in majesty. This alludes both to baptism by which we are clothed with Christ the light, and also to the sayings of John 6, which we saw in the last lesson. One extract may recall them to mind: "I am the living bread which came down from heaven. If any man eat of this bread, he shall live for ever; and the bread that I will give, is My flesh, for the life of the world." (John 6:51-52)

The third section commences with Psalm 112 "Happy the man who fears the Lord." It refers to men, and might be thought to be particularly well-suited to the funeral of a male, yet the sentiments in this part of the Psalm can all be equally well applied to women. There is no third prayer, but rather a third hymn, which is followed by the *Hoosoye*, the incense prayer we considered in lesson 13.

This opens by recalling God's awe-inspiring power over life and death:

> ... the Living One spoke, and we came to life. He created Adam and fashioned him in the image of His majesty. By His command He deprives Adam of this life and sends him back to his former state: the dust from which he was made. Then He recalls him, raises him, renews him, adorns him, and grants him an inheritance with his angels.

It goes on to remind us that while God can see us, we cannot see Him:

> You are light and new life. You are the Creator of the universe, time, and all that changes. You are awesome, exalted and praised in Your commands, yet patient and kind in Your mercy. Innermost thoughts are revealed and laid bare before You, yet Your ways are unsearchable.

It also includes a very apt description of life here on earth as being a pilgrimage: "... we offer you prayers for the soul of our brother (his name) who has left this earthly life of pilgrimage so that the angels of peace may guide him to the place of rest." "Pilgrimage" comes from the word "pilgrim" which means "one who journeys (usually a long distance) to some sacred place as an act of religious devotion." The "pilgrimage" is the journey made by the pilgrim. This could be us, travelling to the sacred place which is heaven.

This prayer also asks God to rescue the deceased from the "second death." Although this phrase is found in the Bible only in the Book of Revelation, it is also known in late Jewish books which were not included in Scripture. The "second death" is the punishment which follows the judgment of the wicked. Revelation 21:8 states that: "… the fearful, and unbelieving, and the abominable, and murderers, and whoremongers, and sorcerers, and idolaters, and all liars, they shall have their portion in the pool burning with fire and brimstone, which is the second death."

Then follows a hymn (the *qolo*), which gives in three short sentences what the Christian should aim to do: "He was baptised, he consumed you, he has followed Your precepts." This is followed by the *3etro* prayer and a prayer before the Epistle and the Gospel.

Funeral Ceremony for a Female

As with the service for a male, there is the glorification of God, then comes an opening prayer asking for mercy for the departed. Then follows Psalm 51 and the first prayer. This has some interesting imagery. It says of Christ: "You are the door to mercy, the road to peace, the way of righteousness, the haven of life and the abode of life." This relates to the idea of the pilgrimage, and that life is a journey which brings us home. The first hymn asks God to count the departed among the wise virgins (see below). This is clearly themed for women.

This is followed by Psalm 63 "… You are my God, for you I long, for you my soul is thirsting," a second prayer and a second hymn which commemorates the triumph of Our Lord over death. The final section begins with Psalm 16 "Preserve me God, I take refuge in You," and the third hymn. The *Hoosoye*, like these hymns and prayers, repeats the themes we have seen. But one interesting section in the Arabic only says: "For our life is like a fever and chaff (in the wind)." Chaff is the outer part of grain. We cannot eat it, so we sift it from the grain by throwing the wheat into the air. The chaff, being lighter, then floats away on the breeze.

I cannot see any real distinction between the services for a man and a woman, they are equal in religious feeling, desire for the Kingdom, and compassion for the deceased. It is just that slightly different texts are used: those for a male perhaps picture an ideal man, and so emphasise activity in the world a little more, and those for a female address the qualities of an ideal woman. This helps to honour something about their specific individuality.

After this, one can proceed to the Eucharistic Celebration, followed by another hymn, a few prayers, and the sprinkling of the coffin with holy water. This means that the body of the deceased faithful is taken from the altar of God to the earth, where we trust that they will sleep until awakened and called to His heavenly altar.

The life of a Christian is a movement from baptism at the altar to this farewell from the altar. At baptism, Christ becomes the invisible robe of glory in which, we pray, we may be raised after death.

Commemorations

These funeral services are distinct from commemorative services, the *jinnairz* of the Maronite Church. These would be said on the seventh and fortieth days after the death, and on the annual anniversaries, especially the first year. It is still a good custom to keep up: it reminds us of our dead, renews our love, gives us cause for hope, and recalls us to our own worldly duties.

To attend a commemoration is to recall that we too shall die. It is to be reminded that we are mortal, as are all others: it is not for us to judge and condemn human frailty. If we do truly love those who have died, let us imitate their good points, learn from their errors, and pray for them. People never forget when someone was prompt and diligent to remember the dead with charity, and to pray for them, especially arranging the Divine Sacrifice of the Mass. Those people are more likely to be remembered after they too have passed.

22.4 The Parable of the Ten Virgins

This parable is told in Matthew 25:

> "Then the kingdom of heaven will be comparable to ten virgins, who took their lamps and went out to meet the bridegroom. Five of them were foolish, and five were prudent. For when the foolish took their lamps, they took no oil with them, but the prudent took oil in flasks along with their lamps. Now while the bridegroom was delaying, they all got drowsy and began to sleep. But at midnight there was a shout: "Behold, the bridegroom! Come out to meet him." Then all those virgins rose and trimmed their lamps. The foolish said to the prudent: "Give us some of your oil, for our lamps are going out." But the prudent answered: "No, there will not be enough for us and you too; go instead to the dealers and buy some for yourselves." "And while they were going away to make the purchase, the bridegroom came, and those who were ready went in with him to the wedding feast; and the door was shut. Later the other virgins also came, saying: "Lord, lord, open up for us." But he answered: "Amen I say to you, I do not know you." Be on the alert then, for you do not know the day nor the hour. (Matthew 25:1-13)

The five foolish maids probably represent the Old Testament Law (expressed in the five books of Moses), who were without oil (faith) when the bridegroom (Jesus the Messiah) came. The five alert ones who had the oil in their flasks represent the New Testament believers who accept the Lord. He, of course, is the bridegroom. His coming is a reference to the Second Coming, often referred to as the *Parousia*. You will recall that we studied the Creed in lesson 2. It says, among other things:

> For our sake He (Jesus) was crucified under Pontius Pilate, He suffered death and was buried, and rose again on the third day in accordance with the Scriptures. He ascended into heaven and is seated at the right hand of the Father. He will come again in glory to judge the living and the dead and His kingdom will have no end. ... we look forward to the resurrection of the dead and the life of the world to come. Amen.

The message of this parable is powerful, but we need to interpret it, which means that we need to make it our own. For example: we surely all hope to see ourselves as like the wise virgins. But what makes them wise? It is often said that they remained awake and did not sleep, but that it is not it. *All ten of the virgins slept* and then awoke at midnight.

What differentiated the wise from the foolish virgins was that the wise ones were *prepared*. They had *thought in advance*. They were prepared for the possible delay. They had done their work during the day.

So too, we should do good deeds while we can. We should think good thoughts and prepare our souls, not putting off confession or leaving past errors uncorrected. The oil the women needed for their lamps is the light and grace we need for our souls.

Questions for Contemplation

1. Where do I see myself in this parable? Can I identify, in any way, with either set of women?

2. Can I apply it to myself in any way?

3. Do I understand the teaching of the Second Coming, when Jesus shall return to judge the living and the dead?

Lesson 23

Maronite "Village" Spirituality

23.1 Introduction

23.2 "Village" Spirituality: Patron Saints, Vows and the *Mazar*

23.3 The Lord Raises Lazarus

23.1 Introduction

"Spirituality" is a living relationship with God which means something to us in our daily lives. "Spirituality" implies that there is an upwards movement within my soul. A tourist can enter a church and, looking through the eyes of a tourist, see only artwork and architecture. But that is not a spiritual experience, although it can lead to one, or be understood more deeply when the spiritual life appears. On the other hand, a believer can see a new-born baby, and say inside his heart, with a thrill of joy: "My Lord made this wonderful child!" That is spirituality. "Spirituality" lives in our connexion with our religion, our faith and our God.

"Spirituality" can also mean all those feelings and aspirations we have which relate us to something higher than the material world. A purely secular culture and an utterly materialist outlook can never be "spiritual." Our spirituality is a way of living in the world while being mindful of the supernatural realities. In the *Hoosoye* for Tuesdays of Pentecost (cycle 2), the priest prays:

> Jesus Christ our Lord and God, you created heaven and earth
> and, by your will, you continuously watch over them. Heaven,
> radiant with light, sings hymns to you. Earth and all of creation

praise you. We thank you on behalf of all visible creation, and ask that we may come to understand, even though in an imperfect way, those things which we cannot see in that world which does not pass away.

There is so much to consider in this short passage. It teaches that both heaven and earth were created by God, and that He watches over them. It petitions God to allow us to understand even a little of the invisible world. This is quite critical: to have a spirituality one really needs to have a sense of *levels*, of *above* and *below*, for example:

1. Heaven, paradise, the spiritual world.
2. This earth.
3. Hell, the infernal, the demonic.

This is basically the world-view of the ancient Semites which has come down to us through the Bible, both Old Testament and New Testament. Some people see the Greek conception as having been different, but I think that the essence of the two are the same. In the Greek world you had:

1. Elysium (the abode of the blessed).
2. This world.
3. Hades, the underworld (the abode of the damned).

These worlds are populated, and have their own laws or order:

1. God, his angels and his saints, directly ruled by the Will of God.
2. Earth, humanity, and the activities of the inhabitants of the worlds above and below, indirectly ruled by the Will of God. Subject to the laws of nature, one of which is the "law of accident," and a second of which is the "law of grace."
3. Hell, the devil and his fallen angels, indirectly ruled by the Will of God, but given over to chaos.

In this earthly sphere, everything considered as a whole, in its beginning and its end, depends indirectly upon the Will of God. God has willed that the world should be ruled by laws, and that there should be an order to the world. It is worth pondering this: if everything in the universe came about by chance, how is it that the principles, the laws of physics and chemistry, are so orderly and regular? The laws of earth are referrable to and depend upon the will of the Creator. The order we see here, imperfect as it is, reflects the more divine order of heaven.

This leads us to the concept of natural law, which the Latin Church developed from ancient philosophy, especially the thought of Plato and Aristotle. Entire shelves have been written about this: we might leave it here as being too far removed from our main concern, the Maronite tradition.

Together with the laws there is free will, and there is *accident*, even if some people cannot see this, and say that everything was "meant to be." Our free will allows us to choose between different courses of action which are offered to us in accordance with God's laws.

Accident is when different courses of action, or lines of cause and effect, which are not connected by any cause, come together. For example, you are stopped at traffic lights, and another car rams into yours. It just happened that you were there, and the other person's bad driving was not at all connected with your presence there.

The entire universe is like a network of actions, causes and effects, and we are always at a crossroads. Sometimes we have the ability to choose which course of action we will take (free will), and sometimes we collide with the world (accident).

In addition to these laws, history witnesses phenomena of an entirely different order: she witnesses *miracles*. Once more, we do not stop and think about this enough. The fact that there can be some miracles means that the author of the miracles allows the laws to continue working. If you are playing a game, and you can stop the game whenever you like, then the entire game depends upon your will. The existence of miracles is something like that. The Maronite liturgy of Great Lent has several weeks of miracles. In the course of these the priest prays in the Opening:

> Lord Jesus, make us worthy to praise and thank you for all you
> have done for us; your signs, miracles and saving deeds, for you
> are abundantly rich in good gifts. You granted speech to the mute,
> hearing to the deaf, sight to the blind, cleansing to lepers, strength
> to the disabled, health to the sick and resurrection to the dead.

The world in which we live, therefore, manifests the will of God in the laws of nature, in the miracles which punctuate it like so many reminders that the vast panoply we see depends upon the Divine Creator, and in the principle or "law" of accident, which, oddly enough, allows for flexibility, change, and even a certain freedom from the laws. But of course the greatest freedom from the laws of the world comes from *grace*.

Together with this goes the concept of the world as a distraction. In the Third Diaconal Prayer of Monday *Safro* in the Season of Pentecost, it is said:

> May we collect our minds, Lord, when they wander in the
> distracting ways of the world. Awaken our interior presence,
> that we may hear the life-giving voice which whispers your
> commandments. As we grow older, we learn what it is to be lost,
> but also to be more sensitive to the inner voice, and to ask for
> the help of your illuminating grace. May our hearts be cleansed
> of attachment to ephemeral works, and we shall present to you
> our oblations of worship in your lordly and sacred temple, now
> and for ever.

We can relate this to the magnificent material from Jacob of Sarug which we saw in lesson 17. This all lends itself to the symbolism of "lost and found," for it is we who were lost and must be found, as in the well-known parable of the Good Shepherd. In the same office, one of the hymns states: "The world had seemed lost, but now sings in adoration, for it is found." Once you start to follow one thread of the spiritual life, it leads to all of the others.

23.2 "Village" Spirituality: Patron Saints, Vows and the *Mazar*

The villages were the cradles of the Maronite Church. The specifics of village life have left an indelible mark on the Maronite character. Sometimes these village ways merge with other customs. One example of this mingling is the traditional devotion to a patron saint.

Many people have a special devotion to a patron saint. It is often Our Lady, the person's name saint, or the patron of their village in Lebanon. But it does not have to be. Someone might take St Matthew as their patron because once when reading his Gospel they were struck by a line, or a feeling came over them.

The system of patron saints for villages and districts is an important aspect of Maronite spirituality. Let us say one hails from a village where the patron saint is Saint Moura. One is baptised in her church, attends it as a child, and makes first holy communion there. As one grows up, one sees other people being baptised and making confession there.

A lot of memories are bound up with the church, even though we rarely stop and think about them. As children, we are taken to the Divine Liturgy by our parents. It is a business getting dressed up, having our face scrubbed, helping prepare our younger brothers and sisters, or otherwise being spruced up by them. Then we walk to church together, or pile into the car. On the way we see people we know heading in the same direction. We even remember the impression of seeing all these people we know and some we don't know walking in the direction of the church. It is like streams coming from every point of the compass to flow into the church. Then, when we have arrived at church, it is as if everyone we know is there. All are more or less united in respect.

This is true for all people from religious families who attend church, but is especially true, I think, for Eastern Christians such as Maronites for several reasons. First, these families tend to place more emphasis on wearing your Sunday best. It used to be the custom everywhere, but Anglo-Celtic Christians have, by and large, lost it. Second, it is more likely that the entire Maronite family will go. Third, Maronites are more likely to have brothers and sisters! Fourth, we are more likely to meet people we know going to church. Fifth, and this is especially true in the village, it is a communal activity in Lebanon. The rate of Mass attendance is relatively high. Also in Lebanon, people are more likely to meet each other as they are walking to the Church, because they live closer.

The crowds which flock in for funerals and commemorative liturgies, and to offer condolences add a special solemnity to those occasions, already grave enough by reason of the fact that people we know, perhaps our parents and uncles and aunts, are sitting out the front, in black, and very serious. When we are children we are often sent to someone's place for all or part of the mourning, and this also made it strikingly different.

These impressions should not be dismissed. They are a part of our emotional makeup and provide the basis for a feeling that it is natural for people to go to Mass. Little keeps the faith as strong as the feeling that the faith is natural. Children do accept it as natural, and are comfortable with it, and even feel close to God, until they are changed by the world.

But while this is all true, I want to point out that it is this sort of experience or "education by accident," which provides us with the feeling of a special relationship to the patron saint of the town. If the patron is Saint Moura, then all of this takes place in her name, as it were. We see her icon. We hear that she was a disciple of Saint Maroun. We know very little about her except that she was a nun and a hermit. But that doesn't matter: we feel her presence. We could almost believe that she watches over us.

When we grow older we look for more sophisticated reasons to take patron saints: we may be struck by an incident in their lives, or there may be something they said or did which helps us come to terms with the difficulties we face in the world, or we feel peaceful when we see their picture. Any of this is possible, and it is not uncommon for Maronites to have a series of patron saints.

The relationship with the patron saint is another aspect of what I think is one of the characteristics of the Maronite approach to spirituality: the belief, and more than the belief, the feeling and conviction that God is here and the divine is in our very midst. This has to be balanced with the Maronite understanding that we still have efforts to make. Yes, God and his saints are here, but we have to open our eyes to see them, and to obtain the favour of God. For this reason, Maronites often went on pilgrimages to the shrines of saints, especially if they had an urgent prayer to make, or sought the healing of their illnesses and the resolution of their problems.

These pilgrimages often went hand in hand with the system of the *nadir* or "vow." The roots of this actually go back to ancient Phoenicia and the Old Testament. The *New Interpreter's Dictionary of the Bible* states:

> Vow ... specifically refers to a person's explicit commitment to perform a favour for a deity if the deity will respond to his or her request for a favour. ... Vow making was typically motivated by a desire for divine help in daily life, particularly in distress. Vows undertaken at a sanctuary in a compliant ritual in connection with a prayer for deliverance would be fulfilled with the complementary ritual of thanksgiving, including public praise of God as well as sacrifice (Psalm 22:23-26) ... No one was obliged to make a vow, but once spoken, a vow was irrevocably in force, and failure to fulfil it could have negative consequences.[226]

In our tradition, the vows might be made for the intercession of a saint. It is not quite right to say that the person making the vow undertakes to perform a favour for God or the saint. But they do intend to do something pleasing to them, even if only to erect a public

---

[226] *NIDB* 5.793.

testament to the faithfulness of God or the saint. It is also essential to the idea of a vow that a person not already be obliged to perform the act in question. For example, a man would not make a vow to God to be a good father: that is already his duty. But he could vow to walk 20 miles in order to obtain the grace to be a better father.

What adds to the value of a vow is, partly, that it binds the will. Of course a person can promise to do something at any time. But they can also change their mind, or simply fail to perform it. A vow is different: you not only promise to do something, you bind *yourself*. It is not merely a solemn promise. It is a commitment of yourself. Further, as the vow is made to God (even through the intercession of a saint) then it is an act of *worship*. The same cannot be said of just any promise. Being an act of religion, the vow adds merit to the good deed.

The Church has the authority to dispense a person from a vow, or to commute it. It *dispenses* when a vow should be forgotten (e.g. as being contrary to another duty), and it *commutes* it when it alters the subject of the vow. For example, some people make a vow to baptise their children in a certain church, But if this church is not their parish church, this is against ecclesiastical law. That vow can therefore be dispensed with altogether, or else a priest might commute it so, for example, that the person attends three Divine Liturgies at that church.

On this subject, it is necessary to say something about the Maronite tradition of the roadside shrine or *mazar*, which is literally a "place of visiting." I doubt that very many people who visit Lebanon for the first time do not notice these shrines by the side of the road. Some of the them are old and dilapidated, some are minor works of art and well cared for, while most are probably somewhere in-between. People place flowers there, and light candles. Some people have a special *mazar* which they tend, and make sure that it is clean with a candle lit there once a day, and sometimes even burn incense there.

This seemingly minor phenomenon of village life presents several interesting aspects:

1. It brings a sign of the divine presence into the street.
2. Through it, the neighbourhood expresses its religious character.
3. The local people can tend for it: it is even a *ministry*.
4. Once it has been established it is low maintenance.

Included in, but transcending all of these things, the *mazar* is a reminder. I remember walking along the village streets as evening was falling, and my eye was attracted by a small light in one of these humble shrines. It was an unforgettable reminder. The light of God is always burning.

As stated, it allows people to express their local character: thus in Kfarsghab you see numerous shrines to many saints, but especially to St Awtel, its patron saint. I shall deal with the saints in the next lesson.

23.3 The Lord Raises Lazarus

This miracle is recounted only in the Gospel of St John: there is a theory that Lazarus was still alive when the other three Gospels were written, and it was felt to be too personal to tell while he was living.

> Now a man named Lazarus was sick. He was from Bethany, the village of Mary and her sister Martha. ... On his arrival, Jesus found that Lazarus had already been in the tomb for four days. ... When Martha heard that Jesus was coming, she went out to meet him, but Mary stayed at home. "Lord," Martha said to Jesus: "if you had been here, my brother would not have died. But I know that even now God will give you whatever you ask."

> Jesus said to her: "Your brother will rise again. ... I am the resurrection and the life. The one who believes in me will live, even though they die; and whoever lives by believing in me will never die. Do you believe this?" "Yes, Lord," she replied: "I believe that you are the Messiah, the Son of God, who is to come into the world." ...

Jesus, once more deeply moved, came to the tomb. It was a cave with a stone laid across the entrance. "Take away the stone," he said. "But, Lord," said Martha, the sister of the dead man: "by this time there is a bad odour, for he has been there four days." Then Jesus said: "Did I not tell you that if you believe, you will see the glory of God?" So they took away the stone. ... Jesus called in a loud voice: "Lazarus, come out!" The dead man came out, his hands and feet wrapped with strips of linen, and a cloth around his face. Jesus said to them: "Take off the grave clothes and let him go." (from John 11)

Questions for Contemplation

1. What does this tell us about Jesus' humanity?
2. What does it say about his love for humanity?
3. Why did Jesus work this miracle?

Lesson 24
The Maronite Saints

24.1 Saint Maroun

There is no figure in history quite like the elusive figure which is St Maroun. Apart from the less well-known apostles, few figures are both so important in the history of Christianity, and yet so invisible. No other purely Catholic rite is, is far as I know, exclusively named after one person: the other rites are named after a language (e.g. the Latin rite), a people (the Armenians), or an institution (the Melkites, named after the king). But our entire rite is named after our god-father, this great, yet shadowy figure. We can be compared to children who wake up after father has gone to work. The father's presence fills the house, and the children sense him – their very existence speaks of him – but during the day, they neither see nor hear him.

I shall try and present St Maroun as he appears in history: a hermit teaching in the mountains of what is now Syria until his death (probably sometime before 425AD); a man of a holiness which was absolutely magnetic, a priest who was able to make the great breakthrough nobody before him had. I will suggest that St Maroun's breakthrough was this: he was the first Christian teacher to be able to make a significant and enduring impact upon the people of the Syrian and Lebanese countryside and mountains. He did this because (1) he possessed the richness of Greek Christianity, but naturally expressed it in the Aramaic language of these people; (2) his example was such that he inspired young people of the region to follow him into the religious life; and (3) his life, and the lives of his religious disciples, demonstrated to the lay people, that in Christianity there had come a religion greater than the polytheism they had known.

We do not know when St Maroun was born, except that it was sometime in the 300s. He almost certainly died between 410 and 425, but we have no clue as to his age at death. One can hardly envisage him having been less than 40 years old, but he have been 100 years old. We simply do not know. And, in any event, that is not significant.

The critical fact about St Maroun is that he lived as a hermit, and he died, atop a hill in Syria, probably at Kaluta. St Maroun was the first hermit known to spend his days in the open air. He chose a site which had been a place of pagan worship: it included a temple, although the text I translate below is suggestive that not only the temple but perhaps the entire hilltop, had been sacred. The polytheists are known to have had sacred groves, trees, fish ponds and stones. There was often, if not always, a temple nearby. St Maroun is said to have dedicated those precincts to God, which may mean that he performed an exorcism, turned the temple into a church, and blessed the rest of the area. For protection against rain and snow, St Maroun relied upon a tent made of animal hides. This way of life made a big impression on the people.

What did St Maroun occupy himself with? There seem to have been two sides to his life at Kaluta: a private life of prayer and spiritual exercise, and a public life with his many visitors, which included many diverse matters: conversation, advice, teaching, healing and exorcism. Our source, Theodoret, says that St Maroun tended to his spiritual life with "the customary labours" and other exercises which he himself conceived. Theodoret speaks of this as "gathering together the wealth of *philosophia*." In the translation below, I have rendered *philosophia* as "wisdom," for our modern term "philosophy" is too narrow to encompass the arts and sciences of the soul which St Maroun pursued.

Theodoret's account is short, but it highlights St Maroun's magnetism in a few deft strokes. First, we have the references to the ascetic disciplines which he undertook. When Theodoret speaks of the "customary labours," he appears to have in mind prayer, fasting, penance, and depriving the body of sleep. Theodoret paid particular attention to any measures which might check the passions and bring the faculties under the control of a Christian will (by "faculties" I mean senses, thoughts and emotions). However, Theodoret does not tell us very much about these inner disciplines, let alone which ones were added by St Maroun. But then, neither, indeed, do many writers describe such disciplines, as they require the assistance and supervision of a teacher, and to write of them could lead some people to attempt exercises which they should not. However, it is clear that St Maroun was a master of these disciplines, and also that he taught various pupils, such as Yakub, Limnaios and – perhaps – Domnina. Theodoret is emphatic on the point that St Maroun was a great teacher: he states that the hermit "planted the paradise which now blooms in the land of Kurros (also known as Cyrrhos or Cyr)."

We are almost totally reliant upon the *History of the Monks of Syria*, by Theodoret, who was bishop of Cyrrhos. Theodoret is uneven in his treatment of the monks, and aimed to relate what he had seen of these monks for himself, or learned from those who had themselves met the relevant monk.[227] Unfortunately for us, it appears that Theodoret did not ever meet St Maroun,[228] and perhaps for this reason, commentators observe that Theodoret's brief account is very thin for such an important monk.[229]

In addition, St John Chrysostom (347-407), the Bishop of Antioch, and later of Constantinople, wrote a letter to a hermit named Maroun, and asked him for his prayers. It is more probable that this was addressed to St Maroun than to someone else of that name. That he enjoyed the confidence of Chrysostom would tell us how impressive a figure he was.

The life of St Maroun is chapter 16 of Theodoret's writings on the holy hermits and monks of Syria.[230] It states:

> 1 After Akepsimas, I will call to mind Maroun, for he adorned the godly troop of the holy ones. Maroun embraced life under the sky, taking for himself a certain hill-top which had long ago been honoured by the impious. And having dedicated to God the sacred precincts of the demons in that place, he passed all of his time there, pitching a small tent, but making little use of it. Maroun did not only employ the customary labours, but he conceived others also, gathering together the wealth of wisdom.

> 2 The judge measured out grace for these labours: so richly did the munificent one grant to him the charism of healing, that Maroun's fame ran about everywhere, and everyone from everywhere was attracted, so that experience taught them the truth of the report. It was seen that fevers were quenched by the dew of his blessing, shudderings ceased, and demons fled – many and varied sufferings were cured by the one remedy. For the race of physicians applies to each illness the corresponding medicine,

---

[227] (Prologue, 11)
[228] Price (1985) 119, n.1.
[229] Price (1985) 119, n.1. Cavinet and Leroy-Molinghen (1979) 28-29, n.1.
[230] *Théodoret de Cyr: Histoire des moines de Syrie*, two volumes, Pierre Canivet and Alice Leroy-Molinghen, Sources Chrétiennes 234, Les éditions du cerf, Paris, 1977 and 1979.

but the prayer of the holy ones is the common antidote to all pathologies.

3 But Maroun healed more than bodily weaknesses alone: he also applied the bountiful cure for souls. He heals the greed of this man, and the anger of that man. For one man, Maroun proffers the teaching which leads to self-control, while for another man he bestows lessons in justice; he tempers the man of intemperance, and arouses the sluggish. Farming in this wise, Maroun cultivated many crops through his wisdom: it was he who planted the paradise which now blooms in the land of Kurros. The great Yakobos (James) was a product of this cultivation: of him and of all the others whom I shall recall individually with God's help, one could rightly apply the famous prophetic saying: "The just man will flower like the palm tree, and will be multiplied like a cedar in the Lebanon."

4 Caring in this way for the garden of God, doctoring to both souls and bodies alike, he patiently suffered but a short illness. Maroun, teaching us the frailty of our nature and strength in commitment, withdrew himself from this life.

Quarrelling broke out between the neighbours over his body, a violent quarrel. A populous bordering village came out in a body, scattered all of the others, and seized this most-desired treasure. They built a great sacred enclosure, and even to this very day they reap the profit, honouring Maroun the victory-bearer with a public feast. And even we, who are at a distance, reap his blessing, for it is not Maroun's tomb which contents us, but his memory.

Note, too, the enigmatic reference to St Maroun's death: he "withdrew himself from this life." Theodoret seems to say that there came a time when St Maroun fell ill, and he deliberately surrendered his soul to his Maker. If this interpretation is correct, it tells us how trusting in God he was, how far above worldly attachments, and how lacking in selfish fear.

Theodoret makes some other comments in odd places about St Maroun, but they are not terribly important. However, now that we have seen the facts about St Maroun, what can we conclude? I suggest that the important considerations are these:

1   In his lifetime, Our Lord taught in southern Lebanon (in particular, he visited Tyre and perhaps Sidon). Our Lord taught these people in Aramaic and perhaps Greek. It is known that some of his teaching was not recorded in the Gospels. Further, some of the sayings, which other sources have reliably recorded, show that not only the name of monasticism, but even the spiritual practices of the monks themselves, can be traced back to Jesus. This evidence bears out a tradition maintained by the monks that Jesus taught them their ways.

2   Some of the sayings attributed to Our Lord bear this out. For example, several sources have preserved his saying "Be good money changers," referring to the need to watch our thoughts and – like a good money changer – not to accept whatever we are offered, but to test it. That is, Jesus taught people to test the quality and value of their own thoughts, and to accept only those which bore the mark of the king. Coins, after all, bore the mark of the sovereign, and our thoughts also betray their origin. Maintaining a careful watch over our thoughts is a foundation of the monastic path. Further, there is reason to believe that Our Lord may even have used the word "monk." Despite ill-informed comments to the effect that it was Gnostic, scholars accept that the Gospel of Thomas, is probably accurate in having Our Lord speak of the "monachos', the monk.[231] This Gospel is thought to have been popular in Syria, and is noteworthy for its emphasis upon ascetic disciplines. And here there is a significant element of continuity between the most ancient church and our own Maronite traditions.

3   After Pentecost, the Apostles travelled, spreading the gospel. St Peter is reliably placed in coastal Lebanon, and is said to have established a bishopric in Byblos. The Pseudo-Clementine *Recognitions* have an interesting passage where St Peter travels to the Phoenician temple on the island of Arwad, and is impressed

---

[231]   The Gospel of Thomas was almost certainly written by heretics, but it was not "Gnostic."

by the massive wooden pillars before it (reminiscent of the pillars before the Temple of Solomon, built for him by Hiram of Tyre). The Phoenician religion, to an extent unparalleled elsewhere, had a doctrine of the death of the god Melqart (and perhaps also of Eshmoun) and his resurrection. This was an intimation or anticipation of Christianity.

4   Christianity spread northwards along the coast to Antioch. Although the Apostles themselves spoke Aramaic (Peter's name was in fact *Kefa* – the Aramaic word for "rock"), they could also communicate in Greek, indeed, this is part of the message of the Pentecost story. Perhaps because they could reach more people by teaching in the cities, the disciples did not have as much success in the countryside as they did in the chiefly Greek-speaking cities. It is known that in Antioch, there were many ordinary men and women who lived lives of celibacy. At this point there is only slim evidence for what we might recognise today as hermits and monks. It is also known that monasticism was a native development in Syria: it was not imported from Egypt. The most likely hypothesis is that eremitism (the condition of being a hermit) and monasticism developed directly from Jesus' example.

5   It seems that St Peter himself was the first bishop of Antioch, although some think that he only appointed the first bishop. When he went to Rome, where he headed the Church, he founded a Greek-speaking congregation. Even in Rome, the language of the Roman church was then Greek. The early Roman texts, too, are all in Greek. For example, the letter of Clement of Rome (later to be Pope, as tradition has it) to the Corinthians was written in Greek. For hundreds of years, the Roman graves of the popes were inscribed in Greek, not Latin. The gospels have survived only in Greek, although there is a tradition that Matthew also wrote in Aramaic.

6   Christianity is not believed to have made much headway in the Syrian and Lebanese countryside. After all, the peasants had little or no Greek. His name: "Maroun" (the Syriac for "little lord"), strongly suggests that he came from a Syriac background. This is significant, the names of most of the other monks and hermits,

and even Theodoret's own name, were Greek. But Maroun's chief disciple was named "Jakoubos." This was originally a Hebrew name, although it was adopted by Greeks, but equally, it was taken over by Syriac speakers.

7   It is not unreasonable to think that St Maroun represented an authentic Syrian Christianity, which can be traced directly back to Our Lord himself and the apostles. That the tradition is not steadily attested is not fatal to this thesis, for so few texts have survived.

The above reconstruction cannot be proven. But there is no evidence against it, and it makes sense of our traditions (not least that a Catholic rite bears his name) and all of the other evidence.

The people of Mount Lebanon shortly afterwards sent to St Symeon for aid, and he set in train a process of converting all of them to Christianity. Given St Maroun's influence on Symeon, this is evidence of a further if indirect link between Maroun and Christianity in Lebanon. The crosses which Symeon told these people to place around their towns were apparently visible in towns such as Ehden and Bsharri until a couple of hundred years ago.

In short, in Mar (St) Maroun there was finally found someone who was a master of the Christian teaching, and who could act as a bridge between the Greek-speaking cities and the Aramaic countryside.

24.2 The Religious Orders

We shall begin our treatment of the religious orders before coming to Saints Charbel and Rafqa, who both belonged to the Lebanese Maronite Order. This order was founded on 10 November 1695, when three Maronites from Aleppo: Abdallah Caraali, Gabriel Hawi and Joseph Al-Batn (being joined later by Germanos Farhat), received the monastic habit from the hands of Patriarch Estphan El-Doueihy. Acceptance of the clothing implied acceptance of the three monastic vows: obedience, chastity and poverty. The new order took St Anthony the Great as its patron. There were, at that time, no monasteries left in Syria, so they travelled to Lebanon (whether for guidance or because they could not live in Syria, I am not sure). They initially stayed at Tamish, then a double monastery (i.e. having rooms for both men and women) for three months, before visiting other monasteries, and finally moving to Mart Moura near Ehidin, where they stayed.

Although this was the founding of a new order, it was not the founding of a new tradition. Rather, the Maronite Church had from the very first been a primarily monastic church, in that the churches were monastery churches. However, these monasteries were originally all autonomous, meaning that they were independent of each other. This new organisation of 1695 would allow for the unification of all monasteries under one directorship, that of a Superior General, who would be assisted by a General Council comprised of four Assistants.

Further, the old monasteries had simply been houses set up at the edge of the town. If you wanted to live the religious life, you just went and stayed there. There are two accounts of the relations of the sexes: according to one, men and women shared the same house, which although it scandalised the Latins, worked perfectly well. In the villages everyone knew and was probably related to each other. It was like living at home with your sister or aunt, and indeed, if any of your sisters and aunts were nuns, they would have been living in that house with you!

On the other hand, the second account states that the men and women had separate, but neighbouring buildings. However, they would share the same chapel, laundry, kitchen and storeroom. It is said that in this type of monastery and convent, the members of the monastery and convent originally came from one family, and the two buildings would be owned by that family. One example is the "double monastery" of the Assaf family, established in 1655, housing four brothers, their sister, and eventually their parents, too.

It is said that in the constitution of the LMO (based on rules attributed to St Anthony the Great), the thought of three monastic saints was particularly influential: Saints Basil the Great (Feast Day 2 January), John Climacus (30 March) and St Ephrem (28 January). However, it is clear that the organisation of the new order was on the model of Western monasticism. The monasteries were segregated, and formed a federation which was centrally managed. The main aim of the LMO was contemplative, while the active life was secondary. Patriarch El-Doueihy approved their constitution on 18 June 1700. Being officially recognised by the Maronite Church, the members could make their solemn profession. They made the triple vow publicly, the first time that this had been done in the Maronite Church.

In May 1727, the Superior General of the LMO, Fr Michael Alexander al-Ehdeni went to Rome to attain pontifical approval of the constitution. Pope Clement XII granted this in 1732. The LMO was now no longer an institute of Patriarchal, but rather of Pontifical Right. Its rules have been the model for other Eastern Catholic orders, Maronite and non-Maronite alike.

In 1770, the LMO was split into two groups, the Aleppine (founded by the sons of the wealthy families of Aleppo) and the Baladites (whose monks were the poor men of the land of Lebanon). In 1969 the Aleppine order became the Mariamite monks (the Maronite Order of the Blessed Virgin Mary).

Meanwhile, in 1700, another monastic order had been founded. I am not sure why it was felt that a new order was needed, but these were to become the Antonines. Their patron was a monk named Isaiah, originally from Aleppo. The Antonine Order of St Isaiah took the Western Rules of St Augustine, but in just 1705, they adopted the rules of St Anthony, which the LMO were using. In 1740, Pope Clement XII approved for them the rules which had been approved for the LMO in 1732.

Therefore, from 1770, there were three Maronite monastic orders, with similar if not identical rules. Then, in 1865, Father John Habib (later the Archbishop of Nazareth) founded a missionary order, the Congregation of Lebanese Missionaries. They take their name "Kraimi" from the monastery of Kraim which Fr Habib purchased from the Armenian Catholics in Ghosta. Their rules, originally based on those of the Redemptorists, were approved by Patriarch Paul Masad. Hence they are of Patriarchal, not Pontifical Right.

The aims of this order were defined as preaching and evangelising, but they also engage in teaching.

24.3 The Maronite Nuns

Fr Abdallah Caraali, one of the original members of the LMO, set about extending his work to nuns, soon after the LMO was founded in 1695. In 1716 he was made Bishop of Beirut, and adapted the monastery of St John the Baptist of Hrache for the nuns. He ensured that monks and nuns were in separate establishments with independent stores and kitchens.

In 1736, the Synod of Mount Lebanon suppressed all double monasteries and forbade the erection of new ones. However, this did not occur for another 100 years! In the interim, Bishop Caraali and the Papal Legate Joseph Simon Assemani founded a convent of St Elie near Jeita, for nuns only, and they would dedicate themselves to prayer and meditation. The first candidates were received on 6 January (the Epiphany) 1740, together with three experienced nuns from St John of Hrache. Later, the LMO monks took charge of these religious sisters. Other convents of this order were opened (St Sassine, Baskinta; St Maroun, Qunaitra; St Simon, Aitou and St Joseph, Jrabta).

At this period, each convent was autonomous, and the nuns were strictly cloistered. They could only leave the convent for a most pressing reason, and with consent. However, they gradually began to become less contemplative, until in 1984, when they became an Order of Pontifical Right, their orientation was to the active life. The same shift from the contemplative to the active life is seen with the Antonine Nuns, who were founded at the convent of St Elie, but under the Antonine Monks. They made the change in 1953, and had it ratified when they became an order of Pontifical Right in 1958.

The Maronite Sisters of the Holy Family were the first all-female institution in the entire Oriental Church. It was founded by Bishop, later Patriarch Elias Howaiek, in 1895 at Jbeil. Later he purchased for them a property at Ibrine where he built their mother convent. This order, unlike the others, was always oriented to the active life, especially to the education of girls, and to teaching them not only religion but also science and other matters. They also worked in training centres, orphanages, hospitals, clinics, elderly care and so on. The congregation is of Patriarchal Right.

As last advised, there are only three enclosed Maronite convents: those of Our Lady of the Fields at Dlebta; the Annunciation at Zouk and the Visitation Convent at Aintoura. They are all Patriarchal, and are independent of each other. There are strictly enclosed and contemplative Poor Clares at Yarze in Beirut. They were originally Latin but are now Maronite.

24.4 St Charbel Makhlouf

Having studied the orders, let us now examine what has flowed from them. St Charbel was the first saint to be canonised under the modern rules. This occurred on 5 December 1965.

Born Youssef Makhlouf in Beqa Kafra on 8 May 1828, he was the fifth child in a a simple farming family. When he was three years old, his father was taken away to work for the Ottoman Army. Youssef was sent to the village school, where he was given to prayer. He knew that he should be a monk, and prayed to Our Lady to make it come to pass. Two of his mother's brothers were already monks. However, he did not leave until 1851, when one of the women of the area took a fancy to him. He left home the next morning, saying nothing to his mother, to enter the monastery of Our Lady of Mayfouq, which was run by the LMO. However, he was pursued there by his uncle, mother and relatives. They begged him to return home, marry, work and look after them. Youssef refused, saying that God wanted him entirely. It is said that in the end his mother told him to be a good monk: if he was going to be mediocre, she said, he should return home.

Youssef took the name of Charbel, a martyr saint who had died about the year 107. At the end of his first year, he was sent to St Maroun's at Annaya for the second year of his novitiate. There, he made his monastic profession and took the three solemn vows in 1853, at the age of 25. When his mother came to visit him, he spoke to her from a window three metres about the ground: he refused to meet her. In those days, the laws against monks speaking to any women were rather strict, and Charbel was determined to keep them. When she asked why he did not wish to meet her, he said that if God wishes, they would be together for eternity.

He was then sent to the Monastery of St Cyprian in Kfifan, the LMO's scholasticate. There he studied philosophy and theology, being ordained a priest, on 23 July 1859, at Bkerke (even then the Patriarchal residence). He was then sent back to Annaya, where he spent 16 years in the community. On arrival, his elderly mother and his relatives were present to greet him as a new priest, and to invite him back to Beqa Kafra to say Mass. He refused. At the end of that 16 years, he chose to retire to the hermitage. It is said that this occurred after the miracle when his lamp remained lit although it contained only water, and no oil.

It is said that as a hermit he was always kneeling before the Blessed

Sacrament. He was said to have always treated even the lowliest person with respect. His fasting was more stringent than the requirements. Another story about him is quite significant: Fr Ignatius Daher saw him once, digging in the fields. Just as he raised his pick in the air, a companion, Fr Makarios, called to him. Charbel lowered the pick at once, not swinging it into the ground. It is, they say, the mark of a master to refrain from doing. That is, the ability to cease something you are doing mid-movement, or to cease speaking mid-word, to refrain from making a point you had been bursting to make, shows the person with true mastery over the self.

There is also a story that when he was working in a remote part of the fields with his brethren, he did not hear the call to lunch, and so he continued working. Only six hours after lunch did someone ask him why he had not eaten. Then they learned what had happened: as he ate only one meal a day, he had been thirty hours without food, working non-stop. Another story goes that one day, again in the fields, a monk heard Fr Charbel cry out for help. The monk left his wheelbarrow, and went to Fr Charbel's aid. When he reached him, he found him calm and silent. Charbel told him that he was alright. A little later he heard Charbel call again, so the monk returned and insisted on knowing what was going on. Quietly, Charbel said to him: "Please forgive me brother, I have been sorely tempted. Pray for me."

Showing his will-power over the body, Charbel wore the poorest clothes, never added extra clothing or wore thicker robes in winter, and ate the worst food: crusts and fruit of the meaner sort. He was vegetarian.

One would hesitate to vouch for the truth of some of the stories. But this one sounds true: a Muslim was searching for the tobacco pouch he had lost. One of the monks told him that Charbel the monk had taken it. The Muslim marched up to him and demanded it back, saying that others had seen him. Charbel's reply was: "Do you see that rock down there at the bottom of the garden? It's been there for centuries and no one has taken it." The Muslim got the point: people don't take things they have no purpose for. It would not have been Charbel, who did not smoke, who took the tobacco.

He prepared his own Mass with great care, and attended the Masses of the other monks, although this was not compulsory. He spent hours before the Eucharist, often for much of the night. He would daily say the prayer: "Father of Truth, your son is here, a victim ready to do your bidding."

Fr Charbel remained in the hermitage until his death. The circumstances of this are quite striking: on 16 December 1898, he was celebrating Mass in the chapel of the hermitage. As he held aloft the chalice for the major elevation, he struck by paralysis. The prayer at that point is:

> O Father of Truth, behold your Son, a sacrifice pleasing to you. Accept this offering of him who died for me. ... Behold his blood shed on Golgotha for my salvation. Accept my offering.

The final illness lasted for eight days. He left this world on 24 December 1898, the vigil of Christmas. I will deal with only one of the miracles worked through him: the miracle that his body was incorrupt for more than 60 years after his death. This is frequently a sign of great holiness.

24.5 Saint Na'amtallah Al-Hardini

In English, this saint's first name is spelled in many ways: Nemetallah, Nehmtallah, Nimattullah and so on. He was beatified on 10 May 1998, and canonised on 16 May 2004 by Saint John-Paul II. We celebrate his feast day on 14 December.

He is the third saint of the Lebanese Maronite Order, after Saint Charbel (1965) and Saint Rafqa (1985). Different dates have circulated for his birth and ordination, but he was born in Hardine in 1810, entered the novitiate on 1 November 1828 at the monastery of St Anthony, Qozhaya, and was ordained a monk on 14 November 1830 by Fr Makarios. He died on 14 December 1858 at the monastery of Saints Cyprian and Justina. He was therefore 48 years old at the time of his death.

Na'amtallah was born and baptised as "Joseph Kassab." His maternal grandfather, Fr Joseph Ra'ad Yaqoub, was a priest of Tannourine. Our Joseph was named after him. There were seven children in the family, four of whom took the religious life. Joseph was the third child: his two elder brothers both became priests, one of them becoming a monk and the other a married priest. The girl after him, Masihiya (Christine) became a nun. He was apparently very bright, and, at age ten, was sent to a local school in Hardine before being sent to an LMO school, St Anthony at Haoub, to learn Arabic, Syriac, mathematics, service of the liturgy, and the hymns and rituals of the church. During this period he stayed with his grandfather the priest. His sister Mariam said that he would take three pieces of bread with him to school, consume two, and always bring the third back. She stated that he was quiet, never fighting or arguing with anyone, and preferred to pray and engage in self-examination rather than play. He did a sort of apprenticeship with his grandfather, accompanying him to church and serving the Mass.

This life continued for three years until he returned home to help his father with manual labour, especially in the fields, but continuing to serve the Mass. He still tended to avoid company, but fortunately had good health and was strong. He remained at home for five years, until, at the age of eighteen, followed the steps of his eldest brother, who had joined the monks at St Anthony, Qozhaya. Apparently the family were relatively well off. Some people would become monks because they had no other options, but he joined the order out of love for God alone. Fr Na'amtallah Al-Kafri wrote about his behaviour at this time:

> He left everything and entered religious life at … Qozhaya. From
> the beginning of his novitiate, he adhered to all the rules and

religious regulations. He was serious about the day and evening prayers, frequently visiting the Blessed Sacrament and staying for hours. Sometimes, he would spend the entire night in church, and when he had to leave the church out of obedience, he would stay in the hall meditating and admiring God.

He was made a monk, but not a priest, in 1830. He was sent to the monastery at Kfifan, were he studied theology with the other seminarians. At that time, seminarians were told that they needed two wings to fly to heaven: the wing of sanctity and the wing of learning. He studied hard, being "obsessed with every small detail," and was so strict on himself, that his superiors became anxious for his health and sent him to the monastery of Saint Moussa Al-Habashi (the Ethiopian) at Dawar in the Matn. He was later allowed to return to Kfifan, presumably when he was out of danger. However, he had not objected to being asked to discontinue his studies: he felt that he was not worthy of being a priest.

Na'amtallah seems to have changed while he was at Dawar, for one of the spiritual directors convinced him that he should desist from avoiding the priesthood. Further, at that monastery they formed the view that his frequent visits to the Blessed Sacrament were made not from madness (as they seem to have thought at Kfifan) but from pure devotion. When he returned to Kfifan after only a few months, he went straight to the top of the class, and became a mentor for the other students, having the capacity of explaining the lessons to them more clearly than the master had. While he was studying, he also had the duty of sewing habits for the monks.

On 22 February 1835, he was one of the monks who signed a petition to the Office of the Propagation of the Faith complaining about some conditions in the LMO (I do not know which those conditions were).

Finally, on 25 December 1835, he was ordained to the priesthood together with 23 other monks. After his ordination, Fr Al-Kafri wrote of him that he went to daily confession as part of his preparation for Mass.

The only exceptions were when he was physically ill, or his pastors advised him not to because there was insufficient need. Even then, he would remember things he had done when young, and seek permission to confess them. He was known, and admired, for the reverent way in which he conducted Mass, pronouncing each word distinctly and with intention. He would not allow the servers to miss anything. In respect of his prayer life generally, Fr Al-Kafri stated:

> ... we could say that he prayed day and night, continuously, either through meditation or through prayers, which he read with great fervour and devotion, without any boredom. He never left prayer, day or night, except for very good reason. Even during his last illness, he never stopped until he became unable to stand. This pious father was in complete union with the Almighty. That is why he liked to be alone, avoiding any occasion that would force him to mingle, isolating himself to communicate with the Almighty.

Saint Na'amtallah had a special devotion to Our Lady. The first aspect of this is that he himself would prayer to her, frequently. He would say the Angelus before he left and when he re-entered his room. He prayed the rosary daily, wore the Carmel scapular, and read books about her, often repeating the prayer: "Blessed be her Immaculate Conception." Even when he was feverish during his final illness, he would repeat this prayer. The second aspect of his Marian devotion is that he urged others to join the Societies of the Sacred Heart of Jesus and that of Mary, distributing membership forms, and introducing the Societies into the monasteries, including Kfifan itself.

Out of devotion to Our Lady he would fast and abstain from all meat on Saturday (which was then followed as Our Lady's day, a practice taken from the Latins). He would also fast during the Triduum of her feasts (the three preceding days, another obsolete practice) and even during the entire month of May. However, it is said that his greatest love was the Eucharist. One side of this fasting must be mentioned, really, as a warning. I do not think that he obtained sainthood *because* of the following, rather, I think that he obtained it *despite* it: we are told that because he fasted so severely, and ate cold food because he ate late, he developed stomach problems, was pale and fragile, and would even vomit his food, evidently being unable to eat it when it was too cold (while the other monks ate around 11.00a.m., he would never eat before 12 noon, which is when he finished his Mass, meditation and thanksgiving).

Additionally, he is known to have had a devotion to St John. In his prayers, he frequently remembered those who were sinners (seeking that they might repent), and those suffering souls in Purgatory who had no one to pray for them. He would ask God for the power to cure the sick, and apparently himself worked cures with holy water. One story was told by Tannous Al-Chidiac of Aytoo, who had visited the monastery of Kfifan when he was eleven years old. He would serve Mass for Na'amtallah, but there came a time when for several days he could not leave his bed because of a fever which had felled him. When he noticed that Tannous failed to attend for Mass, Na'amtallah went to his room. The boy explained that he had a fever, but Na'amtallah ordered the fever to depart, saying: "Sit, my son. Leave him, O Blessed." Tannous immediately arose, completely free of the sickness.[232] Na'amtallah had a special care for the handicapped and the young, even being willing to share with them whatever food and clothing had been given to him.

His main priestly duty was teaching the seminarians. Three times he was elected Assistant General, and served on the General Council of the Order. He did not like the Assistant's position but he accepted it out of obedience. He was not only lacking in ambition for promotion, he avoided it. He could, apparently, have been superior of the Order, but refused, saying that Our Lord and Our Lady did not want him to accept that position. When pressed on the point, he said that Our Lady had

---

[232] When he was 90 years old, Tannous said: "… I still remember the time when the Lord bestowed on me his grace to serve Father's Mass. I remember this very well and the mention of it makes my life happy until death."

told him so. He was known for his obedience. Saint Na'amtallah earnt money for the monastery by repairing and binding books. He would give that money to his Superior, using it only for church purposes. He respected people not for their town, but only for their virtues. He did not favour those he knew over strangers.

He was also an *understanding* man: meaning that he not only knew a lot of facts and lived virtuously, but he was wise, attaining to insights which a high IQ alone will never deliver. Thus, he was not harsh with the novices. When Bishop Joseph Geagea, the Apostolic Visitor to the Order wished to introduce severe rules denying the monks all luxuries, Saint Na'amtallah took the floor to object to banning smoking among the monks. Bishop Geagea was furious, and said: "You cover your eyes with your hood and you object." Saint Na'amtallah answered:

> Your Excellency, we should not be rigid in those things that are lawful and allowable. We should lighten the burden we put on the shoulders and the consciences of the monks. The greater the pressure, the greater the explosion will be. If we tighten the arch too much, it will eventually loosen.

Saint Na'amtallah was also ahead of his time as an educationalist, in that he appreciated the importance of Western languages and educational practices. When the Jesuits opened the seminary of Ghazir in 1846, he persuaded the rector to send some of his students there to obtain a better education. Then, he and the rector would sometimes visit these students, taking them fresh fruit, wine and cheese. This did not compromise his deep devotion to the Eastern tradition, teaching students how to read and recite the hymns of St Ephrem in the original Syriac.

It is said that he began a reform and deepening of the spirituality of the LMO, although I have not seen any specific details of what that reform consisted in. He was the master of St Charbel, who was, we are told, very close to Saint Na'amtallah, and was present at this death.

Saint Na'amtallah chose to be a monk, rather than a hermit, despite his retiring ways, because, he said, he needed the communal life to teach him patience, tolerance and obedience. He especially sought to be patient with others' shortcomings (real or perceived). When his brother, himself possibly a hermit, advised him to become a hermit, he replied:

> Those who struggle with community life in a monastery or convent are virtuous. They need to be patient and obedient and need to put up with the weaknesses of others. Community life in the monastery is, according to the Spiritual Fathers, a constant heroic act. A monk cannot act according to his wishes, but has to be always vigilant not to arouse doubt in others. These are the duties of the monk in the monastery. On the other hand, my brother, the hermit is alone. No one tempts him from the outside. He spends his time praying and cultivating the vineyard. I tell you, we are not all the same. Each has his own vocation. Some were called for the life of isolation and others for community life at the monastery. I adopted my vocation a long time ago.

Saint Na'amtallah did not shirk work: he would get up before others in order to do the washing up, and then would ring the bell for midnight prayer.

His techniques for dealing with temptations of the flesh were not moderate. He always looked down to the ground when he walked, covering his head and forehead. When he knew that a woman might pass, he would cross the road. He avoided women, and when he could not, refused to allow them to kiss his hand. To discipline his body, he wore sackcloth and ate little fruit, possibly because it is sweet. He sometimes slept without a mattress, resting his head on his hand, and lying on a goat skin. He refused to wear additional clothing to protect him in winter, although his feet swelled from the cold.

This led to his death: he allowed himself to become exposed to the bitter winds of Kfifan, and contracted pleurisy. After ten days, during which the usual medicines did not help, he died. Fr Al-Kafri was told by Fr Raphael Al-Bezawy, who was present, that at the time of Na'amtallah's death, a light shone from his mouth (or, in one account, filled the room).

Saint Na'amtallah's experiences as a rigorous seminarian make me think of three related matters in the spiritual life:

1. We should not be too hard on ourselves; we should even have pity on ourselves.
2. We attach too much importance to the wrong things.
3. Someone who has been through a problem can help others better than someone who has not.

In respect of his prayer life, we could note that although he usually knelt at Mass, he sometimes prayed standing up, and it is said that when he was before the Blessed Sacrament, he would remain with his hands up in the air (as in the pictures of him). But more importantly than this, he found that when he was alone, he could communicate better with the divine. This is an important principle: not that we should isolate ourselves, but that if you wish to focus on anything, you have to cut out distractions. People who want to listen to one particular sound have to block other sounds. If you want to study something visually, you magnify what you wish to see, or if you can't do that, you examine it from up close, maybe training a light upon it. This applies also to divine worship and prayer. It is important to observe, however, that his principle can be taken to an extreme, although it is sound in itself: for that reason, as mentioned, he lived with others rather than in a hermitage.[233]

Saint Na'amtallah evidently had a reputation as a holy man, even during his life, and apparently Patriarch Paul Massad spoke highly of him. But he must have had a reputation among the people, because

---

[233] It is the nature of our human consciousness that it magnifies what it rests upon. The positive aspect of this is how, if we direct our attention, we can concentrate and understand something well. But because our consciousness tends to focus on what it sees, once we have a certain idea, it can exclude all others. So two perspectives are ultimately needed: the near and the far.

immediately upon hearing of his death, people came to visit his tomb and touch anything which had been in contact with him. The visitors included not only Maronites but also Orthodox Christians and Muslims. Cures of many diverse illnesses were attributed to his intercession. For over a year, his body showed no deterioration and gave off no rank smell. I can well believe this of a man of whom it was said that he had three concerns, God, His Holy Mother, and books.

Although Saint Na'amtallah did not write any books, he is known to have written letters, of which seven survive. However, they are very brief. The first one reads:

By the Grace of God,

I kiss with honour the hands of Reverend Father Lawrencios Al-Shababy, Lebanese Superior-General, who is honoured and revered, may God keep him.

We present to your goodness, asking God for your well-being. After kissing your blessed hands with respect and asking for your blessing, we present to you what you already know in this area. We are in need of a priest to help us. We beg of you to give us Fr Paul Kfarhatna to help us. Our hope in your goodness is great. We know that you want our comfort. Again we kiss, with great respect your blessed hands, asking God to keep you.

24 January 1851

Your son in his holiness, Na'amtallah Hardini, Lebanese

I shall omit the second letter. The third is a little different:

The honourable Mr Ibrahim, May God keep him.

After bestowing our blessing on you, longing to find you in good health. You had mentioned that you had some books that needed binding. If you can send them now, we can bind them. We are free and work is slow. Record each book by its name. That is all. May God keep you.

2 January 1856

Yours truly, Monk Na'amtallah Hardini, Lebanese

In addition to this, the following additional sayings are attributed to him:

> The monk in his monastery is like a king in his castle. His nation is his religious order, his soldiers are his brother monks, his glory is his virtue, his crown is his love for God and the religious order, his mace is his purity, his armour is his poverty, obedience and prayer; and his robe is his humility.

> The monk must be careful about his reputation and conduct, lest he causes others to doubt him and become suspicious.

> If you have something to say to your brother, go and confront him in the spirit of Christ. Don't allow your tongue any opportunity to blame and accuse.

> The clever person is the one who knows how to save his soul.

> The skilful one is the one who can save his soul.

When some monks said to him that making a daily confession would "lead to madness," he replied:

> Confession is the best preparation for Mass. It is never a madness. If it is not necessary, it is without a doubt very beneficial. If one changes his garment every day, even though it is not dirty, he nevertheless feels better and smells nicer.

Then we come to the question of the miracles. It is said that once, while teaching children, he realised that a wall was about to collapse on them. He commanded it to stop, and it did. He ordered the children out, and once they were gone, it came crashing down. Also, he once insisted that the ten cattle belonging to the monastery be taken out of their stalls immediately. When the last one was led out, the entire structure collapsed. He also apparently knew by clairvoyance when people were waiting beyond the doors for Mass to begin.

There is a tale that two of his pupil monks had been out walking, when they became thirsty. He had ordered them only to speak Syriac.

When they asked a lady for water, in Syriac, she did not understand. One of them then asked her in Arabic (or was it Lebanese?), and she supplied their need. The guilty novice then came to Fr Hardini to tell him, but he said that he already knew, and *not because he had been accused.* That is, he knew it by inspiration.

There is a story that he once gave holy water to someone that was working with the harvest. When it was sprinkled on the ants, they ceased to steal the wheat, and took only the tares (grass which looks like wheat but cannot be eaten). He is said to have miraculously refilled low provisions.

The miracles for his canonisation include that of Michael, a Melkite cripple, who was told that he would never be able to walk again without a miracle. He fell asleep outside the saint's tomb. That night, a monk came to him in his dream and told him to get some grapes for the monks. The monk told him to take "these shoes" and walk, and when he awoke he could walk. Then there is the miracle of André Najam, who was cured of leukaemia. A monk's habit was wiped over the tomb, and when he wore it, he had been cured. He married and had three children, then became a Maronite priest. Rome accepted this miracle.

The other important miracle was of Mousa Saliba, a Greek Orthodox man, whose eyesight was restored after wiping them with a cloth which had been touched to the tomb. Finally, it is said that the son of a Druze woman was restored to life. She had been childless, and had vowed that if the saint interceded for her and she had a child, she would take the child to visit at his tomb. But when the child was born, the father would not consent. The child died. This happened twice. It was about to happen a third time, when the father finally consented. However, the child died on the way. Yet, for two and a half hours the woman carried a corpse, being unwilling to tell her husband. When she placed the child's body by the tomb she left in great fear, but was relieved when a monk came to tell her that her child was crying.

24.6 Blessed Estphan Nehme

Blessed Estphan was born as Youssef Nehme in Lehfed, on 8 March 1889 a village in the Byblos area, which had once been the seat of the Patriarch, and whose patron saint is St Stephen. The youngest boy in a family of four boys and two girls, he lost his father in 1903 (while about 14 years old), and was orphaned only about two years later when his mother died. In 1905, he entered the Lebanese Maronite Order monastery of Saints Cyprian and Justina, Kfifan. When he became a novice about a week later, he took the name Estphan. When Estphan's elder brother learned where he was, he travelled to the monastery, asking his brother to return. However, he replied: "I have entered this monastery and I will die here." Those words proved prophetic: although he spent periods in different monasteries, he did in fact die there.

On 23 August 1907, after the two year novitiate, he pronounced his vows of obedience, chastity and poverty, and became a religious members of the Lebanese Maronite Order. He never became a priest, but always remained a "lay-brother." He was put to work in the fields at the monasteries of Our Lady of Mayfouq, Saint Challita of Qattarah, Our Lady of Perpetual Succour in Byblos, and possibly also at Saint Anthony of Haboub. His death came about because in the summer of 1938, he had been called to return to the monastery at Mayfouq to settle a dispute between the farmers and the monastery over certain land. When Estphan had been there earlier, the stone boundary posts were visible, but they had become covered with time. Estphan remembered where they were, and was asked to go to the fields, and uncover them. He did so, but the work was hard, and on his return home, he fell ill with a fever. He died, at age 49, of a cerebral haemorrhage, and was buried in the monastery vaults.

In 1950, Dr Louis Zoghbi examined the corpse, and found it supple. He could even make the deceased sit up. When the vaults were re-opened on 10 March 1951, someone noticed that his corpse was still intact. Not only the body, but even the clothes in which he reposed, were incorrupt. The news spread and attracted the curiosity of the villagers, so the vaults were closed up. On 29 September 1962, the body was inspected by a doctor, who found the corpse intact and almost entirely without decomposition: limbs, muscles and the skin of the belly were all still supple, and the hair of his head and beard were intact.

In what did Blessed Estphan's spirituality consist? It is said that from his childhood, he would often say: "God is watching me." That is, he lived with a constant sense of the presence of God. This is also shown by another saying attributed to him: "Monastic life is a total union with God and with the Virgin Mary."

He was pious, and was known to be generous, feeding the poor during times of famine. He was a willing worker, and also a good one, being competent in the fields, at carpentry and in the winery.

There is no need to go into details about the miracles attributed to his intercession, although one of them relates to an Australian boy. Another involved his niece, a nun. She had cancer and asked to be given water from a spring he had discovered, known as the "Badger's Spring," because he had followed a badger into a hole, noticed that there was moisture in the hole, and had enlarged it. She was cured by drinking and being washed in that water. He was beatified on 27 June 2010.

24.7 St Rafqa

As with St Charbel, little is known of her life. The very ordinariness and simplicity of their lives is part of their sainthood. Her true name was Boutroussieh (Petra) Khoury on 29 June 1832, the Feast of Saints Peter and Paul. She was born in Himlaya near Bikfaya in the northern Matn of Lebanon. Her mother's name was Rafqa El-Gemayel, and she was baptised by Fr Hanna El-Rayes eight days after birth (7 July 1832). When she was only seven years old, her mother died, and she remained at home with her father for the next four years or so.

Not only were all the Christians of Lebanon suffering from the disturbances we will mention in connection with the Massabki brothers, but her family was especially poor. To provide for her, her father had to send her to Damascus where she served in the house of Assad Badawi. She was there from 1842 to 1846. In the interim, her father remarried and had two children, so that when she returned home at the age of 14 she felt a little distanced from them. She went to stay with her cousins from the Gemayel family in Bikfaya, and there fell under the spell of her uncle, Fr Youssef Gemayel (1824-1892), who was only eight years older than she was.

Fr Youssef had founded a congregation in collaboration with the Jesuits. She would visit his community, although her real desire was to become a contemplative nun at the monastery of St Elias at Shwaya. However, she entered his congregation at Our Lady of Deliverance at Bikfaya in 1853, but not as a nun. They were known as "The Congregation of the Daughters of Mary," and had taken St Dorothy (died about 304) as their patron. They professed four vows: obedience, chastity, poverty and mission.

Meanwhile, her stepmother and aunt were quarrelling over who she should marry. Indeed, their very fighting was one of the things which made her decide to enter the convent. This is interesting for what it says about vocations: that together with a call, one can legitimately take into factors forcing one from the world. Another interesting aspect is that she mentioned her desire to three of her friends, and asked them if they would like to join with her. Two said that they would, while the third said yes on the proviso that the other three joined and remained in the convent. So in May 1859, the Rafqa and her first two friends presented themselves at the convent of Our Lady of Deliverance. It is said that when Rafqa saw the icon, she heard a voice saying: "You will become a nun." The Mother Superior accepted Rafqa at once, but told the other two to return later. Rafqa had not told either her father or her stepmother of her decision. She refused to see them when they came.

She spent one year performing ordinary chores in the convent. On 19 March 1861, she was made a novice, which entailed wearing a robe. On 19 March 1862 she made her temporary monastic vows. The mission was to be in the Jesuit school in Ghazir. She spent several years working in the school kitchen. She would prepare food for the students, among whom was the future Patriarch Elias Al-Howayek. She also learnt Arabic, calligraphy and mathematics during her spare time.

In 1860 she was sent to the monastery of Dayr Al-Qamr, where she witnessed the massacres. She saved a boy by hiding him beneath her robes when the soldiers came looking for him. At the end of that year, she was returned to Ghazir, and then in 1863 to Byblos, teaching girls. At the church of St John-Mark, she was renowned for her good voice and her ability with music.

In September 1863 she was sent to Maad to educate young girls in reading, writing, catechism and mathematics. She also taught them how to behave themselves in Mass. Apparently, she refused to follow the time-hallowed tradition of using corporal punishment, and she did not raise her voice to the girls. She would visit only the sick parents of her students; otherwise, she lived a cloistered life until 1871. However, each year she and the other nuns would meet at the convent of Our Lady of Deliverance.

Due to financial problems, the congregation was merged with that of the Sacred Heart in Zahleh, to form a "Congregation of the Holy Hearts of Jesus and Mary." The crisis in the order continued, until, in 1871, she went to the church of St George in Maad to pray about it. There she felt a hand touch her shoulder and tell her that she would become a nun. When she left the church, she met the philanthropist with whom she was staying, and told him that she wished to become a Baladite

(LMO) nun. That night she had a dream in which she saw three men: a monk with a white beard holding a stick, a soldier and an old man. The monk touched her with the stick and commanded her to join the Baladites. Soon after, she left for the convent of Saint Simon, El-Qarn, Aito. On 6 July 1871 she was accepted into the monastery. On 12 July she took the robe of a novice. On 25 August 1872 she pronounced the solemn vows of obedience, poverty, chastity and humility.

From 1871 to 1914 she would live a secluded life, dedicated to contemplation and work. The period from 1871 to 1897 was at Aito, and from 1897 to 1914 at the convent of St Joseph, Jrabta. Those nuns would fast until noon almost every day of the year, would attend Mass and receive communion daily. They would spend half an hour in contemplation each morning, and read spiritual books each evening. Among other work they performed at the convent, they raised silkworms and sewed.

Rafqa was, apparently, struck by the hard life of the other nuns: how they suffered from the harsh weather, poor nutrition and mortifications. She would say: "God is tempting my sisters, some with blindness, and others with sickness, but I am being left healthy." However, at some time between 1876 and 1878 she developed a stomach abscess. It is testified that when she was sick, she would pray: "For God's glory, in participation with the Passion of Jesus."

In 1885 she asked God why he did not send her pain. "Have you forgotten me?," she asked. That very night she felt a terrible pain in her head and above her right eye, and to a lesser degree in her left. She accepted medical help only under orders. In 1899, after disastrous medical treatment, she became totally blind. She would stay indoors, as light was so painful, but when it was possible, she would perform chores.

The move to the convent of St Joseph in Jrabta, indeed the building of that convent, were apparently to meet her needs. The details of her suffering are painful. She became paralysed in 1911. When she had a shoulder wound, from the bones piercing the skin, she would say: "For God's glory, in participation with the Shoulder Wound of Jesus" (a reference to what he suffered when he bore his Cross to Calvary).

She knew when she was dying, and bade farewell to the nuns. Her last words were: "Jesus, Mary and Joseph. I give you my heart and myself. Take my soul." She died on 23 March 1914, Ash Monday. She was canonised on 10 June 2001.

24.8 The Blessed Massabki Brothers

The Blessed Massabki brothers, Francis, Abdel Moati and Rafael, were Maronite martyrs, slain in Damascus in 1860 in part of a dramatic anti-Christian uprising in Syria and Lebanon from April to July of that year, when more than sixty villages were destroyed in the Shouf and the Matn. Around 2,600 Christians were slaughtered in Deir El-Qamr with the connivance, if not the help, of the Turkish authorities. Estimates are that some 12,000 were slain in Lebanon, and 11,000 in Syria.

Economic jealousy was perhaps the chief reason for the massacres: the Christians were perceived as being undeservedly wealthy, and prospering in Muslim lands while many Muslims were in poverty. Further, in 1856, the Turkish Empire had lifted many legal restrictions on Christians. Many Muslims became envious simply because the Christians were no longer oppressed to the same degree as before. This resentment may have been at least a contributing factor to the slaughter of the Massabkis, who were from a prominent wealthy Syrian family. Although they were esteemed for their piety, wealth and willingness to aid the poor and the needy, these virtues might even enrage, rather than pacify, an envious person.

Francis and Abdel Moati were each married with children. Raphael, the youngest, who was not well, remained single. They had another brother, the priest Fr Abdallah, who was not with them at the time of their martyrdoms. Of the brothers, Francis was the best known. He was a generous man and a successful silk trader, famous in Lebanon and Syria alike. He represented the Maronite Patriarch when his Beatitude needed to conduct business in Syria. All three were known for their diligence and fervour in prayer. They performed much of their charitable work from the Franciscan monastery in Damascus.

When the 1860 attacks and massacres by Muslims in Damascus and Druze in parts of Lebanon started, Muslims set fire in the Christian neighbourhood of Damascus, and the brothers, along with a large crowd of Christians, took refuge in the Franciscan monastery. There, they prayed and celebrated the Mysteries of Forgiveness (confession) and the Eucharist for the last time.

While Francis was alone in the Church, kneeling and praying before the statue of Our Lady of Sorrow, he was filled with supernatural hope. After midnight, a band of armed Muslim rioters broke into the monastery. The Christians were terrified: some managed to run away, and others hid themselves. The murderers said to him: "Sheikh Abdallah has sent us to save you from death; you, your brothers, your families, and all those who depend upon you for protection, on the condition that you deny your faith and convert to Islam." Francis courageously replied: "Sheikh Abdallah can take the money I lent him, he can also take my life; but my faith, no one can make me deny. I am a Maronite Christian and in the faith of Christ I will die. As our Lord Jesus commanded, we do not fear those who can kill the body." As he began to pray, they massacred him with swords and daggers. He had lent the sheikh eight hundred thousand pounds! It was a vast fortune in those days.

Abdel Moati was seized at the chapel door, and ordered to deny his faith in order to save his life. In a clear voice, he said: "I am a Christian, kill me, I am ready." Raphael was found and given the same choice – convert or die. He fell to his knees in prayer. Both of them, like their brother, were cut down. They were later buried with the

Franciscan priests who had also been martyred. But Christ crowned their martyrdom.

On 10 July 1860, his Holiness Pope Pius IX declared them Blessed. On 10 October 1926 they were beatified, thanks largely to the efforts of Bishop Bechara Al Chemaly, the Maronite Archbishop of Damascus. The campaign for their canonisation was spearheaded by his Excellency's letter to Pope Pius XI, noting that the beatification would be a source of grace for the Damascus community, and could help to revive Christian life in the hearts of the Eastern faithful. On 7 October 1926, His Holiness Pius XI proclaimed the beatification of the three brothers, saying: "By the power of these lines are named Most Blessed Martyrs the servants of God: Francis, Abdel Moati, and Raphael Massabki, Maronites of Damascus. ... and we hereby permit the display of their relics before all the devout, and the celebration, on their day of remembrance, of the Liturgy of the Martyrs.

Their feast day is 10 July. The cause for their canonisation is proceeding.

24.9 Maronite Hermits

Lebanon was once a field flowering with hermits. In fact, it was once said, perhaps facetiously, that there were too many: monks who wanted escape work would become hermits, and the monasteries were emptying. With the increasing influence of the Latin Church, by the early 20th century, there were few hermits left in the Maronite Church. However, Fr Chayna is credited with having restored the ancient tradition to public notice. The last Miriamite hermit was Fr Tarabay, who died in 1998. Today there are at least three hermits in Lebanon, and possibly more.

The hermit can acquire a tremendous force, because he must always test and tame his desires. It is traditional for the hermit to eat but one meal a day, and to never eat meat. Hermits are an ancient part of the Maronite system, for their witness is of great importance: we know that somewhere in the world there is someone who has left everything to devote himself to God. He is of course, still in the world, but he is as far from it as possible. This is why they tend to prefer heights, caves, forests or both. The most famous location of Maronite hermits is the Qadiša Valley.

The eremitic life was brought to Qadiša by Ibrahim Kawrachi, and, some say, by St Simeon Stylites, however, this must be a mistake. It is possible that they meant "pupils of St Simeon", because I can find no reliable evidence that he ever left his pillar. However, before his death in 459, a man named Theodosius, who had visited St Simeon, travelled to the Qadiša, and there introduced the Egyptian style of organising the hermits, both male and female, in separate houses but around a central chapel. Many, perhaps most hermits, were friars, that is, they could not say Mass. Rather, they went to the central chapel for the liturgy. During the Middle Ages, this eremitic centre at Qadiša served as the Patriarchal residence.

No one may know the full history of eremitism, but there may have been a break between the first hermits, and 1228, when Patriarch El-Doueihy mentions Yuhanna (John) of Qnat, in Qannoubine in the Qadiša Valley. In 1393 there was a hermit, Elisha of Hadeth who lived in the Monastery of St Sarkis, near the Monastery of St John the Little, overlooking Qadiša. But the most celebrated of all was Younan Al-Mitriti, who was a hermit for 50 years, ate only each second day (and in Lent only two days a week: Saturday and Sunday), and carried out 24,000 prostrations during Holy Week.[234]

Also well-known from the Church of St Elisha in the Qadiša, is the French hermit Francois de Chasteuil, who began at Mar Yaacoub

---

[234] Prostrations are still used in the Orthodox Churches. I do not presently know whether they were originally part of the Maronite tradition. I would guess that, even if they were, the practice was abandoned under Latin influence.

in Ehden before moving to St Elisha's. He was very learned, reading the scriptures in Semitic languages. However, most hermits spent their time in praying and working in the fields, depriving themselves of sleep to the greatest possible extent. However, there must have been more hermits than these: for example, El-Doueihy says that Patriarch Yaacoub al-Hadthy (elected 1445) had been raised in a hermitage. How would this be possible?

The hermit is usually found near a monastery. First, he is usually tested as a monk. He is allowed to live as a hermit for a certain period, after he has spent five years as a monk. Then, sometimes immediately, but sometimes after two or three of these periods, he can enter the hermitage for the rest of his life. It was once unknown for a Maronite hermit to leave his hermitage. Today, however, this happens, depending upon the hermit.

Questions for Contemplation

1. Which saints' stories especially touched you?
2. Do you feel that it is possible to imitate these saints in any way?
3. What did you learn about how to approach life from their example?

Lesson 25

Contemporary Issues in Ethics

1. The Changing World
2. The Family
3. The Maronite Experience of Coexistence
4. Social Justice
5. The Environment
6. Discrimination and Racism (Indigenous People)
7. Health and the Purpose of Human Life

1. The Changing World

God's creation is fundamentally good (as we saw when we discussed the creation account in Genesis). The world was created by Him according to a natural order which would support and sustain that goodness. This order should be exemplified in our souls, in our families, and in our larger social groupings. We can approach that natural order in several ways, but we can always *religiously* align ourselves with it by keeping to the *types*, the divine models which are expressed most perfectly in the life of Christ. The very word "religion" seems to mean "re-binding," that is, reuniting what had been separated. We have been separated from God and from the natural order He created.

The theme of this chapter will be the need to remain close to the natural order, and to interfere as little as possible with it. Further, some practices of civilisation and culture have impacts upon nature and the individual which can be sustained, while others do not. While being absolutely natural is impossible for us, first and foremost as a result of the Fall, we can desist from meddling with the natural order in intolerably damaging ways.

So from the outset there is a paradox: the natural order we aspire to align ourselves with is the harmonious state of coexistence which God had intended for humanity, but the human nature we have to work with is wounded. Our fallen nature is in a less than harmonious condition, indeed, human nature can be so perverted as to actually revolt against the natural order and its desirable harmony.

Yet the clear fact is that we benefit not only mentally and emotionally from contact with nature, but even physically. There is something very deep in human nature, "the soul," which finds peace and comfort in the continuous rhythm of day and night, the action of the wind, the blue of the sky, the gleam of the stars, and the swaying of the sea. Nature has elements of both stability and change, but over the course of individual lives, the stability of nature is probably more marked. Features of the landscape are generally permanent within our lifetimes, and when they are not, the agent of rapid change is more likely than not to have been human activity. We have the sense that in the greatness of the natural world, some powerful heart abides. Therefore, the Bible speaks of the seeming eternity of the mountains as a blessing and sign of God's care for us:

> ... because of your father's God, who helps you,
> because of the Almighty, who blesses you
> with blessings of the skies above,
> blessings of the deep springs below,
> blessings of the breast and womb.
> Your father's blessings are greater
> than the blessings of the ancient mountains,
> than the bounty of the age-old hills. (Genesis 49:25-26)

Nature displays cycles of change. The atmosphere which is

dramatically turned upside down by a thunderstorm returns to normal when the sun reappears. Further, if we place human agency on one side, the vicissitudes of the natural world are caused from within that natural world by only a few phenomena: sun, wind, rain, storm and wave. Occurrences such as fire, landslide, earthquake, tsunami and hurricane are rarer; but even when they occur, they occur in accordance with natural laws.

Our human society, however, is forever changing, irrevocably, and seemingly in default of decided action: as a general rule, people do things randomly and the effects add up. The pace of change is abnormally accelerating, but no one ever said: "Let's cause these changes to come faster and faster." The fact that matters could have been anticipated, but were not, is itself an issue. And then there have been occasions where pernicious doctrines have been introduced into the world: the totalitarian and atheistic teachings of the modern world come to mind. However well-intentioned and sincere the proponents of these views may have been, the result has been not only bloodshed (e.g. Mussolini's Italy, Hitler's Germany, Stalin's Russia, Mao's China and Pol Pot's Cambodia) but also an ever-increasing lack of the sense that life has a purpose, and that God wills us to face our challenges rather than avoid them. It is impossible to think that this sea-change in society has not contributed to the tragic wave of drug-abuse and suicides which is afflicting the contemporary world.

This social plague has justly been termed "the culture of death," in opposition to the "culture of life," which is opposed to the culture of Christianity.

If the social changes we see can be described in a single neutral word, it is, I suggest: "ab-natural." This is not the same as "unnatural," or against nature, but rather: "departing from the natural." This applies not only to our personal lives but to our social lives as individuals, and our existence as nations, cultures and civilisations.

This is of grave concern to the Church, because the Church has before her eyes the divine model for creation, and it grieves her to see it abandoned, and then this departure from God's good path is celebrated as "freedom" and "making my own rules". Some superficially say that man is part of nature, and therefore whatever he does must be natural. But man is the only part of nature which can choose to violate her rhythms, to exploit, deplete her and to destroy her. Humans can and do ravage entire forests and kill the fish life in rivers. This is not natural, it is ab-natural, being a transgression of good order.

The world in which Our Lord lived was not so very different from the world that had existed 1500 years before or 1500 years after His time. The realities of daily life were effectively unvarying until the time of the birth of modern science in Italy made possible the Industrial Revolution, which began in England. With the harnessing of electricity, which has made possible computer technology, and then nanotechnology and other new methods of production, the world has undergone unprecedented changes.

The result is clearest in the pollution and destruction of the environment, the rapid extinction of species, and in global warming. The Church has met much criticism for daring to venture an opinion on the human factor in global warming. However, just as there is no effect without a cause, so too there is no cause without an effect. I do not believe that anyone can seriously doubt that burning fossil fuels and destroying natural means of absorbing heat could cause some global warming. If it is conceded that human activity is a possible cause of planetary warming, the only question can be whether this cause is too small to have an effect.

Equally, it is wrong that climate change should be seized upon by some for anti-human agendas, especially those tied to the culture of death. Even if human activity has some impact on global temperatures, that fact can never be used as a justification for something like population control, forced sterilizations and one-child policies.

To strike the right balance between individual liberty and common good is always a question for judgment and prudence. Political ideologies are too narrow to draw the line where it should be. For wisdom, we need to broaden our vision to include God, His natural order, and the imperative need to avoid sin. Evil can never be justified by appeals to "the greater good."

We debate questions of politics and civil liberties in a society where individuals can now single-handedly massacre hundreds and even thousands in unprecedented ways, not only with guns, and high-powered explosives, but also by using trucks and airplanes as bulldozers. The water and electricity supplies of cities are carefully guarded because the chances of their being ravaged by one renegade are real. When the twentieth century opened, if you had an argument with someone in your neighbourhood, he might attack you. By the time the twentieth century closed, he could wipe out your entire family in seconds. War was once waged by nations: now it can be waged by groups. Then, when people combine, the available dangers increase significantly.

The greater speed and volume of connections within society and around the world also means that we are more vulnerable because of our dependence upon those connections, and their reliance upon the internet. We are vulnerable not only as individuals but as societies, because the modern world, to an unparalleled extent, is interconnected and uses electricity and the internet for this purpose. Certain individual liberties, such as privacy, may need to be curtailed, especially when we are mixing in public areas, because of the significant damage one person can do.

We also live in an age of previously unknown mixing of races and religions. There were great upheavals after WWII. These had barely settled when the refugee crises of the third millennium burst upon an unprepared world. Together with the continuous Muslim immigration into Europe and the West which had preceded it, and the decline of

Christianity in those same countries, the growth of Islam and alteration of national identity are well under way, with sometimes quite substantial breakdowns in law and order.

The answers to particular questions can and, I would say, must be developed from sound principles. Then, people working constructively and impartially, trying to assist society in finding a shape which corresponds to the natural order and grants justice to all, can make progress on those issues. It is impossible to specify all answers in advance. All that can be done in general is to speak in general.

But we can say this: the life of the family, under God, and adhering to His commandments, is the natural life for humanity. And the closer we remain to the natural life, the more soundly based our lives will be, and the better equipped we shall be to spiritually and emotionally deal with the issues which shall arise before us. This includes, of course, the option of remaining single, whether as a cleric or a lay-person.

It is vital for Christians to acknowledge their duty, to God, to others and to themselves. The conscientious discharge of one's duty (whether it is in the form of a job or otherwise) is a wonderful principle of continuity. It helps us deal with each day: I have a duty to discharge today. Good, let me do it well.

I do not only work well because I am contractually obligated to. Rather, I work with a will and a conscience because I am a Christian and I love God. As the Lord said in the parable of the talents: "Well done, good and faithful servant! You have been faithful with a few things; I will put you in charge of many things. Enter into the joy of your master!" (Matthew 25:21 and 23).

The same applies to my obligations to my family, except that here it is even easier to see how I should love to be responsible, and to act accordingly. In the family, and among the people I meet, I should strive to naturally be an example. I do not need to lecture everyone, although I may need to say a word to those people for whom I am responsible, rather, I model the behaviour and standards I expect from others, and show the character to rise above the weaknesses of the age and the culture.

The narrative of my life, the day to day activity, provides some order. And the unbreakable golden thread which runs through it is the love and service of God.

2. Changes in the Family

Other once unimaginable changes have arisen even in the area of the family, once the stable pillar in a shifting society: whatever else might happen, you would think that short of treachery or massacre, your family would also be there, and that "family" was a constant within society, too. But with scientifically devised methods of fertilisation and new models of parenting, one no longer needs a father and mother to have children, let alone to raise them: one merely needs the relevant donors and a woman to be obliging, as it were, with her womb. So now children can be raised by two fathers or two mothers, or one parent alone. No parent or combination of the parenting collective (for there are sometimes more than two parents) need be of any specific gender in this strange new world.

External signs of male and female gender can now be changed or erased, at least superficially, by medical means involving surgery and chemicals. Furthermore, the will to undergo so-called "gender reassignment," and even to have the alterations done to one's own children is growing, despite warnings that children are too vulnerable to suggestion and too likely to change their views of their gender to be able to make responsible decisions which will affect the full terms of their lives.[235]

---

[235]   See "Sexuality and Gender: Findings from the Biological, Psychological, and Social Sciences," Lawrence S. Mayer and Paul R. McHugh, *The New Atlantis*, No. 50, Fall 2016, 114-116.

An almost extraordinarily misguided philosophical theory, that of "gender theory," has been used to propagate a revolution in society which, it seems to me, has as its only certain result the confusing of children and the adults which they will become. The educational programmes which have been designed to go with this "gender" revolution, teach or rather strive to indoctrinate children to question their genders. Research into ethics courses has suggested that despite the theory that such classes would help people become better citizens, they may in fact make them worse, because they teach them more ways to justify their desired "unethical" behaviour.[236] Applying this to "gender instruction", it is to be feared that it will confuse rather than enlighten. One can only feel compassion for those people who believe that they are born with the wrong gender, but attempting to change their nature is not a radical answer: it is an evasion. After all, if, as some suggest, genitals do not determine gender, then why do some have operations to change their genitals to make them artificially accord with their "new genders"? Our desire is that all people may lead stable and healthy lives. Surely this is better by done by facing one's nature, and adjusting to reality, difficult as that may appear.

One school teacher who was willing to discuss the topic told me that they have one child "transitioning" and that the other children knew there was something different about that child, and did not believe teachers' assertions that the child was an ordinary boy. The children were not helped by their "education," rather they were bewildered. This sort of situation can only lead to a lack of credibility in their teachers, and maybe even a scepticism about their very educations.

From Mayer and McHugh's study I shall only reproduce some conclusions:

- "While there is evidence that biological factors such as genes and

---

[236] Much of this study, at least those portions most accessible to me, have been conducted by Prof. Eric Schwitzgebel. The question of whether instruction in philosophical and ethical areas actually works seems to me to be rather frequently avoided.

hormones are associated with sexual behaviours and attractions, there are no compelling causal biological explanations for human sexual orientation. While minor differences in the brain structures and brain activity between homosexual and heterosexual individuals have been identified by researchers, such neurobiological findings do not demonstrate whether these differences are innate or are the result of environmental and psychological factors.

- Longitudinal studies of adolescents suggest that sexual orientation may be quite fluid over the life course for some people, with one study estimating that as many as 80% of male adolescents who report same-sex attractions no longer do so as adults (although the extent to which this figure reflects actual changes in same-sex attractions and not just artifacts of the survey process has been contested by some researchers).

- Compared to heterosexuals, non-heterosexuals are about two to three times as likely to have experienced childhood sexual abuse.

- The hypothesis that gender identity is an innate, fixed property of human beings that is independent of biological sex — that a person might be "a man trapped in a woman's body" or "a woman trapped in a man's body" — is not supported by scientific evidence.

- According to a recent estimate, about 0.6% of U.S. adults identify as a gender that does not correspond to their biological sex.

- Children are a special case when addressing transgender issues. Only a minority of children who experience cross-gender identification will continue to do so into adolescence or adulthood.

- There is little scientific evidence for the therapeutic value of interventions that delay puberty or modify the secondary sex characteristics of adolescents, although some children may have improved psychological well-being if they are encouraged and supported in their cross-gender identification. There is no evidence that all children who express gender-atypical thoughts or behaviour should be encouraged to become transgender."[237]

Once more, this gender revolution shows the danger of departing too far from the natural order. If doctors all took the view that it is better to help people to adapt to their natures than to attempt to alter their natures, this would accord with the natural order. Even some who champion so-called "reassignment" surgery which often involves a permanent mutilation of the body, have been known to say that biology will return even if you try and change it. This calls to mind the saying by the Roman writer Horace: "You can drive out Nature with a pitchfork, but she keeps on coming back."

There are disorders of sexual development which invite some type of medical intervention, such as when someone is born with ambiguous genitalia, although even here the tendency among doctors has been, apparently, to be more cautious to intervene.[238] However, to damage healthy and functional reproductive systems in order to make a person appear to belong to the other sex, is an abuse of medicine, for it wounds a functioning body to satisfy an anti-natural desire. Were it possible to really change a gender, ongoing treatment would not be required to maintain the new physical features.

How far we are seeing a revolt against reality, is shown by the phenomenon of "otherkins" and "therianthropes" . "Otherkins" are "people who believe and live as if they are partly other-than-human, for example part-dragon, unicorn, vampire, angel ... or other mythological or supernatural creature."[239] "Therianthropy" is believing and living

---

[237] http://www.thenewatlantis.com/publications/executive-summary-sexuality-and-gender accessed 3 February 2017.

[238] See "Gender Reassignment" by N. Tonti-Filippini (undated), http://www.jp2institute.org/index.php/49-gender-reassignment/file, accessed 2 February 2017. I am not saying that medical intervention is warranted, only that it is to be considered because of the very nature of the objective condition.

[239] Carole M. Cusack, "Spirituality and self-realisation as 'other-than-human': The Otherkin and Therianthropy communities," in Carole M. Cusack and Pavol Kosnac (eds), *Fiction, Invention and Hyper-reality*, Taylor and Francis, 2016, 40-57, 40.

as if partly animal, e.g. partly "wolf, horse, eagle, ram and so on".[240] People can sincerely believe that they have an identity which does not accord with reality. We, as Christians, should encourage and help them to come to the truth, using prudence, wisdom and charity.

Another issue affecting the family is the ready availability of contraception or, perhaps even more significantly, what is called the "contraceptive mentality." Once more, the failure to understand the teaching of the Church on this topic is due in large part to the failure to understand that the natural order is critical to human well-being, physical and emotional as well as spiritual. For the entirety of recorded history, it was normal for men to do the physically most demanding work, a labour which often took them out of the house. Women, on the other hand, did the domestic work. This made sense: it is women, not men, who bear children and who lactate, their milk being the ideal food for children.

It is only really with the industrial revolution that this began to change, or more precisely, that the possibility of change appeared. It took many generations for the desire to change to gain traction, and for the new roles of men and women which were now possible to be imagined and for the necessary political changes to be advocated.

The marketing of a contraceptive pill in the 1960s snapped the link between sexual relations and childbirth more completely than had ever before been possible. As a result, the way our society views sex, gender and sexual activity has undergone a revolution.

The sexual act should never be detached from its God-given purpose, and neither should the union of man and woman lose its intended life-long perspective. When pleasure is exalted as the sole reason for sex and becomes the ultimate justification for the choosing and exchanging of partners, then commitment becomes tied to ongoing satisfaction. Promiscuity is acid to permanence.

---

[240] Carole M. Cusack, "Spirituality and self-realisation as 'other-than-human'," 40.

The Catholic Church, of course, continues to adhere to the natural order as being the divinely appointed framework for human life. For this she necessarily suffers substantial misunderstanding and criticism. She is not defending outdated customs. Rather, she is teaching the natural order, as God has provided it.

It is not necessary to describe and judge every variation from the legitimate way of satisfying sexual desires. If one desires Christian love, then by necessary implication all other paths are closed. But the capacity for love and affection, and the sensitivity to human existence which comes with the sex drive remains, and these can be put to good use outside of marriage in ordinary human relations. In such cases, the energy which would have gone into physical sexual expression is transformed into a responsive and selfless charitable impulse, which provides the Christian with a powerful fountain of force.

Before leaving this area, the scourge of pornography should be briefly noted. The manufacture, distribution and use of pornography is sinful. It is a violation of the marital vows, makes people secretive, renders them unable to see each other as anything but objects for their selfish satisfaction, causes them to abuse their own bodies, deprives them of the grace of God, makes them lose control of their own appetites, renders their reason feeble and their judgement skewed

Further, pornography is addictive. It introduces a power of imagination into the head, poisoning a person's view of sex and, ultimately, of humanity. No pornography will ever bridge the gap between fantasy and reality. It will always disappoint in the end, while magnetising the user. It can and has destroyed lives. But it can be beaten. Again, it is not natural: it works by exciting natural impulses to an unnatural pitch.

Finally here, I might mention bioethics, a new field of ethics which seeks to apply the fundamental principles to novel situations. I refer to Bishop Antoine-Charbel Tarabay's first volume of his study of bioethics and its intellectual and religious foundations in Christianity and Islam.[241] The second volume, which considers specific problems in bioethics, is being prepared for publication.

3. The Maronite Experience of Coexistence

These changes in society cannot all be reversed. The deep geopolitical changes of population will be the longest acting. The age of mixing of peoples in which we live will irrevocably change the face of many countries, particularly in Europe. That is a new reality which we must confront, and the only possible answer is neither along the lines of deportation nor containment, but of a tolerant society under the rule of law. That is a course wherein Maronites have a good track-record: coexistence between Christian, Druze and Muslim has long been a feature of Lebanese life. There have been hiccups along the way, sometimes to the point of ruinous civil war, although even this can perhaps be explained as having at least been aggravated by the presence of an extraneous power on Lebanese soil: the Palestinians, and the battle between Israel and the Palestine Liberation Army being fought on Lebanese soil.

There has been one major difference between the situation in Lebanon and that in the West. In Lebanon, the people are aware that religion does matter. So they live in a system which is openly and avowedly confessional. It is easy to criticise it as being a violation of individual rights, but the individuals are members of religions or confessions, and in safeguarding these, the individual is protected not less securely than in secular Western societies. Because religion does not matter to the politicians and opinion makers of the West, they either assume that religion does not matter to anyone, or that those to whom it is important are wrong-headed. And so there follows a demand that people of faith must conform to the secular model.

---

[241] *Bioethics at the Crossroads of Religions: Thoughts on the Foundation of Bioethics in Christianity and Islam*, Connor Court, Ballarat, 2015.

We Maronites can teach the West, from our own experience, that rather than pretend that a person does not have a religion, or demand that their religion be of no civil significance, it should be recognised, and clear guidelines as to how that religion will affect the law of the land be put in place and maintained. In Lebanon, for example, there are religious courts for Christians, Druze, Sunni and Shiite Muslims. These have their proper spheres of action, can be invoked or bypassed, and the State system covers the balance of the field. In Israel, where there are Jewish, Druze, Muslim and several Christian courts, the situation is similar, but even more complex, yet it seems to work. This is not the only possible solution, and I do not suggest that it should be adopted anywhere. But it is an option, and it deserves careful study. My point is that recognising religion and striving for mutual respect may be more rational social policy than trying to remove it from public life.

Fortunately, most religious systems tend to be close to the natural order. It is atheistic and philosophical systems which most depart from it, and so give rise to the friction I have been discussing.

Further, and perhaps most importantly, if through an understanding of typology we could come to see that the true model of our lives is the divine template for creation, especially as expressed in the life of the Lord and His Church, we could attempt to live by that more natural model, not by slavish imitation of life in first century A.D. Galilee, but by applying the principle of sane and natural order to ourselves and our own.

4.   Social Justice

"Social justice" is the virtue of working to establish and maintain social institutions which work for the common good, in accord with the social teaching of the Catholic Church. There are many social virtues which we cannot go into here, which are instances of the common good in operation, such as the principle of "subsidiarity." According to that principle, dear to the heart of the Church, decisions should be made by the people who will be affected by them, or at least as close to them as possible, e.g. a question of garbage collection in a council should be made at the council level rather than by the national government, all things being equal (a corrupt council might be a reason to depart from the ideal).

But this also has the upshot that if a matter does not have to be regulated, then it should not. It might be a good idea that everyone have a pair of slippers and keep them by their bed. But to legislate to that effect would be tyrannical.

Why is "social justice" made so much of today in the Church, to the extent that it is given first place and almost swallows up ethics, at least in some people's minds? It is perhaps because social institutions have far more power in our everyday lives than they once had, and because the connections between us, our houses and our activities are so much more pervasive and intense. International travel was far harder and more expensive than it is today. News travelled more slowly before the radio and t.v. We were not even aware that inhaling someone else's cigarette smoke was a hazard. Today we live under the shadow of the internet: it cannot be escaped for too long. Hence, there is a real reason why social justice should be of increasing importance to us.[242] Also, the greater power of State institutions, and the more effective weapons of war available, which are increasingly accessible not only by nations but by individuals, justify the same trend.

But also, I believe, the social teaching of the Church is found to be less embarrassing than other aspects of its ethical teaching. Even to contend that sexual relations should be restricted to within marriage, as a matter of morality, is to court unpopularity and rejection in today's world. Yet, any failure to promote the entirety of the Church's teaching

---

[242] Incidentally, modern problems of addiction to electronic media exist. These can be serious issues, and turn once functional households into a collection of apartments. But I cannot go into that here.

is short-sighted. The point is our principles: since they are sound, then they should be consistently promoted and carried out. To restrict ourselves to social justice is to betray all our ethics by abandoning our principles.

5. The Environment

To the Christian, the world in which we live manifests the will of God in the laws of nature, in the miracles which punctuate it like so many reminders that the vast panoply we see depends upon the Divine Creator, and the principle or "law" of accident, which, oddly enough, allows for flexibility, change, and even a certain freedom from the laws. But of course the greatest freedom from the laws of the world comes through *grace*.

We shall come to grace soon, but first, let us consider what is said about the praise offered to God by all creation. The roots of this idea are biblical. We find it in Psalm 19:2-3, for example:

> The heavens proclaim the glory of God;
> and the sky manifests the work of His hands.
> Day unto day pours forth speech,
> and night unto night unfolds knowledge.

In Psalm 96:11-12 (to which Psalm 98:7-8 is almost identical) not only the elements but also the trees join in:

> Let the heavens rejoice and the earth be glad;
> the sea and what fills it thunder;
> the highland and everything on it exult.
> Then all the woodland trees will shout for joy.

The idea is that God is speaking through nature. This is not the superstition that God is nature itself, but that He is present *in* and *through* it, and that in some mystical fashion, the universe is praising Him in return.

I have gone into this in some detail, because it seems to me that this idea that the divine is present in and through the world, and that the universe is echoing the call of God is intrinsic to the Maronite view of the world, even if it is rarely articulated. Very often, the deepest ideas are the ones you take for granted.

Psalms 148, 149 and 150, which are said each morning in the Maronite Office, are songs of praise and worship. Consider Psalm 148:1-10, which brings together the themes of the praise of God and the divine ordering of creation:

> Praise the Lord from the heavens, give praise from the heights.
> Praise Him all you angels, praise Him all His soldiers!
> Praise Him, sun and moon; praise Him, all stars of morning!
> Praise Him, heaven of heavens, you waters above the heavens.
> Let them all praise the Lord's name; for the Lord commanded and they were created.
> He stationed them from all time to eternity;
> He issued a decree and it shall never pass away.
> Praise the Lord from the nether world, you sea monsters and all you depths!
> Fire and hail, snow and smoke, storm wind executing His command.
> You mountains and all hills, fruit trees and all cedars.
> You animals wild and tame, you creatures that crawl and fly.

I am especially touched by the reference to the storm wind which executes God's commands! This psalm includes the three-level view of the universe, first addressing celestial beings, then the nether world and the abysses, and finally terrestrial creatures. The power of this scheme of the universe is that it tells us *where we are*, and what is above us and what below, thus telling and warning us of our possible futures and failures.

There is another famous example of the cosmic praise in Daniel 3, when the angel of the Lord joins Azariah and Daniel's companions in the furnace, and there they call upon "all you works of the Lord" to praise Him, including in their summons angels, heavens, waters, sun, moon, stars, rain and dew, wind, fire, heat, cold, chill, frost, ice, snow, nights, days, light, darkness, lightnings, clouds, dolphins and all water creatures: "priests of the Lord", "spirits and souls of the just," and "holy men of humble heart," among others.

These Psalms influenced the hymns of the Maronite Divine Office. The Monday *Safro* or morning office of the Season of Pentecost can serve as an example. In one of the hymns we read:

> On the morning of the second day of creation,
> You ordered the vastness of the celestial bodies, such is Your splendour, Lord.
> Waters above, waters below, and in the midst of them – sky!
> The luminaries of the cosmos eloquently raise hymns of glory to You.

The anaphoras of the Maronite Liturgy are replete with this sentiment of universal praise. For example, the Eucharistic Prayer of the Anaphora of St James reads:

> Truly it is right and just to glorify you, bless you, praise you, adore you, and give you thanks, O Maker of all things visible and invisible. The highest heavens and all its powers praise you; the sun, the moon and all the stars, the earth, the seas and all that is in them, the heavenly Jerusalem and the assembly of the firstborn who are enrolled in heaven; the angels, archangels and heavenly hosts all sing, praising your majestic glory with triumphant hymns, with never-ending voices, and with acclamations.

Incidentally, the only inanimate objects here are the sun and the moon, but even here, I suspect, these are seen as being moved by angels. The unseen angelic presence behind the visible creation is an ancient motif. Hence, in the oldest Maronite art, there was always the sun in the top left and the moon in the top right corner. Some people were scandalised by this, or at least dubious of it. One such person painted over the sun and moon in the picture of Our Lady of Elige, replacing the luminaries with the heads of cherubim.

Returning to the anaphora of St James, note that it states: "Truly it is right and just to glorify you ...." This is because to glorify God is in accordance with the nature both of the universe and of our moral selves. Worship is the highest end of which humanity is capable.

The Anaphora of St John Maroun contains the same idea, developing it to include our adoration of God:

> We praise and thank You with our mouths that have been blessed by Your holy word and cleansed with Your forgiving hyssop. Those who glorify You are countless: cherubim and seraphim, thousands of spiritual beings standing before You and myriads of fiery ranks serving Your majesty. They sing triumphant hymns with harmonious voices. O Lord, although we are Your weak and sinful children, make us worthy, through the gift of Your grace, to sing with them and proclaim: *Holy, holy, holy* ... etc.

The world in which we live is the antetype of heaven. It is the Garden of Eden in a fallen condition. It is our tremendous privilege to be stewards of it. We must not abuse our trust.

5.   Discrimination and Racism (Indigenous People)

Discrimination, in itself, simply means "the power of observing differences accurately."[243] It is necessary: I have to discriminate between products when I go to a shop. I have to ask which one I will purchase and why. I consider whatever is relevant (e.g. the value of the product and how it matches my needs), and I try to dismiss from my mind irrelevant considerations (e.g. wanting to impress the person on the cash register with how much money I have). A discriminating person is one who makes a prudent choice. Discrimination is not only a necessary, it is also a useful part of life.

Discrimination can be based on irrational factors, such as trying to impress someone whom I don't even know. It can also be based on a

---

[243]   *The Shorter Oxford Dictionary.*

range of emotions from preference and affection on the one hand to antipathy and hatred on the other. To be clear, sometimes emotions such as affection are properly taken into consideration, such as for example in deciding who I will marry. But I always have a duty to be impartial. Our objective must always be to make decisions on the basis of principles and – to the degree that emotions are present – to exclude the emotions that prevent us judging on principle, and allow the emotions that assist us to judge on principle. Any considerations which make me swerve from impartiality are "irrational," whether or not they are based on liking, disliking or some other factor.

When these irrational factors cause or support discrimination in the case of other people, this is sinful. It is an offence against the image of God which we share equally with all people, despite their race, colour, gender, state of health, fame, social status, age, background, associates, past mistakes, clothes, language, manner of speaking or behaviour, sexuality, marital status, occupation, political views, philosophy or religion. This sort of discrimination is criticised time and again in the New Testament. Thus St James said:

> My brothers and sisters, believers in our glorious Lord Jesus Christ must not show favouritism. Suppose a man comes into your meeting wearing a gold ring and fine clothes, and a poor man in filthy old clothes also comes in. If you show special attention to the man wearing fine clothes and say: "Here's a good seat for you," but say to the poor man: "You stand there" or "Sit on the floor by my feet," have you not discriminated among yourselves and become judges with evil thoughts? (James 2:1-4)

It also offends against the Golden Rule which Our Lord taught: "Do unto others as you would have them do unto you" (Matthew 7:12 and Luke 6:31).

So discrimination of this irrational kind is sinful, and, on some occasions, criminal. However, in striving to avoid irrational discrimination, we must be careful not to fall into another extreme, equally injurious, that of avoiding rational discrimination. Part of the reason I stressed that in the parable of the Good Samaritan, Our Lord did not say "everyone is your neighbour" (lesson 13) is because we do have to give priority to those who are closest to us. If my own children are hungry, I cannot refuse to feed them on the grounds that there are children in some part of the world who are even hungrier, and I will feed them first. We are made to love ourselves, hence the commandment to love your neighbour as yourself (Matthew 22:39, Mark 12:31 and Luke 10:27) has meaning. If we were not so, and if it was not right to do so, then it would be a vain saying.

Imagine a world where everyone brushed anyone else's teeth except their own. It would be madness. So too, our duties begin with ourselves and our immediate families. It is because *everyone* has that same duty that others can be attended to. So, working in concentric circles, we assist our extended family, and then others. So, if for example, I have an aunt who needs assistance, it would be better for me to help her than to go off and assist poor people overseas if that meant neglecting my aunt. I am bound by ties of family love to that aunt. Even if I dislike her, she is still closer to me, just as others will be closer to the people in foreign parts. If nothing else, it is simply more practical, and hence a more efficient charity, for us to help those who are closest to us, both physically and metaphorically. Then, when our family is alright, it is a good thing to seek out the most wretched and the most helpless and give them charity in a way which will help them to help themselves, where that is possible. We should seek out those who are homeless or without family or friends, that is, without someone who can help them.

Although it is unfashionable to say so, this also has the corollary that, all things being equal, we will help Catholic charities and other Christians first and foremost. It is not that we would never help non-Christians. We are duty bound to, as Our Lord taught us in the parable of the Good Samaritan. But if we care for our own people, and other faiths and people of none, care for their own, that would be a sensible and efficient arrangement. The first Christians took great pains to care for other Christians. They did not neglect others, but the Christians were their own first priority. Then, when we see people with no one to care for them, we adopt them as our own.

So we have a duty to use wisdom in our charitable work, and not be satisfied with platitudes. Instead of making empty statements of recognition and acknowledgement, *do* something, and encourage others to do something specific. The great danger is that we will be satisfied with vacuous proclamations and neglect action.

6.   Health and the Purpose of Human Life

We have a duty to look after our health. We also have a duty to look after the health of our dependents, and not to do anything which will harm others' health. These duties are intimately related to God's role as the nourisher of the universe, and our role as His steward on the earth (Genesis 1:28). Jacob of Sarug stated that God bears the title of "Nourisher" (*zâyûnâ*), for He not only created the world, but cares for it in a *continuing creation*. God has providentially prepared a food for every creature.[244]

It follows from first principles that we are not to give children and the vulnerable food which has harmful effects, even if those harmful effects are gradual and take a while to be felt. I would contend, in fact, that the very gradualness of the evils caused by foods such as sugar and tobacco, to name probably the two most notorious, is all the more reason why we have a duty to warn and educate people, and not to produce or deal in them.

Yet, there remains a very fine question of judgment, for not every step which could keep a person alive must necessarily be taken to avoid sin. A person can even choose death, e.g. as a martyr for the

---

[244]   Tanous Bou Mansour, *La théologie de Jacques de Saroug*, vol. 1, Kaslik, 1993, 42-43.

faith. We have an obligation to employ ordinary means in order to restore our health. Only if the ordinary means cause an extraordinary difficulty can we be allowed to refuse them. If we have dependents then we must prudently weigh up, with the best medical advice we can obtain, what is the likely prognosis, and how that would impact upon our dependents?

It is wrong to hurry from life, and it is sinful to seek to take our own lives. Life is a divine gift. To arrogate to ourselves the right to decide when and how we will die is effectively to deny the gift of God. Every person has an individual work to do. He may not find it, but I am sure that he will stumble on it, for God places it in our paths.

In the course of our lives we establish certain tendencies of various strength: one can think of it as a certain momentum. Some of these tendencies continue even during sleep: we may wake up with a problem resolved, or alternatively, with an awareness of anxiety which we had not had. A psychological momentum has been at work, notwithstanding our unawareness of it. The same sort of thing can happen during other states of unconsciousness. It only stands to reason that these tendencies will continue to the moment of death.

Further, this momentum which we find in our lives will, I suggest, take us beyond even the curtain of death. As we have lived, so will we die. Nature is full of cycles: the water, the nitrogen, the oxygen cycle and so on. Our bodies return to the earth and become components in the material makeup of the earth, its plants and its animals. Nothing is wasted, not even our souls and the tendencies formed in them.

I came across an instance of a good old woman who had been working around the farm and playing with her children until the very day that she fell into a coma. That coma lasted some eight months. However, she regained consciousness on some occasions, and when she did I was privileged to be there. She could not speak, but she was aware, and she could smile. And more than that: she had a new presence. She would openly show her love. She was at peace with all. Something had happened. I believe that God had done some special soul work with her. I have since had some experience of other people who have been in comas, and although this by no means is always the case, so far as I can see, yet it sometimes is. Not even death can end that work, for our lives continue: whether in heaven, hell or purgatory. It would be a mistake to think that only our physical bodies are left when we die, to be recycled and through recycling find a place in new organisms. The same is true of our souls, but their new life is not in this world, it is in the next.

In the Syriac tradition, our lives are seen as antetypes of the life of Christ. His life is the type, the model. This gives us another approach to immortality: our lives cannot end while He lives, for they are shadows of His eternal life. Therefore, we too are meant for eternity.

The purpose of life, surely then, is to live so that our small lives will continue to grow into the reality which is the divine life. It is to live in such a way that when we die we are worthy either immediately or afterwards, of standing in His presence and enjoying the beatific vision: the eternal blissful sight of God.

The desire to live with purpose is imparted to each of us. It is part of the order of creation which God established. At every point of our lives, whenever there are difficult situations before us, we can return to the teaching of the Lord, and find our way.

Appendix: Some Prayers

The Sign of the Cross (Maronite Version)

Glory be to the Father, and to the Son, and of the Holy Spirit, One God. Amen.

The Sign of the Cross (Latin Catholic)

In the name of the Father, and of the Son, and of the Holy Spirit. Amen.

The "Our Father" (The Lord's Prayer)

Our Father, who art in heaven

Hallowed be Thy Name.

Thy kingdom come,

Thy will be done,

on earth as it is in heaven.

Give us this day our daily bread,

and forgive us our trespasses,

as we forgive those who trespass against us;

and lead us not into temptation,

but deliver us from evil. Amen.

Note: When used liturgically in the Eastern Churches, the ancient custom prevails of adding the words: "for the kingdom, the power and the glory are yours, now and forever," just before the closing "Amen." However, these words are not found in chapter 6 of the Gospel of Matthew, from where we take this prayer, and are not properly part of the prayer: they are a liturgical addition. Note also, that in the original Greek, and in the Syriac and Arabic, it says: "Thy will be done, as in heaven, so on earth." That is significant, because the true movement of God's will is from heaven to earth, and the higher should be mentioned before the lower.

The "Hail Mary" (The Angelic Salutation)

Hail Mary, full of grace. The Lord is with thee. Blessed art thou among women, and blessed is the fruit of thy womb, Jesus. Holy Mary, Mother of God, pray for us sinners, now and at the hour of our death. Amen.

The "Glory Be"

Glory be to the Father, and to the Son, and to the Holy Spirit. As it was in the beginning, is now, and ever shall be, world without end. Amen.

A Morning Prayer

Heavenly Father, who created and formed us, we worship You especially upon this morning, when You have aroused us from the sleep of nature so that we might awaken to Your spiritual life. Grant to us that we may stand on Your right side on that great morning when we arrive at the mansions of life, where we shall worship in the radiance of Your presence, with Your Only Son and your Holy Spirit, for ever. Amen.

Prayer at Noon

Most High Lord, who has witnessed my doings today, patiently allow me to pause my activities in peace of heart and mind, and to collect myself in tranquillity. Strengthened by Your refreshing Spirit, may I renew my intention to live in holiness, and return to the world to serve You. Amen.

Evening Prayer

Grant us, Lord, security in the evening, and at night, calm rest and the sleep of the just. May we lie down in peace, knowing that Your eye protects us from all evil. May we awaken refreshed in the morning to perform Your will, and to fill our day with works of righteousness. You are the hope of our lives, Lord Jesus, and You are our saviour. To You be the glory, and to Your Father and Your Holy Spirit, for ever. Amen.

Prayer Before Study

Come, Holy Spirit, Lord and Giver of Life, to hover over our bodies, our souls and our minds. Purify our thoughts, cleanse our hearts, and enlighten our consciences. Grant us Your light that by it we may perceive the divine pattern and order in creation, understand what we study, and apply it to fulfil our purpose and mission in this life. Amen.

Prayer After Study

Holy Spirit of wisdom and understanding, help me to remember and profit from the lessons I learn in life and faith, so that I do not repeat the mistakes of the past. As I grow in knowledge, may I also increase in the wisdom to instruct the ignorant and counsel the doubtful. May I find joy in understanding and teaching. Amen.

Ashraqa n-nouru (The light has arisen) attributed to St Ephrem

The light of the just and joy of the upright is Christ Jesus, Our Lord. Begotten of the Father, He manifested Himself to us. He came to rescue us from darkness and to fill us with the radiance of His light.

Day is drawing upon us; the power of darkness is fading away. From the true Light there arises for us the Light which illumines our darkened eyes. His glory shines upon the world and enlightens the very depths of the abyss. Death is annihilated, night has vanished, and the gates of Sheol are broken.

Creatures lying in darkness from ancient times are clothed in light. The dead arise from the dust and sing because they have a Saviour. He brings salvation and grants us life. He ascends to His Father on high. He will return in glorious splendour and shed His light on those gazing upon Him.

Our King comes in majestic glory, Let us light our lamps and go forth to meet Him. Let us find our joy in Him, for He has found joy in us. He will indeed rejoice us with his marvellous light.

Let us glorify the majesty of the Son and give thanks to the almighty Father, who, in an outpouring of love, sent Him to us, to fill us with hope and salvation. When He manifests Himself, the saints awaiting Him in weariness and sorrow, will go forth to meet him with lighted lamps. The angels and guardians of heaven will rejoice in the glory of the just and upright people of the earth; together, crowned with victory, they will sing hymns and psalms.

Stand up then and be ready! Give thanks to our King and Saviour, who will come in great glory to gladden us with His marvellous light in His Kingdom.

Glory be to the Father and to the Son and to the Holy Spirit, now and for ever. Amen. Alleluia!

A Prayer for the Family

Saint Joseph, noble protector of the Holy Family, please pray that all parents may receive the grace to be good examples for their children, and to bring them up to know, love and serve God. We ask you to pray that those who take the lives of unborn innocents, disrespect fatherhood, and attack the dignity of motherhood may come to see the error of their ways, and that all men may value the holiness of Christian family life. Amen.

Prayer to my Guardian Angel

Heavenly being who looks up the face of God, to whose care I have been committed: watch over my steps, guard my thoughts and grant me peace, so that I may know and follow God's will for me.

The Rosary

There are many instructions as to how to pray the Rosary. Some have additional prayers, known as the "trimmings on the rosary." They are not needed, although they can be useful. It is no sin to use them, and it is no sin to omit them. But the essence of the Rosary is this: five decades of prayers.

Each decade is made up of first, an Our Father, then ten Hail Marys, then the Glory Be, and finally the Fatima Prayer. The Fatima Prayer is now part of the Rosary, having been added at the request of Our Lady of Fatima in 1917. The Fatima Prayer, as used today, is:

O my Jesus, forgive us our sins. Save us from the fires of hell. Lead all souls to Heaven, especially those in most need of thy mercy.

It is also usual to meditate upon one of these twenty Mysteries of the Rosary, while praying it.

The Joyful Mysteries

1. The Annunciation of the Angel Gabriel to Our Lady (Luke 1:26-39)

2. The Visitation of Our Lady to her cousin Elizabeth (Luke 1:39-56)

3. The Nativity of Our Lord (the Gospels of Matthew and Luke)

4. The Presentation of Our Lord in the Temple (Luke 2:22-40)

5. The Finding of Our Lord in the Temple (Luke 2:41-52)

The Luminous Mysteries

1. The Baptism of Our Lord in the Jordan (all Gospels)

2. The Wedding at Cana (John 2:1-11)

3. Our Lord proclaims the Kingdom of God (all Gospels)

4. The Transfiguration of Our Lord (Matthew, Mark, Luke and 2 Peter)

5. Our Lord's Institution of the Eucharist (Matthew, Mark, Luke and 1 Cor.)

The Sorrowful Mysteries (all Gospels)

1. The Agony in the Garden

2. The Scourging at the Pillar

3. The Crowning with Thorns

4. Our Lord carries his Cross

5. The Crucifixion

The Glorious Mysteries

1. The Resurrection (all Gospels)

2. The Ascension (Mark 16:19; Luke 24:50-53; Acts 1:9-11)

3. The Descent of the Holy Spirit on Pentecost (Acts 2:1-31)

4. The Assumption of Our Lady into Heaven (Gen. 3:15 and 1 Cor. 15:54)

5. The Coronation of Our Lady as Queen of Heaven and Earth (Rev. 12:1)

It is customary, since St John-Paul II's Apostolic Letter *Rosarium Virginis Mariae*, of 16 October 2002, to pray the Joyful Mysteries on Monday and Saturday, the Sorrowful Mysteries on Tuesday and Friday, the Glorious Mysteries on Wednesday and Sunday, and the Luminous Mysteries on Thursday. Of course, this is only a recommendation, and one may pray more than five decades, on any day of the week.

Grace Before Meals

Bless us, Lord, bless this food, those who prepared it, and those who will eat. May it be granted to us to share our bread and our joy with those less fortunate than ourselves. Amen.

Grace After Meals

We give you thanks, almighty God, for all your benefits, who live and reign for ever and ever. May the Lord grant us His peace, and life everlasting. Amen.

Prayer of the Christian Soul

Remember, Christian soul, that you have this day and every day of your life ...

God to glorify,

Jesus to imitate,

A soul to save,

A body to mortify,

Sins to repent of,

Virtues to acquire,

Hell to avoid,

Heaven to gain,

Eternity to prepare for,

Time to profit by,

Neighbours to edify,

The world to despise,

Devils to combat,

Passions to subdue,

Death perhaps to suffer,

Judgement to undergo.

Therefore, child of Jesus and Mary, avoid sin and all its occasions.[245] Pray often, and go frequently to Confession and Holy Communion.

Prayer for Protection during the Night

Visit, we beg you, Lord, this house, and drive from it all the snares of the enemy. Let your holy angels remain here to preserve us in peace. Bless the rest I am going to take in order to renew my strength, so that I may be better able to serve you. Intercede for me, all you holy saints and angels, and chiefly you, Mother of God! Intercede for me this night and throughout my life, but particularly at the hour of my death. May the divine assistance remain always with us. Amen.

A Prayer for Faith

Lord, as the sun rises on the earth anew to nourish it with its light, so kindle anew in me the light of faith so that my soul may be nourished and the world around me enlightened through me. Amen.

---

[245] Avoiding the occasion of sin is avoiding those situations wherein we sin. For example, if certain so-called friends offer me drugs, then staying away from those people is avoiding the occasion of sin.

I Confess

I confess to Almighty God, to blessed Mary Ever-Virgin, to blessed Michael the Archangel, to the holy Apostles Peter and Paul, to blessed Saint Maroun, Saints Charbel, Rafqa and Nemetallah, and to all the saints, that I have sinned exceedingly in thought, word and deed (*one may strike one's breast three times in token of contrition*), through my fault, through my fault, through my most grievous fault. Therefore, I beseech blessed Mary Ever-Virgin, blessed Michael the Archangel, the holy Apostles Peter and Paul, blessed Saint Maroun, Saints Charbel, Rafqa and Nemetallah, and all the saints to pray to the Lord our God for me. May the Almighty and Merciful Lord grant me pardon, absolution, and remission of my sins. Amen.

Prayer for the Newly Born

Lord, bless this child of your grace (Name), this soul you have created, this person you have sent into our world. Fill this child with holiness, happiness and health. May we love this child as you love him/her. May we care for this child without any selfishness, desiring only that he/she fulfil the potential and use the talents you have allotted him/her. May he/she grow upright before you like the fragrant cedars of Lebanon, and serve you as the righteous of every age have served, with faith, hope and charity. Grant him/her a holy life, and a heart in which you may rejoice, so that when he/she leaves this world, he/she may be united to you in eternity. Amen.

An Act of Spiritual Communion

Lord Jesus, I believe that you are present in the Most Holy Sacrament. I seek to love you above all things, and I desire to receive you into my soul. Since I cannot at this very moment receive you sacramentally, I invite you to come spiritually into my heart. May I sense your presence filling me with faith, hope and charity. May my will be united to yours. Never permit me to be separated from you.

Note: This prayer is particularly to be said when one desires to attend Mass and receive communion, but cannot.

Prayer to Saint Maroun

Great Saint Maroun, who while living in the world cut all your attachments to it, and through your virtuous example became the father of a spiritual nation, intercede for us, that we may attain to the spirit of compassion, humility and simplicity, and so enter the Kingdom of Heaven through the grace of God. Amen.

Prayer to St Charbel

Holy Saint Charbel, who chose God before all others, who lived in a world of sanctified silence and honest labour, help us to find the joy in discharging our duty to God, family and our neighbour, without stinting and without regret. Through your prayers, may we receive the grace to live not for worldly goods but for eternity in the presence of God. Amen.

Prayer to St Rafqa

Humble Saint Rafqa, who sought suffering as a token of God's love, remember us in the courts of heaven. Now that your pain has ended and all been turned to bliss, intercede for we who struggle with sickness, illness, loss and death. Grant that our hearts and minds may be illuminated with the light of faith, and we may always remember that our aim is to attain to eternal life with God and His most holy Mother. Amen.

Prayer to St Nemetallah

Pious and self-effacing St Nemetallah, you said that "the clever man is he who saves his soul." Pray for us, before the throne of God, that the spirit of divine wisdom may enter our souls and so guide our lives. Amen.

Prayer to the Blessed Massabki Brothers

Blessed Massabki Brothers, Abdal-Moati, Francis and Raphael, pray to the Lord our God for me and for my family, that, like you, I may persevere in love and courage until the destined end should find me, whatever that may be. May I fear only that which kills the soul, never that which only afflicts the body. Amen.

Prayer to Blessed Estphan Nehme

"God Sees Me," you would say, Blessed Estphan. May we live with that awareness each day: not doing, saying or thinking anything which is shameful. May all the work of our hands and the fruits of our minds be such as we would be proud to show to Our Lord. Remember us here below, and kindly intercede for us before our Divine Master. Amen.

Prayer to Blessed Yaqoub Al-Kabouchi

Pray for us, Blessed Yaqoub, you who diligently discharged your duty, placing God first, and for love of Him, teaching His little ones to be devoted to Him in His Holy Sacraments and in His teachings and commandments. May our lives be entirely occupied, as yours was, with performing our daily work so that we might receive out supernatural bread. Amen.

Prayer to the Venerable Patriarch Estphan El-Doueihy

Venerable Estphan El-Doueihy, who served God and His people as Patriarch, scholar and leader, do not forget us who are lonely and in need of understanding as we journey through this world. May we serve Him, as you did, in our churches, in our homes and wherever we may work. Intercede to Our Lord for us, that we may remain together in His Holy Church, together with all the faithful, both here and in heaven. Amen.

Prayer from the Maronite Office of the Epiphany (Sunday Morning)

Lord Jesus, Light of the World, your radiance burst forth at your godly baptism in the River Jordan, and your splendour dispersed the darkness which had enfolded us for long ages. You manifested yourself to us in your essential unity with the Father and the Holy Spirit, and they witnessed to you from heaven. Dispel the shadows of ignorance from all around us, in the descent of your Spirit and the effulgence of your illumination. So shall we glorify you, and your Father and your Holy Spirit, now and for ever. Amen.

Prayer from the Maronite Office of Easter (Sunday Vigil)

Make us worthy, Lord God, in your grace and abundant mercy, to praise your resurrection with pure hearts, to laud your victory with holy mouths, and to declare your glory with cleansed tongues. Then, with the heavenly throng, we shall extol your divine dignity. We thank and praise you for your compassion, and that of your Father and your living Holy Spirit, the Good One whom we adore, the Vivifier, who is equal with you in essence, now and at every moment for ever. Amen.

Prayer from the Maronite Office of Pentecost (Tuesday Morning)

May we awaken to you first of all each morning, Lord Creator of All, seeking your grace, mercy and kindness. We beseech you to put forth your light, and to illumine our minds, hurling far from us the shadows of sin. Lead our steps along the path of your righteousness, the road to your eternal mansions of light; and we shall glorify you, your Son, and your Holy Spirit, for ever. Amen.

Prayer for the Sick

Blessed Trinity, Father, Son and Holy Spirit, One God, heal, I beseech you, your sick and suffering people, especially my beloved (name). Grant them the fullness of physical health you wish for them, but above all them, console their minds, ease their emotions, and bring them to an understanding and acceptance of your will. Heal their souls which long for you more than for lesser, passing goods. Amen.

Act of Acceptance of Death

My Lord and my God, this day and for each day of my granted life until its end, I humbly and willingly accept from your holy hands the release of death when and how it pleases you to send it to me. May the suffering of death be the kind stroke which frees me from lingering attachment to this world.

Most Holy Trinity which dwells in unimaginable light, I surrender my soul to you.

Blessed Virgin Mary, St John the Beloved and you holy women who stood at the foot of the Cross, assist me in my last agony.

All you saints, hermits, monks and nuns, holy men and women who lived in this world and have passed into heaven, may I breathe forth my soul in peace.

Lord Jesus, send forth your holy angels to meet me on the road. Amen.

Prayer for the Departed

God our Father, Your power brings us to birth, Your providence guides our lives, and by Your command we return to dust. Lord, those who die still live in Your presence, their lives change but do not end. I pray in hope for my family, relatives and friends, and for all the dead known to You alone.

In company with Christ, Who died and now lives, may they rejoice in Your kingdom, where all our tears are wiped away. Unite us together again in one family, to sing Your praise forever and ever. Amen.